PHARMACY AND THE LAW

By Carl T. DeMarco, B.S. Pharm., J.D.

Aspen Systems Corporation
Germantown, Maryland
1975

Library of Congress Catalog Card Number: 75-34698
ISBN: 0-912862-16-5

Printed in United States of America.

*This book is dedicated
to my mother Rose,
whose personal sacrifices, early encouragement
and continuing guidance laid the early foundation
for the writing of this book.*

TABLE OF CONTENTS

PART III — CONTROLLED SUBSTANCES 151

Part IV — PROFESSIONAL LIABILITIES 195

PREFACE

PHARMACY AND THE LAW IS WRITTEN FOR PRACTICING PHARMACISTS AS A BOOK-shelf reference and for students as a textbook. It is written broadly enough to be used by pharmacists in community practice, hospital practice, research or teaching. Specific information has also been incorporated in order to be useful in specialty areas of practice. The book does not include any major discussion of business or commercial law nor the law as it relates to the employment relationship.

The book is divided into four main parts. The first part, The Professional Practice of Pharmacy, zeros in on pharmacy practice itself. It discusses who may practice pharmacy and what is expected of pharmacy practitioners. Part I is the largest part of the book because of its direct and unique application to the profession of pharmacy.

Part II, Drug Laws, concentrates on the regulation of drug products. It is a broad, yet highly complex area of law and pharmacists should have a working knowledge of these legal principles and rules.

Part III, Controlled Substances, deals with a law that is basically a criminal statute, the Controlled Substances Act. This law contains many specific rules that must be followed by pharmacists, for failure to comply may result in serious consequences.

Part IV, Professional Liabilities, analyzes the law as it applies to pharmacists whose professional activities may result in a transgression of law or result in injury to a patient. Hopefully, an awareness of the legal principles at work in this area will help the pharmacist avoid liability.

An Expanded Outline has been included in lieu of an index. It will facilitate use of the book by minimizing the difficulty in finding sections where material of interest is covered. The Expanded Outline will also aid the pharmacist or student by placing the subject of immediate concern into context within the overall body of law affecting pharmacy.

Another helpful aid in understanding the law is the extensive use of appendices. The applicable text of as many major laws as practicable

ix

have been included for direct consideration and analysis. The text also quotes liberally from many federal and state laws and regulations, where appropriate. Nevertheless, all laws are not incorporated. The reader should have copies of, and be familiar with, his state's pharmacy laws as well as federal laws. This book should assist in understanding and interpreting these laws as applied to questions of practice.

In addition to an expanded outline and extensive appendices, a Table of Cases and Selected References have been included. These additions contain citations to cases or references mentioned in the text. The table will be of assistance to those readers who wish to further examine a case and delve into the reasoning used by the court involved. The references allow further reading in the areas discussed in the book.

Attorneys familiar with the applicable areas of law and pharmacy practice have reviewed the text to ensure accuracy and relevance.

A word of caution is in order. This text will not make attorneys out of pharmacists. If a serious legal problem should arise, pharmacists are advised to seek the advice of competent counsel. Failure to do so could result in undesirable civil or criminal consequences.

Nor will this book take the place of keeping up-to-date on the rapid changes occurring in the health care field. For example, in July, 1975, new Maximum Allowable Cost (MAC) regulations were issued by the Department of Health, Education, and Welfare concerning the maximum allowable reimbursement of drugs. When the HEW's MAC regulations came out the American Medical Association brought suit in Chicago to declare the regulations invalid, in whole or in part. In other areas there are pending lawsuits brought by the American Medical Association, the American Hospital Association, and the American Pharmacological Association against HEW officials to prevent implementation and enforcement of regulations in the areas of utilization review, health care financing and preadmission certification.

These and other issues will be more fully discussed in future editions. Meanwhile, they should be followed carefully to determine their day-to-day effect upon the professional practice of pharmacy.

Carl T. DeMarco
Bethesda, Maryland
October, 1975

ACKNOWLEDGMENTS

THIS BOOK WAS NOT WRITTEN WITHOUT HELP. THE ASSISTANCE OF THE FOLLOW-
ing friends and associates is expressly acknowledged for their excellent
review, comment and suggestions.

Joseph A. D'Arco, B.S. Pharm., J.D., Attorney at Law; formerly
Attorney, Office of Chief Counsel, Drug Enforcement Administration,
U.S. Department of Justice; formerly Staff Attorney, American Phar-
maceutical Association.

Joseph L. Fink III, B.S. Pharm., J.D., Member, Pennsylvania Bar;
Assistant Professor of Pharmacy Administration, Philadelphia College
of Pharmacy and Science; Chairman, Steering Committee, American
Society for Pharmacy Law.

Robert F. Steeves, B.S., Pharm., J.D., Attorney at Law, Washington, D.C., formerly Director, Legal Division, American Pharmaceutical
Association, author of *A Pharmacist's Guide to Liability.*

Joseph G. Valentino, B.S. Pharm., J.D., Executive Associate,
United States Pharmacopeial Convention, Inc.; formerly Assistant to
the Director, Division of Case Guidance, Bureau of Regulatory Compliance, Food and Drug Administration, U.S. Department of HEW;
Member of the Bar in New Jersey and Maryland.

Jaxon A. White, B.S. Pharm., J.D., Assistant Director, Medical
Affairs, Scientific Apparatus Makers Association; formerly Staff Attorney, American Society of Hospital Pharmacists.

Acknowledgment is also due to the following organizations for permission to reprint their materials in this book: American Medical
Association, *Medicolegal Forms;* American Pharmaceutical Association, *APhA Code of Ethics,* "Drug Product Selection Authorization
Forms;" Joint Commission on Accreditation of Hospitals, *Accreditation Manual for Hospitals;* National Association of Boards of
Pharmacy, *Survey of Pharmacy Laws.*

Last, but not least I acknowledge with love the patience, understanding and sacrifice of my wife, Mary Ann and of our children, Lisa and
Carl.

EXPANDED OUTLINE

Part II — DRUG LAWS

Chapter 7 — THE REGULATION OF DRUGS, DEVICES, AND COSMETICS

Part III — CONTROLLED SUBSTANCES

Part IV — PROFESSIONAL LIABILITIES

PART I
THE PROFESSIONAL PRACTICE
OF PHARMACY

PART I COVERS THOSE LAWS THAT MOST DIRECTLY AFFECT THE PHARMACIST AS A professional practitioner. In relating to the pharmacist as a provider of professional services, these chapters discuss who may provide such services, the types of services that are expected and the quality of those services. The more important federal, state and professional standards applicable to these questions are identified and discussed.

The liabilities involved for failure to meet the various requirements expected of pharmacists are not fully examined in Part I. Both civil and criminal liabilities are treated in Part IV. For particular areas of interest with respect to liabilities see the Expanded Outline.

1

CHAPTER 1
THE PHARMACIST

Section 1
LICENSURE REQUIREMENTS

IN ADOPTING THE UNITED STATES CONSTITUTION, THE STATES RESERVED FROM those powers granted to the federal government the basic police power necessary to protect the health, safety and welfare of the citizens of their respective states. This power includes the right to deny or grant a franchise (generally called licenses or permits) to persons who provide services that have a great impact on the health and safety of the people. By limiting certain practices to licensees, a state can assure a certain level of competence and quality of service. At the same time, unqualified persons and substandard practices can, hopefully, be eliminated.

Since pharmaceutical services have a profound effect upon health and safety, it is necessary to be licensed to practice pharmacy. The federal government does not issue licenses to practice pharmacy; each state does its own licensing. In order to practice pharmacy within an individual state it is necessary to obtain a license from that state. Accordingly, each state has a pharmacy law which sets forth its requisites for licensure. While there may be a substantial degree of similarity among the various state laws, it is imperative to carefully examine the law of the state in which licensure is desired. The following discussion deals with licensure requirements that are generally applicable. It does not include all variations that exist.

One basic requirement for licensure is that the applicant be a graduate of an accredited college of pharmacy. Pharmacy schools are accredited by the American Council on Pharmaceutical Education (ACPE). In order to be accredited the curriculum must provide certain basic courses in pharmacy, chemistry, biology and mathematics. Minimum standards concerning faculty, facilities, equipment and library resources necessary to properly educate future pharmacists must be met by the school.

3

The Attorney General of Pennsylvania advised its Board of Pharmacy on March 23, 1972, that an applicant may not be denied licensure because his degree was not granted from a school accredited by the ACPE. This is based upon the theory that reliance on a private agency could constitute an improper delegation of authority and that the Board of Pharmacy, as an agency of the state, must exercise its own judgment if there is any doubt. Since the ACPE does not accredit foreign pharmacy schools this factor could be important where the applicant was educated in a school outside the United States.

Early in the development of our system, a pharmacist was not required to have a college degree. As the body of pharmaceutical knowledge grew and became more complicated, a post high school course was required. Over the years it was increased to two years, three years, a full four year baccalaureate program and finally to its present-day five year curriculum. Some schools also offer a six year program which leads to a Pharm. D. degree, while others grant this degree for a duration of study for not less than two years following completion of the five year program.

In addition to a college education, states generally require some practical training and experience. This usually takes the form of an internship or residency. Sometimes the internship may occur during the college years, but many states require all or some of the training to take place after graduation. Six-month or one year internships are common. There is a trend to place this requirement under the supervision of the college of pharmacy.

Subsequent to college graduation an applicant for licensure must successfully pass the state administered examination. The total examination process is generally divided into theoretical and practical exams. The theoretical portion is most frequently given immediately after graduation, while practical abilities are tested after completion of the internship. Examination fees usually run from $15 to $100.

In 1968, the National Association of Boards of Pharmacy (NABP) created the Blue Ribbon Committee to develop an examination for licensure to be used by the states. A standard examination has since been developed and administered to pharmacy candidates. At last count, all but five states use all or portions of the standard test.

In addition to education, training and examination requirements, most states require an individual to be 21 years of age in order to practice pharmacy. A few set the age at 18 or 19, and two states have no specification. The applicant must not have been convicted of a felony or abuse alcohol or other drugs. A minimal initial certificate fee is charged in some states.

Most states require the applicant to be a full citizen or have made a legal declaration of intention to become a citizen. In recent years, this licensure requirement has also been questioned along with the prerequisite of a degree from an ACPE accredited school. On March 23, 1972, the Attorney General of Pennsylvania advised the Pennsylvania Board of

Pharmacy that the requirement that an applicant be a citizen of the United States is unconstitutional and unenforceable because it deprives noncitizens of equal protection of laws within the meaning of the Fourteenth Amendment of the United States Constitution.

A relatively recent trend in pharmacy has been to require continuing education in order to maintain an active license. Such laws require the accumulation of a certain number of continuing education credits. This requirement is based upon the desire to maintain a certain level of competency among pharmacy practitioners. This movement has been paralleled in other health professions as well in order to ensure high quality patient services. In 1967 the states of Florida and Kansas adopted laws requiring continuing education for relicensure. At least ten states now have such laws including California, Indiana, Minnesota, Nevada, New Jersey, Ohio, Oklahoma, and Washington.

It quickly becomes evident that national interests in such laws would not be served if the various states passed laws with radically different requirements and substantially different mechanisms for implementation. Many pharmacists are licensed in more than one state and should be able to fulfill all continuing education requirements in one process. To fulfill such a requirement in each state would be difficult unless the same continuing education programs were acceptable for credit in the various states. Similarly, sponsors of continuing education programs would find it ever difficult to fulfill the requirements of different states with one program if the standards differed too greatly. It could also become impossible for program sponsors to meet the continuing education needs of practitioners from different parts of the country if the sum of the fees charged to obtain accreditation in each state were oppressive. This process could have a retardant effect upon attendance at national meetings, reduce the exchange of ideas from various areas of the country and fragmentize the trend toward high level national standards in favor of state or regional standardization.

Hence, in 1970 the American Association of Colleges of Pharmacy called for the creation of a Tripartite Committee on Continuing Education composed of representatives from the American Association of Colleges of Pharmacy, the National Association of Boards of Pharmacy (NABP) and the American Pharmaceutical Association. The Tripartite Committee recommended the development of flexible legislation and implemented regulations. Following these meetings, NABP adopted, in 1972, a Uniform Professional Continuing Education Act. (See Appendix A.)

Although a uniform act has been prepared and promoted, there are still outstanding questions. Does attendance at seminars and lectures ensure continuing competence? Should not continuing education programs be accredited by a national body, such accreditation qualifying the program for all states? These and other questions need answering before a unified national answer to the continuing education issue can be found.

Section 2

LICENSURE BY RECIPROCITY

As the United States expanded across the continent, its population acquired a great mobility that continued long after the continent was spanned. Farmers moved from the country to urban centers, the suburbs swelled, and citizens moved to different regions for a change of climate or better job opportunities without regard to state boundaries. The founding fathers, in their desire to facilitate travel among the various states incorporated a provision in the United States Constitution that provides that a citizen of the United States is automatically a citizen of the state in which he resides.

Nevertheless, separate licensure in each state tends to diminish the ability of pharmacists to freely move from one state to another and still practice their profession. Furthermore, it became readily apparent that it would be unrealistic to require a person licensed to practice pharmacy in one state to undertake a similar and at times identical, extensive and time consuming examination process in his newly adopted state in order to practice his chosen profession. Hence, most state laws contain provisions for licensure by reciprocity. California, Florida and Hawaii do not.

The first and foremost requirement to qualify for reciprocity is that one be licensed under state law. An unlicensed person cannot obtain a pharmacist's license by reciprocity. In addition, the license upon which the reciprocity is based must have been obtained by examination. For example, if one is originally licensed in Maryland by examination and receives licensure by reciprocity in Texas, a license by reciprocity in Washington must be obtained by reliance on the license in Maryland and not on the license obtained in Texas.

The second overall requirement is that the pharmacist seeking reciprocity meet substantially the same legal requirements in his state of original licensure as he would have had to meet in the reciprocating state for original licensure. This requirement creates a system of relative comparability and creates a grandfather effect in the reciprocation system.

This type of requirement was challenged in a 1972 reciprocation case. A pharmacist licensed in Utah sought certification in Arizona. Although the applicant otherwise qualified, the license was denied because he had not practiced for one year in Utah. This provision is contained in the Rules and Regulations of the Arizona State Board of Pharmacy.

The applicant challenged the board's ruling on a number of legal grounds. The first claim was that the Board of Pharmacy exceeded the authority granted by the legislature. The law did not expressly require one year of practice in the state of licensure; that requirement was added by the Board of Pharmacy in its regulations. The second challenge was that the standards of due process were not met concerning the applicant. The regulations allow the Board of Pharmacy to waive failure to comply with the rules. Since the applicant had, in addition to his two and one-half months in Utah, practiced for eighteen years elsewhere, he had a great deal of practical experience and equity was, therefore, with the applicant. The last argument centered around equal protection. This regulation creates two classes of applicants, those who have practiced for one year and those who have not. Such classifications are unconstitutional, particularly where fundamental personal rights are concerned unless the state can show that such classification| must be upheld in all cases in order to properly protect the public health and welfare. Since the applicant had over eighteen years of experience there was no rational basis for enforcing the one year rule.

After a formal hearing and the filing of a legal brief by counsel in *In re Cloyd Sorensen, Jr.*, the Board of Pharmacy granted the license and no further proceedings took place.

In addition to having been previously licensed and having met equivalent standards, the reciprocating state usually requires the applicant to appear before its board of pharmacy to answer questions designed to satisfy the board that the pharmacist has a working knowledge of local state law. This is important since state laws vary on any number of specific points.

There are some limitations on the type of examination that may be given by the reciprocating state. A recent reciprocity case, *In re Stephenson*, involved an attorney. The court held that the state of reciprocation could not administer a national exam designed for recent graduates but rather had to use an exam that was suitable to an attorney who was licensed and practicing for an number of years. Whether this principle will apply to pharmacy and the NABP standard examination is not known at this time.

Another major requirement built into reciprocation laws is that the state from which the applicant is reciprocating will also honor licensees from the reciprocating state. In order for each state to provide the greatest degree of flexibility and mobility to its registrants, it behooves each state to permit reciprocity from each other state. In this manner, other states will honor applicants from the reciprocating state. This is truly the essence of a "reciprocal" license.

Since California, Florida and Hawaii do not permit licensure by reciprocation, pharmacists from these states may not use these licenses as the basis for reciprocating to other states. The practical hedge against the future by pharmacists from these states is to obtain licensure by examination in a reciprocating state soon after graduation. Hence, California pharmacists may obtain a license by examination in the bordering states of Nevada, Colorado or Utah and use that license for future reciprocation.

The National Association of Boards of Pharmacy has developed a system to facilitate the reciprocity process. The NABP is an organization whose membership is composed of state boards of pharmacy. In order to reciprocate, an applicant would provide information to the NABP who in turn would verify certain facts relating to licensure. All the necessary information is provided to the reciprocating state by the NABP and to the board of pharmacy of the state from which reciprocation is being made. The reciprocating state board of pharmacy then exercises its independent judgment as to whether the applicant meets that state's requirements for reciprocity.

Although pharmacist licenses are granted by each state, the reciprocal licensing system facilitates movement from state to state. However, reciprocation is a cumbersome process and has become quite expensive. Furthermore, it is necessary to continue to maintain a license in the state of original licensure in case further reciprocation is necessary. Because of the inherent difficulties in the reciprocation system there have been suggestions to establish a system of national licensure by the federal government. Then a pharmacist could practice in any state. The NABP Standard Examination may be a step in this direction.

Section 3

SPECIALIZATION

It is becoming more and more difficult, in the practice of pharmacy, to keep up with the increase in the depth and expansion of knowledge in the field of pharmaceutical science. Likewise it becomes increasingly desirable to specialize in specific subjects of this knowledge.

In recognition of this pressure within the profession, the American Pharmaceutical Association (APhA) appointed, in 1971, a Task Force on Specialties in Pharmacy. The purpose of the task force was to identify existing or potential areas of specialization in pharmacy, set forth the means by which specialties can be identified, and develop the mechanism to certify individuals as specialists.

The report of the Task Force was presented at the APhA Annual Meeting on April 18, 1974. It did not identify any existing specialties. It did, however, set forth criteria for recognizing areas of specialization and proposed a Board of Pharmaceutical Specialties to certify programs and individuals. This report was not universally welcomed and was challenged on various points. What its effect will be in the future on a pharmacist's qualifications cannot be determined at this point in time.

Despite the fact that there are no officially recognized specialties in pharmacy, there are, nevertheless, references in various standards that relate to a pharmacist's special skills. The Medicare Conditions of Participation for Hospitals, which are regulations of the Social Security Administration, in explaining competent supervision in a hospital pharmacy state, "The pharmacist is trained in the specialized functions of hospital pharmacy." The Conditions of Participation for Skilled Nursing Facilities define pharmacist as follows:

20 C.F.R. §405.1101(p)

(p) *Pharmacist.* A person who:
(1) Is licensed as a pharmacist by the State in which practicing, and
(2) Has training or experience in the specialized functions of institutional pharmacy, such as residencies in hospital pharmacy, seminars on institutional pharmacy, and related training programs.

Similarly, the Joint Commission on Accreditation of Hospitals in their *Accreditation Manual for Hospitals* on interpreting Pharmacy Standard I states that:

[The pharmacist] should be oriented to the specialized functions of hospital pharmacies or have completed a hospital pharmacy residency program approved by the American Society of Hospital Pharmacists.

Professional societies that represent what are considered to be specialty interests are also active in this area. The American Society of Hospital Pharmacists has an extensive accreditation program for residency training in hospital pharmacies. The purpose of such residencies is "to improve the professional competence of hospital pharmacy practitioners through organized educational training programs." Residents receive training and experience in pharmacy administration, drug distribution and control, sterile and nonsterile compounding, and quality control as applied in hospital practice.

The American Board of Diplomates in Pharmacy (ABDP) is an organization of limited membership which was established along the guidelines used by medical specialty boards. In order to obtain fellowship, a pharmacist must meet certain criteria of education, training, and professional recognition. After successful completion of an oral interview and written examinations, an applicant may then be certified by the Board of Directors of the ABDP. The American Society of Consultant Pharmacists also has a program of accreditation for consultant pharmacists who serve skilled nursing facilities.

Section 4

SUPPORTIVE PERSONNEL

It becomes clear from the foregoing discussion that it is not easy to become a pharmacist. It takes years of training and rigorous study. This is as it should be considering the tremendous responsibilities entrusted to pharmacists. Pharmacists' duties range from inventory and recordkeeping, labeling and packaging, drug compounding, monitoring drug therapy, drug use control and advising patients, physicians and other health care professionals. In order to adequately achieve total performance expectations, it is not unusual nor unexpected for pharmacists to look for assistance. An area of growing interest and legal controversy concerns the use of nonpharmacists in a pharmacy. The question at this point is whether supportive personnel may be lawfully engaged in a pharmacy and, if so, in what capacity. (Note: Liability considerations in the use of technicians are discussed in Chapter 22.)

It is necessary to distinguish at this point between supportive personnel such as technicians, clerks, assistants, etc. and interns and residents. Interns are future pharmacists obtaining the practical experience necessary to qualify for licensure. Generally they are either pharmacy students or graduates performing specified functions under direct supervision of a licensed pharmacist who has met certain qualifications. Residents are pharmacy graduates, most often already licensed to practice, who are engaging in special areas of study, hospital pharmacy, for example, in order to gain expertise. The activities of interns and residents in a pharmacy are lawful if, in the case of interns, the stipulations of law are met, and in the case of residents, they are licensed. The discussion that follows relates to the use of supportive personnel other than interns and residents.

The profession itself has tried to resolve the question of supportive personnel. The published reports of these endeavors discuss in detail the assignment of various functions or tasks to supportive personnel. An examination of what is being done in other countries has also been made.

In seeking guidance on this question a natural starting place is state law. State law as expounded in statutory, regulatory, and decisional law, has a controlling influence in this area. Some state statutes still authorize the use of licensed pharmacy assistants. In such instances it is safe to utilize such personnel without violating the law. However, many states are no longer licensing new assistants. Thus the number of licensed assistants is fixed or diminishing. In most instances, pharmacy technicians will be unlicensed, and certain precautions must be observed.

At the highest level, only a licensed pharmacist may practice pharmacy. Thus the definition of the practice of pharmacy in a state's pharmacy act serves as a basic point of reference. Generally, the issue which emerges is whether a manipulative or mechanical task falls within the definition of the practice of pharmacy. Some state legislatures have very carefully defined the practice of pharmacy to such an extent as to almost eliminate the use of supportive personnel. In Colorado, compounding which is restricted to pharmacists is defined:

Colo. Rev. Stat. Ann. §12-22-102
(10) "Compound" means to interpret a prescription or chart order, measure, mix, weigh, or otherwise prepare, ingredients, as specified in the prescription or chart order of a practitioner,

in accordance with the acts of pharmacy, prepare a label i accordance with the prescription or chart order and place in or securely attach such label to the medicine container.

On the other hand, where the technicians perform mere mechanical or manipulative tasks with proper supervision or control, the courts have not found the use of supportive personnel to be a violation of law. For example, the Court of Common Pleas of Franklin County, Ohio, held in the case of *In re Toledo Health and Retiree Center, Inc.,* that the typing of labels did not constitute the practice of pharmacy. The court said:

There is no doubt but that the public health is directly concerned with accurate dispensing of drugs, and the utmost care must be exercised to avoid fatal error in the preparation and distribution of drugs, which includes the proper labeling of any drug container. No drug should be delivered to a patient that has not been checked for accuracy as to content and as to instruction for use, and this responsibility must be placed in, and remain with, the registered pharmacist at all stages between the receipt of the prescription order and the delivery of the order to the patient. Most of the procedures fall appropriately within the field of training of a registered pharmacist. The typing of a label is a procedure which falls within the field of training of a typist, and not necessarily that of a registered pharmacist. No matter who does the mechanical job of typing a label, the registered pharmacist who dispenses the drug to the patient is responsible to make as many checks as he believes are required to protect the life and safety of the prospective patient who will use the packaged drug. He must see to it that proper ingredients are contained in the package and that it is properly labeled. We see no danger in making use of experienced personnel, or in making use of modern and efficient processes so long as the responsibility for proper compounding and delivery of drugs is properly placed upon the registered pharmacist who receives the prescription.

In *Arkansas Board of Pharmacy v. Whayne,* the court went further. It held that typing a label and affixing it to the dispensing container and delivering the bulk medicine to the pharmacist did not constitute a violation of the pharmacy law.

The Attorney General of Iowa interpreted the Iowa Narcotic Drug Act to permit a nurse to dispense and administer narcotic and dangerous drugs under the supervision of a medical practitioner. Whether this interpretation would apply to the pharmacy law is not clear. The opinion is also questionable in light of the fact that Iowa's Narcotic Drug Act has subsequently been repealed and replaced with the Uniform Controlled Substances Act.

The Florida Supreme Court held in *Parr v. Spires*, that there was no violation of Florida's pharmacy law, for an unlicensed person in a hospital drug room may measure, weigh, count, wrap and label prescribed drugs or medicines and deliver them to the patient. In a subsequent Florida case, *Hall v. Florida Board of Pharmacy*, however, the court noted that the result in the Spires case would probably be different under a subsequent amendment to the Florida Pharmacy Act which additionally defines the practice of pharmacy as including, "any other act, service, operation or transaction incidental to or forming a part of compounding, dispensing or advising, requiring, involving or employing the science or art of any branch of the pharmaceutical profession, study or training." The adoption of an "institutional pharmacy" law in Florida further compounds the issue in that state. [Note: The Florida institutional pharmacy law is discussed in Chapter 6, Section 1.]

In other states, such as Michigan and Pennsylvania, the boards of pharmacy have not waited for the courts to rule on the issue. They have taken steps to identify the manner in which technicians may be properly used.

The employment of pharmacy technicians has created special problems in hospital pharmacies. In an attempt to free themselves to engage in greater patient contact, physician and nurse consultation, and to provide greater professional services, hospital pharmacists have engaged technicians in various activities, most notably in tasks involving repetitive, manipulative procedures. The technicians prepare reports, maintain records, prepackage drugs and deliver medications to other areas of the hospital.

Virtually all states require that a pharmacy, drug store or other place where prescriptions are compounded be under the supervision of a registered or licensed pharmacist. The Michigan Attorney General has held that its state pharmacy law applies to institutions and that institutions maintaining pharmacies were held subject to the provision of the act requiring a registered pharmacist to be in charge of every pharmacy or drug store. Similarly, the Minnesota Attorney General has held that the section of Minnesota pharmacy law prohibiting the compounding or dispensing of prescriptions except under the personal supervision of a pharmacist was violated where a physician's prescription was filled and dispensed in a hospital by nurses who were not supervised by a registered pharmacist or the prescribing physician.

In a few states certain hospitals may be exempted from similar requirements. For example, in Iowa the pharmacy law exempts licensed hospitals from the pharmacy business license law; in Kansas, the pharmacy law removes the drug room from the definition of "pharmacy." The Kansas law also provides that a registered pharmacist or a registered nurse may be in charge of a hospital's drug supply, but the hospital must obtain a pharmacy permit to compound prescriptions.

In addition to what may be found in state laws, the Joint Commission on Accreditation of Hospitals, in its *Manual,* also recognizes the need for lay help in the hospital pharmacy. The interpretation of Standard I, Pharmaceutical Service, states, in part:

> . . . The director of pharmaceutical service should be assisted by additional qualified pharmacists and ancillary personnel as needed.

> If trained pharmacy assistants are employees, they should be carefully selected and shall work under the supervision of a pharmacist. They shall not be assigned duties that should be performed only by registered pharmacists. Clerical and stenographic assistance should be provided as needed to assist with records, reports and correspondence.

The Conditions of Participation for Hospitals also permit the use of supportive personnel.

20 C.F.R. §405.1027(c)

(c) *Standard; personnel.* Personnel competent in their respective duties are provided in keeping with the size and activity of the department. The factors explaining the standard are as follows:

(1) The pharmacist is assisted by an adequate number of additional registered pharmacists and such other personnel as the activities of the pharmacy may require to insure quality pharmaceutical services.

(2) The pharmacy, depending upon the size and scope of its operations, is staffed by the following categories of personnel:

(i) Chief pharmacist.

(ii) One or more assistant chief pharmacists.

(iii) Staff pharmacists.

(iv) Pharmacy residents (where a program has been activated).

(v) Nonprofessionally trained pharmacy helpers.

(vi) Clerical help.

Based on the language of state laws defining pharmacy and application of the law by courts, it seems that supportive personnel may be used as called for by the standards of the Joint Commission on Accreditation of Hospitals and the federal government's Medicare regulations. However, such personnel may not, as recognized in the foregoing standards, direct or manage a hospital pharmacy. Nor may they exercise the consultative or decisional powers of pharmacists concerning compounding, dispensing and drug usage. Support personnel should be restricted to performing manipulative or mechanical tasks with appropriate checks and quality controls in effect.

When it is permissible to employ nonpharmacists and their tasks have been defined, their remains the question of supervision. Everyone agrees that there must be supervision based, at least, on principles of good management if not, indeed, on pharmaceutical needs. Phrases such as "personal supervision" or "direct supervision" or "close supervision" are frequently encountered in laws, regulations, and literature. One extreme example was a case in which a board of pharmacy member felt that necessary supervision required the pharmacist to watch over a typist's shoulder as the label was typed; the pharmacist could not be on the other side of the same workbench. This is obviously an untenable position. If the pharmacist must stand and watch, what advantage is gained by employing such individuals? Under such circumstances, there is no savings in time nor improvement of performance.

The important aspect of supervision is that appropriate in-process and terminal controls be used to ensure quality. This is exactly what is done in manufacturing where nonpharmacists make the millions of dosage forms that are used in the United States today. Doesn't this manufacturing process pose more of a public health danger because of the large number of individuals who could be harmed by an error than a pharmacy technician assisting to prepare prescription orders? Even a single personal injury is undesirable, but the point is that proper controls and checks are generally acceptable as a means of ensuring quality. In pharmacy the same principles are applicable.

The other supervisory question concerns the ratio of pharmacists to supportive personnel. Recommended ratios have run from 1:1 to 1:3 or more. The prior selection of a given ratio is arbitrary. The number of individuals needed and the number of technicians that can be properly supervised depends upon the given job. Control procedures in use at the time are also important. Whether these ratios turn out to be unlawfully arbitrary or unreasonable remains to be seen. In any event, pharmacy should not fix arbitrary ratios so firmly that it becomes unnecessarily difficult to change them. As the court in the *Toledo Health and Retiree* case pointed out, the pharmacist must ". . . make as many checks *as he believes are required* to protect the life and safety of the prospective patient who will use the packaged drug." (Emphasis added.)

CHAPTER 2
STANDARDS OF PRACTICE

THERE ARE MANY STANDARDS APPLICABLE TO THE PRACTICE OF PHARMACY. These standards are embodied in laws, regultions, codes of ethics, official statements of practice developed by professional societies of pharmacists or are general conditions of practice that have emerged from within the community of pharmacy. Other standards are dictated by the courts in rendering judgment on the relative rights, duties and obligations of the parties to a law suit.

The standards discussed in this chapter are those that affect the type of professional services pharmacists should render but which do not fall within some other identifiable area of law or practice dealt with in other portions of this book.

Section 1
STATE LAW

In discussing state laws, it would be impossible, without reproducing every state pharmacy act, to list all those duties and standards embodied in state law. (Appendix B contains a state-by-state compilation of citations to state laws important to pharmacy.) Selected principles of importance embodied in state pharmacy practice acts are identified and illuminated. This section does not deal with state law covering specific topics which are discussed in other sections of the book such as clinical pharmacy (Chapter 3), drug product selection (Chapter 4), quality assurance (Chapter 5), and operating a pharmacy (Chapter 6). State laws such as drug laws, controlled substances acts, etc., are examined in other parts of the book.

It is under the police power which states reserved for themselves that they can regulate the practice of pharmacy, medicine, nursing, dentistry, and other professions and occupations serving the public. Ac-

15

cordingly, the federal government does not directly regulate the professional practice of pharmacy. This is not to say, however, that federal laws dealing with interstate commerce and the distribution of federal funds do not have their impact on the practice.

Every state has a pharmacy practice act which regulates the profession. Most pharmacy laws are old. Of all state pharmacy laws only nine were originally enacted in the 20th Century. All others were first adopted in the previous century, the earliest one, Kentucky's, in 1874. Since most pharmacy laws were created at a time when pharmacy was not thought of as a science but was engaged primarily in the procurement and extraction of drugs and preparation of finished dosage forms for administration to patients, these laws are basically oriented to the production of a product and regulation of the place of preparation.

In the years since these laws were enacted the practice of pharmacy has been and is still changing. It has matured as a science and has spawned a gigantic drug industry. Pharmacy is evolving from a practice of drug production, presently consisting primarily of counting and pouring, to a service-oriented profession, providing drug-related services to patients, physicians and other health professions.

Pharmacy laws, despite amendments that have been added over the years, are seriously in need of updating. Many of the laws are based upon the 1921 version of a "Model Modern Pharmacy Law." In an attempt to fill this need, the National Association of Boards of Pharmacy has undertaken a project to develop a new uniform model pharmacy act. Such a project would result in a model law which could be adopted, with or without modification to meet local needs, by the states. A model law would bring greater uniformity to state pharmacy laws while at the same time making them more relevant to modern practice.

Laws are enacted by legislatures composed of elected representatives of the people. In drafting a law, it is impossible to cover every conceivable situation that may be affected by the law. There will always be room for interpretation and argument. Such laws, therefore, generally authorize, and create if necessary, an administrative agency to carry out the intent and purpose, as well as the letter of the law. In the areas of pharmacy, such agencies are generically known as boards of pharmacy. These boards implement the pharmacy law by promulgating regulations, and they enforce the law and regulations. In discussing state law, then, it is important to also include regulations of boards of pharmacy, which are extendors of the law.

The following principles from state pharmacy laws are not universal. They have been assembled from a sampling of various state laws. The law of the state of practice must be examined to determine a specific rule for that state. (See Appendix B.) Every pharmacist should obtain a copy of his state's laws and regulations and become familiar with them.

In most cases they may be obtained from the state board of pharmacy. (Appendix C is a listing of addresses of such boards.)

A basic element to distill from state pharmacy laws is the definition of the practice of pharmacy. Unfortunately, not every state law includes a definition. Sometimes it is necessary to search board regulations to find one. This is in sharp contrast to the fact that virtually every state law defines a "pharmacy" or "drug store" which is discussed in Chapter 6, below.

One type of definition of the practice of pharmacy is exemplified by New York law.

N.Y. Educ. Law (1974)
§6801. Definition of practice of pharmacy.
The practice of the profession of pharmacy is defined as the preparing, compounding, preserving, or the dispensing of drugs, medicines and therapeutic devices on the basis of prescriptions or other legal authority.

This is a basically "product oriented" definition. Other definitions may be more elaborate to include personal services as well as drug control. The Virginia pharmacy act states:

Va. Code Ann. §54-524.2(26a)
"Practice of pharmacy" is the personal health service that is concerned with the art and science of procuring, recommending, administering, preparing, compounding and dispensing of drugs, medicines and devices used in the diagnosis, treatment, or prevention of disease, whether compounded or dispensed on a prescription or otherwise legally dispensed or sold, and shall include the proper and safe storage and distribution of drugs, the maintenance of proper records therefor, and the responsibility of providing information, as required, concerning such drugs and medicines and their therapeutic values and uses in the treatment and prevention of disease.

The words "drug" and "devices," as used in this definition, shall not include surgical or dental instruments, physical therapy equipment, X-ray apparatus, their component parts or accessories.

The "practice of pharmacy" shall not include the operations of a manufacturer or wholesaler.

One question that arises is whether the practice of pharmacy is a profession. Not all state laws define it as such. Examples of those that do follow. The Texas pharmacy law provides:

Tex. Rev. Civ. Stat. Art. 4542a
Sec. 20 . . . The practice of pharmacy in the State of Texas is declared a professional practice affecting the public health.

safety, and welfare and is subject to regulation and control in the public interest. It is further declared to be a matter of public interest and concern that the practice of pharmacy, as defined in this Act, merit and receive the confidence of the public and that only qualified persons be permitted to practice pharmacy in the State of Texas. This Act shall be liberally construed to carry out these objects and purposes.

The California law states:

Cal. Ann. Bus. & Prof. Code §4046.
In recognition of and consistent with the decisions of the appellate courts of this State, the Legislature hereby declares the practice of pharmacy to be a profession.

The difficulty arises when there is no legislative pronouncement, and the pharmacy act repeatedly refers to a pharmacist's "place of business." Preferably, such laws should speak in terms of "place of practice" as do the laws governing other professions.

Nevertheless, pharmacy is almost universally accepted as a profession. This conclusion has been reflected in many areas of law in court cases. In *Supermarket General v. Sills,* a decision upholding the validity of a New Jersey statute prohibiting prescription drug advertising, the court concluded that the practice of pharmacy is a profession. The court also pointed out why it reached this decision.

In concluding that pharmacy is a profession, I am not unmindful of the fact that over 90% of the prescriptions dispensed are pre-compounded, that is, the pharmacist's function is to count the tablets called for by the prescription and transfer them from the container furnished by the manufacturer into the bottle ultimately dispensed to the purchaser. As will hereinafter appear, however, the role of the pharmacist goes beyond that of the sale of a comodity. In filling a prescription the pharmacist often aids the physician by informing him of the properties and effects of various drugs. If the prescription calls for a generic compound, he chooses the particular brand to be dispensed. Additionally, he may "monitor" each prescription as to dosage, and possibly determine whether the prescribed drug may be antagonistic to another previously prescribed for the patient by another physician.

In the area of labor law the question of professionalism arises in determining bargaining units. Both the National Labor Relations Board in the case of *In re Reynolds Electrical and Engineering Company* and the New York State Labor Relations Board in *University Hospital of New York Medical Center* have held pharmacists to be professionals for purposes of those laws. Their decisions were based upon the many years of education, training and licensure requirements to practice pharmacy as well as the varied and intellectual nature of their activities.

A major professional service performed by pharmacists is the filling of prescriptions. This activity begins with receipt of the drug order and includes its interpretation, verification, and compounding, if necessary, packaging, labeling and finally dispensing the medication to the patient. The definition of a prescription varies somewhat from state to state. The Virginia pharmacy law is typical and defines it in the following manner:

Va. Code Ann. §54-524.2(28)
"Prescription" shall mean and include an order for drugs or medical supplies, written or signed or transmitted by word of mouth, telephone, telegraph or other means of communication to a pharmacist by a duly licensed physician, dentist, veterinarian or other practitioner, authorized by law to prescribe and administer such drugs or medical supplies.

If the prescription is an oral one the Ohio law states:

Ohio Rev. Code Ann. §479.37
Prescriptions received by word of mouth, telephone, telegraph, or other means of communication shall be recorded in writing by the pharmacist and the record so made by the pharmacist shall constitute the original prescription to be filled by the pharmacist. All prescriptions shall be preserved on file at the PHARMACY for a period of THREE years, subject to inspection by the proper officers of the law.

A question in institutional practice that frequently arises is whether drug orders entered in a patient's medical record are prescriptions. How are such orders to be treated, who may fill such orders, and what information is required? Answers to these questions depend upon the particular pharmacy law involved. Many are silent on this point. California law is rather specific. It holds:

Cal. Bus. & Prof. Code §4036.1
An "order," entered on the chart or medical record of a patient registered in a hospital or a patient under emergency treatment in the hospital, by or on the order of a practitioner authorized by law to prescribe drugs, shall be authorization for the administration of such drug from hospital floor or ward stocks furnished by the hospital pharmacy or under licensure granted under Section 4052.1, and shall be considered to be a prescription if such medication is to be furnished directly to the patient by the hospital pharmacy or another pharmacy furnishing prescribed drugs for hospital patients; provided that the chart or medical record of the

patient contains all of the information required by Section 4036 and the order is signed by the practitioner authorized by law to prescribe drugs, if he is present when the drugs are given, or if he is not present, then on his next visit to the hospital.

A basic question concerning prescriptions is who may lawfully order legend drugs? The Virginia Code, above, refers to a "duly licensed physician, dentist, veterinarian or other practitioner, authorized by law to prescribe and administer such drugs or medical supplies." Since practice of the professions is regulated by state law, the authorization referred to is state licensure. Laws licensing various health care practitioners, such as physicians, osteopathic physicians, dentists, podiatrists, chiropractors, etc., would have to be examined in each state to determine which drugs a class of practitioners is authorized to prescribe. Foreign-licensed physicians are not generally considered practitioners who may prescribe. This is also true of newly emerging classifications such as physician assistants, pediatric nurses and the like. The statutes enabling these individuals to practice should also be examined on a state-by-state basis. Nurses are licensed by law to administer legend drugs but licensure usually does not include authority to prescribe such drugs. Hence, persons not licensed by state law to prescribe may not issue written or oral orders for a legend drug.

Sometimes a pharmacist receives a prescription order of a physician from another state. Under the Federal Food Drug and Cosmetic Act it would be a lawful prescription. On the other hand, each state determines who may practice medicine or, more specifically, who may prescribe medication. Like pharmacists, physicians licensed to practice in one state may not practice in another state unless also licensed in the second state. Sometimes out-of-state licenses are recognized for emergency treatment or consulting with colleagues, but this is not universal. A few states, such as California and Illinois, specifically prohibit a pharmacist from filling prescriptions written by practitioners not licensed in the state. The existence of such laws settle the matter. If, however, there is no appropriate law, pharmacists should be careful to ascertain the prescriber's authority and whether the medication was ordered in the course of practice. If there is doubt, the prescription should be refused.

In order to assist both prescribers and dispensers concerning the information that should be included in prescription orders and on prescription labels, the American Pharmaceutical Association and the American Society of Internal Medicine have adopted a "Statement on Prescription Writing and Prescription Labeling." This statement appears in the *Journal of the American Pharmaceutical Association*.

The question of out-of-state prescribers directly leads to the subject of mail order prescriptions. In this instance not only is the physician probably not known but neither is the patient. What generally happens is that a patient mails his prescription to a pharmacist who fills the order and mails the medication back to the patient. The professional acceptability of this practice is questionable. Section 7 of the APhA Code of Ethics recognizes the importance of the pharmacist's opportunity to establish a personal relationship with the patient. Nevertheless, this activity is prevalent among retired persons who obtain their prescriptions by mail.

Under state law, unless mail order prescriptions are prohibited, either in the statutes or by opinion of the attorney general, or by a court of law, the practice is permissible. In Oklahoma's pharmacy law an example of this type of prohibition may be found.

59 Okla. Stat. Ann. §353.24 Unlawful Acts
It shall be unlawful for any person, firm or corporation:
* * *

(d) To engage in any "mail order" prescription business in which prescriptions are solicited and received through the mails for dispensing, or in which prescriptions are dispensed and delivered by mail to customers other than those personally known to the pharmacist in charge of a pharmacy and under circumstances clearly dictating that such method of delivery is in the best interests of the health and welfare of the customer.

In addition to state laws, federal postal law also regulates mailing of drugs and is discussed in Chapter 2.

Another question that sometimes arises is who "owns" the prescription. Of course, the only time there is a question is when a patient gives the prescription to a pharmacist. Somewhere between the transfer of the piece of paper and the receipt of and payment for the medication, a binding, legal contract arises. It is possible to discuss many fine legal points as to exactly when a contract arises, what constitutes satisfactory performance in dispensing, etc., but more important from a professional point of view is a consideration of the legal rights that attach to prescriptions. Both pharmacist and patient have certain continuing rights in relation thereto.

For example, a patient has a right to have the order refilled if the physician so designated on the prescription. However, the Controlled Substances Act places specific limitations on this right which the pharmacist is legally bound to observe. The patient should also have a right to obtain a copy of the prescription just as he would have a right to a copy of his medical record as maintained by a physician. On the other hand, the pharmacist would have a duty not to disclose information in the prescription and to maintain its confidentiality. These are the rights and duties significant in practice, not whether one party or the other owns the prescription.

If the drug order is not being filled by a pharmacist, may he keep the prescription, destroy it, or deface it in some manner? This may be thought necessary if a pharmacist believes the prescription to be a forgery or if he detects a drug interaction which he thinks may be detrimental to the patient. Some feel this intervention is a professional duty.

Generally, until a pharmacist accepts a prescription to fill it, there is no contract that gives him any right to the piece of paper. If he accepts the prescription and then destroys or defaces it, he does so at his own risk. The risk is that the patient would have a civil cause of action against the pharmacist, if the prescription is not a forgery or if following it would not result in an interaction with some other medication, and if the patient suffers an injury because of the pharmacist's failure to return the order or because he has defaced it.

If there is any doubt, the pharmacist should inquire of the physician or patient in an attempt to learn more about the situation. He might first consult with a physician or issue a warning to the patient. Secondly, he could refuse to fill the prescription. Only if he is absolutely certain about the facts and it is essential to the patient's health or safety should he attempt to keep the order unfilled, or deface it in such a manner that no other pharmacist could fill it.

In completing a prescription order, pharmacists must be certain the dispensing container is properly labeled. In addition to requirements of various federal laws, state pharmacy acts also specify the information that must be included. The California code contains the following requirements:

Cal. Bus. & Prof. Code §4047.5
A pharmacist shall not dispense any prescription except in a container correctly labeled with the following:

(a) Except where the prescriber orders otherwise, the trade name of the drug, or if there is no trade name, the generic name and the name of the manufacturer. Commonly used abbreviations may be used. Preparations containing two or more active ingredients may be identified by a brand or commonly used name or the principal active ingredients.

(b) The directions for the use of the drug.

(c) The name of the patient.

(d) The name of the prescriber.

(e) The date of issue.

(f) The name and address and prescription number of the furnisher.

(g) The strength of the drug or drugs prescribed.

(h) The quantity of the drug or drugs prescribed.

Expiration dating may also be required as in California:

Cal. Bus. & Prof. Code §4048
The label on any drugs furnished to a patient under the provisions of Section 4051 of this chapter, or dispensed on

prescription by a pharmacist as provided in this chapter, shall, in addition to any other information required to be stated thereon, contain the expiration date of the effectiveness of the drug if such information is required on the original label of the manufacturer of the drugs.

Once a prescription is processed, the order must be initialed, numbered and filed, usually for a specified number of years. New Jersey law indicates:

N.J. Stat. Ann. §45:14-15. Prescriptions to be numbered and filed; removal of original prescriptions by board or agents.
The registered pharmacist compounding, dispensing, filling, or selling a prescription shall place the original written prescription in a file kept for that purpose for a period of not less than five years if such period is not less than two years after the last refilling, and affix to the container in which the prescription is dispensed, a label bearing the name and complete address of the pharmacy or drug store in which dispensed, the date on which the prescription was compounded and an identifying number under which the prescription is recorded in his files, together with the name of the physician, dentist, veterinarian or other medical practitioner prescribing it and the directions for the use of the prescription by the patient, as directed on the prescription of the physician, dentist, veterinarian or other medical practitioner licensed to write prescriptions. Every registered pharmacist who fills or compounds a prescription, or who supervises the filling or compounding of a prescription by a person other than a pharmacist registered in this State, shall place his name or initials on the original prescription or on the label affixed to the container in which the prescription is dispensed or in a book kept for the purpose of recording prescriptions. The board of pharmacy or any of its agents is hereby empowered to inspect the prescription files and other prescription records of a pharmacy and to remove from said files and take possession of any original prescription; *providing,* that the authorized agent removing or taking possession of an original prescription shall place in the file from which it was removed a copy certified by said person to be a true copy of the original prescription thus removed; *provided further,* that the original copy shall be returned by the board of pharmacy to the file from which it was removed after it was served the purpose for which it was removed.

State laws also provide special standards for sale of nonprescription poisons. The poisons are often specified in the law by name. In addition, they may be referred to by toxicity and listed in appropriate schedules. For example, Schedule A poisons are sometimes defined as those that are liable to be destructive to adult human life in doses of five grains or less, and Schedule B poisons may be defined as substances liable to be destructive to adult human life in doses of sixty grains or less.

Before a poison may be sold the pharmacist must be sure that the purchaser is above the age specified in the poison law, anywhere from twelve years old and up, that the purchaser knows the poisonous nature of the substance, and that it will be used for a lawful purpose. A poison register or book must be maintained indicating the date and time of sale, the name and address of the purchaser, the substance and quantity sold, the purpose for which the poison is required, and the name of the dispenser. In addition, the bottle or packaging must be distinctively marked with a red label stating the name of the substance plus the word "POISON."

The foregoing specific requirements are representative and may vary somewhat from state to state. They generally do not apply to non-pharmacy outlets that sell poisonous chemicals and substances for use in agriculture, mining, the arts and similar commercial or economic uses.

Other articles that come under special control are prophylactics. These include drugs and devices used for the prevention of venereal disease. In many states they may only be sold at retail through pharmacies, for which a special permit is required. Their advertisement or display is frequently prohibited as is their sale through vending machines. Wholesalers may also be required to obtain a special license to sell prophylactics at wholesale.

In addition to poisons and prophylactics, hypodermic syringes and needles are often singled out. These and other devices that are adaptable to illicit use in drug abuse situations require special control. Generally, they may be sold only in registered pharmacies pursuant to written prescriptions. Such prescriptions must contain the name and quantity of the device required. These prescriptions should be filed and maintained along with other prescriptions.

Many states also prohibit the sale of drugs, both prescription and OTC medications, through vending machines. The Nebraska law provides:

Neb. Rev. Stat. §71-1147.15 Drugs; automatic or vending machine; dispense or vend; unlawful.
It shall be unlawful to distribute dispense or vend any drug by automatic or vending machines; Provided, that this prohibition shall not apply to institutions duly licensed under the provisions of sections 71-2017 to 71-2029.

It should be noted that this prohibition does not apply to institutions, because automatic equipment is used frequently in hospitals to provide security and control as well as to provide access to emergency medications at times when the pharmacy is not open. Generally special cards or other coded devices are needed to operate the machines, and only professional personnel have access to them.

Lastly, the prohibited acts section of state pharmacy laws shed some light on the practices *not* expected from pharmacists. Oklahoma law specifies the following items.

Okla. Stat. Ann. tit. 59 §353.24 Unlawful acts.

It shall be unlawful for any person, firm or corporation:

(a) To forge or increase the quantity of drug in any prescription, or to present a prescription bearing forged, fictious or altered information or to possess any drug secured by such forged, fictious or altered prescription.

(b) To sell, offer for sale, barter or give away any unused quantity of drugs obtained by prescription.

(c) To sell, offer for sale, barter or give away any drugs damaged by fire or water without first obtaining the written approval of the Board of Pharmacy and the State Department of Health.

(d) To engage in any "mail order" prescription business in which prescriptions are solicited and received through the mails for dispensing, or in which prescriptions are dispensed and delivered by mail to customers other than those personally known to the pharmacist in charge of a pharmacy and under circumstances clearly dictating that such method of delivery is in the best interests of the health and welfare of the customer.

(e) To enter into any arrangement whereby prescription orders are received or prescriptions delivered at a place other than the pharmacy in which they are compounded and dispensed. However, nothing in this section shall prevent a pharmacist or his employee from personally receiving a prescription or delivering a legally filled prescription at a residence, office or place of employment of the patient for whom the prescription was written. Laws 1961, p. 452, § 24.

Some or all of the foregoing prohibitions may be contained in other state pharmacy laws. Variations exist and each state's laws should be examined for applicability.

Section 2

FEDERAL LAW

The federal government does not regulate professional practice. This area of regulation is reserved, under the U.S. Constitution, to the states. Nevertheless, federal laws have an effect on practice. (Appendix D is a list of selected federal laws, regulations and agencies of great interest to pharmacy.) The federal budget for health care amounts to billions of dollars. Most federal health activity is centered in the

Department of Health, Education and Welfare (HEW), a cabinet level department. HEW's health programs are scattered among the Public Health Service, the Food and Drug Administration, the National Institutes of Health, Center of Disease Control, the Consumer Product Safety Commission, the Social Security Administration, the Social and Rehabilitation Service, the Office of Professional Service Review and others. Various programs of these agencies have a direct or indirect effect upon the practice of pharmacy. Some are discussed in depth in other sections of the book.

The programs of greatest interest at this point are those of the Social Security Administration (SSA) and the Social and Rehabilitation Service (SRS). The SSA administers the Medicare program, federal health insurance for the aged, while the SRS implements the Medicaid program, a medical assistance program. In order to qualify to receive reimbursements for professional services rendered to individuals participating in these programs, providers, including pharmacists, must meet certain standards. These standards are designed to assure a certain level of service and to contain costs.

Subsequent to adoption of the 1965 Medicare Amendments to the Social Security Act, the SSA promulgated regulations commonly referred to as Conditions of Participation. These regulations set forth the conditions that must be met in order to qualify for reimbursement for services rendered. The conditions that apply to pharmaceutical services provided in hospitals follow.

20 C.F.R. §405.1027
Condition of Participation — Pharmacy or Drug Room. —
The hospital has a pharmacy directed by a registered pharmacist or a drug room under competent supervision. The pharmacy or drug room is administered in accordance with accepted professional principles.

(a) Standard; Pharmacy Supervision. — There is a pharmacy directed by a registered pharmacist or a drug room under competent supervision. The factors explaining the standard are as follows:

(1) The pharmacist is trained in the specialized functions of hospital pharmacy.

(2) The pharmacist is responsible to the administration of the hospital for developing, supervising, and coordinating all the activities of the pharmacy department.

(3) If there is a drug room with no pharmacist, prescription medications are dispensed by a qualified pharmacist elsewhere, and only storing and distributing are done in the hospital. A consulting pharmacist assists in drawing up the correct procedures, rules, and regulations, for the distribution of drugs, and visits the hospital on a regularly scheduled basis in the course of his duties. Wherever possible the pharmacist, in

dispensing drugs, works from the prescriber's original order or a direct copy.

(b) Standard; Physical Facilities. — Facilities are provided for the storage, safeguarding, preparation, and dispensing of drugs. The factors explaining the standard are as follows:

(1) Drugs are issued to floor units in accordance with approved policies and procedures.

(2) Drug cabinets on the nursing units are routinely checked by the pharmacist. All floor stocks are properly controlled.

(3) There is adequate space for all pharmacy operations and the storage of drugs at a satisfactory location provided with proper lighting, ventilation, and temperature controls.

(4) If there is a pharmacy, equipment is provided for the compounding and dispensing of drugs.

(5) Special locked storage space is provided to meet the legal requirements for storage of narcotics, alcohol, and other prescribed drugs.

(c) Standard; Personnel. — Personnel competent in their respective duties are provided in keeping with the size and activity of the department. The factors explaining the standard are as follows:

(1) The pharmacist is assisted by an adequate number of additional registered pharmacists and such other personnel as the activities of the pharmacy may require to insure quality pharmaceutical services.

(2) The pharmacy, depending upon the size and scope of its operations, is staffed by the following categories of personnel:

(i) Chief pharmacist.

(ii) One or more assistant chief pharmacists.

(iii) Staff pharmacists.

(iv) Pharmacy residents (where a program has been activated).

(v) Nonprofessionally trained pharmacy helpers.

(vi) Clerical help.

(3) Provision is made for emergency pharmaceutical services.

(4) If the hospital does not have a staff pharmacist, a consulting pharmacist has overall responsibility for control and distribution of drugs and a designated individual(s) has responsibility for day-to-day operation of the pharmacy.

(d) Standard; Records. — Records are kept of the transactions of the pharmacy (or drug room) and correlated with other hospital records where indicated. Such special records are kept as are required by law. The factors explaining the standard are as follows:

(1) The pharmacy establishes and maintains, in cooperation with the accounting department, a satisfactory system of records and bookkeeping in accordance with the policies of the hospital for:

(i) Maintaining adequate control over the requisitioning and dispensing of all drugs and pharmaceutical supplies, and

(ii) Charging patients for drugs and pharmaceutical supplies.

(2) A record of the stock on hand and of the dispensing of all narcotic drugs is maintained in such a manner that the disposition of any particular item may be readily traced.

(3) Records for prescription drugs dispensed to each patient (inpatients and outpatients) are maintained in the pharmacy or drug room containing the full name of the patient and the prescribing physician, the prescription number, the name and strength of the drug, the date of issue, the expiration date for all timedated medications, the lot and control number of the drug, the name of the manufacturer (or trademark) and (unless the physician directs otherwise) the name of the medication dispensed.

(4) The label of each outpatient's individual prescription medication container bears the lot and control number of the drug, the name of the manufacturer (or trademark) and (unless the physician directs otherwise) the name of the medication dispensed.

(e) Standard; Control of Toxic or Dangerous Drugs. — Policies are established to control the administration of toxic or dangerous drugs with specific reference to the duration of the order and the dosage. The factors explaining the standard are as follows:

(1) The medical staff has established a written policy that all toxic or dangerous medications, not specifically prescribed as to time or number of doses, will be automatically stopped after a reasonable time limit set by the staff.

(2) The classifications ordinarily thought of as toxic or dangerous drugs are narcotics, sedatives, anticoagulants, antibiotics, oxytocics, and cortisone products.

(f) Standard; Committee. — There is a committee of the medical staff to confer with the pharmacist in the formulation of policies. The factors explaining the standard are as follows:

(1) A pharmacy and therapeutics committee (or equivalent committee), composed of physicians and pharmacists, is established in the hospital. It represents the organizational line of communication and the liaison between the medical staff and the pharmacist.

(2) The committee assists in the formulation of broad professional policies regarding the evaluation, appraisal, selection, procurement, storage, distribution, use, and safety procedures, and all other matters relating to drugs in hospitals.

(3) The committee performs the following specific functions:

(i) Serves as an advisory group to the hospital medical staff and the pharmacist on matters pertaining to the choice of drugs;

(ii) Develops and reviews periodically a formulary or drug list for use in the hospital;

(iii) Establishes standards concerning the use and control of investigational drugs and research in the use of recognized drugs;

(iv) Evaluates clinical data concerning new drugs or preparations requested for use in the hospital;

(v) Makes recommendations concerning drugs to be stocked on the nursing unit floors and by other services; and

(vi) Prevents unnecessary duplication in stocking drugs and drugs in combination having identical amounts of the same therapeutic ingredients.

(4) The committee meets at least quarterly and reports to the medical staff.

(g) Standard; Drugs To Be Dispensed. — Therapeutic ingredients of medications dispensed are included (or approved for inclusion) in the United States Pharmacopoeia, National Formulary, United States Homeopathic Pharmacopoeia, New Drugs, or Accepted Dental Remedies (except for any drugs unfavorably evaluated therein), or are approved for use by the pharmacy and drug therapeutics committee (or equivalent committee) of the hospital staff. The factors explaining the standard are as follows:

(1) The pharmacist, with the advice and guidance of the pharmacy and therapeutics committee, is responsible for specifications as to quality, quantity, and source of supply of all drugs.

(2) There is available a formulary or list of drugs accepted for use in the hospital which is developed and amended at regular intervals by the pharmacy and therapeutics committee (or equivalent committee) with the cooperation of the pharmacist (consulting or otherwise) and the administration.

(3) The pharmacy or drug room is adequately supplied with preparations so approved.

Sections relating to nursing from the conditions of participation for hospitals are also relevant for they deal with administration of medications.

20 C.F.R. 405.1024(g)

(5) Only (i) a licensed physician or a registered professional nurse or (ii) a licensed practical nurse, a student nurse in an approved school of nursing, or a psychiatric technician, when these three classes of personnel are under the direct supervision of a registered professional nurse, is permitted to administer medications, and in all instances, in accordance with the Nurse Practice Act of the State.

* * *

(7) Blood transfusions and intravenous medications are administered in accordance with State law. If administered by

registered professional nurses, they are administered only by those who have been specially trained for this duty.

Some state inspectors have maintained that drug administration programs run by hospital pharmacies do not comply with the regulations. Officials at SSA have made it clear, however, that it is not their intent to prohibit drug administration programs that are centralized within and under the supervision of the department of pharmaceutical services, especially since such programs are usually developed jointly by the pharmacy, nursing and medical staffs. These programs centralize in one department all the activities relating to drugs from the time they enter the institution until they are administered to inpatients, dispensed to outpatients or disposed of in some other way.

In 1973, the Social Security Law was amenaed by P.L. 93-603. One provision requires that federal standards applicable to various health programs such as Medicare and Medicaid as well as others be uniform. As a result, the former conditions of participation for skilled nursing homes and extended care facilities were combined and revised, in 1974, under the name of "Skilled Nursing Facilities" (SNF). The conditions for pharmaceutical services in SNF read:

20 C.F.R. §405.1127 Condition of participation—pharmaceutical services.

The skilled nursing facility provides appropriate methods and procedures for the dispensing and administering of drugs and biologicals. Whether drugs and biologicals are obtained from community or institutional pharmacists or stocked by the facility, the facility is responsible for providing such drugs and biologicals for its patients, insofar as they are covered under the programs, and for ensuring that pharmaceutical services are provided in accordance with accepted professional principles and appropriate Federal, State, and local laws. (See §405.1124 (g), (h), and (i).)

(a) *Standard: Supervision of services.* The pharmaceutical services are under the general supervision of a qualified pharmacist who is responsible to the administrative staff for developing, coordinating, and supervising all pharmaceutical services. The pharmacist (if not a full-time employee) devotes a sufficient number of hours, based upon the needs of the facility, during regularly scheduled visits to carry out these responsibilities. The pharmacist reviews the drug regimen of each patient at least monthly, and reports any irregularities to the medical director and administrator. The pharmacist submits a written report at least quarterly to the pharmaceutical services committee on the status of the facility's pharmaceutical service and staff performance.

(b) *Standard: Control and accountability.* The pharmaceutical service has procedures for control and accountability of all drugs and biologicals throughout the facility. Only approved drugs and biologicals are used in the facility, and are dispensed in compliance with Federal and State laws. Records of receipt and disposition of all controlled drugs are maintained in sufficient detail to enable an accurate reconciliation. The pharmacist determines that drug records are in order and that an account of all controlled drugs is maintained and reconciled.

(c) *Standard: Labeling of drugs and biologicals.* The labeling of drugs and biologicals is based on currently accepted professional principles, and includes the appropriate accessory and cautionary instructions, as well as the expiration date when applicable.

(d) *Standard: Pharmaceutical services committee.* A pharmaceutical services committee (or its equivalent) develops written policies and procedures for safe and effective drug therapy, distribution, control, and use. The committee is comprised of at least the pharmacist, the director of nursing services, the administrator, and one physician. The committee oversees pharmaceutical service in the facility, makes recommendation for improvement, and monitors the service to ensure its accuracy and adequacy. The committee meets at least quarterly and documents its activities, findings, and recommendations.

Under these new regulations the pharmacist must also be a participant in the institution's infection control committee.

With this current revision, three important drug standards were transferred from the former pharmacy condition to the new nursing condition. Prior to this update, all drug related standards were found in one place, the condition dealing with pharmaceutical services. One central location for drug related matters was important because it clarified pharmacist responsibility, made it easy to find all drug standards, and facilitated comparison of various standards. The reason the drug standards were fragmented in the 1974 revision is to make it easier for nursing personnel to find these drug standards that relate directly to their activities in administering medication, complying with the drug order, and properly storing medication at the nursing station. These transferred standards are below.

20 C.F.R. §405.1124 Condition of participation — nursing services

* * *

(g) *Standard: Administration of drugs.* Drugs are administered in compliance with State and local laws. Procedures are established by the pharmaceutical services committee (see § 405.1127 (d)) to ensure that drugs are checked against physicians' orders, that the patient is identified prior to administration of a drug, and that each patient has an individual medication record and that the dose of drug administered to that patient is properly recorded therein by the person who administers the drug. Drugs and biologicals are administered as soon as possible after doses are prepared, and are administered by the same person who prepared the doses for administration, except under single unit dose package distribution systems (See § 405.1101 (h).)

(h) *Standard: Conformance with physicians' drug orders.* Drugs are administered in accordance with written orders of the attending physician. Drugs not specifically limited as to time or number of doses when ordered are controlled by automatic stop orders or other methods in accordance with written policies. Physicians' verbal orders for drugs are given only to a licensed nurse, pharmacist, or physician and are immediately recorded and signed by the person receiving the order. (Verbal orders for Schedule II drugs are permitted only in the case of a bona fide emergency situation.) Such orders are countersigned by the attending physician within 48 hours. The attending physician is notified of an automatic stop order prior to the last dose so that he may decide if the administration of the drug or biological is to be continued or altered.

(i) *Standard: Storage of drugs and biologicals.* Procedures for storing and disposing of drugs and biologicals are established by the pharmaceutical services committee. In accordance with State and Federal laws, all drugs and biologicals, are stored in locked compartments under proper temperature controls and only authorized personnel have access to the keys. Separately locked, permanently affixed compartments are provided for storage of controlled drugs listed in Schedule II of the Comprehensive Drug Abuse Prevention & Control Act of 1970 and other drugs subject to abuse, except under single unit package drug distribution systems in which the quantity stored is minimal and a missing dose can be readily detected. An emergency medication kit approved by the pharmaceutical services committee is kept readily available.

The SNF regulations also define drug administration and dispensing.

20 C.F.R. §405.1101

* * *

(h) *Drug administration.* An act in which a single dose of a prescribed drug or biological is given to a patient by an authorized person in accordance with all laws and regulations governing such acts. The complete act of administration entails removing an individual dose from a previously dispensed, properly labeled container (including a unit dose container), verifying it with the physician's orders, giving the individual dose to the proper patient, and promptly recording the time and dose given.

(i) *Drug dispensing.* An act entailing the interpretation of an order for a drug or biological and, pursuant to that order, the proper selection, measuring, labeling, packaging, and issuance of the drug or biological for a patient or for a service unit of the facility.

Drugs which are reimbursible under Medicare and Medicaid are also indicated.

20 C.F.R. §405.1101

* * *

(b) *Approved drugs and biologicals.* Only such drugs and biologicals as are:

(1) In the case of medicare:

(i) Included (or approved for inclusion) in the United States Pharmacopoeia, National Formulary, or United States Homeopathic Pharmacopoeia; or

(ii) Included (or approved for inclusion) in AMA Drug Evaluations or Accepted Dental Therapeutics, except for any drugs and biologicals unfavorably evaluated therein ; or

(iii) Not included (nor approved for inclusion) in the compendia listed in paragraphs (b) (1) (i) and (b) (1) (ii) of this section, may be considered approved if such drugs:

(A) Were furnished to the patient during his prior hospitalization, and

(B) Were approved for use during a prior hospitalization by the hospital's pharmacy and drug therapeutics committee (or equivalent), and

(C) Are required for the continuing treatment of the patient in the facility.

(2) In the case of Medicaid, those drugs approved by the State Title XIX agency.

Lastly, these regulations contain a standard relating to the use of outside resources.

20 C.F.R. §405.1121 (i)

* * *

(i) *Standard: Use of outside resources.* If the facility does not employ a qualified professional person to render a specific service to be provided by the facility, there are arrangements for such a service through a written agreement with an outside resource—a person or agency that will render direct service to patients or act as a consultant. The responsibilities, functions, and objectives, and the terms of agreement, including financial arrangements and charges, of each such outside resource are delineated in writing and signed by an authorized representative of the facility and the person or the agency providing the service. The agreement specifies that the facility retains professional and administrative responsibility for the services rendered. The financial arrangements provide that the outside resource bill the facility for covered services (either Part A or B for Medicare beneficiaries) rendered directly to the patient, and their receipt of payment from the program(s) to the facility for the services discharges the liability of the beneficiary or any other person to pay for the services. The outside resource, when acting as a consultant, apprises the administrator of recommendations, plans for implementation, and continuing assessment through dated, signed reports, which are retained by the administrator for follow-up action and evaluation of performance. (See requirement under each service—§§ 405.1125 through 405.1132.)

This provision deals with both business and professional matters. It requires contracts for outside services to be in writing. Such providers must bill the facility rather than the patient receiving the service, and federal government payment to the facility alleviates the patient from paying the provider. Continuing written reports are also required.

The practice standard that is difficult to assess is the requirement that the agreement specify that the facility retain "professional and administrative responsibility for the services rendered." How can an administrator properly assess professional services? Who does the patient sue if injury results? Are any laws broken if a pharmacist agrees to this transfer of professional responsibility?

Another set of federal standards of importance also resulted from the 1973 amendments to the Social Security Law and relate to Intermediate Care Facilities (ICF). The relevant provision does not even refer to pharmaceutical services but rather speaks of "drugs and biologicals."

45 C.F.R. §249.12   The facility:

* * *

(8) Implements methods and procedures relating to drugs and biologicals which assure that:

(i) If the facility does not employ a licensed pharmacist, it has formal arrangements with a licensed pharmacist to provide consultation on methods and procedures for ordering, storage, administration and disposal and recordkeeping of drugs and biologicals;

(ii) Medications administered to a resident are ordered either in writing or orally by the resident's attending or staff physician. Physician's oral orders for prescription drugs are given only to a licensed nurse, pharmacist, or physician. All oral orders for medication are immediately recorded and signed by the person receiving them and are countersigned by the attending physician in a manner consistent with good medical practice;

(iii) Medications not specifically limited as to time or number of doses when ordered are controlled by automatic stop orders or other methods in accordance with written policies and the attending physician is notified;

(iv) Self-administration of medication is allowed only with permission of the resident's attending physician;

(v) A registered nurse reviews monthly each resident's medications and notifies the physician when changes are appropriate. Medications are reviewed quarterly by the attending or staff physician; and

(vi) All personnel administering medications must have completed a State-approved training program in medication administration.

* * *

Other "Pharmacy Services" conditions apply to ICFs that treat the mentally retarded or persons with related conditions.

45 C.F.R. §249.13

* * *

(7) *Pharmacy services.* (i) Pharmacy services shall be provided under the direction of a qualified licensed pharmacist. There shall be a formal arrangement for qualified pharmacy services, including provision for emergency service, by means appropriate to the facility.

(ii) There shall be a current pharmacy manual that:

(A) Includes policies and procedures, and defines the functions and responsibilities relating to pharmacy services; and

(B) Is revised annually to keep abreast of current developments in services and management techniques.

(iii) There shall be a formulary system approved by the responsible physician and pharmacist, and by other appropriate facility staff. Copies of the facility's formulary and of the American Hospital Formulary Service shall be located and available, as appropriate to the facility.

(iv) Upon admission of the resident, a medication history of prescription and nonprescription drugs used shall be obtained where possible, preferably by the pharmacist, and this information shall be entered in the resident's record for the information of the staff. The pharmacist shall:

(A) Receive the original, or a direct copy, of the physician's drug treatment order;

(B) Maintain for each resident an individual record of all medications (prescription and nonprescription) dispensed, including quantities and frequency of refills;

(C) Participate, as appropriate, in the continuing interdisciplinary evaluation of individual residents for the purposes of initiation, monitoring, and follow-up of individualized habilitation programs; and

(D) Establish quality specifications for drug purchases, and insure that they are met.

(v) A pharmacist or RN shall regularly review the record of each resident on medication for potential adverse reactions, allergies, interactions, contraindications, rationality and laboratory test modifications, and advise the physician of any recommended changes with reasons, and with an alternate drug regimen.

(vi) Written policies and procedures that govern the safe administration and handling of all drugs shall be developed by the responsible pharmacist, physician, nurse and other professional staff, as appropriate to the facility. There shall be a written policy governing the self-administration of drugs, whether prescribed or not. The compounding, packaging, labeling, and dispensing of drugs, including samples and investigational drugs, shall be done by the pharmacist, or under his supervision, with proper controls and records. Each drug shall be identified up to the point of administration. Wherever possible, drugs that require dosage measurement shall be dispensed by the pharmacist in a form ready to be administered to the resident.

(vii) Medications shall not be used by any resident other than the one for whom they were issued. Only appropriately trained staff shall be allowed to administer drugs.

(viii) Drugs shall be stored under proper conditions of sanitation, temperature, light, moisture, ventilation, segregation, and security. All drugs shall be kept under lock and key except when authorized personnel are in attendance. The security requirements of Federal and State laws shall be satisfied in storerooms, pharmacies, and living units. Poisons, drugs used externally, and drugs taken internally shall be stored on separate shelves or in separate cabinets, at all locations. Medications that are stored in a refrigerator containing things other than drugs shall be kept in a separate compartment with proper security. If there is a drug storeroom separate from the pharmacy, there shall be a perpetual inventory of receipts and issues of all drugs by such storeroom.

(ix) Discontinued and outdated drugs, and containers with worn, illegible, or missing labels, shall be returned to the pharmacy for proper disposition.

(x) There shall be automatic stop orders on all drugs. There shall be a drug recall procedure that can be readily implemented. Medication errors and drug reactions shall be recorded and reported immediately to the practitioner who ordered the drug. There shall be a procedure for reporting adverse drug reactions to the Federal Food and Drug Administration.

(xi) There shall be an emergency kit readily available to each living unit and constituted so as to be appropriate to the needs of its residents.

These latter conditions do not become effective before March 18, 1977. This gives affected ICFs plenty of time in which to comply with these innovative, service-oriented regulations. Unlike state pharmacy practice acts, the emphasis is ultimately on what the pharmacist is providing in terms of service and not merely on the product or the place.

The last major federal law specifying the services that pharmacists are to provide is the Health Maintenance Organization Act of 1973, P.L. 93-222. This law defines a health maintenance organization (HMO) as "a legal entity which (1) provides basic and supplemental health services to its members in the manner prescribed, and (2) is organized and operated in the manner prescribed." The act then goes on to identify which services are basic and which are supplemental. The law includes the provision of prescription drugs prescribed in the course of basic or supplemental health services and goes on to say:

A health maintenance organization is authorized, in connection with the prescription or provision of prescription drugs, to maintain, review, and evaluate (in accordance with regulations of the Secretary) a drug use profile of its members receiving such services, evaluate patterns of drug utilization to assure optimum drug therapy, and provide for instruction of its members and of health professionals in the use of prescription and non-prescription drugs.

The Senate-House Conference Report, No. 93-621 explains this language.

The conferees agreed that to achieve the prime goal of an HMO—to provide high quality care most efficiently with the greatest cost effectiveness—the high incidence of adverse drug reactions and interaction encountered in the practice of medicine should be avoided. Experience has shown that utilization of a clinical pharmacist—to establish patterns of patient drug utilization, to maintain such patterns under surveillance, and to provide evaluation and review as well as maintain a drug-use profile for individual patients—has proven highly effective in reducing the incidence of such adverse reactions and interactions. The conferees did not wish to dictate the staffing patterns of each HMO and for that reason deleted language in the Senate bill which would have required the utilization of a clinical pharmacist as part of the basic benefits package. The conferees, however, are cognizant of the important role the clinical pharmacist can play in encouraging the development of rational drug therapy programs for HMO's and for educating patients and professionals in drug use and abuse, and urge that such professionals should be used to the maximum feasible extent.

Regulations were promulgated pursuant to the Health Maintenance Organization Act of 1973 by the Public Health Service on October 18, 1974. Under these regulations, HMOs must provide drugs, medication, and biologicals to inpatients as part of the basic health services rendered. They need not be provided as part of basic services incidental to outpatient care. As part of the HMO's supplemental health services prescription drugs must be offered on an optional basis.

The regulations provide for drug use profiles as required by the law.

42 C.F.R. 110.103

* * *

(b) A health maintenance organization is authorized, if it so elects, in connection with the prescription or provision of prescription drugs, to maintain, review, and evaluate a drug use profile of its members receiving such services, evaluate patterns of drug utilization to assure optimum drug therapy, and provide for instruction of its members and of health professionals in the use of prescription and nonprescription drugs. Each health maintenance organization providing such services shall insure that:

(1) The program is developed jointly by the physicians and pharmacists associated with the health maintenance organization;

(2) The objectives of the program are explained to all health professionals and members of the health maintenance organization;

(3) Individual rights are protected and that all information regarding and identifying an individual is available only to appropriate health professionals of the health maintenance organization, and to the individual member at his request;

(4) The primary thrust of the program is optimum drug therapy for the individual member of the health maintenance organization; and

(5) The information obtained in drug utilization review is utilized in educational programs for professionals and members of the health maintenance organization.

Section 3

PRIVATE, QUASI-LEGAL, AND PROFESSIONAL STANDARDS

In addition to state and federal law, perhaps even more standards of practice are found in private, quasi-legal and professional standards. One type of private standard that has been in use for centuries is represented by a Code of Ethics. Such codes date back to the days of guilds in medieval time before the advent of public laws and regulations. These private codes were the means by which members of guilds could assure the public that services or goods provided by guild members were of a high quality. They were the keystone of self-regulation and voluntary compliance and have become one of the benchmarks of a profession.

Pharmacy has a code of ethics. It was first developed by the American Pharmaceutical Association (APhA) in 1852, and has been periodically revised and updated, most recently in 1968. Most state pharmaceutical associations also have codes of ethics. The APhA Code of Ethics, with commentary, follows.

APhA Code of Ethics

PREAMBLE

These principles of professional conduct for pharmacists are established to guide the pharmacist in his relationship with patients, fellow practitioners, other health professionals and the public.

The Preamble provides an introduction to the code and defines its purposes and areas of application—general principles of professional conduct established to guide the pharmacist in his relationship with patients, fellow practitioners, other health professionals and the public. Each section of the code applies to these four relationships unless specifically limited. The guidance of the code is intended for pharmacists generally and the Preamble is so stated that application of the code is not restricted to the community practitioner.

SECTION 1

A pharmacist should hold the health and safety of patients to be of first consideration; he should render to each patient the full measure of his ability as an essential health practitioner.

Section 1 specifies that the primary obligation of the pharmacist is the health and safety of patients and that an equally important obligation of the pharmacist, in his capacity as an essential health practitioner, is to serve each patient to the best of his ability. This section thus contains the fundamental principles of the code; upon these principles the following sections build in providing ethical guidance for pharmacists to fulfill these primary obligations of ethical professional practice.

SECTION 2

A pharmacist should never knowingly condone the dispensing, promoting or distributing of drugs or medical devices, or assist therein,

which are not of good quality, which do not meet standards required by law or which lack therapeutic value for the patient.

Section 2 adopts a standard for drugs and medical devices which the pharmacist may ethically dispense or make available for dispensing. The standard is that of good quality—a term embracing a complex of considerations and a dynamic concept allowing the ethical standard to advance as the science of pharmacy advances. As a minimum, this section adopts those standards required by law which would include, among others, standards elaborated by official compendia. And to further emphasize the responsibility of the pharmacist to patients in supplying beneficial drugs and medical devices, this section recognizes that it is unethical for the pharmacist to offer, or further the distribution of any drug or medical device which he knows, or which he should know, lacks therapeutic merit.

SECTION 3

A pharmacist should always strive to perfect and enlarge his professional knowledge. He should utilize and make available this knowledge as may be required in accordance with his best professional judgment.

This section recognizes that the service provided by the pharmacist largely depends on the professional knowledge at his command. It establishes that the pharmacist has a continuing obligation to acquire and maintain his professional knowledge; and that the pharmacist has a duty to employ this knowledge at times when it is required for the benefit of patients, fellow practitioners, other health professionals, and the public. This section also allows the pharmacist to make his professional knowledge available, voluntarily on request, when it is appropriate according to his professional judgement. While this section is not intended to derogate from the role of the physician in providing medical care to patients, it does allow the pharmacist to make his professional knowledge available to patients in circumstances where it is in the best interest of the patient as determined according to the professional judgment of the pharmacist.

SECTION 4

A pharmacist has the duty to observe the law, to uphold the dignity and honor of the profession, and to accept its ethical principles. He should not engage in any activity that will bring discredit to the profession and should expose, without fear or favor, illegal or unethical conduct in the profession.

Section 4 recognizes the duty of the pharmacist to observe national and state laws, to uphold the dignity and honor of the profession and to accept the ethical principles of the profession. This section also recognizes that a pharmacist should not engage in any activity which will bring discredit to the profession and, moreover, that a pharmacist has an ethical obligation to expose illegal or unethical conduct in the profession.

SECTION 5

A pharmacist should seek at all times only fair and reasonable remuneration for his services. He should never agree to, or participate in transactions with practitioners of other health professions or any other person under which fees are divided or which may cause financial or other exploitation in connection with the rendering of his professional services.

Section 5 states that a pharmacist should seek only fair and reasonable remuneration for his services. Yet the decision as to the specific amount will continue to be made by the individual pharmacist. This section further provides that a pharmacist should not agree to divide his remuneration with practitioners of other health professions or any others. This is in agreement with the ethics of other health professions which prohibit the dividing of fees. This section also provides that a pharmacist should not agree to arrangements with anyone which involve a reasonable probability that they may result in exploitation of the patient.

SECTION 6

A pharmacist should respect the confidential and personal nature of his professional records; except where the best interest of the patient requires or the law demands, he should not disclose such information to anyone without proper patient authorization.

A pharmacist may ethically disclose information from his patient and prescription records where it is in the best interest of the patient. He should disclose such information when it is required by law or when it is properly authorized by the patient. He may also release information for legitimate research purposes where the obligation of confidentiality to the patient is not compromised.

SECTION 7

A pharmacist should not agree to practice under terms or conditions which tend to interfere with or impair the proper exercise of his professional judgment and skill, which tend to cause a deterioration of the quality of his service or which require him to consent to unethical conduct.

Section 7 applies to all pharmacists; it especially applies to employee pharmacists. This section thus applies to the circumstances of employment of the pharmacist and to circumstances of his practice. Inherent in this section is the recognition of the pharmacist-patient-prescriber relationship and the importance of the pharmacist's opportunity to establish a personal relationship with the patient. In addition, Section 7 establishes that a pharmacist is responsible for the unethical conduct of an employer respecting pharmacy by consenting to that conduct through a continuing employment relationship.

SECTION 8

A pharmacist should not solicit professional practice by means of advertising or by methods inconsistent with his opportunity to advance his professional reputation through service to patients and to society.

Section 8 discourages solicitation of professional practice by means of advertising or other methods which are inconsistent with the opportunity of the pharmacist to advance his professional reputation through service to patients and to society. This section does not affect the commercial element of the traditional community pharmacy nor does it infringe upon the legitimate public interest in knowing where professional pharmaceutical services may be obtained. The section merely recognizes that solicitation of professional practice to be unethical which is inconsistent with the professional status of the pharmacist or which is contrary to the best interest of the public health and welfare.

SECTION 9

A pharmacist should associate with organizations having for their objective the betterment of the profession of pharmacy; he should contribute of his time and funds to carry on the work of these organizations.

Section 9 recognizes the importance to the profession of the professional unity necessary to advance the ethical and professional interests of the profession. And this section also recognizes that through the professional organization pharmacists can better achieve objectives which will be beneficial not only to the profession but to those whom the profession has an obligation to serve.

Many codes of ethics have some type of mechanism for enforcement of the code. The APhA has a judicial board that interprets the Code, applies it to specific fact situations, and renders advisory opinions. It has expressed opinions in the area of mail order pharmacies, practice in physician-owned pharmacies, and pharmacists' responsibilities in the sale of over-the-counter medications that might be used as adjuncts in narcotic addiction.

Sanctions that may be applied to those who transgress the principles of a code of ethics include censure, reprimand, suspension of membership, or expulsion from the professional association. In addition to violation of specific standards contained in a code of ethics, professional societies may also expel members for criminal activity, unethical conduct, and gross immorality. This has occurred in medical and legal associations and may, doubtlessly, occur in pharmacy associations.

A word of caution is in order concerning enforcement of codes of ethics. Just as boards of pharmacy must meet standards of due process in dealing with its licentiates, so too must professional associations administer their codes of ethics with due process. In the case of *McCune v. Wilson,* which considered the expulsion of a real estate appraiser from membership in a nonpublic, nonprofit, incorporated association, the court said:

> . . . Professional organizations, although voluntary in nature, often attain a quasi-public significance. In public view, membership in such organizations may appear to be a tangible demonstration of professional competence and skill, professional responsibility, and acceptance by one's professional peers. The fact that an individual member expelled from membership may not be prohibited from practicing his chosen occupation or profession is not a sufficient test to determine whether he needs and is entitled to judicial protection from unfair proceedings or arbitrary actions. When a voluntary association achieves this quasi-public status, due process considerations come into play. Such is the policy of the judicial decisions and statutes of this state.

> Disciplinary action against a member of a professional organization, although falling short of expulsion from occupation, may have an import which transcends the organization itself because it conveys to the community that the disciplined member was found lacking by his peers. For this reason, it is suitable and proper that an organization, whether a domestic or foreign nonprofit corporation, or a nonchartered corporation, or a nonchartered nonprofit association, be held to reasonable standards of due process and fairness, especially those inherent in its own bylaws, rules, or customs.

> While the courts should be loath to intervene in purely private organizational matters, nonintervention is not justified where a quasi-public organization takes action and imposes public sanctions. It is clear that not all private associations must observe due process standards. However, such standards must be observed when a private association becomes quasi-public, assumes a public purpose of its own, incorporates and seeks the tax shelters and other protections of public law, or otherwise assumes a larger purpose or stature than pleasant, friendly, and congenial social relationships.

In addition to codes of ethics, professional societies also develop standards of practice that amount to pronouncements concerning the manner in which the practice should be conducted. The American Society of Hospital Pharmacists has been very active in this area. Some of the statements the Society has prepared include:

Guidelines for Institutional Use of Controlled Substances
Statement on Unit Dose Drug Distribution Systems
Statement on Supportive Personnel in Hospital Pharmacy
Statement on Clinical Pharmacy and its Relationship to the Hospital
The Hospital Pharmacist and Drug Information Services
Guidelines for Single-Unit Packages of Drugs
Statement on Hospital Drug Control Systems
Statement on Research in Hospital Pharmacy
Statement of Guiding Principles on the Operation of the Hospital Formulary System
Statement on Principles Involved in the Use of Investigational Drugs in Hospitals
Statement on the Competencies Required in Institutional Pharmacy Practice
Minimum Standard for Pharmacies in Hospitals with Guide to Application
Statement on Pharmacy and Therapeutics Committee
Guidelines for Scientific Research in Hospital Pharmacy

The American College of Apothecaries has published proposed minimum practice standards as have some state and local associations.

Lastly, quasi-legal, quasi-governmental agencies have a role in the establishment of standards. The Joint Commission on Accreditation of Hospitals (JCAH) is such an organization. As medical care became more scientific and exacting, it became necessary to have available an environment that provided the requisite cleanliness, equipment, personnel and support services to care for the acutely ill. Earlier in this century the American College of Surgeons began a program of hospital standardization. The American College of Surgeons was joined by the American Medical Association and the American Hospital Association in this effort through the JCAH. The JCAH establishes standards affecting all phases of hospital care and operates a voluntary program in which a special inspection team enters a hospital, examines its plant and equipment, policies and procedures, personnel, and services to determine if it qualifies for accreditation.

One of the areas of concern to the JCAH is the pharmacy service. The basic principles affecting the service are contained in the chapter on pharmaceutical services in the *Manual on Accreditation of Hospitals* and are set forth below.

PHARMACEUTICAL SERVICES
Principle

The hospital shall maintain a pharmaceutical service that is administered in accordance with accepted ethical and professional practices.

Standards

Standard I   — Organization and Staffing
Standard II   — Facilities and Operations
Standard III   — Scope of Service and Accountability
Standard IV   — Intrahospital Drug Distribution System
Standard V   — Safe Administration of Drugs

STANDARD I

The pharmaceutical service shall be directed by a professionally competent and legally qualified pharmacist. It shall be staffed by a sufficient number of competent personnel, in keeping with the size and scope of services of the hospital.

INTERPRETATION

There shall be a director of the pharmaceutical service who is legally and professionally qualified, and who is responsible to the chief executive officer. The director should be a graduate of a recognized college of pharmacy and may be employed either part time or full time as the activity of the service requires. He should be oriented to the specialized functions of hospital pharmacies or have completed a hospital pharmacy residency program approved by the American Society of Hospital Pharmacists. The director of pharmaceutical service should be assisted by additional qualified pharmacists and ancillary personnel as needed.

If trained pharmacy assistants are employed, they should be carefully selected and shall work under the supervision of a pharmacist. They shall not be assigned duties that should be performed only by registered pharmacists. Clerical and stenographic assistance should be provided as needed to assist with records, reports and correspondence.

The organizational structure of the pharmaceutical service will vary, depending upon the size and complexity of the hospital. If the hospital does not have an organized pharmacy, pharmaceutical service shall be obtained from another hospital having such service, or from a community pharmacy. Prepackaged drugs then should be stored in, and distributed from, the hospital drug storage area under the supervision of the director of pharmaceutical service.

STANDARD II

There shall be equipment and supplies provided for the professional and administrative functions of the pharmaceutical service, as required to ensure patient safety through the proper storage and dispensing of drugs.

NTERPRETATION

Hospitals with an organized pharmaceutical service should have the necessary equipment and physical facilities for compounding and dispensing drugs, including parenteral preparations.

Drugs stored within the pharmacy, and throughout the hospital, must be under the supervision of the pharmacist. They must be stored under proper conditions of sanitation, temperature, light, moisture, ventilation, segregation and security. There should be adequate and properly controlled drug preparation areas, as well as locked storage areas, on the nursing units. These areas, which should be well lighted, should be located in a place where the nursing personnel will not be interrupted when handling drugs. The pharmacist, or his designee, must make periodic inspections of all drug storage and medication centers on nursing care units. A record of these inspections should be maintained in order to verify that:

- Disinfectants and drugs for external use are stored separately from internal and injectable medications.

- Drugs requiring special conditions for storage to ensure stability are properly stored. For example, biologicals and other thermolabile medications should
  . be stored in a separate compartment within a refrigerator that is capable of maintaining the necessary temperature.

- No outdated drugs are stocked.

- Distribution and administration of controlled drugs are adequately documented.

- Emergency drugs are in adequate and proper supply.

- Metric-apothecaries' weight and measure conversion charts are posted wherever they are needed.

Materials and equipment necessary for the administration of the service should be provided. Effective messenger and delivery service should connect the pharmacy with appropriate parts of the hospital.

Up-to-date pharmaceutical reference material should be provided in order to furnish the medical and nursing staffs with adequate information concerning drugs. As a minimum, the following should be available: *United States Pharmacopeia, National Formulary, American Hospital Formulary Service*, and *A.M.A. Drug Evaluations.*[1]

In addition, there should be current editions of text and reference books covering theoretical and practical pharmacy; general, organic, pharmaceutical and biological chemistry; toxicology; pharmacology; bacteriology; sterilization and disinfection; as well as other related matters important to good patient care. Authoritative, current antidote information should be readily available in the pharmacy for emergency reference, along with the telephone number of the regional poison control center.

STANDARD III

The scope of the pharmaceutical service shall be consistent with the medication needs of the patients and shall include a program for the control and accountability of drug products throughout the hospital.

INTERPRETATION

Policies and procedures relative to the selection and distribution, as well as to the safe and effective use, of drugs shall be developed by the medical staff in cooperation with the pharmacist and with representatives of other disciplines, as necessary. Such policies and procedures should be approved by the medical staff. All drugs and chemicals should be obtained and used in accordance with these established policies. Such products shall meet the standards of quality of the *United States Pharmacopeia* or *National Formulary*. Drugs for bona fide clinical investigations may be exceptions.

Within this framework, the director of the pharmaceutical service should be responsible for at least the following:

---

[1] *American Hospital Formulary Service* (Washington, D.C.: American Society of Hospital Pharmacists, 1959).
A.M.A. Drug Evaluations (Chicago: American Medical Association, 1970).
National Formulary (Easton, Pa.: Mack Publishing Co., 1970).
U.S. Pharmacopeia (Easton, Pa.: Mack Publishing Co., 1965).

- Preparing and sterilizing parenteral medications that are manufactured in the hospital.

- Admixture of parenteral products, when feasible.

- Manufacturing pharmaceuticals when this is done in the hospital.

- Establishing specifications for the procurement of all approved drugs, chemicals and biologicals.

- Participating in the development of a hospital formulary. The existence of a hospital formulary does not preclude the use of unlisted drugs.

- Dispensing drugs and chemicals.

- Filling and labeling all drug containers issued to departments/services from which medications are to be administered.

- Implementing the decisions of the pharmacy and therapeutics committee.

- Maintaining and keeping available the approved stock of antidotes and other emergency drugs, both in the pharmacy and in patient care areas. Authoritative, recent antidote information, as well as the phone number of the regional poison control center, should be readily available in the areas where these drugs are stored.

- Maintaining records of the transactions of the pharmacy as required by law and as necessary to maintain adequate control and accountability of all drugs. This should include a system of controls and records for the requisitioning and dispensing of supplies to nursing care units and to other departments/services of the hospital as well as records of all prescription drugs dispensed.

- Cooperating in the teaching and research programs of the hospital.

STANDARD IV
Written policies and procedures that pertain to the intrahospital drug distribution system shall be developed by the medical staff in cooperation with the pharmacist and representatives of other disciplines, as necessary.

INTERPRETATION

Drug compounding and dispensing shall be restricted to the pharmacist, or to his designee under the direct supervision of the pharmacist. It is desirable for the pharmacist to review the prescriber's original order, or a direct copy, before the initial dose of medication is dispensed.

Written policies and procedures that are essential for patient safety, and for the control and accountability of drugs, should include, but should not be limited to, provision that:

- All drugs shall be labeled adequately, including the addition of appropriate accessory or cautionary statements, as indicated.

- Discontinued and outdated drugs and containers with worn, illegible or missing labels shall be returned to the pharmacy for proper disposition.

- Only the pharmacist, or authorized pharmacy personnel under the direction and supervision of the pharmacist, shall dispense medications, make labeling changes, or transfer medications to different containers.

- Only prepackaged drugs shall be removed from the pharmacy when the pharmacist is not available. These drugs shall be removed only by a designated nurse or physician, and in amounts sufficient for immediate therapeutic needs. A record of such withdrawals shall be made.

- There shall be a drug recall procedure that can be readily implemented.

- At the time of dispensing the prescription, the pharmacist should note on the prescription order the source and lot number of the medication and the name or initials of the dispensing pharmacist.

- Medications to be dispensed to inpatients about to be discharged should be labeled as for outpatient prescription.

- A system should be established to ensure accurate identification of outpatients.

- Outpatient prescription labels should bear the following information:
  Name, address and telephone number of the hospital pharmacy;
  Date and pharmacy's serial identifying number for the prescription;
  Full name of the patient;
  Name of the drug, strength and number of tablets, capsules, etc.;
  Directions for use to the patient;
  Name of the physician prescriber;
  Initials of the pharmacist dispenser;
  The required BNDD cautionary label on controlled substance drugs; and
  Such other accessory cautionary labels as may be indicated.

STANDARD V

Written policies and procedures that govern the safe administration of drugs shall be developed by the medical staff in cooperation with the pharmacist and with representatives of other disciplines, as necessary.

INTERPRETATION

Written policies, which are essential for the safe administration of drugs to patients, shall include at least the following:

- Drugs shall be administered only upon the orders of an individual who has been assigned clinical privileges or who is an authorized member of the house staff.

- All medications shall be administered by appropriately licensed personnel in accordance with any laws and regulations governing such acts.

- Acceptable precautionary measures for the safe admixture of parenteral products shall be developed. Whenever drugs are added to intravenous solution, a distinctive supplementary label shall be affixed that indicates the name and amount of the drug added, the date and time of the addition and the name of the person who prepared the admixture.

- Each dose of medication administered shall be properly recorded in the patient's medical record.

- Medication errors and drug reactions shall be reported immediately to the practitioner who ordered the drug. An entry of the medication given and/or the drug reaction shall be properly recorded in the patient's medical record. Hospitals are encouraged to report any unexpected or significant adverse drug reactions to the Hospital Reporting Program of the Federal Food and Drug Administration and to the manufacturer.

- If patients bring their own drugs into the hospital, these drugs shall not be administered unless they can be identified, and written orders to administer these specific drugs are given by the responsible practitioner. If the drugs that the patient brought to the hospital are not to be used while he is hospitalized, they should be packaged, sealed, stored and returned to the patient at the time of discharge, if such action is approved by the responsible practitioner.

- Self-administration of medications by patients shall be permitted only when specifically ordered by authorized house staff members and/or individuals who have been granted clinical privileges.

●Investigational drugs properly labeled shall be used only under the direct supervision of the principle investigator and should be approved by an appropriate medical staff committee. Nurses may administer these drugs only after they have been given basic pharmacologic information about the drug. A central unit should be established where essential information on investigational drugs is maintained.[2]

●Orders involving abbrevations and chemical symbols should be carried out only if the abbreviations and symbols appear on a standard list approved by the medical staff.

References

A.M.A. Drug Evaluations 1971, American Medical Association, 535 North Dearborn Street, Chicago, Illinois 60611.

National Formulary American Pharmaceutical Association, 1970, Mack Publishing Co., Easton, Pennsylvania.

Statement of Guiding Principles on the Operation of the Hospital Formulary System, 1964, American Society of Hospital Pharmacists, 4630 Montgomery Avenue, Washington, D.C. 20014.

Statement on Hospital Drug Distribution Systems, 1964, American Society of Hospital Pharmacists.

Statement of the Pharmacy and Therapeutics Committee, 1959, American Society of Hospital Pharmacists.

Statement of Principles Involved in the use of Investigational Drugs in Hospitals, 1957, American Hospital Association, 840 North Lake Shore Drive, Chicago, Illinois 60611, and American Society of Hospital Pharmacists.

U.S. Pharmacopeia, 1965, Mack Publishing Co.

---

2 For further guidance, refer to *Statement of Principles Involved in the Use of Investigational Drugs in Hospitals*, approved by the American Hospital Association and the American Society of Hospital Pharmacists. (Washington, D.C.: The Society, 1957).

(Other standards in the *Manual* may also have an affect on pharmacy practice and are referred to elsewhere in this book, when appropriate.)

The United States Pharmacopeial Convention is another such quasi-legal organization whose standards are important to pharmacists. It is an organization whose membership represents both medicine and pharmacy. Its purpose is to publish a set of standards for the production of drugs, which is known as the United States Pharmacopeia (U.S.P.). The Food, Drug and Cosmetic Act officially recognizes the standards of the U.S.P., and drug manufacturers, pharmacists and others preparing drug products must comply with them.

CHAPTER 3
CLINICAL PHARMACY

Section 1

EMERGING TRENDS

FOR YEARS PHARMACY HAS BEEN A PRODUCT ORIENTED PRACTICE. IT concentrated on the collection of drug source material, extraction of medicinal agents and preparation of finished dosage forms suitable for human uses. Proper packaging, labeling, and drug control have also been important. Over the years, as drug manufacturers assumed an ever increasing role in drug preparation, pharmacists adjusted their focus to bring the patient more clearly within the area of professional concern.

Attention to actual drug use in therapeutics is a natural extension of the education and training of pharmacists. As far as the public health and safety is concerned it is not enough to produce a quality product. Proper and safe use of such products is equally important in achieving the desired end result, the cure or mitigation of disease in the patient.

This area of professional endeavor is of growing importance to pharmacists, educators and regulators as well as to other professionals such as physicians and nurses. Pharmacists are assuming an important role as active members of the health care team. They are no longer functioning solely within the confines of the "pharmacy." Factors such as manpower shortage or maldistribution, the nature of modern potent pharmacological agents, as well as a greater desire to utilize acquired professional skills, have resulted in the expanded activities of pharmacists.

In addition to the traditional activities of drug ordering, preparation, distribution, and pharmacy administration, and recordkeeping, pharmacists are becoming involved in other activities generically referred to as "clinical pharmacy." Clinical pharmacy includes activities such as taking medication histories, monitoring drug use, contributing to drug therapy, drug selection, patient counseling, drug

51

administration programs, and surveillance for adverse reactions and interactions.

These additional activities were recognized by the court in *Supermarket General Corp. v. Sills* which stated:

> . . . the role of the pharmacist goes beyond that of the sale of a commodity. In filling a prescription, the pharmacist often aids the physician by informing him of the properties and effects of various drugs. If the prescription calls for a generic compound, he chooses the particular brand to be dispensed. Additionally, he may monitor each prescription as to dosage, and possibly determines whether the prescribed drug may be antagonistic to another previously prescribed for the patient by another physician.

In addition to improving patient care or providing it more efficiently, these activities are important from a legal standpoint and may possibly create problems regarding scope of practice under professional practice acts. The broad legal question of concern is whether certain activities are lawful for pharmacists to undertake. Rather than try to speak generically of "clinical pharmacy," this chapter attempts to distill for discussion discreet clinical functions or specific clinically oriented services performed by pharmacists.

One last point in considering new roles for all health care personnel is that all professional practice acts must be considered. This includes pharmacy laws, nursing practice acts and medical practice laws, as well as the many laws discussed throughout this book, which affect the practice of various health care professionals.

Section 2

DRUG INFORMATION

Drug information is a broad term. It could include information, advice and other communications with patients and/or various health professionals. Physicians and others, however, are independent practitioners who must exercise independent judgments concerning patient care. As used in this chapter drug information embraces patient communications which have taken on a whole new light in pharmacy in recent years.

Patient communication begins with taking a medication history at the initiation of treatment or upon the patient's admission to a hospital or clinic and extends to counseling the patient on how to take his medication at home or after discharge. Counseling may involve drug monitoring or advising ambulatory patients or patients being served through a hospital home care program on drug usage. It may extend to the pharmacist having complete responsibility for therapeutic regimens and follow-up care, especially for, but not necessarily limited to, patients with chronic conditions.

Medication histories are important for they identify drugs a patient may be taking, specific allergies, etc., all of which assit in diagnosis and treatment. A study by Covington and Pfeiffer, *The Pharmacist-Acquired Medication History,* designed to compare pharmacist-acquired medication histories with the medication histories obtained from the same patients by physicians revealed that:

> . . . Physicians did not generally obtain a comprehensive medication history. The pharmacist was more proficient in acquiring comprehensive medication histories. Much of the information obtained in the pharmacist-acquired medication history revealed that a significant percentage of patients were poorly informed about many aspects of drug therapy.

Such activities and studies may eventually affect the standard of care expected of pharmacists involved in drug therapy.

Generally state pharmacy laws do not state that pharmacists are authorized to take medication histories, but that does not mean pharmacists may not do so. As a matter of fact, pharmacists acquire information from patients almost every day. Sometimes they must know a patient's full name, an address missing from a prescription, or a patient's age—in pediatrics age may be very important. Many pharmacists know the medication history of their clientele simply because they have served them for so many years. Merely because a more formal type of medication history may be required in present day practice, it does not alter the fact that pharmacists gather information to assist them in adequately rendering professional service.

A recognition of the usefulness of taking medication histories has already seeped into federal regulations. The Conditions of Participation for Intermediate Care Facilities for the mentally retarded (discussed more fully in Chapter 2) state:

> **45 C.F.R. 240.13**
> (7) (iv) Upon admission of the resident, a medication history of prescription and nonprescription drugs used shall be obtained where possible, preferably by the pharmacist, and this information shall be entered in the resident's record for the information of the staff . . .

After the patient's medication history is prepared, a diagnosis made and a therapeutic regimen chosen, pharmacists may be called upon to discuss drug therapy with the patient. Whether direct pharmacist advice to patients concerning drug therapy has legal authorization depends, by and large, on state law. Some laws speak specifically on this point. For example, the Maryland Pharmacy Law defines the practice of pharmacy as:

Md. Ann. Code Art. 43 §250(a)
. . . the practice that is concerned with . . . the responsibility of providing information, as required, concerning such drugs and medicines and their therapeutic values and uses in the treatment and prevention of disease . . . .

Other state pharmacy laws, including those in Colorado, Illinois, Michigan, Nebraska, New Mexico, Pennsylvania, Virginia, and Washington, have similar provisions. In these states patient consultation by pharmacists concerning therapeutics and drug usage seems clearly within the law.

In Florida, the practice of pharmacy provides for rendering therapeutic advice about dispensed drugs "whether pursuant to prescriptions, or in the absence and entirely independent of such prescriptions or orders . . ." Thus, Florida law expressly encompasses legend and OTC medicines. Other state laws have similar indications.

Some state laws, such as those of Idaho, Maryland and West Virginia, require a pharmacist to personally discuss the nature of poisonous, habit-forming or dangerous drugs or medical supplies with the purchaser at the time of sale. This type of language is broad enough not only to include traditional poisons as defined by law but also to encompass virtually all legend drugs. After all, a drug is classified as a prescription drug because it is habit-forming or is toxic or otherwise unsafe for use without supervision by a physician. This interpretation of the West Virginia Code is reflected in the Amended Rules and Regulations of the West Virginia Board of Pharmacy, Article 15, Rules of Professional Conduct, which states:

> 14. Duties. It shall be the duty of a registered pharmacist in every pharmacy to perform the following duties.
>
> *   *   *
>
> f. Discuss with patient matters pertaining to the drug, its reasons for usage, contraindications or answer questions regarding the practitioner's intent.

Authority to supply drug information or to counsel patients is sometimes found in sections of the regulations prohibiting unauthorized disclosure of information. The California regulation, Section 1764, states:

> No pharmacist shall exhibit, discuss, or reveal the contents of any prescription, nor shall he discuss the therapeutic effect thereof, or the nature, extent, or degree of illness suffered by any patient served by him, *with any person other than the patient or his authorized representative,* the prescriber or other licensed practitioner then caring for the patient, or a person duly authorized by law to receive such information. (Emphasis added.)

Regulations in Florida, Maine, New York, Tennessee and Vermont have similar provisions.

In Arizona and Minnesota, regulations pertaining to the duties that must be performed by pharmacists speak of patient communications. Arizona regulations provide that:

§4.1100 The following . . . shall be performed only by a pharmacist, or a pharmacy intern under the immediate personal supervision of a pharmacist:

* * *

(11) Giving instructions to the patient whenever good professional judgment requires it.

In Georgia, authority is found in a prohibition against diagnosis or treatment contained in the Rules of the Georgia Board of Pharmacy.

§480-11-.01(d) Diagnosis or Treatment. No pharmacist or employee of a retail drug establishment shall diagnose, treat, prescribe for, or attempt to do so, any disease, illness or organic disorder. *This limitation shall not be construed to prevent a registered pharmacist from advising individuals on matters concerning simple ailments, first aid measures, sanitary measures, or the merits and qualities of patent medicines as defined by Sec. 79A-102 (p) Ga. Code.* (Emphasis added.)

Recently, the board of pharmacy of the state of Washington promulgated a regulation that requires pharmacists to discuss with the patient the directions for use and additional information for each new prescription. If necessary, he must transmit such information in writing or by telephone. The regulation follows.

WAC 360-16-250 Patient Information Required.
(1) With each new prescription dispensed after January 1, 1974, the pharmacist, in addition to labeling the prescription in accordance with the requirements of RCW 18.64.246, must orally explain to the patient or the patient's agent the directions for use and any additional information, in writing if necessary, to assure the proper utilization of the medication or device prescribed. For those prescriptions delivered outside the confines of the pharmacy, the explanation shall be by telephone or in writing, PROVIDED, That this shall not apply to those prescriptions for patients in hospitals or institutions where the medication is to be administered by a nurse or other individual licensed to administer medications, or to those prescriptions for patients who are to be discharged from a hospital or institution.

(2) To ensure proper information is available to each pharmacist, each pharmacy and/or pharmacist shall maintain current reference material on drug interactions.

In summary, statutes and regulations in state law may affect information and patient consultation by pharmacists. The statutory sections and/or regulations are diverse and can be found in at least the following states:

Arizona	Nebraska
California	New Mexico
Colorado	New York
Florida	North Carolina
Georgia	Oregon
Idaho	Pennsylvania
Illinois	Tennessee
Maine	Vermont
Maryland	Virginia
Michigan	Washington
Minnesota	West Virginia

In addition to state law, federal laws and agency actions also deal with the subject of drug information. The Health Maintenance Organization Act of 1973 requires "instructions of its members [patients] . . . in the use of prescription and non-prescription drugs." The report of the Senate-House Conference Committee emphasizes the role of the clinical pharmacist in educating patients in drug use and abuse. (See discussion on HMOs in Chapter 2.)

Studies and publications of the U.S. Department of Health, Education and Welfare have also dealt with this issue. The *Final Report of the Task Force on Prescription Drugs,* at pages 19 and 20, states:

At the other end of the spectrum, it is also becoming evident that appropriately trained pharmacists may become new and vital members of the total health team by serving as drug information specialists.

Some community pharmacists are already providing such services. They do not prescribe, but they discuss practical details of drug administration, possible side-effects, and other facets of drug use with each patient to whom a prescription drug is dispensed. They maintain patient or family records which contain data on drugs which have been dispensed to each patient, allergic responses, and adverse reactions. They call to the attention of the physician any prescriptions which may have been written for the same patient by other physicians, and they refer to him any prescriptions which may involve drug-interaction, synergism, or similar effects.

Some hospitals—especially teaching institutions and those major medical center complexes—are already using pharmacists as consultants on drug therapy. They serve not only as drug distributors, but also as sources or drug data for physicians, interns, residents, and nurses. They may participate in ward rounds with the staff, providing valuable drug information on both old and new drug products. Although they do not prescribe for patients, they enable the physicians who do prescribe for patients to keep up more effectively with drug information.

The R_x Legend, An FDA manual for pharmacists, counsels:

A pharmacist should be familiar with the active ingredients and labeling of over-the-counter drugs he sells, as well as the drugs he dispenses on prescription. As the licensed expert on drugs, the pharmacist is professionally competent to answer the questions of his patrons about such drugs, without, of course, attempting to diagnose or to prescribe.

Any drug that does not bear the Rx Legend can be sold without a prescription. The consumer has the responsibility for reading and heeding the directions and warnings, if any, which appear on the package. But the pharmacist may render a professional service by calling attention to such directions and warnings.

The FDA's "Primer on Medicines," which appeared in *FDA Consumer,* December, 1973-January, 1974, advises consumers to "ask your pharmacist's advice." The article points out that "Pharmacists are well-trained professionals who can help their customers understand how to buy and use drugs." Concerning the use and storage of medicines it states:

Directions. Continue taking an Rx drug for the entire time ordered by your doctor, even if you're feeling better. You might prevent the drug from doing a complete job and find yourself sick again. With both Rx and OTC drugs, follow very carefully the directions about when and how much to take. Ask your pharmacist for help if you need it.

Side effects. Bear in mind that sometimes certain people react adversely to a particular medicine. If you find that an Rx drug causes a side effect, perhaps a rash, headache, nausea, or dizziness—talk to your doctor. Your pharmacist can help too. The drug may be discontinued, the dose changed, or another drug substituted.

Combining drugs. Consult your doctor or pharmacist before you take two drugs together. If you're taking any medicines at all, don't drink alcohol without first asking your doctor. It could be dangerous.

See also the discussion of patient package inserts in Chapter 9, Section 2.

In addition to state and federal laws, regulations and interpretations, the courts have also recognized the pharmacist's role in drug information and patient advisory duties. In the case of *Krueger v. Knutson* the court said:

> It has been held that where the druggist knows that a drug, harmless in itself, is to be mixed with or used in connection with, another which would then have an injurious effect, of which the purchaser has no knowledge, he should advise the purchaser of it, and a failure to do so would make him liable for the consequences.

Lastly, official statements of professional societies of pharmacists have made drug information a component of pharmacy practice. Section 3 of APhA's Code of Ethics states that the pharmacist should utilize and make available his knowledge as may be required in accordance with his best professional judgement. The interpretation of this section states, in part:

> This section also allows the pharmacist to make his professional knowledge available, voluntarily or on request, when it is appropriate according to his professional judgement. While this section is not intended to derogate from the role of the physician in providing medical care to patients, it does allow the pharmacist to make his professional knowledge available to patients in circumstances where it is in the best interest of the patient as determined according to the professional judgment of the pharmacist.

This principle is embodied in the Rules and Regulations of the North Carolina Board of Pharmacy, Article 7, Code of Professional Conduct.

State codes of ethics should also be consulted. For example, the Code of Ethics of the Maine Pharmaceutical Association states:

> The Pharmacist shall make no attempt to prescribe or treat diseases and he should refrain from any practice which might be construed as trespassing into the field of Practicing Medicine.

The American Society of Hospital Pharmacists, in 1968 adopted a "Statement on the Hospital Pharmacist and Drug Information Services" which deals with this subject in the hospital setting.

When all factors are taken into account, despite some negative evidence on this point, there is more than adequate authority upon which to conclude that as a general rule pharmacists may and in fact in many instances have a positive duty to advise patients about drugs they are taking. Even if the pharmacy laws and regulations do not expressly apply to such activities, they must be interpreted in light of the profession's education, training standards and current practices. No laws or regulations can cover every facet of practice, especially emerging trends, and laws and regulations must be interpreted with this in mind.

Section 3
RATIONAL DRUG USE

Along with taking patient drug histories and advising patients on drug usage, another major area of clinical practice deals with drug therapy surveillance which includes protecting patients from drug reactions and drug interactions. This activity can range from mere literature searches in response to questions posed by physicians to monitoring the patient's therapy. These activities can have a significant effect upon drug therapy decisions up to and including the actual prescribing of medications.

In order to prevent an adverse drug reaction it is necessary to know a patient's allergies and sensitivities. To detect possible drug-drug interactions, drug-lab test interactions or drug-food interactions it is imperative to know all the drugs, lab tests and diets being given to the patient. Any type of monitoring requires the collection and analysis of pertinent data. Increasingly, pharmacists are maintaining patient medication profiles. These records contain information that will enable the above functions to be performed effectively.

In fact, at least one state requires all pharmacists to maintain such records. The New Jersey Board of Pharmacy in 1972, promulgated a regulation requiring the maintenance of patient profile records which must include: (1) the family name and the first name of the person for whom medication is dispensed (the patient); (2) the complete address of the patient; (3) the patient's birthdate; (4) all known allergies and idiosyncrasies of the patient and other chronic conditions which may relate to drug utilization; (5) the original date the medication is dispensed pursuant to the receipt of a physician's prescription, the date(s) of renewal (refilling); (6) the number assigned the prescription; (7) the prescriber's name; (8) the name, strength and quantity of the drug dispensed; and (9) the initials of the dispensing pharmacist. In the hospital setting, these records should be made available to the Pharmacy and Therapeutics Committee for drug utilization review studies. This regulation has been upheld in court in the case of *Rite Aid v. Board of Pharmacy*.

Once the necessary data has been collected it must be put to use. At the federal level, the Conditions of Participation for Skilled Nursing Facilities, require that "the pharmacist reviews the drug regimen of each patient at least monthly, and reports any irregularities to the medical director and administrator." The Conditions of Participation for Intermediate Care Facilities engaged in the treatment of the mentally retarded are more elaborate. They state:

45 C.F.R. §249.13
(7) *Pharmacy services*

* * *

(iv) . . . The pharmacist shall:

* * *

(B) Maintain for each resident an individual record of all medications (prescription and nonprescription) dispensed, including quantities and frequency of refills;

(C) Participate, as appropriate, in the continuing interdisciplinary evaluation of individual residents for the purposes of initiation, monitoring and follow-up of individualized habilitation programs; and

* * *

(v) A pharmacist or RN shall regularly review the record of each resident on medication for potential adverse reactions, allergies, interactions, contraindications, rationality and laboratory test modifications, and advise the physician of any recommended changes with reasons, and with an alternate drug regimen.

These federal regulations clearly specify that pharmacists must maintain records of and monitor drug therapy. These regulations are consistent with state law and principles of professional practice.

The courts, in various cases, have recognized the pharmacist's role in drug monitoring. In *Supermarkets General Corporation v. Sills,* the New Jersey Supreme Court, in upholding the validity of a New Jersey statute prohibiting prescription drug advertising stated, when confronted with a challenge to the professional services performed by pharmacists:

Additionally, he may 'monitor' each prescription as to dosage, and possibly determine whether the prescribed drug may be antagonistic to another previously prescribed for the patient by another physician.

In another price advertising case, *Patterson Drug Co. v. Kingery,* a federal court said:

Some pharmacists, probably a minority, systematically monitor prescriptions by family records to avoid allergic reactions or the simultaneous use of antagonistic drugs, of which the patient's doctor may not be aware. Although monitoring is not completely effective because of the mobility of customers and the availability of nonprescription drugs which may be antagonistic, it is a benefit to the public.

In some cases, such as *Pennsylvania State Board of Pharmacy v. Pastor* and *Maryland Board of Pharmacy v. Sav-a-lot,* the courts acknowledge that such activities are not a major practice at the present time.

Section 4
DRUG ADMINISTRATION AND PRESCRIBING

A third new area of activity involves drug administration. This activity centers in hospitals. Some hospitals have placed their drug administration programs under the direction and supervision of the pharmacy department. By doing this responsibility for all of the functions relating to drugs, from the time they enter the hospital to the time they are disposed of, including administration, are placed in one hospital department. Such programs are usually developed through the joint effort of pharmacists, nurses and physicians. These programs relieve nurses of medication duties and allow them to concentrate on nursing care. The identification, measurement, mixing, or other preparation of drugs is accomplished through the pharmacy department. However, no laws have been found specifically authorizing pharmacists to administer medications although they are authorized to compound and dispense medications.

The JCAH standards regarding pharmaceutical services offer some guidance on the administration of medications. Standard V states:

> Written policies and procedures that govern the safe administration of drugs shall be developed by the medical staff in cooperation with the pharmacist and with representatives of other disciplines, as necessary.

The interpretation goes on to state:

> All medications shall be administered by appropriately licensed personnel in accordance with any laws and regulations governing such acts.

By not limiting drug administration to specified persons, the JCAH standards leave room for development of drug administration programs by the hospital staff, and, specifically by the medical staff and pharmacist.

Unfortunately, the Conditions of Participation for Hospitals seem to limit drug administration to physicians, registered nurses, licensed practical nurses, and student nurses and psychiatric technicians under the direct supervision of a registered nurse. On the other hand, the newer skilled nursing facility conditions do not specify who may administer drugs. They merely say that it must be done in compliance with state and local laws. It is interesting to note that, according to these conditions, procedures relating to drug administration are to be established by the pharmaceutical services committee which is comprised of at least the pharmacist, the director of nursing services, the administrator, and one physician. In an intermediate care facility (ICF), all personnel administering medication must have completed a state-approved training program in medication administration, according to the conditions of participation. If an ICF treats the mentally retarded, written policies and procedures that govern the safe administration and handling of all drugs shall be developed by the responsible pharmacist, physician, nurse and other professional staff, as appropriate to the facility.

In addition to the JCAH standards and federal regulations, it is, again, important to look at state law. Pharmacy acts do not directly authorize pharmacists to administer medications. They do, however, permit "dispensing" of prescription drugs. Dispensing is not always defined by law but may be considered to be the issuance of multiple doses of medication in a properly labeled container. If a pharmacist may give to a patient more than one dose at a time and may instruct the patient how to take the medication, why can't he also offer the patient one dose each time it is to be administered? It is not disputed that pharmacists must have some additional training in the administration of parenteral preparations, but this training is certainly minimal when compared to the pharmacist's overall knowledge of drugs. On the other hand, nurses need relatively greater training in the pharmacology and therapeutics of drugs than pharmacists. It would certainly seem to be efficient to use pharmacists in drug administration programs.

The last area of clinical practice that deserves mention is drug "prescribing." One area of activity related to prescribing that seems well-settled concerns drug product selection. An ASHP Product Selection Survey study shows that in 68.4% of the hospitals surveyed, pharmacists prepare the drug specifications and in 74.2% of the hospitals, the pharmacists select sources of supply for these hospitals. Drug selection has not reached the point at which the pharmacist actually prescribes based upon a physician's diagnosis. But pharmacists are providing, with increasing frequency, information and advice upon which prescribers base their decisions.

The federal government's Task Force on the Pharmacist's Clinical Role had the following to say about drug prescribing by pharmacists.

> The physician determines if drug therapy is indicated and usually chooses the drug to be used as part of his overall therapy. Under certain circumstances the pharmacist does

assist in planning drug therapy, and at times may prescribe medications at the request of the physician.

1. Pharmacists, in reissuing prescriptions designated to be refilled at the request of the patient (p.r.n.), may be regarded as performing a prescribing function.
2. Pharmacists, in complying with "standing orders" of the physician, may be performing an independent prescribing function. "Standing orders" refers to a prearranged plan or understanding between the physician and the pharmacist which permits the latter to dispense medications under certain circumstances without the immediate concurrence of the physician.
3. Pharmacists and pharmacy residents often help medical students to plan drug regimens.
4. Physicians may share responsibility for prescribing with the pharmacist when the latter has demonstrated competence. This may include the selection of drugs, the dosage forms and frequency of use, based upon the physician's diagnosis.
5. Pharmacists prescribe over-the-counter (OTC) drugs. Also, by recommending against the purchase and/or use of OTC drugs, they enter into the prescribing function.
6. Pharmacists prescribe medications in emergency situations when it appears to be in the best interest of the patient.
7. Pharmacists, after consultation with the prescriber, may select and dispense a drug other than the one prescribed by the physician, when they practice under the authority of the drug formulary system.
8. Pharmacists may be considered to be performing a prescribing function when they reply to inquiries from patients about continued use of medications previously prescribed.

Whether pharmacists will one day come to prescribe medications for patients may depend to a large extent on how well they perform current clinical functions.

CHAPTER 4
DRUG PRODUCT SELECTION

Section 1
LAWS PROHIBITING SUBSTITUTION

BEFORE THE DAYS OF LARGE SCALE DRUG MANUFACTURING, PHYSICIANS WROTE prescription orders using drug or chemical names. Pharmacists took the prescribed amount of medical agents and "compounded" them into a finished dosage form which was then dispensed to the patient. Most state laws at that point in time, prohibited the substitution of one drug or chemical for another drug or chemical. If aspirin were prescribed, it was unlawful to dispense phenacetin; aspirin had to be used.

In the 20th century, drug manufacturers became more involved in prefabricating finished dosage forms intended to be dispensed to patients as obtained from the manufacturer. In order to protect their individual investments, reputations, processes and products, drug manufacturers, like other manufacturers, applied trade names to their products. Thus the APC compound was marketed as "Empirin," chloral hydrate was called "Noctec," papaverine became known as "Pavabid," and so forth.

An important question arose as drug manufacturers became more involved in prefabrication of finished dosage forms. If a drug was prescribed by a particular brand or trade name, was it a violation of the antisubstitution law if the pharmacist dispensed the same drug produced by another manufacturer and marketed under its generic name or some other trade name? Apparently, many people thought such practice was not illegal, because a large scale mid-century legislative campaign took place to amend antisubstitution provisions to expressly prohibit brand as well as drug substitution. The movement had the backing of drug manufacturers, organized medicine and pharmacy, and regulatory agencies and was, naturally, very successful. As a result, all fifty states adopted antisubstitution laws.

65

Under present law, drug substitution may be defined as the dispensing of a different drug or brand of drug in the place of the one ordered or prescribed without the express permission of the prescriber. State statutory prohibitions, which generally appear in the pharmacy law or food and drug law, fall into three categories: those prohibiting substitutions absolutely; those prohibiting substitution except where there is prior notification to, or consent from the prescriber; and those prohibiting substitution except where the authorization of the prescriber is manifested on the prescription or order.

Penal sanctions, as well as loss of license, are imposed for violation of such laws. In order to protect their products it became a rather common practice for some drug manufacturers to file complaints with boards of pharmacy when they discovered pharmacists substituting. In one case, *Kaufman v. A.H. Robins*, a drug company which had failed to prove a substitution was subsequently sued by the exonerated pharmacist for malicious prosecution. The Supreme Court of Tennessee held that such a claim was actionable and remanded the case for trial.

In addition to state law, it is important to examine federal law on the question of substitution. The Federal Food, Drug and Cosmetic Act protects the public by prohibiting the adulteration or misbranding of drugs. For example it states:

§501. A drug or device shall be deemed to be adulterated—
. . . (d) If it is a drug and any substance has been . . . (2) substituted wholly or in part thereof.
§502. A drug or device shall be deemed to be misbranded—
(a) If its labeling is false or misleading in any particular.
(1) . . . (3) if it is offered for sale under the name of another drug.

The Federal Trade Commission Act must also be considered, for the Federal Trade Commission has held it to be unlawful to substitute merchandise even though it is equivalent in grade, quality and appearance to that ordered.

The last major area of potential conflict concerns trademark law. The problem may occur when a company's proprietary name appears on the prescription order and the dispensing label, but the product dispensed is another brand or nonproprietary drug. The contents would, under such circumstances, be passed off as the product of another manufacturer and the company's trademark rights would be violated.

Section 2

BRAND SELECTION

In recent times, it became apparent that pharmacists had little say in the selection of drugs to be used and could not even select the suppliers of their drugs. Pharmacists had to stock every manufacturer's products that were prescribed by physicians in their market area. This created a great deal of duplication of inventory. It also prevented use of a product of higher quality or one that might be less expensive. Of course, the converse was also true. Present day pharmacists seeking to make better use of their knowledge and understanding of drug products have been concerned whether their selection of brand products would result in violation of any laws.

Under state antisubstitition laws, in order for there to be a violative substitution or adulteration, there must, in the first instance, be a substitution. Court interpretation of this principle is hard to come by, but attorneys general have rendered opinions on this subject. In 1965, the attorney general of California said that a pharmacist may not substitute another brand or pharmaceutical for the one prescribed without advising the physician. Nevertheless, if the prescription blank, as signed by the physician, had typed on it "or USP, NF, NND, or generic equivalent," another brand product might lawfully be dispensed. This question arose because prescription blanks for use in the California Medical Assistance Program contained the quoted phrase in close proximity to the physician's signature line. Thus, if the physician signed the blank, as he must if it is to be a lawful prescription, he granted written authorization for brand selection. Presumably, if the physician crossed out the quoted language, the pharmacist would not be permitted to dispense another brand. Likewise, if the prescription were an oral one and no mention of substitution was made, it would not be lawful to do so.

In a 1973 opinion, the attorney general of Oregon viewed this matter differently. He determined that a physician may give prior authorization for brand selection only if the physician specifies the brands that may be used in place of a specific brand-named product which the prescriber may later designate in a prescription.

Based on this principle of physician consent, written agreements were sought from physicians providing prior authorization for brand selection by pharmacists. To assist pharmacists in this area, the American Pharmaceutical Association developed a number of model authorization agreements. They are set forth in Exhibits 1 through 4.

Exhibit   1

DRUG PRODUCT SELECTION AUTHORIZATION
FORM A

I, _____, a practitioner licensed to prescribe in
the State of _____, hereby authorize _____,
a pharmacist licensed in the same state, and all similarly licensed pharmacists associated with him in practice at_____,
to dispense a drug product other than that I may prescribe by brand
name, under the following conditions:

1. The drug product dispensed must be of the same established
   (generic) name as the drug product prescribed;

2. The drug product dispensed must be, in the professional opinion
   of the pharmacist, a high quality product from a reputable source
   of manufacture.

3. In the event my prescription is handwritten and specifies a manufacturer's name in addition to the brand or established name of
   the drug product, the pharmacist will dispense only the drug
   product thus prescribed;

4. Modification of this authorization, if any, is attached hereto.

This authorization shall continue in effect until modified or terminated by me in writing.

_____

Agreed to and accepted _____

_____
(date)

Exhibit   2

DRUG PRODUCT SELECTION AUTHORIZATION
FORM B

AUTHORIZATION FOR SPECIFIED DRUG ENTITIES

I, _____, a practitioner licensed to prescribe
in the State of _____, hereby authorize _____,
a pharmacist licensed in the same state, and all similarly licensed pharmacists associated with him in practice at _____,
to dispense a drug product other than that I may prescribe by brand
name, under the following conditions:

1. The drug product dispensed must be of the same established
   (generic) name as the drug product prescribed;

2. The drug product dispensed must be, in the professional opinion

Exhibit 2 *(continued)*

of the pharmacist, a high quality product from a reputable source of manufacture.

3. In the event my prescription is handwritten and specifies a manufacturer's name in addition to the brand or established name of the drug product, the pharmacist will dispense only the drug product thus prescribed;

4. Modification of this authorization, if any, is attached hereto.

This authorization shall continue in effect until modified or terminated by me in writing.

Agreed to and accepted _____

_____
(date)

The DRUG PRODUCT SELECTION AUTHORIZATION, page one of this agreement, applies ONLY to prescriptions for the _____ _____ drug entities listed below by established (generic) name.^(number)

Those drug entities to which this agreement applies are:

1. _____

2. _____

3. _____

4. _____

5. _____

Exhibit 3

DRUG PRODUCT SELECTION AUTHORIZATION
FORM C
AUTHORIZATION LIMITED TO SPECIFIED DRUG ENTITIES
AND
SPECIFIED DRUG PRODUCTS

I, _____, a practitioner licensed to prescribe in the State of _____, hereby authorize _____, a pharmacist licensed in the same state, and all similarly licensed pharmacists associated with him in practice at _____, to dispense a drug product other than that I may prescribe by brand name, under the following conditions:

1. The drug product dispensed must be of the same established (generic) name as the drug product prescribed;

Exhibit　3 *(continued)*

2. The drug product dispensed must be, in the professional opinion of the pharmacist, a high quality product from a reputable source of manufacture.

3. In the event my prescription is handwritten and specifies a manufacturer's name in addition to the brand or established name of the drug product, the pharmacist will dispense only the drug product thus prescribed;

4. Modification of this authorization, if any, is attached hereto.

This authorization shall continue in effect until modified or terminated by me in writing.

Agreed to and accepted _____

_____
(date)

The DRUG PRODUCT SELECTION AUTHORIZATION, page one of this agreement, applies ONLY to prescriptions for the _____ _____ drug entities listed below and only where the product
(number)
dispensed is selected from among the drug products listed.

The _____ drug entities and the respective drug products
(number)
which may be dispensed are as follows:

1. When a _____ drug product is prescribed, the drug product dispensed shall be chosen from among the following:

   a) _____   f) _____
   b) _____   g) _____
   c) _____   h) _____
   d) _____   i) _____
   e) _____   j) _____

2. When a _____ drug product is prescribed, the drug product dispensed shall be chosen from among the following:

   a) _____   f) _____
   b) _____   g) _____
   c) _____   h) _____
   d) _____   i) _____
   e) _____   j) _____

3. When a _____ drug product is prescribed, the drug product dispensed shall be chosen from among the following:

   a) _____   f) _____
   b) _____   g) _____
   d) _____   h) _____
   c) _____   i) _____
   e) _____   j) _____

Exhibit 4

DRUG PRODUCT SELECTION AUTHORIZATION
FORM D

AUTHORIZATION FOR ALL BUT SPECIFIED DRUG ENTITIES

I, _____, a practitioner licensed to prescribe in the State of _____, hereby authorize _____, a pharmacist licensed in the same state, and all similarly licensed pharmacists associated with him in practice at_____, to dispense a drug product other than that I may prescribe by brand name, under the following conditions:

1. The drug product dispensed must be of the same established (generic) name as the drug product prescribed;

2. The drug product dispensed must be, in the professional opinion of the pharmacist, a high quality product from a reputable source of manufacture.

3. In the event my prescription is handwritten and specifies a manufacturer's name in addition to the brand or established name of drug product, the pharmacist will dispense only the drug product thus prescribed;

4. Modification of this authorization, if any, is attached hereto.

This authorization shall continue in effect until modified or terminated by me in writing.

Agreed to and accepted _____

(date)

The DRUG PRODUCT SELECTION AUTHORIZATION, page one of this agreement, applies to all drug entities and their respective drug products EXCEPT the following:

1. _____

2. _____

3. _____

4. _____

5. _____

The need for pharmacist brand selection has also been recognized by a national scientific organization. Based upon recommendation of its drug research board, the National Academy of Sciences adopted the following resolution.

> *"WHEREAS,* The patient's welfare should be the ultimate goal of statutes and regulations concerning drug product selection, which in operational terms means the best product for the lowest cost, and
> *"WHEREAS,* The physician must have the ultimate responsibility and authority in drug product selection, since he has the fullest knowledge of the patient's needs and responses with attendant obligation to be held accountable for his selection of particular drug products, and
> *"WHEREAS,* The pharmacist may, in some situations, have greater knowledge of drug products than other health professionals, including knowledge of both quality and costs, and
> *"WHEREAS,* It is appropriate that decisions with regard to the choice of drug products be made by the health professional possessing the greatest amount of information involved in the particular selection in question, with the attendant accountability, therefore be it
> *"RESOLVED,* That the physician, having selected the chemical entity to be used for therapy, should be required either to delegate to the pharmacist, or explicitly to retain to himself, selection of the particular drug product to be dispensed and received by the patient."

Since there is some doubt about the legality of drug product selection agreements between pharmacists and physicians, other than those contained in the actual prescription order itself, there has been a recent trend for states to attenuate, to varying degrees, the impact of their antisubstitution laws. In most instances this has been achieved by adoption of formulary laws. In one state, Michigan, the antisubstitution prohibition itself was removed.

The following amendments to state laws have already been adopted and other states are considering similar laws.

Arkansas: Public Act No. 872 (H.B. 963) 1973

Section 3. PROGRAM RESTRICTORS. The Director of the Department of Social and Rehabilitative Services and the Commissioner of the Social Services Division are hereby authorized to implement a Prescription Drug Program for the State of Arkansas. Such program shall be limited to the funds appropriated by Sections 1 and 2 of this Act. Said officials are hereby authorized to make contracts with private, non-profit corporations for the administration of said program subject to the approval of the Chief Fiscal Officer of the State. In addition, the Chief Fiscal Officer of the State shall be authorized to prescribe any rules and regulations necessary to insure administering said Prescription Drug Program. It is the intent of the General Assembly that the Director of the Department of Social and Rehabilitative Services and the Commissioner of the Social Services Division shall negotiate an amount to be paid each participating pharmacist for each prescription filled under this program, but in no event shall this pharmacist fee exceed two dollars ($2.00). *It is further declared to be the intent of the General Assembly that the drugs provided under this program shall be prescribed and dispensed as generic drugs whenever possible.* (Emphasis added.)

CONNECTICUT: Public Act No. 73-242 (S.H.B. No. 8754) 1973 An act concerning the labeling of drugs.

Be it enacted by the Senate and House of Representatives in General Assembly convened:

Section 2 of number 15 of the public acts of 1972 is repealed and the following is substituted in lieu thereof: Any physician, surgeon or other person authorized to prescribe drugs within this state, who prescribes a drug, shall in each such prescription, oral or written, include the generic name thereof, if any, unless such physician, surgeon or other person authorized to prescribe drugs, in the exercise of his professional judgment, prescribes a specific brand name drug. The physician, surgeon or other person so authorized shall state to the patient for whom a drug is being prescribed, or to his parent or guardian, the name of the drug or medicine being prescribed, either orally or in writing, and all licensed pharmacists dispensing prescriptions and all health care institutions or facility pharmacies shall label the container containing said medication or prescription with the name as provided by the physician, surgeon or other person so authorized, the strength of each dose prescribed and the date of refill if said prescription is a refill, except if the physician, surgeon or other person so authorized expressly forbids the placing of said drug or medicine name on the prescription label or package. On all prescriptions, whether or not a generic name is stated, the physician, surgeon or other person so authorized shall, if the patient is over the age of sixty-five, include a notation to that effect.

KENTUCKY: Ky. Rev. Stat. §217.822 (Supp. 1972) Substitution of Equivalent Drug for Brand Name Drug—Labeling— Substitution Forbidden

(1) When a pharmacist receives a prescription for a brand name drug for which one or more equivalent drugs are listed in the formulary prepared by the drug formulary council, he may dispense any one (1) of the tested products and shall do so if the purchaser so requests, provided however that if such

substitution is made, the label on the container of the drug shall show both the name of the prescribed drug and the name of the drug dispensed in lieu thereof. (2) If, in the opinion of a practitioner, it is to the best interest of his patient that an equivalent drug should not be dispensed, he may indicate in the manner of his choice on the prescription "DO NOT SUB-STITUTE," except that the indication shall not be preprinted on a prescription.

MARYLAND: Md. Ann. Code art. 43, §273A (Supp. 1972) Dispensing Different Drug Product from That Specified in Prescription.

(a) As used in this section, *"brand name"* means the proprietary name the manufacturer places upon a drug product or on its container, label or wrapping at the time of packaging; and *"established name"* shall have the same meaning as assigned that term by the Federal Food, Drug and Cosmetic Act as amended, Title 21 U.S.C. 301 et seq.

(b) Unless the physician or other authorized prescriber explicitly states otherwise when transmitting an oral prescription or in the instance of a written prescription, indicates in his own writing or by initialing an appropriate imprinted statement, a different brand name or nonbrand name drug product of the same established name may be dispensed by a pharmacist provided, however, that such action by the pharmacist shall be authorized only if in each case the pharmacist immediately transmits notice in writing to the prescriber specifying the drug product actually dispensed and the name of the manufacturer or distributor.

(c) The provisions of this section shall only apply to those drug products included in the Maryland Medical Assistance Formulary determined by the Maryland Department of Health and Mental Hygiene on the basis of scientific evidence to be clinically equivalent.

(d) In any instance in which the pharmacist, purusant to this section, dispenses a different drug product from that prescribed, the pharmacist shall pass on the full savings in cost, being the difference between the wholesale prices of the two drug products, to the consumer.

MASSACHUSETTS: Mass. Gen. Laws Ann. ch. 94, §187 (1958, as amended Supp. 1972); ch. 17, §13 (Supp. 1972); ch. 112, §12D (Supp. 1972). "Misbranding" Term Defined When Applied to Drugs, . . .

* * *

For the purposes of said sections an article shall also be deemed to be misbranded:—

In the case of a drug: First, if it is so designated by the United States Food and Drug Administration, or if it is an imitation of or offered for sale under the name of another article . . .

§13. Establishment; Membership; Formulary of Generic and Brand Names of Drugs; List; Judicial Review

There shall be in the department a drug formulary commission, hereinafter called the commission, to consist of five members to be appointed by the governor from lists of eligible names to be compiled and prepared by the commissioner of public health, the commissioner of public welfare and the consumers' council. Members of the commission shall be individuals possessing recognized competence in the rendering of professional services under, or the administration of, state health programs, and a majority of the members shall be practicing members of the professions authorized to render professional health services under state-financed health programs; provided, however, that not more than one member of said commission shall be a registered pharmacist. Each member of the commission shall serve at the pleasure of the governor.

The commission shall prepare a formulary of generic or chemical, and brand names of drugs and pharmaceuticals considered by the commission as therapeutically equivalent. The sources for such document shall include a list of drugs most frequently prescribed by licensed physicians in the commonwealth, the formularies of various hospitals in the commonwealth and any additional formularies available from any agency or department of the United States and of other states, but shall not include drugs which are the subject matter of patent rights issued by the United States Patent Office. The commission shall provide for distribution of copies of such formulary and revisions thereto amongst physicians licensed to practice within the commonwealth and to other appropriate individuals and shall supply a copy to any person on request upon payment of the cost of printing. Such formulary shall be revised from time to time, but in no event less frequently than once a year, so as to include new pertinent information on drugs approved for inclusion or drugs to be deleted and to reflect current information as to the therapeutic efficacy of drugs and pharmaceuticals.

Any person or party in interest aggrieved by a finding or report of the commission shall be entitled to a judicial review thereof as provided in section fourteen of chapter 30 A. For the purposes of this section, the term "brand name" shall mean the name that the manufacturer of such drug places on the container thereof at the time of packaging, and the term "generic name" shall mean the chemical or established name of such drug or pharmaceutical.

Section 13 becomes operative when used in conjunction with ch. 112, §12D (Supp. 1972) as follows:

§12D. Prescriptions of Brand Name Drugs Listed in Formulary; Generic or Chemical Name

Every physician who prescribes by brand name a drug listed in the formulary prepared by the drug formulary commission under section thirteen of chapter seventeen shall, in each such prescription, oral or written, also include the generic name or the chemical name of such drug, if any.

MICHIGAN: Public Act No. 155 (H.B. 4145) 1974

Sec. 1. As used in this act:

(u) "Substitute" means to dispense, without the prescriber's authorization, a different drug in place of the drug ordered or prescribed.

Sec. 14a. (1) When a pharmacist receives a prescription for a brand name drug product, and the purchaser requests a lower cost generically equivalent drug product, the pharmacist may dispense a lower cost but not higher cost generically equivalent drug product if available in the pharmacy, except as provided in subsection (3). If a drug is dispensed which is not the prescribed brand, the prescription label shall indicate both the name of the brand prescribed and the name of the brand dispensed and designate each respectively. If the dispensed drug does not have a brand name, the prescription label shall indicate the generic name of the drug dispensed, except as otherwise provided in section 14b.

(2) If a pharmacist dispenses a generically equivalent drug product, unless the prescription purchase is covered by a "third party pay contract," the pharmacist shall pass on the savings in cost to the consumer. The savings in cost is the difference between the wholesale cost to the pharmacist of the 2 drug products.

(3) The pharmacist shall not dispense a generically equivalent drug product under subsection (1) of this section if

(a) The prescriber, in the case of a prescription in writing signed by the prescriber, writes in his own handwriting "dispense as written" or "D.A.W." on the prescription, or

(b) The prescriber, having preprinted on his prescription blanks the statement "another brand of a generically equivalent product, identical in dosage, form, and content of active ingredients, may be dispensed unless initialed D.A.W.", writes the initials "D.A.W." in a space, box or square adjacent to such statement, or

(c) The prescriber, in the case of a prescription other than one in writing signed by the prescriber, expressly indicates the prescription is to be dispensed as communicated.

(4) A pharmacist may not dispense a drug product with a total charge that exceeds the total charge of the drug product originally prescribed, unless agreed to by the purchaser.

NEW HAMPSHIRE: N.H. Rev. Stat. Ann. ch. 146, Sec. 6-b, Sec. 11.

373:1 Providing of Generic Names in Physicians' Prescriptions. Amend RSA 146 by inserting after section 6-a the following new section:

146:6-b Generic Names Required. Every physician prescribing by brand name a drug listed in the formulary prepared by the director of the division of public health services department of health and welfare, under RSA 146:11, shall in each such prescription, oral or written, also include the words "or its generic equivalent drug listed in N.H. drug formulary" if in the physician's judgment it is medically sound to do so. Any person receiving such prescription from a physician shall have the option of purchasing the prescription drug under either its brand name or its generic name.

373:2 Compiling a List of Brand Names for Drugs and their Generic Equivalents. Amend RSA 146:11, as amended, by striking out said section and inserting in place thereof the following:

146:11 Enforcement; Rules; Inspections. The department of health and welfare, division of public health services, is charged with the enforcement of this chapter. The director may make rules and regulations for the proper enforcement thereof, including as a part of said rules and regulations, when not inconsistent with existing laws, the adoption of such definitions and standards of identity, standards of quality or fill of container as may from time to time be promulgated under the federal food, drug and cosmetic act, also similar adoption of regulations promulgated under the federal meat inspection act. The director shall cause inspections to be made of the quality, condition and branding of foods and drugs, devices or cosmetics, found on sale, possessed of sale, or in process of manufacture or distribution, and shall collect samples for analysis in its laboratories. The director shall compile a formulary of the two hundred most frequently prescribed types of medication of prescription drugs giving both brand and generic names, if any, and cause each formulary to be distributed to all pharmacies and/or drug stores, physicians, and medical students in the state. All inspectors and other employees appointed by said director shall be permitted access at all reasonable hours to all places of business concerned in the manufacture, production, transportation, distribution and sale of foods and drugs, devices or cosmetics, shall have power to open and examine any package or container of any kind containing, or believed to contain, any article of food or drugs, devices or cosmetics, which may be manufactured, distributed, sold or possessed for sale in violation of the provisions of this chapter and to take samples therefrom for analysis, tendering to the manufacturer, distributor or vendor the value thereof.

In Delaware a voluntary formulary system has been developed by a joint effort between the Delaware Pharmaceutical Society and the Delaware Medical Association. It has been reviewed by the U.S. Department of Justice and it has not been found, as conceived, to be in violation of the antitrust laws.

Under the Social Security Act, inhospital drugs are covered under Medicare (Title XVIII) and outpatient drugs are covered under Medicaid (Title XIX). Under Title XIX, approximately seventeen states have developed "formularies" or "drug lists" of those drugs acceptable for use by the states' medical assistance programs. These drug lists are essentially cost-containing devices designed to establish which drugs are covered and to establish upper limits on amounts that will be reimbursed for drugs. At least one state, Illinois, uses a committee to guide its professionals. The Drug and Therapeutics Committee of the Illinois State Medical Society is used to advise on the state's drug manual.

As activity encouraging national health insurance increases, a major issue is whether drugs and pharmaceutical services should be covered. The major concern of Congress and the administration is the tremendous cost that will be involved in a prescription drug program. One possible approach to this problem is the creation of a national formulary. But before the federal government will support such a program, it wants assurances that money will not only be saved but that quality and effectiveness will be maintained. The debate has raged over such concepts as chemical equivalence, bioavailability, therapeutic equivalence, and governmental and compendial standards.

In an attempt to resolve this issue, Congress requested its Office of Technical Assessment to make a suggestion. The Office of Technical Assessment sent a report of its study to Congress on July 15, 1974. Parties on both sides of the generic controversy challenged the report on various specific conclusions and recommendations. Because the issue is political as well as scientific, there may never be agreement on all the answers. However, the issues may be settled when Congress adopts legislation concerning brand selection.

Section 3

HOSPITAL FORMULARY SYSTEM

The first hospital formulary was compiled in 1816 by a New York hospital, four years prior to publication of the United States Pharmacopeia. Because of the long history surrounding hospital formularies, their widespread use in American hospitals and the resultant impact they have had on pharmacy practice, it is important to examine the legal considerations associated with the use of such formularies.

The basic formulary system was established many years ago in the *Statement of Guiding Principles on the Operation of the Hospital*

Formulary System, as adopted by the American Society of Hospital Pharmacists, the American Hospital Association, the American Medical Association, and the American Pharmaceutical Association. In addition to such strong backing by professional associations, such a system for drug selection has also been incorporated in the Standards of the Joint Commission on Accreditation of Hospitals and the Medicare Conditions of Participation.

The core of the formulary system is the pharmacy and therapeutics committee or equivalent committee composed of both pharmacists and physicians. The purposes, organization, and functions and scope of this committee are set forth in another professional policy document, the *Statement of the Pharmacy and Therapeutics Committee,* also adopted by the American Society of Hospital Pharmacists and the American Hospital Association. It is also dealt with by the Joint Commission on Accreditation of Hospitals and the Social Security Administration. Basically, the duties of this committee are:

A. To serve in an advisory capacity to the medical staff and hospital administration in all matters pertaining to the use of drugs.

B To serve in an advisory capacity to the medical staff and the pharmacist in the selection or choice of drugs which meet the most effective therapeutic quality standards.

C. To evaluate objectively clinical data regarding new drugs or agents proposed for use in the hospital.

D. To prevent unnecessary duplication of the same basic drug or its combinations.

E. To recommend additions and deletions from the list of drugs accepted for use in the hospital.

F. To develop a basic drug list or formulary of accepted drugs for use in the hospital and to provide for its constant revision.

G. To make recommendations concerning drugs to be stocked in hospital patient units or services.

H. To establish or plan suitable educational programs for the professional staff on pertinent matters related to drugs and their use.

I. To recommend policies regarding the safe use of drugs in hospitals, including a study of such matters as investigational drugs, hazardous drugs, and others.

J. To study problems involved in proper distribution and labeling of medications for inpatients and outpatients.

K. To study problems related to the administration of medications.

L. To review reported adverse reactions to drugs administered.

M. To evaluate periodically medical records in terms of drug therapy.

The net effect of this system of drug selection is that drugs listed in the hospital formulary are the products dispensed, which may be nonproprietary or of propietary brands different from those brands prescribed. Guiding Principle 5 of the Formulary Statement referred to above states:

> The medical staff shall adopt the policy of, and formulate the procedure for, including drugs in the formulary by their nonproprietary names, even though proprietary names are and will continue to be in common use in the hospital. Physicians may be encouraged to prescribe drugs under their nonproprietary names, although the nomenclature used is entirely a matter of the individual medical practitioner's discretion.

The hospital formulary system is based upon the principle of concurrent consent. Guiding Principle 4 states:

> To insure the maintenance of the responsibility and prerogatives of the physician in the exercise of his professional judgment, the hospital formulary system shall not contain any policies or procedures which, prior to the time of prescribing, provide for consent by the physician to the dispensing of a nonproprietary drug or to the dispensing of a proprietary brand different from the brand which he prescribed. However, *it shall be within his discretion at the time of prescribing to approve or disapprove the dispensing of a nonproprietary drug or the dispensing of a different proprietary brand.* (Emphasis added.)

In the absence of this consent the pharmacist and hospital must comply with the law; Guiding Principle 6 states:

> In the absence of written policies approved by the medical staff relative to the operation of the hospital formulary system, and authorization from the prescribing physician, the pharmacist must dispense the brand prescribed, bearing in mind his professional prerogative to confer with the physician should the prescribed brand be unavailable.

Stronger support for the formulary system is found in the interpretation of Medical Staff Standard IV of the Joint Commission on Accreditation of Hospitals, which states in part:

> The development and surveillance of pharmacy and therapeutic policies and practices, particularly drug utilization within the hospital, must be performed by the medical staff in cooperation with the pharmacist and with representatives of other disciplines, as necessary. Such policies and practices

should ensure optimal drug use, with a minimum potential for hazard to the patient.

A similar statement appears in Pharmaceutical Standard II:

Policies and procedures relative to the selection and distribution as well as to the safe and effective use of drugs shall be developed by the medical staff in cooperation with the pharmacist and with representatives of other disciplines, as necessary. Such policies and procedures should be approved by the medical staff. All drugs and chemicals should be obtained and used in accordance with these established policies. Such products shall meet the standards of quality of the United States Pharmacopoeia or National Formulary. Drugs for bona fide clinical investigations may be exceptions.

Standard IV, Medical Staff, provides a mechanism for implementation of these provisions:

The medical staff shall adopt rules and regulations that should contain specific statements covering procedures that foster optimal achievable patient care, including the care provided in the emergency service area. These statements should be appropriate for the given hospital, and should be such as will be followed by members of the medical staff. As an evidence of having read and understood the bylaws, each member must have signed, on application to the medical staff, an agreement to abide by the current medical staff bylaws, rules and regulations and by the hospital bylaws.

In addition, regulations of the Social Security Administration contain provisions similar to those found in the Joint Commission Standards.

If a hospital formulary system is based upon the Statement of Guiding Principles, Joint Commission Standards, or the Medicare regulations, appropriate medical staff involvement with prescriber consent should exist so as to not violate any substitution or adulteration laws.

To be on the safe side, prescriber consent to the formulary system can be obtained each time a prescription is written by placing on prescription blanks the following language:

Authorization is given for dispensing by nonproprietary name under formulary system unless checked here . . . .

As pointed out above this type of language on the prescription blank has been treated by the Attorney General of California as permitting substitution.

Neither will the mislabeling or trademark laws be violated under a properly functioning formulary system. Guiding Principle 12 advises:

> The labeling of a medication container with the nonproprietary name of the contents is always proper. The use of a proprietary name other than that describing the actual contents is improper if it is used in a manner that can be taken as descriptive of the contents, even though personnel familiar with the hospital formulary system may understand that it is not descriptive. The following format is recommended for labeling individual patient's containers used within hospitals:
>
> (Nonproprietary Name)
>
> (Name of Manufacturer or Distributor)
>
> Note for information of staff:
> Prescription or order for
>
> (Proprietary Name)
>
> dispensed as per formulary policy; contents are same basic drug as prescribed but may be of another brand.

This language on the label of the dispensing container should protect against mislabeling or infringement of a manufacturer's trademark.

What has been the effect of the hospital formulary system on drug product selection by pharmacists? A recent study reveals that among the hospitals surveyed, in 68.4% the hospital pharmacist prepares the drug specifications and in 74.2% of the hospitals the pharmacist selects the sources of supply (*i.e.,* brands). Evidently, the system works.

CHAPTER 5
QUALITY ASSURANCE

Section 1
PRIVATE PROGRAMS

AS PRIVATE AND FEDERAL EXPENDITURES FOR HEALTH CARE INCREASE, SO DOES the public and governmental expectation that the services for which they are paying will be of high quality. Prior to the enactment of any specific quality assurance law, private standards were being developed to assure the quality of health care services.

Private national standards of quasi-legal impact are those developed by the Joint Commission on Accreditation of Hospitals. These standards require the cooperative efforts of the medical and pharmacy staff to ensure optimal drug use. Standard IV, Medical Staff, Interpretation states:

> The development and surveillance of pharmacy and therapeutic policies and practices, particularly drug utilization within the hospital, must be performed by the medical staff in cooperation with the pharmacist and with representatives of other disciplines, as necessary. Such policies and practices should ensure optimal drug use, with a minimum potential for hazard to the patient.

In July, 1973, the JCAH added to its accreditation manual Appendix II entitled "Medical Care Evaluation and Utilization Review" which further formalizes the goals and procedures for a quality assurance program for hospitals.

Also in the private sector both the American Medical Association and the Americal Hospital Association have been forging ahead with their own programs. The Americal Hospital Association published the *Quality Assurance Program for Medical Care in the Hospital* in 1972.

83

This program is not designed to merely apply hindsight on specific problems but rather to upgrade, on a prospective basis, all services being provided.

The American Medical Association program is embodied in two publications, *Utilization Review, A Handbook for the Medical Staff* and *Peer Review Manual.* These standards provide physicians with the means by which to evaluate the quality of medical care.

Pharmacy has yet to develop a quality assurance program for the delivery of pharmaceutical services. National pharmacy organizations are now pursuing this goal, especially in view of the federal PSRO program, discussed in the next section.

Section 2
GOVERNMENT ACTIVITIES

The Social Security Act has required, for a number of years, that some form of utilization review be undertaken concerning services reimbursed by the federal government. Medicare regulations require the establishment of utilization review programs for care provided in hospitals. Although this requirement does not expressly include drug utilization review, the pharmacy conditions do require the hospital's pharmacy and therapeutics committee to formulate policies concerning the evaluation and use of drugs.

Over the years, various government reports and studies have recognized the need for some type of review. In 1973, the HEW Secretary's Commisson on Medical Malpractice, as a means of preventing medical injuries, made the following recommendation.

The Commission recommends that institutional quality control mechanisms of all types be constantly evaluated and, where proven desirable, modified so that the information they generate can be fed into a nationwide information system and into continuing education programs.

More specifically in the area of drugs, the 1969 *Report of the HEW Task Force on Prescription Drugs* called for drug utilization review programs.

The federal government's efforts to ensure the quality of care it purchases culminated in P.L. 92-603, the 1972 amendments to the Social Security Act. Section 249(F) of these amendments requires the creation of "Professional Standards Review Organizations" (PSROs). Basically they are local physician organizations designed to ensure effective, efficient and economical delivery of government reimbursed health care service within the physicians' geographic area of operation. The PSRO program was started as an institutional review program. It may be extended to health care services provided outside institutions if the PSRO petitions the Secretary of HEW to do so and if the PSRO can demonstrate a capability to provide effective review.

In reviewing health care services the PSRO must determine whether:

(a) services and items are or were medically necessary;
(b) the quality of such services meet professionally recognized standards of health care;
(c) services and items proposed to be provided in an institution could be provided on an outpatient basis or in another institution at less cost.

When a PSRO evaluates institutional care, it must use the hospital's review committees and accept their findings if the hospital has an effective and timely mechanism for this purpose. This provision complements the AHA's Quality Assurance Program.

Neither pharmacists nor pharmaceutical services are mentioned in the federal law. Naturally, drug therapy will come under review as part of the broad range of health care review. Pharmacists should have an active role to play in this area. The PSRO law makes provisions for participation by nonphysician health care practitioners.

§1155(b) (1)

To the extent necessary or appropriate for the proper performance of its duties and functions, the professional Standards Review Organization serving any area is authorized in accordance with regulations prescribed by the Secretary to make arrangements to utilize the services of persons who are practitioners or specialists in the various areas of medicine (including dentistry), or other types of health care, which persons shall, to the maximum extent practicable, be individuals engaged in the practice of their profession within the area served by such organization.

The Senate Finance Committee explained this provision in the following manner.

PSROs would be authorized and expected to retain and consult with other types of health care practitioners such as podiatrists to assist in reviewing services which their fellow practitioners provide. However, physicians should not be precluded — in fact they should be encouraged — to participate in the review of services ordered by physicians but rendered by other health care practitioners. For example, physical therapists may be utilized in the review of physical therapy services, but physicians should determine whether the services should have been ordered.

The expertise of pharmacists in matters relating to drug procurement, storage, control, and therapy is indispensible in PSRO activities and the law clearly permits their involvement. Two questions must be faced concerning pharmacist involvement. First, what kind of review should take place; secondly, how will pharmacists fit into the review mechanisms?

In response to the first question, the delivery of pharmaceutical services, *per se,* could be subject to review. This relates to the activities of pharmacists, such as compounding, dispensing, properly storing drugs, keeping effective control, maintaining proper records, repackaging, etc. Pharmacists do all these things and the performance of such tasks can be reviewed to determine the quality of performance. Measuring the performance of these purely pharmaceutical tasks does not, however, reach the purpose for which they are performed, that is, to provide drug therapy to the ill.

The second area for review focuses on the ultimate outcome of drug therapy. Did the patient get better? Was the patient harmed by any drugs? Were the medications really necessary? Was the right dose administered? In this area of medical care evaluation there is direct interaction between various health professionals: physician, pharmacist, nurse, laboratory technician, dietitian and so on. What one professional does may affect what another one does, and close cooperation will be needed as outcome review develops. Nevertheless, pharmacists have an important contribution to make and should not be timid in this regard.

If pharmacists are to contribute to a review, they must develop the appropriate criteria and standards for measurement of their services, and the criteria must fit into the overall review mechanisms. Criteria and standards for pharmaceutical services should be developed by pharmacists, preferably through their national organizations in order to achieve uniform national standards. If not, governmental units will undertake the task on their own.

On the other hand, involvement in review is centered at the state and local level. Broad, general encounter is provided for at the national level, but the real work is at the state and local levels. The law requires the establishment of state level advisory groups to assist statewide PSRO councils. The advisory group may have up to eleven board members, a majority of whom must be nonphysician practitioners. The only nonphysician member identified so far is a dentist, if dental services are subject to review. The question at this point is whether pharmacists will be made members. There is a great deal of competition among the many health professions for the five or six mandatory nonphysician seats. It seems that pharmacy should receive a place on the board because drug therapy is extensively used, can be dangerous if not used properly, and represents a substantial portion of the health care dollar.

CHAPTER 6
OPERATING A PHARMACY

CHAPTER 1 DISCUSSES THE LEGAL REQUIREMENTS THAT MUST BE MET BEFORE AN individual may practice pharmacy. In order to operate a "pharmacy" it is also necessary to comply with certain conditions. This chapter deals with licensure and other technical requirements concerning the operation of a pharmacy.

Section 1
LICENSURE

Under state law, any place wherein drugs are manufactured or dispensed, or where physicians' prescriptions are compounded, or where there are other indications of the apothecary's art, such as show globes or descriptive signs or words, is a pharmacy, drug store or apothecary. Such establishments must be licensed by the state or board of pharmacy or other regulatory agency. Generally, the statute requires an annual fee, inspection by the controlling agency, the keeping of up-to-date formularies, and the maintenance of records of prescriptions. The licenses or permits are required to be posted in a conspicuous place.

Despite the universality of this rule, there are some exceptions. Variations occur in relation to patent medicine stores, hospital pharmacies, and clinics. Patent medicines or proprietary medications are over-the-counter drugs and may be sold without a prescription. Many state laws require that before such medicines may be sold in any establishment other than a licensed pharmacy, that place must first obtain a permit from the state board of pharmacy. For example, the Colorado Pharmacy Law provides:

Colo. Rev. Stat. Ann. §48-1-23
Proprietary or patent medicine dealer.—No one located within this state, except a licensed pharmacy, shall engage in the sale

of proprietary or patent medicines until he has made application for a license as a proprietary or patent medicine dealer. An applicant shall be a person or a partnership of persons, not less than twenty-one years of age, or a corporation.

The other major area in which pharmacy licensing acts are not clearly applicable 'in all cases is the hospital setting. Many state statutes are broad enough to include hospital pharmacies within their scope. For example, the Michigan Attorney General construed Michigan's pharmacy act to apply to hospital pharmacies. In other legal definitions the implication arises that the drugs have to be dispensed "at retail" before the store or place would fit the descriptive wording of the statute. Hospitals may not be subject to these statutes unless they sold at retail. In Louisiana the Attorney General said that state hospitals dispensing drugs in connection with the operation thereof are not required to obtain the permit required of pharmacies, but that only registered pharmacists should be employed.

A recently enacted state law of particular interest is the Florida Institutional Pharmacy Law. Prior to enactment of this law, the Supreme Court of Florida held, in *Parr v. Spires,* that the drug room in a proprietary hospital not selling to the general public, but used only for compounding prescriptions for patients of the physicians owning the hospital, was not a drug store within the meaning of the former pharmacy act. Thus, it was not required to be licensed as such. Under the new law, however, the ruling in this case is no longer viable. In addition to the community pharmacy category, the Institutional Pharmacy Law creates two new institutional pharmacy categories. The Class I institutional classification applies to those institutions that do not have their own pharmacies. The drugs they administer to patients have been prepared in another pharmacy. The Class II license is for those institutions having their own pharmacies. If a Class II pharmacy also dispenses drugs to outpatients, it must also register with the Board of Pharmacy as a community pharmacy.

In addition to this most recent example of legislative action, there exist state regulations of similar thrust, such as Joint Regulation No. 1-70, adopted jointly by the State Board of Pharmacy and State Board of Health in Montana in 1970. Michigan and Pennsylvania also have hospital pharmacy regulations.

In the area of clinics, the court, in *Love v. Escambia County,* held that a city-county indigent outpatient clinic was not a pharmacy, for a nurse dispensed prefabricated medications under the supervision of a physician. No drugs were mixed, prepared or compounded at the clinic and all medications were given free to patients and not otherwise sold at retail or wholesale. Thus, the clinic was not required to obtain a pharmacy license.

A licensure issue that has gained national prominence in recent years is whether a pharmacy may be owned by nonpharmacists. In the early part of this century a number of states passed laws prohibiting the ownership of pharmacies by nonpharmacists. Some laws did not outrightly prohibit pharmacy ownership by nonpharmacists, but instead limited the percentage of the pharmacy's stock that could be in the hands of unlicensed owners. Michigan law requires all pharmacies, drugstores or apothecary shops to be owned by registered pharmacists, and further requires that partnerships and corporations owning such places have 25% of their stock owned by registered pharmacists. However, under exceptions in these two sections and from the language of other sections of the pharmacy law, it appears that pharmacies may be owned in other ways.

An ownership statute was challenged by the Liggett Drug Store Company in Pennsylvania. In 1928, the United States Supreme Court held, in *Ligett Co. v. Baldridge,* that such laws restricting pharmacy ownership violated the Due Process Clause of Section 1 of the Fourteenth Amendment to the Unites States Constitution.

Forty-four years later, in 1972, the North Dakota Board of Pharmacy denied a pharmacy license to Snyder's Drug Stores because they did not comply with the North Dakota Pharmacy Act requiring that the majority of stock of a pharmacy corporation be owned by registered pharmacists in good standing in North Dakota. The North Dakota Supreme Court held, in *Snyder's Drug Stores, Inc. v. Board of Pharmacy,* the requirement to be void because of the *Liggett* ruling of the U.S. Supreme Court. Upon petition by the North Dakota Board of Pharmacy, the Supreme Court justices reversed their earlier *Liggett* opinion and held in *North Dakota Board of Pharmacy v. Snyder's Drug Stores,* that such pharmacy ownership laws were constitutionally sound if such a requirement was deemed by the legislature to be reasonably related to the public health and welfare. Upon rehearing, the North Dakota Supreme Court found that its law is reasonably so related. The court identified seven possible reasons for the ownership requirements.

(1) The professional and ethical standards of pharmacy demand the pharmacist's concern for the quantity and quality of stock and equipment. A drug which has deteriorated because of improper storage facilities can be a detriment to public health. A drug not in stock poses a threat to the individual who needs it now. Decisions made in conjunction with the quantity and quality of stock and equipment by nonregistered-pharmacist owners could be detrimental to the public health and welfare.

(2) Supervision of hired pharmacists by registered-pharmacist owners would be in the best interests of public health and safety.

(3) Responsibility for improper action could be more readily pinpointed when supervision is in registered-pharmacist owners.

(4) The dignity of a profession and the morale and proficiency of those licensed to engage therein is enhanced by prohibiting the practitioner from subordinating himself to the direction of untrained supervisors.

(5) If control and management is vested in laymen unacquainted with pharmaceutical service, who are untrained and unlicensed, the risk is that social accountability will be subordinated to the profit motive.

(6) The term "pharmacy" was intended to identify a particular type of establishment within which a health profession is practiced, and thus was intended to be more than a mere means of making a profit. He who holds the purse strings controls the policy.

(7) Doctor-owned pharmacies with built-in conflict-of-interest problems could be restricted.

As a result of this case there may be increased activity in state legislatures to secure adoption of similar laws.

The North Dakota case highlights a fact of life pharmacy has lived with for years, i.e., incorporation of the practice of pharmacy under general business corporation laws. Problems have resulted from classifying pharmacy in this way. First, it raises serious challenge to the professionalism of pharmacy for no other professionals are legally able to incorporate under the general business laws. If pharmacy can, is it really a profession? Secondly, it contributes to the adoption of that ill-fated concept of "the dual character of pharmacy, part profession and part business." Lastly, it aids the ownership of stock in pharmacies by individual nonpharmacists or large business corporations.

In recent years various states have adopted professional corporation laws that allow professionals to incorporate. Professional corporations offer the same basic tax benefits provided by business corporations. Personal business liabilities are also limited just as they are in general corporations.

Even though they bestow certain tax and business advantages, professional corporation laws do, however, place certain restrictions upon incorporated professionals. Professional corporations are restricted in ownership; only licensed practitioners may participate. Furthermore, each practitioner's liability for professional malpractice is not limited. In some states these laws specify which professions may incorporate. And in some of these statutes pharmacy is not mentioned. This may be due to the fact that pharmacy did not ask to be included or because pharmacy has always used general business corporations.

Now that professional corporation laws have been enacted, it will be interesting to see if pharmacists will convert to the use of this type of corporation or continue to use business corporations.

Section 2
OTHER REQUIREMENTS

Most state pharmacy laws or regulations set forth specific technical standards of practice that must be met. These standards relate to appropriate compounding areas, adequate supplies of pharmaceuticals and drugs, basic pharmaceutical equipment such as a Class A balance and weights, mortars and pestles, spatulas, graduates and other similar equipment, storage facilities with appropriate humidity and temperature controls that will protect the integrity of the products, and other professional and technical equipment for the storage, compounding, and dispensing of drugs and pharmaceuticals. A minimum library is usually required, including such references as the *United States Pharmacopeia, National Formulary* and other pharmaceutical references.

The National Association of Boards of Pharmacy has identified the following minimum technical equipment and stock necessary to properly operate a pharmacy.

XIII. MINIMUM STANDARD OF TECHNICAL EQUIPMENT AND STOCK

Stock of Drugs

Approved by N.A.B.P. (See 1934 and 1962 Proceedings)

The stock of drugs should include such U.S.P., N.F., and other commonly used chemicals, drugs, and preparations sufficient to compound ordinary prescriptions as indicated by experience in the community where the pharmacy is located.

Reference Library

The U.S.P. and Supplements.
The National Formulary.
The Dispensatory.
New and Non-official Remedies.
    (All of the above books to be of the latest editions.)
A Medical Dictionary.
A treatise on each of the following subjects.
    Materia Medica & Therapeutics.
    General Chemistry.
    Botany and Pharmacognosy.
    Practice of Pharmacy.
A book or books of reference covering the subjects of:
    Toxicology—Compounding.
    Incompatibilities—Arithmetic.
Copies of Federal and State Laws governing pharmacy.
    Upon inspection these books should be indelibly stamped with an identifying serial number.
Other books recommended are works on—
    Bacteriology—Endocrinology—
    Vitamin Therapy—Bio-Chemistry—

First Aid—Pharmaceutical Law—
Economics—History of Pharmacy—

A copy of each of Merck's Index and Modern Drug Encyclopedia with supplements.

American Hospital Formulary Service of American Society of Hospital Pharmacists.

Introduction to the Practice of Pharmacy—A Guide for Preceptors and Interns.

Technical Equipment

The necessary equipment for dispensing and compounding should include:

Graduates—capable of accurately measuring volumes from 5 cc. to at least 500 cc.

Mortars and Pestles—Glass—at least one
    —Porcelain—at least two assorted sizes
Wedgewood—at least three assorted sizes

Spatulas—Steel—at least three assorted sizes
    —non-metallic—at least two assorted sizes

Funnels—at least three assorted sizes

Stirring rods—glass or rubber

Test Tubes—assorted sizes

Pill Tile

Ointment Slab

Tripod

Water Bath

Bunsen Burner or Alcohol Lamp

Ring Stand and Rings

Corks—assorted sizes

Filter Paper

Litmus Paper

Powder Papers—pervious and impervious

Evaporating Dishes

Percolator

Sieves

Empty Capsules—various sizes

Ointment Jars—various sizes

Collapsible Tubes—various sizes

Tablet Triturate Mold

Towels

Flasks

Prescription Files

Poison Record Book and Narcotic Record Book

Homeopathic Vials

Bottles—clear glass, amber glass—necessary sizes

Labels

Boxes—Capsule and Powder

Thermometer—for measuring temperature from Zero to 250 degrees centigrade

Scales and Balances—for bulk, medium, and light weighing at least one of which must be sensitive to ½ grain

Weights—apothecary and avoirdupois from ½ gr. to 1 lb. metric from 0.02 Gm. to 1 Kg.

Space and Fixtures

The stock, library and equipment should be housed in a suitable, well lighted and ventilated room or department with clean and sanitary surrounding devoted primarily to the compounding of prescriptions, the manufacture of pharmaceutical preparations, and the operations necessary to determine strength and purity of medicines. The space should be equipped with necessary counters, tables, drawers, shelves and storage cabinets; a sink with hot and cold water, or some facilities for heating water, and proper sewerage outlet; poison cabinet, narcotic drug cabinet; and refrigerator storage equipment of a reasonable capacity. There must be facilities for sterilizing solutions and containers as well as facilities for the proper cleaning of premises, equipment and utensils.

NOTE: Requirements in all states do not conform to minimum recommendations, in all respects. In some states it is not mandatory for pharmacies to have any reference texts or special equipment to weigh, measure, compound, dispense and store drugs. Very few states do not require all or more than the above listed reference texts, equipment and facilities.

An important question in hospital practice is whether any of these pharmacy standards apply to other areas of the hospital or whether they are limited solely to the area called the pharmacy. Simple logic and professional advice tells us that if temperature controls are necessary for the preservation of drugs in the pharmacy, they probably have an effect on the same products in other areas of the hospital, such as the emergency room, nursing stations, and operating rooms. For example, nurses should not store nitroglycerine or other unstable products near heat or moisture in order to protect the potency of the product. And, nurses who measure out doses of medication must have equipment sensitive enough to yield the proper quantities before administering them to patients. In fact, such principles have been carried over into certain standards. For example, state and federal laws require that narcotics be locked wherever they are stored in the institution. The interpretation of Standard II of the Joint Commission on Accreditation of Hospitals deals in detail with this subject:

> Drugs stored within the pharmacy, and throughout the hospital, must be under the supervision of the pharmacist. They must be stored under proper conditions of sanitation, temperature, light, moisture, ventilation, segregation and security. There should be adequate and properly controlled drug preparation areas, as well as locked storage areas, on the

nursing units. These areas, which should be well lighted, should be located in a place where the nursing personnel will not be interrupted when handling drugs. The pharmacist, or his designee, must make periodic inspections of all drug storage and medication centers on nursing care units. A record of these inspections should be maintained in order to verify that:

Disinfectants and drugs for external use are stored separately from internal and injectable medications.

Drugs requiring special conditions for storage to ensure stability are properly stored. For example, biologicals and other thermolabile medications should be stored in a separate compartment within a refrigerator that is capable of maintaining the necessary temperature.

No outdated drugs are stocked.

Distribution and administration of controlled drugs are adequately documented.

Emergency drugs are in adequate and proper supply.

Metric-apothecaries' weight and measure conversion charts are posted wherever they are needed.

Materials and equipment necessary for the administration of the service should be provided. Effective messenger and delivery service should connect the pharmacy with appropriate parts of the hospital.

Up-to-date pharmaceutical reference material should be provided in order to furnish the medical and nursing staffs with adequate information concerning drugs. As a minimum, the following should be available: *United States Pharmacopoeia, National Formulary, American Hospital Formulary Service,* and *A.M.A. Drug Evaluations.*

In addition, there should be current editions of text and reference books covering theoretical and practical pharmacy; general, organic, pharmaceutical and biological chemistry; toxicology; pharmacology; bacteriology; sterilization and disinfection; as well as other related matters important to good patient care. Authoritative, current antidote information should be readily available in the pharmacy for emergency reference, along with the telephone number of the regional poison control center.

Standards established by the profession itself are also applicable. The American Society of Hospital Pharmacists has a published statement entitled "Minimum Standards for Pharmacies in Hospitals with Guide to Application," which sets forth in detail the minimum requirements, as determined by professional practitioners, necessary to properly provide quality pharmaceutical services to patients of hospitals. Of similar importance is the *Statement on Hospital Drug Control Systems.*

PART II
DRUG LAWS

THE ENTIRE STOCK-IN-TRADE IN A PHARMACY IS SUBJECT TO VARIOUS GOVERN-mental controls at the federal, state and local levels. The most important federal law having an impact on pharmacy is the Federal Food, Drug, and Cosmetic Act (FDCA). In *United States v. Sullivan,* the United States Supreme Court held, under the FDCA, that once drugs enter interstate commerce any person subsequently holding them for purposes of resale must comply with the Act. This ruling would apply to drugs held for sale in community pharmacies, hospitals, clinics, HMOs, physicians' offices, and other places.

It is imperative that the pharmacist intern and resident understand the manner in which these articles are regulated. In chain drug stores, the director of professional affairs, store managers and other members of the corporate hierarchy should also be familiar with these laws. This is equally true in the hospital setting for the hospital's administrative staff, hospital attorney, medical staff, and other professional employees.

Books have been written about the FDCA, the Food and Drug Administration (FDA) regulations, and court interpretations of these requirements. This part of the book is not intended to be an in-depth analysis of this body of law. It is designed to familiarize pharmacists with those requirements of the law that most directly affect their practice. Appendix D contains relevant sections of the FDCA for further study and analysis.

In addition to the FDCA, there are a number of other laws that have a relatively minor, yet important affect upon pharmacy practice. These include the laws and regulations covering poison prevention packaging, mailing and shipping of drugs, and alcohol tax. These laws as well as other state drug laws are discussed.

CHAPTER 7
THE REGULATION OF DRUGS, DEVICES, AND COSMETICS

Section 1

HISTORICAL DEVELOPMENT OF THE FEDERAL FOOD, DRUG, AND COSMETIC ACT

GENERAL FEDERAL REGULATION OF DRUGS BEGAN WITH THE ENACTMENT OF THE Food and Drugs Act of 1906. It covered *all United States Pharmacopeia* and *National Formulary* medicines and preparations and prohibited their marketing if adulterated or misbranded, as defined in the law. This law had the dubious distinction of regulating interstate drug traffic until 1938. That year more than one hundred persons died after taking "elixir of sulfanilamide." The elixir was prepared with diethylene glycol, a toxic substance. Thye Food and Drugs Act of 1906 did not require premarket testing for safety, and hence this product was placed on the market with dire results.

The sulfanilamide diaster paved the way for the enactment of the Federal, Food, Drug, and Cosmetic Act of 1938 (FDCA). This new law continued the scheme of prohibiting from commerce adulterated or misbranded items. The FDCA added the requirement that drugs be adequately tested to establish that they are safe for use under the conditions of use set forth in the label. It also required labels to bear warning about the habit-forming nature of certain drugs, adequate directions for use, and other precautionary measures. For the first time, federal law also applied to devices and cosmetics.

In subsequent years Congress amended the FDCA to require batch certification of insulin and antibiotics for the Food and Drug Administration (FDA) before such drugs could be marketed. In 1949, the Act was amended to extend its coverage to products that became adulterated or misbranded after interstate shipment and at all levels of distribution, including retailing.

The Durham-Humphrey Amendment of 1951 is of major importance in pharmacy. Sometimes referred to as the prescription-drug amendments, these changes, among other things, established by law which drugs may only be dispensed by pharmacists pursuant to the order of a practitioner authorized by law to administer such drugs. Congress continued to enhance the protection afforded by FDCA during the 1950s.

In 1962, another drug incident, the "thalidomide disaster," similar to the sulfanilamide episode, resulted in the Kefauver-Harris Drug Amendments of 1962. These amendments introduced the concepts of good manufacturing practices, premarket testing for effectiveness as well as safety, factory inspection every two years, annual manufacture registration, the use of established (generic) names in labeling and advertising, a balanced representation of risks along with benefits, adverse drug reaction reporting, investigational new drug procedures, and informed consent.

More recently, the Drug Listing Act of 1972 requires a current listing of each drug manufactured by a registrant under the FDCA.

The development of the law was accompanied by a comparable development of regulatory sophistication. The FDA is the central regulatory and enforcement agency under the FDCA. Nevertheless, other agencies, by virtue of authority granted by other laws, have jurisdiction over certain aspects of drug marketing as well. Although the FDA retains control over advertising of prescription drugs, the Federal Trade Commission (FTC) regulates advertising of over-the-counter medications similar to the manner in which it regulates advertising of other, nondrug products. Advertising of such products may not be misleading or fraudulent.

In addition to the FTC, the Consumer Product Safety Commission (CPSC) has primary regulatory jurisdiction under the Consumer Product Safety Act and the Poison Prevention Packaging Act.

Although certain provisions of the Federal Food, Drug, and Cosmetic Act specifically apply to intrastate commerce insofar as drugs are concerned, Congress, at various times, has specifically provided for the applicability of state law. Accordingly, most states now have a food, drug and cosmetic law based primarily upon the Uniform State Food, Drug and Cosmetic Bill. State laws vary in specific details from the uniform act or the federal act and must be consulted when determining whether a specific course of conduct is in compliance with all applicable laws.

The foregoing outline of the background of federal drug legislation is but a thumbnail sketch. It does not include legal control of drugs subject to abuse. This area of interest is covered in Part III. Many of the concepts and controls alluded to above are discussed in greater detail throughout Part II because of their impact on the practice of pharmacy.

Section 2

DIFFERENTIATION BETWEEN DRUGS, DEVICES, AND COSMETICS

The difference between drugs, devices, and cosmetics are very important in pharmacy practice because these products are distributed through pharmacies. The FDCA applies to the quality, purity, packaging, labeling, potency, safety, and effectiveness of these products in varying degrees depending on how they are classified. Therefore, it is important to define these terms. The FDCA gives the following definitions of drugs, devices, and cosmetics.

§201. For the purposes of this chapter . . .

(g) (1) The term "drug" means (A) articles recognized in the official United States Pharmacopoeia, official Homeopathic Pharmacopoeia of the United States, or official National Formulary, or any supplement to any of them; and (B) articles intended for use in the diagnosis, cure, mitigation, treatment, or prevention of disease in man or other animals; and (C) articles (other than food) intended to affect the structure or any function of the body of man or other animals; and (D) articles intened for use as a component of any article specified in clauses (A), (B), or (C) of this paragraph; but does not include devices or other components, parts, or accessories.

(h) The term "device" (except when used in paragraph (n) of this section and in sections 331(i), 343 (f), 352 (c), and 362 (c) of this title) means instruments, apparatus, and contrivances, including their components, parts, and accessories, intended (1) for use in the diagnosis, cure, mitigation, treatment, or prevention of disease in man or other animals; or (2) to affect the structure or any function of the body of man or other animals.

(i) The term "cosmetic" means (1) articles intended to be rubbed, poured, sprinkled, or sprayed on, introduced into, or otherwise applied to the human body or any part thereof for cleansing, beautifying, promoting attractiveness, or altering the appearance, and (2) articles intended for use as a component of any such articles; except that such term shall not include soap.

The application of these definitions to specific products has been the subject of significant litigation. The central question in such cases concerns the "intended use" of such products as opposed to the actual use, although the latter may be significant in some instances. In determining the classification of a product all relevant factors are taken into account by the courts. For example, even though therapeutic claims are not made on the label or labeling accompanying a product, other sources, such as newspapers, leaflets and booklets or magazine advertisements may be examined. If these sources contain therapeutic claims which have been adopted by the manufacturer, a court may find that the product is a drug and subject to requirements of the FDCA which are generally more stringent than those applicable to devices or cosmetics.

A number of items that have been held to be drugs, although they might not seem to be drugs to a casual observer, include antibiotic sensitivity discs used in laboratory procedures, diagnostic preparations listed in official compendia, and certain sutures used for tying off blood vessels during surgical procedures. Other items, such as cotton, are drugs by virtue of the fact that they are listed in the *United States Pharmacopeia.*

Whole human blood has also been held to be a drug within the meaning of the Food, Drug and Cosmetic Act and so have plastic bags used for storage of blood and other intravenous substances.

Among the types of products that have been held to be devices are tongue depressors, surgical gloves and instruments, thermometers, syringes, hypodermic needles, various suspensory bandages, and supporters. As with drugs, certain items may become devices depending upon the claims made for their use. Hence, phonograph records that were advertised as sleep aids were held to be devices as were toothbrushes that were claimed to be helpful in curing pyorrhea. Newer types of devices would include heart valves, pacemakers, and intrauterine devices.

Cosmetics include perfumes, make-up, baby oil, bleaching agents, deodorants, depilatories and so forth. Soap, as such, is specifically exempt under the law. However, shaving creams are not exempt. One particular brand of shaving cream was held to be both a cosmetic and a drug because of the claims made for it. Various wrinkle removers have also been held to be drugs because of therapeutic claims.

Section 3

REGULATION OF DEVICES

Devices were not regulated by federal law until enactment of the FDCA. Devices are basically regulated through standards that ensure their integrity, their packaging and labeling, and directions for use. This is achieved through the FDCA's provisions setting forth the circumstances under which a device is deemed to be adulterated or misbranded.

A device is adulterated if it consists of any filthy, putrid, or decomposed substance, if. it was processed or held under unsanitary conditions, or if its strength, purity or quality does not comply with its label.

A device is deemed to be misbranded if its labeling is false, misleading, or does not contain the name and place of business of the manufacturer, or if the label does not contain information required under the FDCA in such terms that it is likely to be read and understood. Misbranding also occurs if its labeling does not contain adequate directions for use, necessary precautions and warnings, or if the device is dangerous to health when used under its labeled directions.

The Act specifies remedies available to the FDA in the case of adulteration or misbranding. The agency may seize such devices, seek injunction against their further distribution, or institute criminal proceedings.

Despite what seems to be rather comprehensive civil and criminal procedures available in the case of offending devices, the shortcoming of such a system is that regulation of an offensive practice comes after the fact. A device must be adulterated or misbranded first; then, the FDA can take action. But even though the agency may take action, it must do so in court which may entail lengthy proceedings over a long period of time.

Obviously, the foregoing regulatory scheme has certain limitations in its capability to protect the public health. Based on the need to provide an ability to control devices before they enter the marketplace and to speed action in the case of offending products, Congress has been considering, since the 1960s, the adoption of amendments to current device legislation. A number of legislative proposals have been introduced to improve the safety and efficacy of devices in commerce.

The bills vary in the type of controls that would be established. Among the concepts the proposed amendments contain are the establishment of good manufacturing practices, registration of manufacturers, and factory inspections. Manufacturers would have to maintain manufacturing records and make experience reports on the effects of their devices. The FDA would be authorized to recognize official names, remove defective or ineffective devices from commerce, classify devices according to their need for premarket clearance, and to establish testing standards. Lastly, advisory councils and information centers for devices would be established.

It is impossible to know what type of law will eventually emerge from Congress. Some or all of these regulatory techniques may be employed. In anticipation of a new device law, the FDA has established a new Bureau of Devices and Diagnostic Products to deal specifically with devices on the market. At the present time special attention is given to products affecting life itself, such as pacemakers.

By increasing controls over devices, the issue of whether an article is a drug or device will diminish.

Section 4

REGULATION OF COSMETICS

Prior to 1938, cosmetics were not covered by federal law. Now cosmetics are regulated in a manner similar to devices. They must meet minimum requirements of purity, safety, packaging and labeling. If not, they may be considered to be adulterated or misbranded.

With the exception of properly labeled coal tar hair dye, a cosmetic is deemed to be adulterated if it contains any poisonous or deleterious substances which may render it injurious to users under labeled conditions, if it consists of any filthy, putrid, or decomposed substance, if it was prepared under unsanitary conditions, if its container is composed of any poisonous or deleterious substance, or if it is not a hair dye that contains a color additive that is unsafe.

Again, like devices, a cosmetic is considered misbranded if its labeling is false or misleading or does not contain certain information such as the name and address of the manufacturer and an accurate statement of the quantity of the contents. In addition, the label information must be such that it will be read and understood by the consumer. Misbranding also occurs if the container is made or filled so as to be misleading or if the packaging or labeling does not conform to the requirements of the Poison Prevention Packaging Act of 1970. When used, color additives must comply with applicable regulations.

Contravention of the cosmetic adulteration and misbranding provisions allows for the same enforcement responses of seizure, injunction and criminal proceedings applicable to devices. The FDA may also request a voluntary "recall" by the manufacturer rather than instituting formal proceedings if the public interest will be adequately served. Naturally, the same shortcomings also exist.

Bills have been introduced to Congress to remedy this situation. Such proposals would require ingredient labeling and premarket testing of cosmetics. Manufacturers would also have to file test reports and reports of adverse reactions.

It is not uncommon for legislative proposals to have long gestation periods. The FDA in the meantime promulgated regulations in 1974 that establish a program of voluntary filing of cosmetic product experiences. The program had to be voluntary because of the lack of statutory authority to require this. The information given to the FDA pertains to the manufacture and composition of cosmetic products as well as consumer adverse reactions. The cosmetic industry, through the Cosmetic, Toiletry and Fragrance Association, has assisted the FDA in preparing the program. If the voluntary program does not work well, as current evidence indicates, the possibility of legislation controlling cosmetics will increase.

Section 5

REGULATION OF DRUGS

Under earlier laws, drugs were subject to the same type of regulatory scheme as presently used for devices and cosmetics. The law was designed to ensure their identity, strength, quality and purity and to regulate their packaging and labeling. If the standards were not met, the drugs, just as devices and cosmetics, were deemed to be adulterated or misbranded.

Drugs are subject to the same adulteration standards that are applicable to devices. In addition, they are subjected to other requirements. A drug may also be deemed adulterated if not produced in accordance with good manufacturing practices, if its container is composed of any poisonous or deleterious substance, if it contains an unsafe coloring, or if it varies from compendial standards unless its label indicates a variation.

Along with extensive adulteration standards, drugs are subject to further misbranding requirements as well. If a drug contains any habit forming ingredients, the label must bear the name and quantity of such ingredients, and next to the name(s) the statement "Warning—May be habit forming" must appear. The label must also bear the drug's established (generic) name, or such names of active ingredients in the case of combination products, in type size at least one-half as large as that used for the trade name. If it is a prescription drug the quantity of active ingredients must be included on the label. If the drug is in an official compendium it must be labeled and packaged in accordance with compendial standards. It may also be misbranded if its package is so filled or formed as to be misleading, if it is an imitation of another drug, or if it is offered for sale under the name of another drug. The manufacturer must be registered with FDA. Advertisements must include the drug's established name in print at least one-half the size of the trade name, must include the quantities of active ingredients, and fairly balance the benefits and risks in using the drug. If the drug is not packaged in accordance with the Poison Prevention Packaging Act it will be deemed to be misbranded. Furthermore, insulin, penicillin and other antibiotics must be from batches certified by the government.

Adulteration and misbranding provisions are not the only way in which drugs are more strictly regulated. They are subject to new drug approvals, investigational new drug exemptions, premarket clearance for safety and effectiveness, and labeling claims for indications, precautions, contraindications, etc., as approved in the new drug application.

The remaining chapters in this part of the book deal with important aspects of these drug controls and their implications to pharmacy practice.

CHAPTER 8
NEW AND INVESTIGATIONAL DRUGS

Section 1
NEW DRUGS

IN ANALYZING THE EFFECT OF THE FDCA ON THE PRACTICE OF PHARMACY, IT IS essential to understand the "new drug" concept. The FDCA defines "new drug" in the following manner:

§201. For the purposes of this chapter . . .

(p) The term "new drug" means—
(1) Any drug (except a new animal drug or an animal feed bearing or containing a new animal drug) the composition of which is such that such drug is not generally recognized, among experts qualified by scientific training and experience to evaluate the safety and effectiveness of drugs, as safe and effective for use under the conditions prescribed, recommended, or suggested in the labeling thereof, except that such a drug not so recognized shall not be deemed to be a "new drug" if at any time prior to the enactment of this chapter it was subject to the Food and Drugs Act of June 30, 1906, as amended, and if at such time its labeling contained the same representations concerning the conditions of its use; or
(2) Any drug (except a new animal drug or an animal feed bearing or containing a new animal drug) the composition of which is such that such drug, as a result of investigations to determine its safety and effectiveness for use under such conditions, has become so recognized, but which has not, otherwise than in such investigations, been used to a material extent or for a material time under such conditions.

Not only newly invented or discovered substances are new drugs. Presently known substances may be new drugs if applied as a drug for

105

the first time. Even "old drugs," those that are generally recognized as safe and effective under the conditions prescribed, recommended or suggested in the labeling, may become new drugs. For example, the newness of a drug may arise by changing the composition of the drug, whether the change affects an active or inactive ingredient. A change from an old drug to a new drug may also occur if a new combination of old drugs is used, if a new proportion of an old combination is prepared, if an old drug is used to treat a different disease or affect another structure or function of the body, if the dosage or duration of administration is altered, or if the drug is used upon a different patient population (e.g., pediatric use) than previously used.

Whether a drug is generally recognized as "safe and effective" is a question of fact that has been tried in a number of cases, including the recent notable case of *U.S. v. Bentex Ulcerine*. This case held that if the drug is not generally recognized as safe and effective it may not be marketed unless it has a New Drug Application (NDA) approved by the FDA. (See Exhibit 5, Form FD 356H.)

The law and regulations establish an elaborate NDA procedure for determining whether a new drug is safe and effective for marketing. Section 505 of the FDCA sets forth the specific kinds of information that must be supplied by the drug sponsor in order to obtain approval of his application.

It is necessary to submit reports of investigations, components used to make the drug, composition of the drug, descriptions of the manufacturing processes, samples of the drug, and examples of the labeling.

The NDA must contain a summary of material information accompanying the application. The summary must cover: the chemistry of the drug; scientific rationale and purpose the drug is to serve; preclinical studies; pharmacology data; toxicology and pathology information and clinical studies, including special studies not described elsewhere, dose-range studies, controlled and other clinical studies, and clinical laboratory studies related to effectiveness and safety; and a synopsis of the literature and unpublished reports on the drug.

In addition to the summary, the NDA must contain a complete and thorough evaluation of the safety and effectiveness of the drug. This evaluation should include favorable and unfavorable information plus a tabulation of side effects and adverse reactions. Copies of the proposed label and labeling must accompany the application. The prescription or over-the-counter (OTC) status must be indicated as well as a full list of articles, chemicals, etc., used in making the drug and the full composition of the drug. The entire manufacturing process must be described and samples submitted. All clinical and preclinical data as well as a list of investigators has to be included.

If an NDA is already approved and the holder wishes to make changes in labeling, formulations or manufacturing processes, a supplemental or Abbreviated New Drug Application (ANDA) may be filed.

An ANDA must contain the information specified in items 1 (table of contents), 4 (labeling), 5 (Rx or OTC statement), and 6 (components) of the NDA. In lieu of the full information required in items 7 and 8 of an NDA the ANDA may contain a brief statement concerning the drug's components, the suppliers of active ingredients, the place of manufacture, conformity with current good manufacturing practices, compliance with compendial specifications and tests, biological availability data, especially if formulation is for sustained action, and clinical data on adverse reactions.

ANDAs are sometimes requested by the FDA if it finds bioavailability problems with drugs on the market. For example, when digoxin problems were identified, a manufacturer had to withdraw his product unless he submitted an ANDA demonstrating the bioavailability of his product.

Exhibit 5

DEPARTMENT OF HEALTH, EDUCATION, AND WELFARE
PUBLIC HEALTH SERVICE
FOOD AND DRUG ADMINISTRATION
ROCKVILLE, MARYLAND 20852

Form Approved
OMB No. 57-R0003

NEW DRUG APPLICATION *(DRUGS FOR HUMAN USE)*
(Title 21, Code of Federal Regulations, § 130.4)

Name of applicant _____

Address _____

Date _____

Name of new drug_____

☐ Original application (regulation § 130.4).

☐ Amendment to original, unapproved application (regulation § 130.7).

☐ Abbreviated application (regulation § 130.4(f)).

☐ Amendment to abbreviated, unapproved application (regulation § 130.7).

☐ Supplement to an approved application (regulation § 130.9).

☐ Amendment to supplement to an approved application.

The undersigned submits this application for a new drug pursuant to section 505(b) of the Federal Food, Drug, and Cosmetic Act. It is understood that when this application is approved, the labeling and advertising for the drug will prescribe, recommend, or suggest its use only under the conditions stated in the labeling which is part of this application; and if the article is a prescription drug, it is understood that any labeling which furnishes or purports to furnish information for use or which prescribes, recommends, or suggests a dosage for use of the drug will contain the same information for its use, including indications, effects, dosages, routes, methods, and frequency and duration of administration, any relevant warnings, hazards, contraindications, side effects, and precautions, as that contained in the labeling which is part of this application in accord with § 1.106(b) (21 CFR 1.106(b)). It is understood that all representations in this application apply to the drug produced until an approved supplement to the application provides for a change or the change is made in conformance with other provisions of § 130.9 of the new-drug regulations.

Attached hereto, submitted in the form described in §130.4(e) of the new-drug regulations, and constituting a part of this application are the following:

1. Table of contents. The table of contents should specify the volume number and the page number in which the complete and detailed item is located and the volume number and the page number in which the summary of that item is located (if any).

2. Summary. A summary demonstrating that the application is well-organized, adequately tabulated, statistically analyzed (where appropriate), and coherent and that it presents a sound basis for the approval requested. The summary should include the following information: (In lieu of the outline described below and the evaluation described in Item 3, an expanded summary and evaluation as outlined in §130.4(d) of the new-drug regulations may be submitted to facilitate the review of this application.)
   a. Chemistry.
   i. Chemical structural formula or description for any new-drug substance.
   ii. Relationship to other chemically or pharmacologically related drugs.
   iii. Description of dosage form and quantitative composition.
   b. Scientific rationale and purpose the drug is to serve.
   c. Reference number of the investigational drug notice(s) under which this drug was investigated and of any notice, new-drug application, or master file of which any contents are being incorporated by reference to support this application.
   d. Preclinical studies. (Present all findings including all adverse experiences which may be interpreted as incidental or not drug-related. Refer to date and page number of the investigational drug notice(s) or the volume and page number of this application where complete data and reports appear.)
   i. Pharmacology (pharmacodynamics, endocrinology, metabolism, etc.).

   ii. Toxicology and pathology: Acute toxicity studies; subacute and chronic toxicity studies; reproduction and teratology studies; miscellaneous studies.
   e. Clinical studies. (All material should refer specifically to each clinical investigator and to the volume and page number in the application and any documents incorporated by reference where the complete data and reports may be found.)
   i. Special studies not described elsewhere.
   ii. Dose-range studies.
   iii. Controlled clinical studies.
   iv. Other clinical studies (for example, uncontrolled or incompletely controlled studies).
   v. Clinical laboratory studies related to effectiveness.
   vi. Clinical laboratory studies related to safety.
   vii. Summary of literature and unpublished reports available to the applicant.

3. Evaluation of safety and effectiveness. a. Summarize separately the favorable and unfavorable evidence for each claim in the package labeling. Include references to the volume and page number in the application and in any documents incorporated by reference where the complete data and reports may be found.
   b. Include tabulation of all side effects or adverse experience, by age, sex, and dosage formulation, whether or not considered to be significant, showing whether administration of the drug was stopped and showing the investigator's name with a reference to the volume and page number in the application and any documents incorporated by reference where the complete data and reports may be found. Indicate those side effects or adverse experiences considered to be drug-related.

4. Copies of the label and all other labeling to be used for the drug (a total of 12 copies if in final printed form, 4 copies if in draft form):

FD FORM 356H (4/71)   PREVIOUS EDITION MAY BE USED UNTIL SUPPLY IS EXHAUSTED.

Exhibit 5 *(Continued)*

a. Each label, or other labeling, should be clearly identified to show its position on, or the manner in which it accompanies, the market package.

b. If the drug is to be offered over the counter, labeling on or within the retail package should include adequate directions for use by the layman under all the conditions for which the drug is intended for lay use or is to be prescribed, recommended, or suggested in any labeling or advertising sponsored by or on behalf of the applicant and directed to the layman. If the drug is intended or offered for uses under the professional supervision of a practitioner licensed by law to administer it, the application should also contain labeling that includes adequate information for all such uses, including all the purposes for which the over-the-counter drug is to be advertised to, or represented for use by, physicians.

c. If the drug is limited in its labeling to use under the professional supervision of a practitioner licensed by law to administer it, its labeling should bear information for use under which such practitioners can use the drug for the purposes for which it is intended, including all the purposes for which it is to be advertised or represented, in accord with §1.106(b) (21 CFR 1.106(b)). The application should include any labeling for the drug intended to be made available to the layman.

d. If no established name exists for a new-drug substance, the application shall propose a nonproprietary name for use as the established name for the substance.

e. Typewritten or other draft labeling copy may be submitted for preliminary consideration of an application. An application will not ordinarily be approved prior to the submission of the final printed label and labeling of the drug.

f. No application may be approved if the labeling is false or misleading in any particular.

(When mailing pieces, any other labeling, or advertising copy are devised for promotion of the new drug, samples shall be submitted at the time of initial dissemination of such labeling and at the time of initial placement of any such advertising for a prescription drug (see §130.13 of the new-drug regulations). Approval of a supplemental new-drug application is required prior to use of any promotional claims not covered by the approved application.)

5. A statement as to whether the drug is (or is not) limited in its labeling and by this application to use under the professional supervision of a practitioner licensed by law to administer it.

6. A full list of the articles used as components of the drug. This list should include all substances used in the synthesis, extraction, or other method of preparation of any new-drug substance, and in the preparation of the finished dosage form, regardless of whether they undergo chemical change or are removed in the process. Each substance should be identified by its established name, if any, or complete chemical name, using structural formulas when necessary for specific identification. If any proprietary preparation is used as a component, the proprietary name should be followed by a complete quantitative statement of composition. Reasonable alternatives for any listed substance may be specified.

7. A full statement of the composition of the drug. The statement shall set forth the name and amount of each ingredient, whether active or not, contained in a stated quantity of the drug in the form in which it is to be distributed (for example, amount per tablet or per milliliter) and a batch formula representative of that to be employed for the manufacture of the finished dosage form. All components should be included in the batch formula regardless of whether they appear in the finished product. Any calculated excess of an ingredient over the label declaration should be designated as such and percent excess shown. Reasonable variations may be specified.

8. A full description of the methods used in, and the facilities and controls used for, the manufacture, processing, and packing of the drug. Included in this description should be full information with respect to any new-drug substance and to the new-drug dosage form, as follows, in sufficient detail to permit evaluation of the adequacy of the described methods of manufacture, processing, and packing and the described facilities and controls to determine and preserve the identity, strength, quality, and purity of the drug:

a. A description of the physical facilities including building and equipment used in manufacturing, processing, packaging, labeling, storage, and control operations.

b. A description of the qualifications, including educational background and experience, of the technical and professional personnel who are responsible for assuring that the drug has the safety, identity, strength, quality, and purity it purports or is represented to possess, and a statement of their responsibilities.

c. The methods used in the synthesis, extraction, isolation, or purification of any new-drug substance. When the specifications and controls applied to such substance are inadequate in themselves to determine its identity, strength, quality, and purity, the methods should be described in sufficient detail, including quantities used, times, temperatures, pH, solvents, etc., to determine these characteristics. Alternative methods or variations in methods within reasonable limits that do not affect such characteristics of the substance may be specified.

d. Precautions to assure proper, identity, strength, quality, and purity of the raw materials, whether active or not, including the specifications for acceptance and methods of testing for each lot of raw material.

e. Whether or not each lot of raw materials is given a serial number to identify it, and the use made of such numbers in subsequent plant operations.

f. If the applicant does not himself perform all the manufacturing, processing, packaging, labeling, and control operations for any new-drug substance or the new-drug dosage form, his statement identifying each person who will perform any part of such operations and designating the part; and a signed statement from each such person fully describing, directly or by reference, the methods, facilities, and controls in his part of the operation.

g. Method of preparation of the master formula records and individual batch records and manner in which these records are used.

h. The instructions used in the manufacturing, processing, packaging, and labeling of each dosage form of the new drug, including any special precautions observed in the operations.

i. Adequate information with respect to the characteristics of and the test methods employed for the container, closure, or other component parts of the drug package to assure their suitability for the intended use.

j. Number of individuals checking weight or volume of each individual ingredient entering into each batch of the drug.

k. Whether or not the total weight or volume of each batch is determined at any stage of the manufacturing process subsequent to making up a batch according to the formula card and, if so, at what stage and by whom it is done.

l. Precautions to check the actual package yield produced from a batch of the drug with the theoretical yield. This should include a description of the accounting for such items as discards, breakage, etc., and the criteria used in accepting or rejecting batches of drugs in the event of an unexplained discrepancy.

m. Precautions to assure that each lot of the drug is packaged with the proper label and labeling, including provisions for labeling storage and inventory control.

Exhibit 5 *(Continued)*

n. The analytical controls used during the various stages of the manufacturing, processing, packaging, and labeling of the drug, including a detailed description of the collection of samples and the analytical procedures to which they are subjected. The analytical procedures should be capable of determining the active components within a reasonable degree of accuracy and of assuring the identity of such components. If the article is one that is represented to be sterile, the same information with regard to the manufacturing, processing, packaging, and the collection of samples of the drug should be given for sterility controls. Include the standards used for acceptance of each lot of the finished drug.

o. An explanation of the exact significance of the batch control numbers used in the manufacturing, processing, packaging, and labeling of the drug, including the control numbers that appear on the label of the finished article. State whether these numbers enable determination of the complete manufacturing history of the product. Describe any methods used to permit determination of the distribution of any batch if its recall is required.

p. A complete description of, and data derived from, studies of the stability of the drug, including information showing the suitability of the analytical methods used. Describe any additional stability studies underway or contemplated. Stability data should be submitted for any new-drug substance, for the finished dosage form of the drug in the container in which it is to be marketed, including any proposed multiple-dose container, and if it is to be put into solution at the time of dispensing, for the solution prepared as directed. State the expiration date(s) that will be used on the label to preserve the identity, strength, quality, and purity of the drug until it is used. (If no expiration date is proposed, the applicant must justify its absence.)

q. Additional procedures employed which are designed to prevent contamination and otherwise assure proper control of the product.

(An application may be refused unless it includes adequate information showing that the methods used in, and the facilities and controls used for, the manufacturing, processing, and packaging of the drug are adequate to preserve its identity, strength, quality, and purity in conformity with good manufacturing practice and identifies each establishment, showing the location of the plant conducting these operations.)

9. Samples of the drug and articles used as components, as follows: a. The following samples shall be submitted with the application or as soon thereafter as they become available. Each sample shall consist of four identical, separately packaged subdivisions, each containing at least three times the amount required to perform the laboratory test procedures described in the application to determine compliance with its control specifications for identity and assays:

i. A representative sample or samples of the finished dosage form(s) proposed in the application and employed in the clinical investigations and a representative sample or samples of each new-drug substance, as defined in §130.1(g), from the batch(es) employed in the production of such dosage form(s).

ii. A representative sample or samples of finished market packages of each dosage form of the drug prepared for initial marketing and, if any such sample is not from a commercial-scale production batch, such a sample from a representative commercial-scale production batch; and a representative sample or samples of each new-drug substance as defined in §130.1(g), from the batch(es) employed in the production of such dosage form(s).

iii. A sample or samples of any reference standard and blank used in the procedures described in the application for assaying each new-drug substance and other assayed

components of the finished drug: *Provided, however,* That samples of reference standards recognized in the official U.S. Pharmacopeia or The National Formulary need not be submitted unless requested.

b. Additional samples shall be submitted on request.

c. Each of the samples submitted shall be appropriately packaged and labeled to preserve its characteristics, to identify the material and the quantity in each subdivision of the sample, and to identify each subdivision with the name of the applicant and the new-drug application to which it relates.

d. There shall be included a full list of the samples submitted pursuant to Item 9a; a statement of the additional samples that will be submitted as soon as available; and, with respect to each sample submitted, full information with respect to its identity, the origin of any new-drug substance contained therein (including in the case of new-drug substances, a statement whether it was produced on a laboratory, pilot-plant, or full-production scale) and detailed results of all laboratory tests made to determine the identity, strength, quality, and purity of the batch represented by the sample, including assays. Include for any reference standard a complete description of its preparation and the results of all laboratory tests on it. If the test methods used differed from those described in the application, full details of the methods employed in obtaining the reported results shall be submitted.

e. The requirements of Item 9a may be waived in whole or in part on request of the applicant or otherwise when any such samples are not necessary.

f. If samples of the drug are sent under separate cover, they should be addressed to the attention of the Bureau of Medicine and identified on the outside of the shipping carton with the name of the applicant and the name of the drug as shown on the application.

10. Full reports of preclinical investigations that have been made to show whether or not the drug is safe for use and effective in use. *a.* An application may be refused unless it contains full reports of adequate preclinical tests by all methods reasonably applicable to a determination of the safety and effectiveness of the drug under the conditions of use suggested in the proposed labeling.

b. Detailed reports of the preclinical investigations, including all studies made on laboratory animals, the methods used, and the results obtained, should be clearly set forth. Such information should include identification of the person who conducted each investigation, a statement of where the investigations were conducted, and where the underlying data are available for inspection. The animal studies may not be considered adequate unless they give proper attention to the conditions of use recommended in the proposed labeling for the drug such as, for example, whether the drug is for short- or long-term administration or whether it is to be used in infants, children, pregnant women, or women of child-bearing potential.

c. Detailed reports of any pertinent microbiological and *in vitro* studies.

d. Summarize and provide a list of literature references (if available) to all other preclinical information known to the applicant, whether published or unpublished, that is pertinent to an evaluation of the safety or effectiveness of the drug.

11. List of investigators. *a.* A complete list of all investigators supplied with the drug including the name and post office address of each investigator and, following each name, the volume and page references to the investigator's report(s) in this application and in any documents incorporated by reference, or the explanation of the omission of any reports.

b. The unexplained omission of any reports of investigations made with the new drug by the applicant, or

Exhibit 5 *(Continued)*

submitted to him by an investigator, or the unexplained omission of any pertinent reports of investigations or clinical experience received or otherwise obtained by the applicant from published literature or other sources, whether or not it would bias an evaluation of the safety of the drug or its effectiveness in use, may constitute grounds for the refusal or withdrawal of the approval of an application.

12. Full reports of clinical investigations that have been made to show whether or not the drug is safe for use and effective in use. a. An application may be refused unless it contains full reports of adequate tests by all methods reasonably applicable to show whether or not the drug is safe and effective for use as suggested in the labeling.

b. An application may be refused unless it includes substantial evidence consisting of adequate and well-controlled investigations, including clinical investigations, by experts qualified by scientific training and experience to evaluate the effectiveness of the drug involved, on the basis of which it could fairly and responsibly be concluded by such experts that the drug will have the effect it purports or is represented to have under the conditions of use prescribed, recommended, or suggested in the proposed labeling.

c. Reports of all clinical tests sponsored by the applicant or received or otherwise obtained by the applicant should be attached. These reports should include adequate information concerning each subject treated with the drug or employed as a control, including age, sex, conditions treated, dosage, frequency of administration of the drug, results of all relevant clinical observations and laboratory examinations made, full information concerning any other treatment given previously or concurrently, and a full statement of adverse effects and useful results observed, together with an opinion as to whether such effects or results are attributable to the drug under investigation and a statement of where the underlying data are available for inspection. Ordinarily, the reports of clinical studies will not be regarded as adequate unless they include reports from more than one independent, competent investigator who maintains adequate case histories of an adequate number of subjects, designed to record observations and permit evaluation of any and all discernible effects attributable to the drug in each individual treated and comparable records on any individuals employed as controls. An application for a combination drug may be refused unless there is substantial evidence that each ingredient designated as active makes a contribution to the total effect claimed for the drug combination. Except when the disease for which the drug is being tested occurs with such infrequency in the United States as to make testing impractical, some of the investigations should be performed by competent investigators within the United States.

d. Attach as a separate section a completed Form FD-1639, Drug Experience Report (obtainable, with instructions, on request from the Department of HEW. Food and Drug Administration, Bureau of Drugs *(BD-200)* Rockville, Maryland 20852), for each adverse experience or, if feasible, for each subject or patient experiencing one or more adverse effects, described in Item 12c, whether or not full information is available. Form FD-1639 should be prepared by the applicant if the adverse experience was not reported in such form by the investigator. The Drug Experience Report should be cross-referenced to any narrative description included in Item 12c. In lieu of a FD Form 1639, a computer-generated report may be submitted if equivalent in all elements of information with the identical enumerated sequence of events and methods of completion; all formats proposed for such use will require initial review and approval by the Food and Drug Administration.

e. All information pertinent to an evaluation of the safety and effectiveness of the drug received or otherwise obtained by the applicant from any source, including information derived from other investigations or commerical marketing (for example, outside the United States), or reports in the scientific literature, involving the drug that is the subject of the application and related drugs. An adequate summary may be acceptable in lieu of a reprint of a published report which only supports other data submitted. Reprints are not required of reports in designated journals, listed in §130.38 of the new-drug regulations, about related drugs; a bibliography will suffice. Include any evaluation of the safety or effectiveness of the drug that has been made by the applicant's medical department, expert committee, or consultants.

f. If the drug is a combination of previously investigated or marketed drugs, an adequate summary of pre-existing information from preclinical and clinical investigation and experience with its components, including all reports received or otherwise obtained by the applicant suggesting side effects, contraindications, and ineffectiveness in use of such components. Such summary should include an adequate bibliography of publications about the components and may incorporate by reference information concerning such components previously submitted by the applicant to the Food and Drug Administration.

g. The complete composition and/or method of manufacture of the new drug used in each submitted report of investigation should be shown to the extent necessary to establish its identity, strength, quality, and purity if it differs from the description in Item 6, 7, or 8 of the application.

13. If this is a supplemental application, full information on each proposed change concerning any statement made in the approved application.

Observe the provisions of §130.9 of the new-drug regulations concerning supplemental applications.

(Applicant)

Per ————————————————
(Responsible official or agent)

(Indicate authority)

(Warning: A willfully false statement is a criminal offense. U.S.C. Title 18, sec. 1001.)

NOTE: This application must be signed by the applicant or by an authorized attorney, agent, or official. If the applicant or such authorized representative does not r e s i d e or have a place of business within the United States, the application must also furnish the nar, and post office address of and must be countersigned by an authorized attorney, agent, or official residing or maintaining a place of business within the United States.

Section 2

INVESTIGATIONAL DRUGS

If a drug is neither generally recognized as safe and effective nor is the subject of an approved NDA, it may not be shipped in interstate commerce unless it is under investigation and complies with the important "investigational use" exception to the new drug provisions:

Sec. 505

* * *

(i) The Secretary shall promulgate regulations for exempting from the operation of the foregoing subsections of this section drugs intended solely for investigational use by experts qualified by scientific training and experience to investigate the safety and effectiveness of drugs. Such regulations may, within the discretion of the Secretary, among other conditions relating to the protection of the public health, provide for conditioning such exemption upon—

(1) the submission to the Secretary, before any clinical testing of a new drug is undertaken, of reports, by the manufacturer or the sponsor of the investigation of such drug, or preclinical tests (including tests on animals) of such drug adequate to justify the proposed clinical testing;

(2) the manufacturer or the sponsor of the investigation of a new drug proposed to be distributed to investigators for clinical testing obtaining a signed agreement from each of such investigators that patients to whom the drug is administered will be under his personal supervision, or under the supervision of investigators responsible to him, and that he will not supply such drug to any other investigator, or to clinics, for administration to human beings; and

(3) the establishment and maintenance of such records, and the making of such reports to the Secretary, by the manufacturer or the sponsor of the investigation of such drug, of data (including but not limited to analytical reports by investigators) obtained as the result of such investigational use of such drug, as the Secretary finds will enable him to evaluate the safety and effectiveness of such drug in the event of the filing of an application pursuant to subsection (b) of this section.

Such regulations shall provide that such exemption shall be conditioned upon the manufacturer, or the sponsor of the investigation, requiring that experts using such drugs for investigational purposes certify to such manufacturer or sponsor that they will inform any human beings to whom such drugs, or any controls used in connection therewith, are being administered, or their representatives, that such drugs are being used for investigational purposes and will obtain the consent of such human beings or their representatives, except where they deem it not feasible or, in their professional judgment, contrary to the best interests of such human beings. Nothing in this subsection shall be construed to require any clinical investigator to submit directly to the Secretary reports on the investigational use of drugs.

An elaborate regulatory scheme has been developed to implement this section of the law. Pharmacists involved in the investigation of new drugs should become thoroughly familiar with investigational new drug (IND) procedures.

The IND procedure begins by filing Form FD 1571, "Notice of Claimed Investigational Exemption for a New Drug." (See Exhibit 6.) Detailed information concerning the drug itself, including name, quantitative composition, method of manufacture, and quality controls, must be furnished. Adequate information on preclinical investigations, including studies on laboratory animals which demonstrate that the drug is safe for testing on humans, must be supplied. The results of literature research are also required. The names and a summary of the training and experience of clinical investigators must be included along with investigator executed forms. (See Exhibit 7.) A complete outline of the three phases of clinical trials is essential. Phase 1 relates directly to establishing human toxicity, metabolism, absorption, elimination and other pharmacological action. Phase 2 covers initial trials on a limited number of patients for treatment of specific diseases. Phase 3 consists of broad clinical testing to assess the drug's safety and effectiveness and to establish dosage schedules.

An important aspect of the IND procedure that deserves highlighting relates to patient use of new drugs. The clinical investigator must certify that the drugs will be used only on subjects under his personal supervision or under the supervision of investigators responsible to him. The investigator must further certify that he will inform any patients or their representatives that the drugs being used are for investigational purposes and that he will obtain their informed consent.

For IND purposes, consent of the patient must be obtained whether the administration of the drug is for purely scientific purposes or for the treatment of the patient. Exceptional circumstances under which consent is not required occur when it is physically impossible to obtain the consent of the patient or his representative and it is imperative to administer the drug without delay or when, as a matter of professional judgment exercised in the best interest of the patient, it would be contrary to that patient's welfare to obtain his consent. (See Exhibit 8.)

Exhibit 6

DEPARTMENT OF HEALTH, EDUCATION, AND WELFARE
PUBLIC HEALTH SERVICE
FOOD AND DRUG ADMINISTRATION

Form Approved
OMB No. 57-R0030

NOTICE OF
CLAIMED INVESTIGATIONAL EXEMPTION
FOR A NEW DRUG

Name of Sponsor_____

Address _____

Date _____

Name of Investigational Drug _____

Commissioner
Food and Drug Administration
Bureau of Drugs (BD-26)
5600 Fishers Lane
Rockville, Maryland 20852

Dear Sir:

The sponsor, _____ , submits this notice of claimed investigational exemption for a new drug under the provisions of section 505(i) of the Federal Food, Drug, and Cosmetic Act and §130.3 of Title 21 of the Code of Federal Regulations.

Attached hereto, in triplicate, are:

1. The best available descriptive name of the drug, including to the extent known the chemical name and structure of any new-drug substance, and a statement of how it is to be administered. (If the drug has only a code name, enough information should be supplied to identify the drug.)

2. Complete list of components of the drug, including any reasonable alternates for inactive components.

3. Complete statement of quantitative composition of drug, including reasonable variations that may be expected during the investigational stage.

4. Description of source and preparation of, any new-drug substances used as components, including the name and address of each supplier or processor, other than the sponsor, of each new-drug substance.

5. A statement of the methods, facilities, and controls used for the manufacturing, processing, and packing of the new drug to establish and maintain appropriate standards of identity, strength, quality, and purity as needed for safety and to give significance to clinical investigations made with the drug.

6. A statement covering all information available to the sponsor derived from preclinical investigations and any clinical studies and experience with the drug as follows:

a. Adequate information about the preclinical investigations, including studies made on laboratory animals, on the basis of which the sponsor has concluded that it is reasonably safe to initiate clinical investigations with the drug: Such information should include identification of the person who conducted each investigation; identification and qualifications of the individuals who evaluated the results and concluded that it is reasonably safe to initiate clinical investigations with the drug and a statement of where the investigations were conducted and where the records are available for inspection; and enough details about the investigations to permit scientific review. The preclinical investigations shall not be considered adequate to justify clinical testing unless they give proper attention to the conditions of the proposed clinical testing. When this information, the outline of the plan of clinical pharmacology, or any progress report on the clinical pharmacology, indicates a need for full review of the

preclinical data before a clinical trial is undertaken, the Department will notify the sponsor to submit the complete preclinical data and to withhold clinical trials until the review is completed and the sponsor notified. The Food and Drug Administration will be prepared to confer with the sponsor concerning this action.

b. If the drug has been marketed commercially or investigated (e.g. outside the United States), complete information about such distribution or investigation shall be submitted, along with a complete bibliography of any publications about the drug.

c. If the drug is a combination of previously investigated or marketed drugs, an adequate summary of pre-existing information from preclinical and clinical investigations and experience with its components, including all reports available to the sponsor suggesting side-effects, contraindications, and ineffectiveness in use of such components: Such summary should include an adequate bibliography of publications about the components and may incorporate by reference any information concerning such components previously submitted by the sponsor to the Food and Drug Administration. Include a statement of the expected pharmacological effects of the combination.

7. A total of three copies of all informational material, including label and labeling, which is to be supplied to each investigator: This shall include an accurate description of the prior investigations and experience and their results pertinent to the safety and possible usefulness of the drug under the conditions of the investigation. It shall not represent that the safety or usefulness of the drug has been established for the purposes to be investigated. It shall describe all relevant hazards, contraindications, side-effects, and precautions suggested by prior investigations and experience with the drug under investigation and related drugs for the information of clinical investigators.

8. The scientific training and experience considered appropriate by the sponsor to qualify the investigators as suitable experts to investigate the safety of the drug, bearing in mind what is known about the pharmacological action of the drug and the phase of the investigational program that is to be undertaken.

FD FORM 1571 (5/71)   PREVIOUS EDITIONS ARE OBSOLETE.

Exhibit 6 *(Continued)*

9. The names and a summary of the training and experience of each investigator and of the individual charged with monitoring the progress of the investigation and evaluating the evidence of safety and effectiveness of the drug as it is received from the investigators, together with a statement that the sponsor has obtained from each investigator a completed and signed form, as provided in subparagraph (12) or (13) of this paragraph, and that the investigator is qualified by scientific training and experience as an appropriate expert to undertake the phase of the investigation outlined in section 10 of the "Notice of Claimed Investigational Exemption| for a New Drug."; (In crucial situations, phase 3 investigators may be added and this form supplemented by rapid communication methods, and the signed form FD 1573 shall be obtained promptly thereafter.)

10. An outline of any phase or phases of the planned investigations and a description of the institutional review committee, as follows:

a. Clinical pharmacology. This is ordinarily divided into two phases: Phase 1 starts when the new drug is first introduced into man—only animal and in vitro data are available--with the purpose of determining human toxicity, metabolism, absorption, elimination, and other pharmacological action, preferred route of administration, and safe dosage range; phase 2 covers the initial trials on a limited number of patients for specific disease control or prophylaxis purposes. A general outline of these phases shall be submitted, identifying the investigator or investigators, the hospitals or research facilities where the clinical pharmacology will be undertaken, any expert committees or panels to be utilized, the maximum number of subjects to be involved, and the estimated duration of these early phases of investigation. Modification of the experimental design on the basis of experience gained need be reported only in the progress reports on these early phases, or in the development of the plan for the clinical trial, phase 3. The first two phases may overlap and, when indicated, may require additional animal data before these phases can be completed or phase 3 can be undertaken. Such animal tests shall be designed to take into account the expected duration of administration of the drug to human beings, the age groups and physical status, as for example, infants, pregnant women, premenopausal women, of those human beings to whom the drug may be administered, unless this has already been done in the original animal studies.

b. Clinical trial. This phase 3 provides the assessment of the drug's safety and effectiveness and optimum dosage schedules in the diagnosis, treatment, or prophylaxis of groups of subjects involving a given disease or condition. A reasonable protocol is developed on the basis of the facts accumulated in the earlier phases, including completed and submitted animal studies. This phase is conducted by separate groups following the same protocol (with reasonable variations and alternatives permitted by the plan) to produce well-controlled clinical data. For this phase, the following data shall be submitted:

i. The names and addresses of the investigators. (Additional investigators may be added.)

ii. The specific nature of the investigations to be conducted, together with information or case report forms to show the scope and detail of the planned clinical observations and the clinical laboratory tests to be made and reported.

iii. The approximate number of subjects (a reasonable range of subjects is permissible and additions may be made), and criteria proposed for subject selection by age, sex, and condition.

iv. The estimated duration of the clinical trial and the intervals, not exceeding 1 year, at which progress reports showing the results of the investigations will be submitted to the Food and Drug Administration.

(The notice of claimed investigational exemption may be limited to any one or more phases, provided the outline of the additional phase or phases is submitted before such additional phases begin. This does not preclude continuing a subject on the drug from phase 2 to phase 3 without interruption while the plan for phase 3 is being developed.)

Ordinarily, a plan for clinical trial will not be regarded as reasonable unless, among other things, it provides for more than one independent competent investigator to maintain adequate case histories of an adequate number of subjects, designed to record observations and permit evaluation of any and all discernible effects attributable to the drug in each individual treated, and comparable records on any individuals employed as controls. These records shall be individual records for each subject maintained to include adequate information pertaining to each, including age, sex, conditions treated, dosage, frequency of administration of the drug, results of all relevant clinical observations and laboratory examinations made, adequate information concerning any other treatment given and a full statement of any adverse effects and useful results observed, together with an opinion as to whether such effects or results are attributable to the drug under investigation.

c. Institutional review committee. If the phases of clinical study as described under 10a and b above are conducted on institutionalized subjects or are conducted by an individual affiliated with an institution which agrees to assume responsibility for the study, assurance must be given that an institutional review committee is responsible for initial and continuing review and approval of the proposed clinical study. The membership must be comprised of sufficient members of varying background, that is, lawyers, clergymen, or laymen as well as scientists, to assure complete and adequate review of the research project. The membership must possess not only broad competence to comprehend the nature of the project, but also other competencies necessary to judge the acceptability of the project or activity in terms of institutional regulations, relevant law, standards of professional practice, and community acceptance. Assurance must be presented that neither the sponsor nor the investigator has participated in selection of committee members; that the review committee does not allow participation in its review and conclusions by any individual involved in the conduct of the research activity under review (except to provide information to the committee); that the investigator will report to the committee for review any emergent problems, serious adverse reactions, or proposed procedural changes which may affect the status of the investigation and that no such change will be made without committee approval except where necessary to eliminate apparent immediate hazards; that reviews of the study will be conducted by the review committee at intervals appropriate to the degree of risk, but not exceeding 1 year, to assure that the research project is being conducted in compliance with the committee's understanding and recommendations: that the review committee is provided all the information on the research project necessary for its complete review of the project; and that the review committee maintains adequate documentation of its activities and develops adequate procedures for reporting its findings to the institution. The documents maintained by the committee are to include the names and qualifications of committee members; records of information provided to subjects in obtaining informed consent, committee discussion on substantive issues and their

Exhibit 6 *(Continued)*

resolution, committee recommendations, and dated reports of successive reviews as they are performed. Copies of all documents are to be retained for a period of 3 years past the completion or discontinuance of the study and are to be made available upon request to duly authorized representatives of the Food and Drug Administration. (Favorable recommendations by the committee are subject to further appropriate review and rejection by institution officials. Unfavorable recommendations, restrictions, or conditions may not be overruled by the institution officials.) Procedures for the organization and operation of institutional review committees are contained in guidelines issued pursuant to Chapter 1-40 of the Grants Administration Manual of the U.S. Department of Health, Education, and Welfare, available from the U.S. Government Printing Office. It is recommended that these guidelines be followed in establishing institutional review committees and that the committees function according to the procedures described therein. A signing of the Form FD 1571 will be regarded as providing the above assurances. If the institution, however, has on file with the Department of Health, Education, and Welfare, Division of Research Grants, National Institutes of Health, an "accepted general assurance," and the same committee is to review the proposed study using the same procedures, this is acceptable in lieu of the above assurances and a statement to this effect should be provided with the signed FD 1571. (In addition to sponsor's continuing responsibility to monitor the study, the Food and Drug Administration will undertake investiga-

tions in institutions periodically to determine whether the committees are operating in accord with the assurances given by the sponsor.)

11. It is understood that the sponsor will notify the Food and Drug Administration if the investigation is discontinued, and the reason therefor.

12. It is understood that the sponsor will notify each investigator if a new-drug application is approved, or if the investigation is discontinued.

13. If the drug is to be sold, a full explanation why sale is required and should not be regarded as the commercialization of a new drug for which an application is not approved.

14. A statement that the sponsor assures that clinical studies in humans will not be initiated prior to 30 days after the date of receipt of the notice by the Food and Drug Administration and that he will continue to withold or to restrict clinical studies if requested to do so by the Food and Drug Administration prior to the expiration of such 30 days. If such request is made, the sponsor will be provided specific information as to the deficiencies and will be afforded a conference on request. The 30-day delay may be waived by the Food and Drug Administration upon a showing of good reason for such waiver; and for investigations subject to institutional review committee approval as described in item 10c above, an additional statement assuring that the investigation will not be initiated prior to approval of the study by such committee.

Very truly yours,

SPONSOR	PER
	INDICATE AUTHORITY

(This notice may be amended or supplemented from time to time on the basis of the experience gained with the new drug. Progress reports may be used to update the notice.)

ALL NOTICES AND CORRESPONDENCE SHOULD BE SUBMITTED IN TRIPLICATE.

Exhibit 7

DEPARTMENT OF HEALTH, EDUCATION, AND WELFARE PUBLIC HEALTH SERVICE FOOD AND DRUG ADMINISTRATION 5600 FISHERS LANE ROCKVILLE, MARYLAND 20852	STATEMENT OF INVESTIGATOR	Form Approved OMB No. 57-R0029
TO: SUPPLIER OF DRUG *(Name and address, include Zip Code)*	NAME OF INVESTIGATOR *(Print or Type)*	
	DATE	
	NAME OF DRUG	

Dear Sir:

The undersigned, _____,
submits this statement as required by section 505(i) of the Federal Food, Drug, and Cosmetic Act and §130.3 of Title 21 of the Code of Federal Regulations as a condition for receiving and conducting clinical investigations with a new drug limited by Federal (or United States) law to investigational use.

1.   STATEMENT OF EDUCATION AND EXPERIENCE

a. COLLEGES, UNIVERSITIES, AND MEDICAL OR OTHER PROFESSIONAL SCHOOLS ATTENDED, WITH DATES OF ATTENDANCE, DEGREES, AND DATES DEGREES WERE AWARDED

b. POSTGRADUATE MEDICAL OR OTHER PROFESSIONAL TRAINING *(Indicate dates, names of institutions, and nature of training)*

c. TEACHING OR RESEARCH EXPERIENCE *(Indicate dates, institutions, and brief description of experience)*

d. EXPERIENCE IN MEDICAL PRACTICE OR OTHER PROFESSIONAL EXPERIENCE *(Indicate dates, institutional affiliations, nature of practice, or other professional experience)*

e. REPRESENTATIVE LIST OF PERTINENT MEDICAL OR OTHER SCIENTIFIC PUBLICATIONS *(Indicate titles of articles, names of publications and volume, page number, and date)*

FD FORM 1573 (5/71)   PREVIOUS EDITION MAY BE USED UNTIL SUPPLY IS EXHAUSTED.

Exhibit 7 *(Continued)*

2a. If the investigation is to be conducted on institutionalized subjects or is conducted by an individual affiliated with an institution which agrees to assume responsibility for the study, assurance must be given that an institutional review committee is responsible for initial and continuing review and approval of the proposed clinical study. The membership must be comprised of sufficient members of varying background, that is, lawyers, clergymen, or laymen as well as scientists, to assure complete and adequate review of the research project. The membership must possess not only broad competence to comprehend the nature of the project, but also other competencies necessary to judge the acceptability of the project or activity in terms of institutional regulations, relevant law, standards of professional practice and community acceptance. Assurance must be presented that the investigator has not participated in the selection of committee members; that the review committee does not allow participation in its review and conclusions by any individual involved in the conduct of the research activity under review (except to provide information to the committee) that the investigator will report to the committee for review any emergent problems, serious adverse reactions, or proposed procedural changes which may affect the status of the investigation and that no such change will be made without committee approval except where necessary to eliminate apparent immediate hazards; that reviews of the study will be conducted by the review committee at intervals appropriate to the degree of risk, but not exceeding 1 year, to assure that the research project is being conducted in compliance with the committee's understanding and recommendations; that the review committee is provided all the information on the research project necessary for its complete review of the project; and that the review committee maintains adequate documentation of its activities and develops adequate procedures for reporting its findings to the institution. The documents maintained by the committee are to include the names and qualifications of committee members, records of information provided to subjects in obtaining informed consent, committee discussion on substantive issues and their resolution, committee recommendations, and dated reports of successive reviews as they are performed. Copies of all documents are to be retained for a period of 3 years past the completion or discontinuance of the study and are to be made available upon request to duly authorized representatives of the Food and Drug Administration. (Favorable recommendations by the committee are subject to further appropriate review and rejection by institution officials. Unfavorable recommendations, restrictions, or conditions may not be overruled by the institution officials.) Procedures for the organization and operation of institutional review committees are contained in guidelines issued pursuant to Chapter 1-40 of the Grants Administration Manual of the U.S. Department of Health, Education, and Welfare, available from the U.S. Government Printing Office. It is recommended that these guidelines be followed in establishing institutional review committees and that the committees function according to the procedures described therein. A signing of the Form FD 1573 will be regarded as providing the above necessary assurances; however, if the institution has on file with the Department of Health, Education, and Welfare, Division of Research Grants, National Institutes of Health, an "accepted general assurance," and the same committee is to review the proposed study using the same procedures, this is acceptable in lieu of the above assurances and a statement to this effect should be provided with the signed FD 1573. (In addition to sponsor's continuing responsibility to monitor the study, the Food and Drug Administration will undertake investigations in institutions periodically to determine whether the committees are operating in accord with the assurances given by the sponsor.)

b. A description of any clinical laboratory facilities that will be used. (If this information has been submitted to the sponsor and reported by him on Form FD 1571, reference to the previous submission will be adequate).

3. OUTLINE THE PLAN OF INVESTIGATION *(Include approximation of the number of subjects to be treated with the drug and the number to be employed as controls, if any; clinical uses to be investigated; characteristics of subjects by age, sex and condition; the kind of clinical observations and laboratory tests to be undertaken prior to, during, and after administration of the drug; the estimated duration of the investigation; and a description or copies of report forms to be used to maintain an adequate record of the observations and tests results obtained. This plan may include reasonable alternates and variations and should be supplemented or amended when any significant change in direction or scope of the investigation is undertaken.)*

Exhibit 7 *(Continued)*

4. THE UNDERSIGNED UNDERSTANDS THAT THE FOLLOWING CONDITIONS, GENERALLY APPLICABLE TO NEW DRUGS FOR INVESTIGATIONAL USE, GOVERN HIS RECEIPT AND USE OF THIS INVESTIGATIONAL DRUG

a. The sponsor is required to supply the investigator with full information concerning the preclinical investigations that justify clinical trials, together with fully informative material describing any prior investigations and experience and any possible hazards, contraindications, side-effects, and precautions to be taken into account in the course of the investigation.

b. The investigator is required to maintain adequate records of the disposition of all receipts of the drug, including dates, quantities, and use by subjects, and if the investigation is terminated to return to the sponsor any unused supply of the drug.

c. The investigator is required to prepare and maintain adequate and accurate case histories designed to record all observations and other data pertinent to the investigation on each individual treated with tne drug or employed as a control in the investigation.

d. The investigator is required to furnish his reports to the sponsor of the drug who is responsible for collecting and evaluating the results obtained by various investigators. The sponsor is required to present progress reports to the Food and Drug Administration at appropriate intervals not exceeding 1 year. Any adverse effect that may reasonably be regarded as caused by, or probably caused by, the new drug shall be reported to the sponsor promptly, and if the adverse effect is alarming, it shall be reported immediately. An adequate report of the investigation should be furnished to the sponsor shortly after completion of the investigation.

e. The investigator shall maintain the records of disposition of the drug and the case histories described above for a period of 2 years following the date a new-drug application is approved for the drug; or if the application is not approved, until 2 years after the investigation

is discontinued. Upon the request of a scientifically trained and properly authorized employee of the Department, at reasonable times, the investigator will make such records available for inspection and copying. The subjects' names need not be divulged unless the records of particular individuals require a more detailed study of the cases, or unless there is reason to believe that the records do not represent actual cases studied, or do not represent actual results obtained.

f. The investigator certifies that the drug will be administered only to subjects under his personal supervision or under the supervision of the following investigators responsible to him,

---

and that the drug will not be supplied to any other investigator or to any clinic for administration to subjects.

g. The investigator certifies that he will inform any subjects, including subjects used as controls, or their representatives, that drugs are being used for investigational purposes, and will obtain the consent of the subjects, or their representatives, except where this is not feasible or, in the investigator's professional judgement, is contrary to the best interests of the subjects.

h. The investigator is required to assure the sponsor that for investigations involving institutionalized subjects, the studies will not be initiated until the institutional review committee has reviewed and approved the study. (The organization and procedure requirements for such a committee should be explained to the investigator by the sponsor as set forth in form FD 1571, division 10, unit c.)

Very truly yours,

(Name of Investigator)

(Address)

(This form should be supplemented or amended from time to time if new subjects are added or if significant changes are made in the plan of investigation.)

Exhibit 8

Form P-31*

AUTHORIZATION FOR TREATMENT WITH DRUG UNDER CLINICAL INVESTIGATION

A.M.
Date_____ Time_____P.M.

I authorize Dr. _____, the attending physician, to

treat _____ with the drug presently identified as
(name of patient)

_____ for the following condition: _____

_____

(Describe symptoms of disease to be treated)
It has been explained to me that the safety and usefulness of the drug in the treatment of patients for the above condition are now being investigated and that the manufacturer or distributor has supplied the drug for the purpose of providing further evidence of its safety and usefulness.

I voluntarily consent to treatment with the drug and release the attending physician from liability for any results that may occur.

Signed _____
(Patient or person authorized
to consent for patient)
Witness_____

*Reproduced by permission from *Medicolegal Forms with Legal Analysis,* Copyright 1973, American Medical Association, p. 75.

The required consent is obtained when the patient has the legal capacity to give consent, is able to exercise free power of choice, and is provided with a fair explanation of pertinent information concerning the drug, including the fact that he may be a control patient. In terms of form, if the investigation is in phase 1 or 2, the consent must be in writing. If the drug is in phase 3 of investigation, the consent may be oral if it is in the patient's best interest, and this fact must be recorded in the medical record of the person receiving the drug.

There seems to be support, however, for the position that patient consent is only necessary for the use of drugs for which there is no approved new drug application. If a drug is already on the market and is being used for clinical studies in the approved dosage range, route of administration, etc., as set forth in the NDA, it may not be necessary to obtain consent.

Since 1973 the U.S. Department of Health, Education and Welfare, through the National Institutes of Health and the Office of the Secretary, has been proposing numerous regulations designed to afford greater protection to human research subjects. On May 30, 1974, one such regulation became final. Then, on July 12, 1974, after lengthy congressional hearings, the National Commission for the Protection of Human Subjects of Biomedical and Behavioral Research was established under Title II of P.L. 93-348, the National Research Service Award Act of 1974. The Commission is charged to identify the ethical principles which should underlie human research, develop guidelines for such research, and recommend administrative policy for research supported by the federal government. More specifically, the Commission shall consider, under Section 202, at least the following:

(i) The boundaries between biomedical or behavioral research involving human subjects and the accepted and routine practice of medicine.
(ii) The role of assessment of risk-benefit criteria in the determination of the appropriateness of research involving human subjects.
(iii) Appropriate guidelines for the selection of human subjects for participation in biomedical and behavioral research.
(iv) The nature and definition of informed consent in various research settings.
(v) Mechanisms for evaluating and monitoring the performance of Institutional Review Boards established in accordance with section 474 of the Public Health Service Act and appropriate enforcement mechanisms for carrying out their decisions.

Another area of investigation of special interest to pharmacists, particularly in the institutional setting, concerns the "institutional review committee." This committee is responsible for initial and continuing review and approval of clinical studies when the subjects of the study are institutionalized or the investigator is affiliated with an institution which agrees to assume responsibility for the study. Members of the committee must come from varying backgrounds: lawyers, clergy, and laymen as well as physicians and scientists. These people may not be chosen by the drug sponsor or investigator. The study protocol must be approved by the committee, and full reports must be made to it. The institutional review committee is required to maintain records of all of its activities for a period of three years past the completion of the study. Pharmacist membership on this committee would seem indicated whether the committee represents a hospital, skilled nursing facility, or intermediate care facility and regardless of whether the pharmacist is a full-time employee of the institution or an independent consultant.

Section 3
APPLICATIONS TO PHARMACY PRACTICE

The new drug application procedure and investigational new drug exemptions are of recurring concern to pharmacists. Since deviation from these procedures may constitute a violation of law or result in civil liability, it is important to analyze and understand the implications these processes have on the practice of pharmacy.

As explained above, only those conditions of use, dosage range, and other prescribing information as approved in an NDA may appear in drug labeling. What if a prescription or drug order calls for an "unofficial" or "nonapproved" use or dose? An example of this may be that the drug methotrexate, an approved antineoplastic, is prescribed for treating psoriasis, an unapproved use.

The question then would be may a physician lawfully prescribe and a pharmacist lawfully dispense an approved drug for a new use? This very issue has been the subject of debate between the FDA and the American Medical Association. Regulation of the practices of medicine or pharmacy is within the police power of the states, as explained in Chapter 1, and is not among the intended purposes of the FDCA. As a general rule, physicians may prescribe and pharmacists may dispense new drugs for uses, in dosages or in different regimens than those set forth in a drug's approved labeling without violating the law.

The FDA is acutely aware of the need for clarification in this area and has tried to do so through its interpretative regulations. In its regulatory proposal on prescribing for uses unapproved by the FDA, the preamble to the proposed regulation states, at 39 F.R. 16503 (Aug. 15, 1972), the current state of the law.

If an approved new drug is shipped in interstate commerce with the approved package insert and neither the shipper nor the recipient intends that it be used for an unapproved purpose, the requirements of section 505 of the Act are satisfied. Once the new drug is in a local pharmacy after interstate shipment, the physician may, as part of the practice of medicine lawfully prescribe a different dosage for his patient, or may otherwise vary the conditions of use from those approved in the package insert, without informing or obtaining the approval of the Food and Drug Administration.

The law at the present time, therefore, does not restrict the prescribing by the physician to the package insert in terms of usage, dosage, frequency, etc., and so it is permissible for a pharmacist to dispense the medication as prescribed.

A similar problem arises when a prescription order is issued for the use of a chemical or other substance that is not marketed or intended to be used as a drug. The label of such a substance may bear a legend that it is not intended for human use or that it is for laboratory or chemical use. These nondrug substances are commonly referred to as "orphan drugs" or "homeless drugs." Examples of this situation are the prescription of lithium carbonate for depression or D-Xylose for use in intestinal absorption tests. Again, physicians may prescribe and pharmacists may dispense "homeless" drugs.

The more important consideration in using approved drugs for nonapproved uses, old drugs for new uses, or chemicals for nonintended drug uses is liability. The pharmacist must judge whether such prescribing and drug use is reasonable, based upon his scientific knowledge and professional experience. The liability aspects of such practices are discussed later in this book.

Whenever a new drug is used in a manner that deviates from official labeling the question as to whether the drug is being used for investigational purposes arises. If the drug is used, in fact, to treat a condition, the use is not investigational. If, on the other hand, the purpose in using the medication is experimental, or to test the product, then the use would be considered investigational. In the latter situation, IND requirements could be applicable.

Since this question is one of purpose or intent it is sometimes difficult to determine the answer. What is the physician's state of mind in so prescribing the product? Some guidance can be obtained by examining the facts of the case. Was the use of the drug an isolated incident, a very occasional occurrence? Was the decision to use the drug based upon a professional or scientific article that espoused use of the drug for treatment? Did the physician expect his patient to respond?

Perhaps the drug was being used on many patients, at various dosage levels, under differing conditions? Were records of results being tabulated and analyzed? Were there double blind studies with placebos? Were tests being conducted to determine rate of absorption, transport, elimination, dosage level, etc.?

These are some of the factors that must be taken into account in deciding whether the use of a drug is for treatment or for investigational purposes. If the use "looks" like an investigational study designed primarily for the accumulation of scientific knowledge concerning drug behavior, body processes, the course of disease, etc., then the IND procedure may be followed. If the use seems to be treatment, which involves medical judgment in caring for the individual patient, then the prescription may be treated as any other prescription.

Aside from the legality of such deviations in the uses of drugs, it is also important to bear in mind the liability question should the prescribed dose be an excessive one or the use be a dangerous one. This matter is treated in Chapter 21.

A third question that has arisen is whether the FDA may require that a prescription drug be dispensed only by physicians, since it has authority under law to stipulate the conditions under which a drug may be marketed. This was the case for many years with the drugs methotrexate and triethyleneamine. Both of these drugs contained, in part, the following caution:

> . . . to be dispensed to patients by physicians only . . . Pharmacists dispense only to physicians, never to patients. Dispense only with full statement of warnings. Physicians should give the drug personally to patients . . .

In an attempt to track down the origin of this warning it was impossible to determine whether it was included by the manufacturer in his NDA submission or whether the FDA required it. The original rationale for including the warning was that these drugs were especially "toxic" and should only be used under the direct supervision of a physician. However, this very reason is the basis of placing drugs in the prescription classification. The FDCA restricts the dispensing, only upon a written or oral prescription of a practitioner, of any drug which

Sec. 503 (b) (1) (B)

. . . because of its toxicity or other potentiality for harmful effect, or the method of its use, or the collateral measures necessary to its use, is not safe for use except under the supervision of a practitioner licensed by law to administer such drug; . . .

Since pharmacists are lawfully entitled to dispense prescription drugs which, by definition, are toxic it is difficult to understand the logic underlying the reason for the cautionary statement. Eventually, after strong prodding by both the FDA and the manufacturer, the warnings were modified.

Another type of marketing restriction that affects pharmacy is the FDA specification of the type of pharmacies that may dispense certain drugs. In an attempt to control diversion of methadone, the FDA issued regulations that restrict distribution of methadone to direct shipments by manufacturers only to approved maintenance treatment programs, to approved hospital pharmacies, and to approved selected community pharmacies. The regulations also restrict shipment of methadone for analgesic purposes to those community pharmacies that are in "remote areas" or where there are no approved hospitals. This regulation was challenged in *American Pharmaceutical Association v. Weinberger*, where the court held it to be an impermissible restriction. This case is being appealed by the FDA.

For years the FDA's long established policy was to maintain the confidentiality of most of the materials contained in NDAs as well as similar data obtained from other sources. In 1966 Congress adopted the Public Information Act (Freedom of Information Act), P.L. 89-487, which amended the Administrative Procedure Act by requiring public access to all federal agency information except limited specified types of information.

Current HEW regulations applicable to the FDA are found at 45 C.F.R. Part 5. Regulations concerning information contained in NDAs give examples of the kind of materials which are exempt from disclosure.

45 C.F.R. 5.85 Appendix A

8. Records of pharmaceutical and related information concerning investigational drugs, revealed to the Department by private sources.

* * *

11. Respecting Food and Drug Administration regulatory activities: Trade secrets or commercial or confidential information voluntarily revealed in requests for opinions and opinions and related records indicating that a person, firm, or product is or is not in compliance with the law; records relating to factory inspections, sample collections, seafood inspection, and other examinations and investigations by the Food and Drug Administration; Investigational New Drug files; New Drug Applications and master files, other than final printed labeling; reports and records relating to individual adverse drug reaction(s); data in support of petitions relating to pesticide chemicals, food standards, food additives, and color additives, and master files relating thereto; files relating to certification of insulin, antibiotics, and color additives, and master files relating thereto; notices of hearing issued to individuals and firms under 21 U.S.C. 335 and records relating thereto; records relating to research in support of

actions to further the law enforcement or regulatory activities of the Food and Drug Administration.
NOTE: Certain documents in some of the above files may be available upon request identifying the particular documents.

More recently, under new regulations by the FDA (39 F.R. 44601, Dec. 24, 1974) all FDA records shall be made available for public disclosure regardless of whether any justification or need for such records has been shown, except: trade secrets and commercial or financial information which is privileged or confidential; inter- or intra-agency memoranda or letters; personnel, medical, and similar files, disclosure of which constitutes a clearly unwarranted invasion of personal privacy; and investigatory records compiled for law enforcement purposes. Even these exemptions have restrictions placed upon them. Exempt information may be disclosed under the following circumstances: if the data and information has been previously disclosed to the public; discretionary disclosure by the Commissioner; disclosure required by court order; disclosure to consultants and advisory committees; disclosures to other federal agencies; administrative or court proceedings or communications with state and local officials; and, disclosures to Congress.

The existence of an IND will not be disclosed by the FDA unless its existence has been publicly disclosed or acknowledged, presumably by the sponsor of the investigation. The data and information contained in an IND file will be available under the same circumstances and to the same extent as the information and data in an NDA file.

An NDA file includes: all data submitted with or incorporated by reference in the NDA, incorporated INDs, supplemental NDAs, reports, and related submissions. The existence of such a file will not be disclosed by the FDA until it has been approved for marketing purposes and an approval letter has been sent, unless its existence has been previously disclosed or acknowledged.

Once the NDA is approved and a letter sent, most of the data contained in the file will be available to the public, including in particular: all safety and effectiveness data previously disclosed to the public; a summary of all other safety and effectiveness data; the study protocol; adverse reaction reports and other experience reports, consumer complaints, etc.; a list of all active ingredients; assay methods; and correspondence and written summaries of oral discussions relating to the NDA file. Under certain specified situations, all safety and effectiveness data may be disclosed.

Certain information contained in the NDA file will not be disclosed, including: manufacturing methods or processes and quality control procedures; production, sales, distribution and similar data; and, quantitative formulas.

CHAPTER 9
LABELING

Section 1
GENERAL REQUIREMENTS

FOR PURPOSES OF THE FDCA, THE TERMS LABEL AND LABELING ARE DEFINED IN the following manner.

§201.

(k) The term "label" means a display of written, printed, or graphic matter upon the immediate container or any article; and a requirement made by or under authority of this chapter that any word, statement, or other information appear on the label shall not be considered to be complied with unless such word, statement, or other information also appears on the outside container or wrapper, if any there be, of the retail package of such article, or is easily legible through the outside container or wrapper.

* * *

(m) The term "labeling" means all labels and other written, printed, or graphic matter (1) upon any article or any of its containers or wrappers, or (2) accompanying such article.

Section 502 of the Act sets forth the information that must appear on the labels or in the labeling of drugs and devices. The label or labeling must contain, among other special information: the name and place of business of the manufacturer, packer, or distributor; the quantity of contents; the name and quantity of any ingredient found to be habit forming along with the statement "Warning—May be habit forming;" the established name of the drug or its ingredients; adequate directions for use; adequate warnings and cautions concerning conditions of use; and special precautions for packaging. If these other applicable requirements of section 502 are not met, the product may be deemed to be misbranded. In addition to the above information, drugs must be labeled as required by the official compendia, the U.S.P. and National Formulary.

The "established name" used in the FDCA means the official name as designated by the Secretary of HEW or the official compendial title of the drug or, if neither of the foregoing exists, the common or usual name of the drug. The established name is often referred to in practice as the "generic name."

Labeling is also affected in a material way by the NDA provisions of the FDCA. The FDA may condition its approval to market a new drug upon specified stipulations and under specified conditions and labeling.

The FDA has extensive regulations (21 C.F.R. 1.106) implementing the various labeling requirements of the FDCA requiring "full disclosure" of prescribing information and adequate directions for use. Adequate directions for use refers to directions under which a layman can safely use a drug for which it is intended. This includes a statement of the conditions for which the drug is intended, quantity of the usual dose, frequency, duration and route or method of administration, and any preparation (i.e., shake-well) necessary prior to use.

Prescription drugs are exempt by the FDA from the requirement that their labeling bear "adequate directions for use for laymen." To be exempt, such drugs must be in the possession of the manufacturer, wholesaler or shipper or warehouses, or in the possession of a retail, hospital or clinic pharmacy or, lastly, under the custody of a practitioner licensed by law to administer or prescribe legend drugs.

The label of prescription drugs must bear: the prescription legend; recommended or usual dose; route of administration, if other than oral; quantity or proportion of each active ingredient; names of all inactive ingredients except flavorings, color additives, and trace substances; and lot or control number.

If the drug container is too small to bear a label with all the information, the label may contain only the quantity or proportion of each active ingredient and the lot or control number. The prescription legend may appear on the outer container of such drug units. The lot or control number may appear on the crimp of a dispensing tube and the remainder of the required label information may appear on other labeling on or within the package.

In addition to the label itself each *legend drug* must be accompanied by labeling, on or within the package from which the drug is to be dispensed, bearing full prescribing information, including: indications; dosages; routes, methods, and frequency of administration; contraindications; side effects; precautions and any other information concerning the intended use of the drug necessary for the prescriber to safely use the drug. This information is usually contained in what is known in the trade as the "package insert." The full official labeling that results from the NDA process is also represented in the package insert. Unless specifically exempted, this prescribing information must accompany the drug.

During 1975, the FDA proposed a regulation designed to standardize the format and content of package inserts for prescription drugs. If this proposal becomes final, practitioners should be able to find comparable information in similar locations in package inserts for different drugs and drug products, thus facilitating comparisons.

As in the case of labeling, the FDA has developed a comprehensive regulatory scheme relating to prescription drug advertisements. Much of the same information from the official labeling must appear in advertisements. This applies to most forms of advertising or other statements made on behalf of the manufacturer. If a statement is made, for example, by a manufacturer's representative or detailman, that relates a use or dosage or other variation from the official labeling the drug can be deemed to be misbranded and subject to action under the Act. One important requirement is that all ads contain a brief summary relating to side effects, contraindications, precautions and effectiveness. The favorable and unfavorable information must be in fair balance.

Certain types of advertisements are exempt from full disclosure. Reminder ads, which merely identify the drug, available dosage forms and which do not include indications or dosage recommendations for the drug, are exempt. Company catalogs fall into this category. Likewise advertisement of bulk-sale drugs and prescription-compounding drugs are also exempt.

Advertisement of OTC drugs is regulated under law by the Federal Trade Commission (FTC). Publicity for such products, along with ads for all other articles of commerce, must be fair and not misleading. Claims made must be substantiated and not false.

Section 2

PHARMACY APPLICATIONS

A concept of critical importance to pharmacists in relation to dispensing and labeling is that of the "prescription legend." Section 503 (b) (1) of the FDCA states:

§503 (b) (1)

(1) A drug intended for use by man which—
   (A) is a habit-forming drug to which section 352(d) of this title applies; or
   (B) because of its toxicity or other potentiality for harmful effect, or the method of its use, or the collateral measures necessary to its use, is not safe for use except under the supervision of a practitioner licensed by law to administer such drug; or

(C) is limited by an approved application under section 355 of this title to use under the professional supervision of a practitioner licensed by law to administer such drug, shall be dispensed only (i) upon a written prescription of a practitioner licensed by law to administer such drug, or (ii) upon an oral prescription of such practitioner which is reduced promptly to writing and filed by the pharmacist, or (iii) by refilling any such written or oral prescription if such refilling is authorized by the prescriber either in the original prescription or by oral order which is reduced promptly to writing and filed by the pharmacist. The act of dispensing a drug contrary to the provisions of this paragraph shall be deemed to be an act which results in the drug being misbranded while held for sale.

Unless state law provides otherwise, drugs that are not subject to this federal dispensing restriction may be sold "over-the-counter" (OTC) without a prescription. Such drugs are commonly referred to as proprietary or patent medications and may be sold over-the-counter. Whether a drug is subject to this section of the law is generally determined at the time an NDA is approved. A drug already subject to this provision may be removed by regulation when such requirements are not necessary for the protection of the public health.

Drugs subject to §503 (b) (1) must bear a special caution on its label in accordance with §503 (b) (4).   .

(4) A drug which is subject to paragraph (1) of this subsection shall be deemed to be misbranded if at any time prior to dispensing its label fails to bear the statement "Caution: Federal law prohibits dispensing without prescription." A drug to which paragraph (1) of this subsection does not apply shall be deemed to be misbranded if at any time prior to dispensing its label bears the caution statement quoted in the preceding sentence.

As this section clearly states, OTC medication may not bear this prescription legend.

This section of the law contains an important exception to the labeling and packaging requirements of the FDCA.

§503 (b) (2)

(2) Any drug dispensed by filling or refilling a written or oral prescription of a practitioner licensed by law to administer such drug shall be exempt from the requirements of section 502 of this title, except subsections (a),(i) (2) and (3), (k), and (l) of said section, and the packaging requirements of subsections (g), (h), and (p) of said section, if the drug bears a label containing the name and address of the dispenser, the serial number and date of the prescription or

of its filling, the name of the prescriber, and, if stated in the prescription, the name of the patient, and the directions for use and cautionary statements, if any, contained in such prescription. This exemption shall not apply to any drug dispensed in the course of the conduct of a business of dispensing drugs purusant to diagnosis by mail, or to a drug dispensed in violation of paragraph (l) of this subsection.

Thus, when a pharmacist dispenses a prescription drug he must place on the dispensing label the following information in order to be in compliance with the FDCA.

1. The name and address of the dispenser
2. The serial number
3. The date of the prescription or its filling
4. The name of the prescriber
5. The name of the patient, if stated on the prescription
6. Directions for use and cautionary statements contained in the prescription

Drugs dispensed and labeled in accordance with this provision need not contain other labeling under the FDCA unless the label is false or misleading, the drug is an imitation of another drug or offered for sale under the name of another drug, or it is an uncertified insulin or antibiotic. Likewise, the dispensed drug is properly packaged if it meets the packaging standards for compendial drugs, special regulatory packaging requirements for unstable drugs, and the packaging and labeling requirements of the Poison Prevention Packaging Act. These exceptions to the labeling and packaging exemptions, because of their rigid requirements, may seem like no exemption at all. However, if it were not for the exemption, pharmacists would have to include the full labeling, including package inserts, with all drugs dispensed pursuant to a prescription.

An important aspect of the foregoing provisions of law concerns the manner in which legend drugs are ordered. If they are ordered in writing there is no particular problem. The physician either writes a prescription or, in the case of a hospital, writes the order on the patient's chart, which serves as an order. If the order is an oral order for the drug, the FDCA states in §503(b) (1) that such prescriptions must be ". . . reduced promptly to writing and filed by the pharmacist . . ." Refills of such drugs must be treated in the same manner. Thus, the use of pharmacy technicians to receive telephone prescription orders from prescribers, or the hospital practice concerning drug orders telephoned to personnel other than a pharmacist may be questionable under the FDCA. For a discussion of who may prescribe drugs see Chapter 2, Section 1.

Along with labeling *per se,* a related issue that has become important to pharmacists in recent years is drug advertisements. Although some courts, *Patterson Drug Co. v. Kingery, Supermarket General Corp. v. Sills,* and *Urowsky v. Bd. of Regents of Univ. of N.Y.,* have upheld prohibitions against advertising drug prices, an increasing number of courts have been declaring such restrictions to be invalid, *Stadnik v. Shell's City Inc., Florida Board of Pharmacy v. Webb's City Inc., Pennsylvania Board of Pharmacy v. Pastor, Maryland Board of Pharmacy v. Sav-a-lot,* and *Virginia Citizens Consumer Council v. State Board of Pharmacy.* There is now a trend among state and municipal governments to require the posting of prices for frequently prescribed legend drugs. As a result, the FDA has proposed price advertisement regulations which exempt such advertisements from full disclosure if the purpose of the ad is to provide price information to consumers, contains the name of the drug, quantity of ingredients, name of the manufacturer, the dosage form, and the price charged for a specific number of dosage units or quantity of the drug product, and further that no representation or suggestion is made concerning the drug's safety, effectiveness or indications for use. The National Drug Code number may also be included. The price stated in the reminder ad must include all charges to the consumer, including, but not limited to, the cost of the drug product, professional fees, handling fees and mailing fees, if any.

The use of the "established name" of the drug has gained interest in pharmacy. It has become the center of the "generic drug" controversy. The question is whether the drug product of one manufacturer bearing the same generic name as the drug product of another manufacturer and, presumably, containing the same active ingredient, is therapeutically equivalent, or bioequivalent, if each product contains the same quantity of active ingredient. The generic name thus becomes a common factor in comparing and possibly equating one product with another. An affirmative answer to this equivalency question is the basic presumption underlying recent enactment of "generic substitution" and "formulary" laws that are discussed in Chapter 4.

Another labeling element of current interest to pharmacists is the name of the manufacturer, packer or distributor. Although the names of different suppliers may appear on different labels of the same drug, they may, in fact, have been produced or fabricated by the same manufacturer. At times, one drug, produced by a manufacturer, is supplied by other manufacturers, packers or distributors at widely differing prices. Based on the assumption that differently labeled drugs will nevertheless be of comparable quality if produced by the same manufacturer, pharmacists desire to discover the name of the actual manufacturer. If they know this information they can purchase a less expensive product of comparable quality and reduce drug costs, thereby saving the consumer money in the purchase of prescription drugs. On this basis at least two states, California and Florida have enacted laws that require labelers to reveal who actually manufactured the product. In California, under Section 26636 of the Health and Safety Code, the name and place of business of the manufacturer that produced the finished dosage forms of specified drugs must be included by the labeler in all advertisements and other descriptive matters. In Florida, the package form of prescription drugs must bear a label containing the name and place of business of the manufacturer of the finished dosage form of the drug and the name and place of business of the packer or distributor.

If states adopt laws with widely varying labeling requirements, the labeling procedures required by each state could become overly burdensome to national distributors. As a result, national legislation is being considered to bring uniformity to such labeling requirements.

The start of a new trend in patient information concerning prescription drugs occured in 1970. The FDA promulgated a regulation requiring patient information to be included in or with the package of oral contraceptives dispensed to the patient. The information consists primarily of a notice that a booklet, which provides further information on the effectiveness and known hazards of the drug, is available upon request from the physician. If this patient notice is not printed on or included with each drug package, it must be printed in leaflets contained in each bulk package with instructions to the pharmacist to distribute a leaflet with each prescription dispensed.

This regulation has not met with universal enthusiasm. The question of concern is whether the FDA intends to expand this type of requirement to other classes of drugs. Some practitioners, in both medicine and pharmacy, feel it to be an intrusion into professional practice, by preempting their judgement as to what information a patient should receive.

CHAPTER 10
DRUG MANUFACTURING

Section 1
GENERAL REQUIREMENTS

UNDER SECTION 510 OF THE FDCA, EVERY PERSON WHO OWNS OR OPERATES ANY establishment engaged in the interstate or intrastate manufacture, preparation, propagation, compounding or processing of drugs must register his name, place of business, and all such establishments with the Secretary of Health, Education and Welfare. The phrase "manufacture, preparation, propagation, compounding, or processing" includes repackaging or otherwise changing the container, wrapper, or labeling of drugs for distribution to others who will make final sale or distribution to the consumer.

In 1972, Congress amended the FDCA to require all manufacturers to file every six months with the government a list of all drugs they manufacture. The Secretary of HEW may assign registration numbers to manufacturers, and he may also assign a listing number to each drug recorded. Numbers assigned to drugs must be the same as the numbers assigned under the National Drug Code. These numbers are used in the identification of drug products and for the processing of third party claim forms.

In addition to registration requirements, other manufacturing obligations under the FDCA are the maintenance of certain records, filing of specified reports, and biennial plant inspections.

A drug is adulterated if it is not manufactured in conformity with current good manufacturing practices. This requirement has been enumerated in regulations. They deal with buildings, equipment, personnel, formula, production and control procedures, product containers, packaging and labeling, laboratory controls, and distribution, stability and complaint records.

Section 2
IMPLICATIONS FOR PHARMACY

Just as in the area of labeling and packaging, the FDCA contains important exemptions from the manufacturing obligations for pharmacists. Section 510, registration of producers of drugs, states in part:

§510 (g)

The foregoing subsections of this section shall not apply to—

(1) pharmacies which maintain establishments in conformance with any applicable local laws regulating the practice of pharmacy and medicine and which are regularly engaged in dispensing prescription drugs, upon prescriptions of practitioners licensed to administer such drugs to patients under the care of such practitioners in the course of their professional practice, and which do not manufacture, prepare, propagate, compound, or process drugs for sale other than in the regular course of their business of dispensing or selling drugs at retail;

(2) practitioners licensed by law to prescribe or administer drugs and who manufacture, prepare, propagate, compound, or process drugs solely for use in the course of their professional practice;

(3) persons who manufacture, prepare, propagate, compound, or process drugs solely for use in research, teaching, or chemical analysis and not for sale;

(4) such other classes of persons as the Secretary may by regulation exempt from the application of this section upon a finding that registration by such classes of persons in accordance with this section is not necessary for the protection of the public health.

Thus, pharmacies, in general, do not have to register as manufacturers.

One issue of importance in the current practice of pharmacy arises under this section. The question is whether compounding drugs and pharmaceuticals in large quantities, the unit dose packaging and relabeling of drugs, or centralized intravenous additive programs constitute "manufacturing" under the FDCA or whether these activities are exempt under §510 (g).

Since the practice of pharmacy is specifically mentioned, the important language in §510 (g) (1) is the last phrase, " . . . and which do not manufacture, prepare, propagate, compound, or process drugs for sale other than in the regular course of their business of dispensing or selling drugs at retail . . ." Language of similar intent and purpose, i.e., the drugs are not being sold to other persons who will sell or distribute them to the ultimate user, appears in other subsections of §510 (g). The exemption seems to apply to pharmacies which prepare large quantities of drugs intended for use by their patients. A similar logic applies for unit dose packaging. The exemption would also seem to hold if, for example, a central university hospital pharmacy supplied drugs to specialized facilities within that complex.

On the other hand, the exception would not apply if a pharmacy were to supply compounded or repackaged drugs to other pharmacies. Similarly, a pharmacy school that manufactures drugs for its affiliated university hospital must register under §510.

There is, however, an established practice in existence that permits the resale of small quantities of drugs, "obliges," to other pharmacies on an emergency basis without nullifying the exemption from the manufacturing classification.

Another question arising in modern day pharmacy practice is whether current good manufacturing practice requirements apply to situations in which a pharmacy engages in bulk compounding or other activities that could be interpreted as manufacturing even though they may not require registration as a manufacturer. This question may be more academic than practical for the FDA has difficulty in adequately inspecting registered manufacturers without diverting presently overworked manpower to review pharmacy establishments.

Good manufacturing practice requirements could be substantially burdensome, if applicable to pharmacy. This does not mean, however, that pharmacy practice should be conducted at a level so low that the public health is jeopardized. A possible solution to the problem of assuring quality service without hindering pharmaceutical services is the development of standards of "current good professional practices." Such standards could be tailored to the needs of pharmacy practice and still provide adequate protection in the compounding, storage, labeling, and quality control testing of drugs as well as assure competent personnel and satisfactory plant and equipment necessary to safeguard the public's interest.

Another issue specifically important to hospital practice under this section of the Act is whether activities of nonprofit cooperative hospital service corporations established under §510 (e) of the Internal Revenue Act for the purpose of centralizing the purchase of drugs constitute manufacturing under the FDCA or whether such activity by hospitals falls within the exemptions of §510 (g). This question cannot be answered clearly for all situations. The particular facts surrounding the organization and operation of the service corporation will determine the answer. It does, however, seem safe to say that if the operation of the service corporation, as a separate and distinct entity, purchases drugs and alters the labeling or packaging in almost any way and resells the drugs to hospitals which will in turn resell the drugs to their patients, the service corporation will most likely be deemed to be a manufacturer under the FDCA and subject to appropriate provisions.

CHAPTER 11
POISON PREVENTION
PACKAGING ACT

Section 1

FEDERAL AND STATE LAW

THE POISON PREVENTION PACKAGING ACT (PPPA) WAS SIGNED INTO LAW AND became effective December 30, 1970. The basis purpose of this law is to provide for special packaging to protect children from serious personal injury or serious illness which could result from handling, using, or ingesting certain household substances. A "household substance" is any substance which is customarily produced or distributed for sale for comsumption or use, or customarily stored by individuals in or about the household and which is: a hazardous substance under the Federal Hazardous Substances Act; an economic poison under the Federal Insecticide, Fungicide, and Rodenticide Act; a food, drug or cosmetic under the FDCA; or a household fuel when stored in a portable container.

At the present time the law is administered by the Consumer Product Safety Commission (CPSC). The CPSC determines which of the foregoing substances are subject to special packaging. It establishes test standards to ascertain whether special packaging is child resistant. Implementation of standards for special packaging requires a determination that the hazard presented to children in availability, by reason of its packaging, is such that special packaging is required to protect them and that the special packaging must be technically feasible, practicable, and appropriate for such a substance. These standards require that a certain number of children cannot open the package within a prescribed time period. The standard does not require the packaging to be 100% child resistant.

The CPSC does not engage in testing nor does it certify that particular packaging meets the requirements of the law. It is incumbent on each packager to be sure that his packaging complies.

Just as in the area of food, drugs, and cosmetics, various states are adopting a state poison prevention packaging act. These laws are often based upon the Model State Poison Prevention Packaging Act which was adopted by the National Drug Trade Conference in 1972. The Model State Act is based upon the federal law, but variations do exist and should be identified in each state.

Section 2

COVERAGE OF THE ACT

Not all products that are presently covered by the PPPA are drug products. The following products have been designated by CPSC for special packaging.

—*Aspirin*—containing products intended to be taken by mouth;

—Products containing any *controlled substance* under the Comprehensive Drug Abuse Prevention and Control Act of 1970;

—*Oral prescription drugs* unless specifically exempted;

—Liquids containing more than 5 percent of *methyl salicylate* (oil of wintergreen);

—Dry household substances containing 10 percent or more of *sodium and/or potassium hydroxide* (lye), and all other household substances containing 2 percent or more of sodium and/or potassium hydroxide;

—Liquid household substances containing 10 percent or more by weight of *turpentine;*

—Prepackaged liquid kindling and/or illuminating preparations such as fuels for cigarette lighters, charcoal, camping equipment, torches, and decorative or functional lanterns, which contain 10 percent or more by weight of *petroleum distillates;*

—Liquid household substances containing 4 percent or more by weight of *methyl alcohol* (methanol);

—Household substances containing 10 percent or more by weight of *sulfuric acid* (not including wet-cell storage batteries);

—Household substances in liquid form containing 10 percent or more of *ethylene glycol;*

—Furniture polishes containing 10 percent or more of *petroleum distillates.*

The foregoing products must be dispensed in packaging that meets the test standards established under this law. Coverage of iron preparations has also been proposed.

This requirement applies to manufacturers, repackagers, relabelers, wholesalers and retailers who repackage or relabel covered products. Pharmacists would be included under the latter category. This rule applies to all dispensing of covered substances for home use whether such dispensing occurs through a community pharmacy, hospital outpatient clinic, emergency room, physician's office or through mail order pharmacies. The type of package does not matter either. It pertains to dropper bottles, unit dose packaging and other forms of special packaging.

Section 3

EXEMPTIONS

Certain products that would otherwise be covered have been specifically exempted from the special packaging rules. These include:

—Sublingual dosage forms of nitroglycerin and isosorbide dinitrate.

—Effervescent tablets containing less than 10% aspirin, other than those intended for pediatric use.

—Unflavored aspirin-containing powders (other than those intended for pediatric use) that are packed in unit doses providing not more than 10 grains of aspirin per unit dose, and that contain no other drug which requires safety packaging.

—Preparations which are packaged in pressurized spray containers and aerosol containers intended for inhalation therapy.

Even though products may require special packaging, they may be packaged in noncomplying packaging under certain conditions. First, the manufacturer or other packer may package one size of each covered product in a noncomplying package provided he also supplies the product in packages which do comply with the standard. The noncomplying package must bear the warning "This Package for Households Without Young Children." If the label is small it may bear the words "Package Not Child-Resistant." This "one-size" exemption is designed to accomodate elderly or handicapped persons unable to use safety packaging.

Another exemption, that more directly affects pharmacists, allows the dispensing of prescription drugs in noncomplying packages if the physician or purchaser request such. Thus, if the physician writes on the prescription order or transmits the request in an oral prescription, which is reduced to writing by the pharmacist, the medication may be dispensed in a noncomplying package. The physician's direction for use of noncomplying packaging can only be validly applied to the drug or drugs actually being dispensed pursuant to the order containing that direction. A blanket order form a physician to dispense all or specified drugs to be prescribed by him would be ineffective.

In the case of consumer requests for noncomplying packaging, pharmacists should retain a written record of the request. This could be achieved in a number of ways. The request could be recorded on the prescription blank. The APhA has suggested use of the following form:

Pharmacist, please do not dispense in safety package.

_____   _____
        patient's signature   date

The patient would sign and date this request.

An alternative to incorporating patient requests on the prescription order would be the maintenance of a record book of requests for noncomplying packaging. Information to be recorded could include the prescription number, the date, the patient's name and address and the patient's initials. Other information could be included, if desired.

Regarding requests from the purchaser, the CPSC has stated that the statutory language is not so limiting as it is concerning physician orders and that a valid request from a purchaser that all of his or her prescriptions be filled in noncomplying packaging would be sufficient to satisfy the requirements of the PPPA. As a matter of policy, however, the practice of obtaining blanket orders and requests for noncomplying packaging should not be encouraged. Congressional intent is for noncomplying packaging to be the exception rather than the rule, and changing circumstances in the household of the purchaser may present young children with the opportunity to gain access to prescription drugs.

CHAPTER 12
MAILING AND SHIPPING OF DRUGS

"MAIL-ORDER PRESCRIPTIONS" IS A TOUCHY SUBJECT. AS DISCUSSED EARLIER, problems with authorization for a mail-order prescription may arise. Despite the relative merits of either side of this issue as they relate to the public health, mail-order prescription services are offered and the regulation of this area of practice should be considered.

In addition to mailing dispensed drugs, it is also necessary to transport drugs and medicines either through the mail or via common carriers such as airlines, railroads, trucks, boats, etc.

As might be expected there are a number of governmental agencies, other than those considered elsewhere, regulating commerce in drugs. The U.S. Postal Service (USPS), the U.S. Department of Transportation (DOT) and the Federal Aviation Administration (FAA) do so. In addition, state laws also contain applicable provisions.

Section 1
FEDERAL LAWS AND REGULATIONS

The United States postal law contains the primary provisions relating to the shipment, via the mail, of injurious articles, including drugs.

18 U.S.C. §1716 Injurious articles as nonmailable

All kinds of poison, and all articles and compositions containing poison, and all poisonous animals, insects, reptiles, and all explosives, inflammable materials, infernal machines, and mechanical, chemical, or other devices or compositions which may ignite or explode, and all disease germs or scabs, and all other natural or artificial articles, compositions, or material which may kill or injure another, or injure the mails or other property, whether or not sealed as first-class matter, are nonmailable matter and shall not be conveyed in the mails

143

or delivered from any post office or station thereof, nor by any letter carrier.

The Postmaster General may permit the transmission in the mails, under such rules and regulations as he shall prescribe as to preparation and packaging, of any such articles which are not outwardly or of their own force dangerous or injurious to life, health, or property.

* * *

The transmission in the mails of poisonous drugs and medicines may be limited by the Postmaster General to shipments of such articles from the manufacturer thereof or dealer therein to licensed physicians, surgeons, dentists, pharmacists, druggists, cosmetologists, barbers, and veterinarians, under such rules and regulations as he shall prescribe.

The transmission in the mails of poisons for scientifc use, and which are not outwardly dangerous or of their own force dangerous or injurious to life, health, or property, may be limited by the Postmaster General to shipments of such articles between the manufacturers thereof, dealers therein, bona fide research or experimental scientific laboratories, and such other persons who are employees of the Federal, a State, or local government, whose official duties are comprised, in whole or in part, of the use of such poisons, and who are designated by the head of the agency in which they are employed to receive or send such articles, under such rules and regulations as the Postmaster General shall prescribe.

Pursuant to its authority to regulate the mailing of poisonous drugs and medicines, the Postal Service has promulgated the following regulations.

39 C.F.R. §124.2 Harmful matter

(a) Except as provided below, any article, composition, or material which may kill or injure another or injure the mail or other property is nonmailable. Harmful matter includes, but is not limited to:

(1) All kinds of poison or matter containing poison;

* * *

(4) Narcotics and other "Controlled Substances" as defined by 21 U.S.C. 801 or the regulations thereunder, and

* * *

(g) *Poisons*—(1) *Highly toxic poisons for scientific use.* Highly toxic poisons for scientific use which are not outwardly or of their own force dangerous or injurious to life, health or property may be shipped only between manufacturers, dealers, bona-fide research or experimental scientific laboratories, and employees of the Federal, State, or local governments who have official use for such poisons. Any such employee must be designated by the head of his agency to receive or send such poisons.

(2) *Highly toxic poisonous drugs and medicines.* Highly toxic poisonous drugs and medicines may be shipped only from the manufacturer thereof or dealer therein to licensed physicians, surgeons, dentists, pharmacists, druggists, cosmetologists, barbers and veterinarians. (See 18 U.S.C. 1716.)

The regulations go on to define controlled substances and narcotics and to declare them injurious.

39 C.F.R. §124.5

(a) *Definitions*—(1) *Controlled substances.* A "controlled substance" is any narcotic, hallucinogenic, stimulant or depressant drug included in Schedules I through V of the "Controlled Substances Act" (Public Law 91-513), 21 U.S.C. 801 et seq., and the regulations thereunder, 21 CFR 1300 et seq.

(2) *Narcotic drugs.* Narcotic drugs as defined in the Controlled Substances Act include opium, cocaine and opiates (synthetic narcotics) and the derivatives thereof.

(b) *Declaration as to injurious nature.* Controlled substances are, by reason of their addictive nature or capacity for abuse, hereby declared to be "Articles, compositions, or materials which may kill or injure another" within the intent and meaning of 18 U.S.C. 1716.

Controlled substances are nonmailable except under the following circumstances.

39 C.F.R. §124.5

(d) *Mailing requirements*—(1) *Authorized mailings.* Controlled substances may be transmitted in the mails between persons registered with the Drug Enforcement Administration or between persons who are exempted from registration such as military, law enforcement and civil defense personnel in the performance of their official duties. Prescription medicines containing nonnarcotic controlled substances may be mailed from a registered practitioner or dispenser to an ultimate user. Prescription medicines containing narcotic drugs may be mailed only by Veterans Administration medical facilities to certain veterans. Parcels containing controlled substances must be prepared and packed for mailing in accordance with the requirements of paragrph (d) (2) of this section.

(2) *Preparation and packing.* (i) The inner container or any parcel containing controlled substances must be marked and sealed in accordance with the applicable provisions of the

Controlled Substances Act, 21 U.S.C. 801, and the regulations promulgated thereunder, 21 CFR 1300 et seq.

(ii) The inner container of prescription medicines containing controlled substances must, in addition to the marking and sealing requirements set forth above, be labeled to show the name and address set forth above, be labeled to show the name and address of the practitioner or the name and address of the pharmacy or other person dispensing the prescription (if other than the practitioner) and the prescription number.

(iii) Every parcel containing controlled substances shall be placed in a plain outer container or securely overwrapped in plain paper.

(iv) No markings of any kind which would indicate the nature of the contents shall be placed on the outside wrapper or container of any parcel containing controlled substances.

(3) *Use of registered mail required.* Parcels containing controlled substances, including those sent to D.E.A. Regional Offices for disposal (see 21 CFR 1307.21), generally must be sent by registered mail, return receipt requested. The Drug Enforcement Administration number or exemption status of the sender shall be set forth in the senders' address section of PS 3806 or PS 3877, as applicable. This information shall appear in the following format:

DEA Registration No. 654321

or

DEA Exempt—Police.

(4) *Regular mail permitted.* The following may be sent by regular mail without regard to the provisions of paragraph (d) (3) of this section.

(i) Prescription medicines containing non-narcotic controlled substances listed in Schedule II in amounts not exceeding 100 dosage units; and

(ii) Prescription medicines containing controlled substances listed in Schedules III, IV and V in amounts not exceeding a 100-day supply or 300 dosage units, whichever is less.

(iii) Physician's samples of medicines containing nonnarcotic controlled substances in amounts not exceeding the limitations set forth in paragraph (d) (4) (i) or (ii) of this section.

(e) *Exempt shipments.* Small quantities of unknown matter suspected of containing controlled substances may be sent by regular mail without regard to the other provisions of §124.5 only when addressed to a federal, state or local law enforcement agency for law enforcement purposes. Such mailings must comply with paragraph (d) (2) (iii) and (iv) of this section.

This law and the regulations leave unanswered the important question of what are "highly toxic poisonous drugs and medicines." Despite the lack of definition in federal law, most state pharmacy laws do define poisons. These provisions are discussed in Chapter 2.

Section 2

STATE LAWS AND REGULATIONS

Many state laws or regulations contain provisions prohibiting the mail-order dispensing of prescriptions. For example, the Oklahoma Pharmacy law contains the following provision.

Okla. Stat. Ann. tit 59, §353.24 Unlawful Acts

It shall be unlawful for any person, firm or corporation:

* * *

(d) To engage in any "mail-order" prescription business in which prescriptions are solicited and received through the mails for dispensing, or in which prescriptions are dispensed and delivered by mail to customers other than those personally known to the pharmacist in charge of a pharmacy and under circumstances clearly dictating that such method of delivery is in the best interests of the health and welfare of the customer.

Regulations of the New Hampshire Board of Pharmacy deal with both mail order prescriptions and other means of receiving and delivering prescriptions.

Rule 13. Mail Order Prescriptions.

It shall be unlawful for any person not authorized to engage in the practice of pharmacy in this state to supply any persons in this state, a drug, medicine, or therapeutic device, on a prescription which has been issued in this state.

Provided however, that this rule shall not prohibit the occasional mailing of prescription drugs to a bonafide customer of any pharmacy when a traditional physician, pharmacist, patient relationship is present.

Traditional Physician Pharmacist Patient relationship means whereby the pharmacist knows either the physician, the patient, or both, and or can readily and easily, in a customary normal procedure check on factors concerning the prescription.

Effective March 13, 1968.

Rule 14. No persons licensed under the provisions of Chapter 318 of the New Hampshire laws, shall enter into or participate in any arrangement or agreement whereby prescriptions may be left at, picked from, accepted by, or delivered to any store or shop not licensed as a pharmacy. Provided, however, that this section shall not prohibit licensee from picking up prescriptions or delivering prescribed medications at the office or home of the prescriber, at the residence of the patient, or at the hospital in which the patient is confined, by means of an employee or by use of a common carrier.

In most instances, the law or regulation controls what may be done within the state. For example, one law may provide that persons within the state may not engage in the mail-order business. This does not, necessarily, mean that persons outside the state may not mail prescriptions into the state. In the 1968 case of *Massachusetts Pharmaceutical Association v. Federal Prescription Services Inc.,* the court ruled that the Iowa based mail-order prescription service was attempting to practice pharmacy in Massachusetts contrary to the requirements of that state's law.

In another earlier case in 1965, the Iowa Board of Pharmacy Examiners was not successful in an attempt to enforce its interpretation of the Iowa Pharmacy law on mail-order operations domiciled and operating within its borders.

CHAPTER 13
ALCOHOL TAX LAWS

Section 1
FEDERAL LAW

UNDER THE INTERNAL REVENUE CODE AND REGULATIONS, HOSPITALS AND LIKE institutions may obtain alcohol tax-free for medical or scientific purposes. The privilege of withdrawing alcohol tax-free under the federal law applies to any permanently established hospital or sanitarium, whether operated for profit or not, and to any nonprofit clinic. The Internal Revenue Code states:

§5214 Withdrawal of Distilled Spirits From Bonded Premises Free of Tax or Without Payment of Tax

(a) Purposes. Distilled spirits on which the internal revenue tax has not been paid or determined may, subject to such regulations as the Secretary or his delegate shall prescribe, be withdrawn from the bonded premises of any distilled spirits plant in approved containers . . .

* * *

(3) free of tax for nonbeverage purposes and not for resale or use in the manufacture of any product for sale . . .

* * *

(C) for use at any hospital, blood bank or sanitarium (including use in making any analysis or test at such hospital, blood bank, or sanitarium), or at any pathological laboratory exclusively engaged in making analyses, or tests, for hospitals or sanitariums; or
(D) for the use of any clinic operated for charity and not for profit (including use in the compounding of bona fide medicines for treatment outside of such clinics or patients thereof); . . .

Regulations of the Internal Revenue Service (IRS) provide for applications to Assistant Regional Commissioners of the Alcohol and Tobacco Tax Division of the IRS, the manner in which the alcohol is to be procured, and the uses to which the alcohol can be put. There are requirements for recording the use of alcohol and for reporting the monthly transactions in alcohol.

Hospitals, sanitariums, and clinics are forbidden from using tax-free alcohol for beverage purposes, in any food products, or in any preparation used in preparing beverage or food products. Furnishing tax-free alcohol in violation of regulations for its use makes a hospital or similar institution liable for the tax on such alcohol. Furthermore, a tax-free permittee who sells alcohol also becomes liable for special tax as a liquor dealer.

Clinics operated for charity and not for profit may furnish medicines made from tax-free alcohol to their patients for use off the premises of the clinics, even though the patients may be required to pay a registration or similar fee entitling them to use all the services of the clinics.

Section 2
STATE REQUIREMENTS

The fact that Congress has taxed and regulated the use of alcohol does not make state statutes taxing and regulating the same activity inapplicable or unconstitutional. The laws of each state also regulate the manufacture, use and sale of alcohol, and control the manner in which a hospital may obtain and use alcohol. Some of these laws grant full exemption from taxation or licensing requirements where there is compliance with federal alcohol regulations; others require licensing with or without the payment of a fee.

PART III
CONTROLLED SUBSTANCES

MAN HAS HAD A NEED FOR DRUGS TO TREAT HIS ILLS AND PROMOTE HIS WELL-being since recorded history. Pharmaceutical knowledge and skills have advanced from the mere use of herbs and preparation of simple galenicals to the application of principles and techniques of modern chemistry. Over the centuries specific chemical substances became identified and associated with pharmacologic responses of the human body. By the 18th century responses currently known by modern terms such as dependence, habituation, and addiction became identified and observed.

During the 19th and 20th centuries, classes of drugs, such as narcotics, were identified as having characteristics that can lead to their excessive abuse. Nonmedical use of such "addicting" drugs create personal and social problems of both an acute and chronic nature. Individuals can suffer impaired mental and psychological functioning as well as deterioration of their physical health resulting ultimately in death. Society may be affected by the economic loss of the abuser's productive capability and may experience drug abuse-related crimes of theft, prostitution, and drug peddling.

These public health and welfare considerations have resulted in an intensified struggle to find an acceptable balance between the need to ensure an adequate supply of drugs for medical use and the desire to reduce, if not eliminate, the social abuse of these same agents. The purpose of this part of the book is to examine the efforts, particularly at the federal level, taken to ameliorate that portion of this public health and welfare problem associated with the prescribing, administering, and dispensing of drugs by practitioners. This need to control certain classes of drugs such as narcotics, depressants, stimulants and other classes of drugs having a potential for abuse is well documented in literature, congressional testimony and governmental studies and investigations.

Of the variety of laws dealing with regulation, enforcement, education, grants to states, etc., that have been created to deal with this problem, the Controlled Substances Act (CSA) is by far the most important to pharmacists. Only the Federal Food, Drug, and Cosmetic Act regulates the distribution of more drugs. The regulatory scheme of the CSA may, nevertheless, have a greater impact on practice, with its inventories, records, labeling, security, and special purchasing requirements. Pharmacists cannot safely practice without a working knowledge of this area of the law.

CHAPTER 14
IDENTIFICATION OF RELEVANT
LAWS AND CONTROLLED
SUBSTANCES

Section 1

BACKGROUND OF DRUG ABUSE CONTROL

PRIOR TO 1970, THERE WAS A PLETHORA OF LAWS SCATTERED THROUGHOUT THE United States Code that controlled narcotics, depressants, stimulants and other "abuse" drugs in one way or another. Tax laws contained provisions of the Harrison Narcotics Act and the Marihuana Tax Act. Drug laws contained control provisions from the Narcotic Drugs Import and Export Act, the Narcotics Manufacturing Act of 1960, and the Drug Abuse Control Amendments of 1965. In addition to applicable provisions of the Judicial Code, the Public Health Service Act and the Community Mental Health Centers Act contained relevant provisions of law. It was at this point in U.S. history that the old system of drug abuse control came to an end and a new era began.

Virtually all of the various laws discussed above were superseded by the Comprehensive Drug Abuse Prevention and Control Act of 1970. In addition to those portions of the law most directly affecting our nation's drug distribution system, such as Title II, the Controlled Substances Act (CSA), the law also deals with rehabilitation under community mental health programs, research in the medical treatment of drug abuse and addiction, and importation and exportation of controlled substances. It also established the Commission on Marihuana and Drug Abuse.

Two years later, the Drug Abuse Office and Treatment Act of 1972 was enacted, which gave statutory support to the Special Action Office for Drug Abuse Prevention and created the National Institute on Drug Abuse and the National Advisory Council on Drug Abuse.

To breathe life into this newly-created regulatory scheme, substantial sums of money were appropriated. In fact, over the years, Congress has exceeded the original appropriations provided for in the CSA. In 1973,

153

the Drug Enforcement Administration alone received more than $100 million.

The Executive Branch of government was no less active in the campaign against drug abuse. With the enactment of the CSA, the former Bureau of Narcotics and the Bureau of Drug Abuse Control were combined to form the Bureau of Narcotics and Dangerous Drugs (BNDD) within the U.S. Department of Justice.

Thereafter, the following executive actions were undertaken:

Executive Order No. 11599 was issued on June 19, 1971, establishing the "Special Action Office for Drug Abuse Prevention" (SAODAP).

Executive Order No. 11641 of February 1, 1972 gave life to the "Office for Drug Abuse Law Enforcement" (ODALE).

Executive Order No. 11676 came forth on July 28, 1972 to create the "Office of National Narcotics Intelligence" (ONI).

Reorganization Plan No. 2 of 1973 reorganized most of the agencies involved in drug abuse control, including BNDD, ODALE, and ONI, into the Drug Enforcement Administration (DEA) within the U.S. Department of Justice.

The Drug Enforcement Administration (DEA) represents the federal government's most unified and coordinated effort at enforcement, intelligence, training, research, and law enforcement assistance in the area of drug abuse.

Subsequent to the adoption of the Single Convention on Narcotic Drugs in 1961, and its amendments, the DEA and its predecessor agencies negotiated with representatives from other nations to develop a meaningful, coordinated response to the drug abuse problem at the international level. These efforts culminated in the Convention on Psychotropic Substances, 1971.

At the present time, the U.S. Senate is actively considering ratification of the Convention and the adoption of proposals to amend the Controlled Substances Act in order to discharge obligations under the Convention.

Section 2

UNIFORM CONTROLLED SUBSTANCES ACT

Prior to the enactment of the Controlled Substances Act, most states had adopted some version of the Uniform Narcotic Drug Act of the Drug Abuse Control Amendments of 1965. Since Congress amended the federal law, the states have been repealing their naroctic and depressant-stimulant laws and replacing them with state controlled substances acts. The new state laws are based upon the Uniform Controlled Substances Act as approved by the National Conference of Commissioners on Uniform State Laws in August, 1970. This uniform law is based upon the CSA.

A number of states have modified the uniform act in various ways. Some variations affect the drugs that are covered. Others contain differing prescription requirements, such as triplicate prescription blanks. The New York law requires the use of prescription blanks printed and numbered by the state. Penalties for violations also vary.

An important difference to keep in mind is the grant of authority to various state enforcement agencies such as the Board of Pharmacy, the Food and Drug Division or a state Board of Health. Division of authority alone could be a major problem in establishing standards and determining compliance.

Section 3

CLASSIFICATION OF CONTROLLED SUBSTANCES

Controlled substances are divided into five schedules. They are defined in Section 812 of the CSA in the following manner:

(b) Except where control is required by United States obligations under an international treaty, convention, or protocol, in effect on the effective date of this part, and except in the case of an immediate precursor, a drug or other substance may not be placed in any schedule unless the findings required for such schedule are made with respect to such drug or other substance. The findings required for each of the schedules are as follows:

(1) Schedule I

(A) The drug or other substance has *a high potential for abuse.*

(B) The drug or other substance has *no currently accepted medical use* in treatment in the United States.

(C) There is a *lack of accepted safety for use* of the drug or other substance under medical supervision.
(Emphasis added.)

This schedule includes: opiates such as dextrorphan, trimeperidine; certain opium derivatives such as acetyldihydrocodeine, heroin, codeine methylbromide, normorphine and thebacon; and hallucinogenic substances known as DET, DMT, STP, THC, LSD, marihuana, mescaline, peyote and psilocybin.

(2) Schedule II

(A) The drug or other substance has *a high potential for abuse.*

(B) The drug or other substance has *a currently accepted medical use* in treatment in the United States or a

currently accepted medical use with severe restrictions.
(C) Abuse of the drug or other substances may lead to *severe psychological or physical dependence.*
(Emphasis added.)

Most of the drugs covered by Schedule II are those that comprised Class A narcotics under former narcotic laws. Additionally, it now includes some nonnarcotic substances in the stimulant category. This schedule includes substances of vegetable origin or chemical synthesis, opiates, and stimulants. Although this classification includes drugs in current medical use, only a sampling is provided.

Schedule II encompasses opium poppy and poppy straw; coca leaves; raw, granulated or powdered opium; extracts or fluid extracts of opium; morphine, codeine, thebaine, and various derivatives or salts thereof. It also includes cocaine and ecgonine as well as any other salts or derivatives of these. Various opiates of chemical syntheses are scheduled such as dihydrocodeine, levomethorphan, pethidine, and phenazocine. Lastly, amphetamine, methamphetamine, phenmetrazine and methylphenidate are included as stimulants.

(3) Schedule III
(A) The drug or other substance has *a potential for abuse less than* the drug or other substances in schedules I and II.
(B) The drug or other substance has *a currently accepted medical use in treatment* in the United States.
(C) Abuse of the drug or other substance may lead to *moderate or low physical dependence* or *high psychological dependence.*
(Emphasis added.)

This schedule consists primarily of substances that were Class B narcotics under former laws or are depressants or stimulants covered by the supplanted Drug Abuse Control Amendments of 1965.

The covered narcotic substances are basically the same as those included in Schedule II but in lesser specified concentrations. Hence codeine itself is in Schedule II, but if it is in a preparation of not more than 1.8 grams per 100 mls. or not more than 90 mls. per dosage unit it is in Schedule III. The same holds true for morphine, ethylmorphine, dihydrocodeine, and dihydrocodeinone, although the concentrations may vary from drug to drug. Nalorphine is also included.

This schedule also includes all substances having a stimulant effect upon the central nervous system unless excepted or covered in another schedule. Depressants are covered in a similar manner and expressly includes: any quantity of barbituric acid, its salts or derivatives; chlorhexadol; glutethimide; lysergic acid; lysergic acid amide; methylprylon; phencyclidine; and sulfonmethane, and its ethyl and diethyl derivatives.

(4) Schedule IV

(A) The drug or other substance has *a low potential for abuse* relative to the drugs or other substances in schedule III.

(B) The drug or other substance has a *currently accepted medical use in treatment* in the United States.

(C) Abuse of the drug or other substance may lead to *limited physical dependence or psychological dependence* relative to the drugs or other substances in schedule III.
(Emphasis added.)

Schedule IV includes only those drugs, in any quantity, that are listed. Only eleven depressants are covered: barbital, chloral betaine, chloral hydrate, ethchlorvynol, ethinamate, methahexital, meprobamate, methylphenobarbital, paraldehyde, petrichloral, and phenobarbital. These drugs were specifically chosen for lesser control because they were considered to have less potential for abuse and have special uses in medicine, such as the use of phenobarbital for the treatment of epilepsy. This separate classification allows greater flexibility to the DEA for their regulation.

(5) Schedule V

(A) The drug or other substance has *a low potential for abuse* relative to the drugs or other substances in schedule IV.

(B) The drug or other substance has *a currently accepted medical use in treatment* in the United States.

(C) Abuse of the drug or other substance may lead to *limited physical dependence or psychological dependence* relative to the drugs or other substances in schedule IV.
(Emphasis added.)

Briefly, Schedule V consists of preparations that were in the former exempt narcotic Class X. They must not contain more than specified concentrations of narcotic drugs plus nonnarcotic active ingredients in sufficient proportion to yield valuable medicinal qualities other than those possessed by the narcotic drug alone. This schedule is intended to cover such preparations as camphorated tincture of opium, elixir terpin hydrate with codeine and other cough preparations and antidiarrheals containing diphenoxylate with atropine sulfate.

Under Section 811, the Attorney General has very broad powers to reschedule a drug, bring an unscheduled drug under control, or remove the controls on scheduled drugs. In doing so, the Attorney General must make his decision based upon a record after opportunity for a hearing. In particular, he must first request from the Secretary of Health, Education and Welfare a scientific and medical evaluation and his recommendations as to whether such drug should be so controlled or removed from control. This authority was exercised by the Attorney

General with the publication in the Federal Register of a final order rescheduling amphetamines from Schedule III to Schedule II.

This process was also initiated when the administration wished to bring chlordiazepoxide (Librium) and diazepam (Valium) under control. Action was initiated on February 6, 1971, with publication of a notice in the *Federal Register* (39 F.R. 2555). Subsequent administrative hearings, court cases, and appeals delayed scheduling these drugs until 1973, when the manufacturers consented to their classification in Schedule IV.

In addition to rescheduling, many preparations have been excluded from coverage of the CSA. Nonnarcotic OTC remedies from the Bronkotabs "family," Tedral "family," and Verequad and Primatene, depressants have been exempted and are not controlled. Likewise, specific depressant and stimulant legend preparations have been excepted. These include many medications (antiacids, bronchodilators, belladonna and synthetic antispasmotics, ergotrate, diphenylhydantoin, digestives, analgesic compounds, vasodilators) in combination with phenobarbital, butabarbital and other barbituates.

Once a substance becomes a controlled substance, it affects any preparation in which it appears. The effect can vary depending upon the schedule the drug or preparation is in, and any substance is subject to scheduling, rescheduling or exemption. The government has no burden to provide a listing of all preparations that are scheduled. How does a pharmacist keep track of all this?

The regulatory system for controlled substances contains an element that is helpful to pharmacists. The label and labeling of all controlled substances packaged after December 1, 1971, must bear identification symbols indicating the schedule in which the product is listed. The following symbols designate the schedule corresponding to it.

Schedule	Symbol
Schedule I	$\mathbb{C}$ or C-I
Schedule II	$\mathbb{C}$ or C-II
Schedule III	$\mathbb{C}$ or C-III
Schedule IV	$\mathbb{C}$ or C-IV
Schedule V	$\mathbb{C}$ or C-V

The word schedule need not be used and no distinction need be made between narcotic and nonnarcotic substances.

The symbol must appear on the label in one of two ways. First, it may appear in the upper right hand corner of the principal panel of the label and must be at least twice as large as the largest type otherwise printed on the label. Alternatively, the symbol may be overprinted on the label at least one-half the height of the label and in a color that contrasts with the background so as to be clearly visible.

This labeling requirement enables pharmacists to know the schedule of any product merely by looking at the label. As an additional aid, the DEA publishes an inventory list, generally on an annual basis. Pharmacists are responsible for proper dispensation of controlled substances and should, therefore, check the scheduling of a product before dispensing it.

CHAPTER 15
REGISTRATION

Section 1
GENERAL INFORMATION

UNDER THE CSA, EVERY PERSON WHO MANUFACTURES, DISTRIBUTES OR DISPENSES controlled substances must annually register with the U.S. Attorney General's office. The terms "manufacture," "distribute," and "dispense" are defined in the CSA and are discussed below.

Certain persons need not register under the law even though they play a role in the distribution or use of controlled substances. These persons are agents or employees of registrants, common carriers or warehousemen, or an ultimate user, *i.e.* patients who lawfully obtain and so possess the substance for his own use or for the use of a member of his household or for an animl owned by him.

Section 2
REGISTRATION OF PRACTITIONERS

In applying the registration requirements to pharmacists, a number of definitions become important. The definition of "practitioner" is of primary concern to pharmacy practice.

§102 (2)

The term "practitioner" means a physician, dentist, veterinarian, scientific investigator, pharmacy, hospital, or other person licensed, registered, or otherwise permitted, by the United States or the jurisdiction in which he practices or does research, to distribute, dispense, conduct research with respect to, administer, or use in teaching or chemical analysis, a controlled substance in the course of professional practice or research.

It should be noted that this definition includes pharmacies and hospitals as practitioners. This is in contrast to former narcotic law which includes registration for "drug stores." Although registration for hospital and community pharmacies is basically the same, they are now included with practitioners who render professional services.

Hospitals were not explicitly included under any of the previous classes of registrants. Under the regulatory scheme established by the former Bureau of Narcotics, hospitals could obtain registration, as practitioners, to administer narcotics to inpatients. They could also obtain registration as retail pharmacies, if they were licensed by the state's board of pharmacy to dispense to outpatients. This was all changed by the explicit recognition of hospitals as practitioners under the CSA. Now one registration as a "hospital/clinic" authorizes hospitals to serve both inpatients and outpatients with controlled substances if they may legally do so under state law.

Pharmacists and other practitioners provide professional service directly to patients. In doing so they do not serve as manufacturers or wholesalers. As such, practitioners are registered to dispense controlled substances. This activity is defined in the following manner.

> **§102 (10)**
> The term "dispense" means to deliver a controlled substance to an ultimate user or research subject by, or pursuant to the lawful order of, a practitioner, including the prescribing and administering of a controlled substance and the packaging, labeling, or compounding necessary to prepare the substance for such delivery. The term "dispenser" means a practitioner who so delivers a controlled substance to an ultimate user or research project.

Clearly, the number of different activities such as prescribe, dispense and administer are lumped together in this one definition. Nevertheless, each person registered to dispense under this provision may only perform those activities in which it is lawful for him to engage under state law. This is usually evidenced by a state license, such as a pharmacy license. The registration also includes dealing with all controlled substances in Schedules II, III, IV, or V unless otherwise restricted. As far as Schedule I substances are concerned, registrants may only deal in those Schedule I substances specifically included in the registration.

As mentioned earlier, the CSA does not require the agents to register who are in the employ of a lawfully registered practitioner. This is especially important to pharmacies or hospitals who employ professionals to provide service to patients. The regulations contain the following parenthetical example:

> **21 C.F.R. §1301.24 (b)**
> . . (For example, a pharmacist employed by a pharmacy

need not be registered individually to fill a prescription for controlled substances if a pharmacy is so registered.)

This principle applies to other professionals as well. Thus, nurses employed in a registered institution would not have to be individually registered to administer controlled substances. Practitioners register on DEA Form 224 (See Exhibit 9).

Exhibit 9

Form DEA – 224
(Jun. 1974)

APPLICATION FOR REGISTRATION
UNDER
CONTROLLED SUBSTANCES ACT OF 1970

PLEASE *print* OR *type* ALL ENTRIES

APPLICANT NAME *(Last, First, Middle; if an individual)*

BUSINESS ADDRESS *(Do not use P.O. Box)*

CITY | STATE | ZIP CODE

RETAIN Copy 3. MAIL Orig. and 1 copy with FEE to:

UNITED STATES DEPARTMENT OF JUSTICE
DRUG ENFORCEMENT ADMINISTRATION
P. O. Box 28083
CENTRAL STATION
WASHINGTON, D. C. 20005

For INFORMATION, Call: 202 382-4876

THIS BLOCK FOR DEA USE ONLY.

REGISTRATION CLASSIFICATION: Submit Check or Money Order Payable to THE DRUG ENFORCEMENT ADMINISTRATION in Amount of $5.00. *DO NOT send CASH or STAMPS.*

FEE MUST ACCOMPANY APPLICATION

1. BUSINESS ACTIVITY: *(Check ☑ one only. Read NOTE before completing.)*
A ☐ RETAIL PHARMACY B ☐ HOSPITAL / CLINIC C ☐ PRACTITIONER *(Specify DEGREE)* D ☐ TEACHING INSTITUTION *(Instructional purposes only)*

2. DRUG SCHEDULES: *(Check ☑ all applicable.)*
SCHEDULE II 1 ☐ NARCOTIC SCHEDULE II 2 ☐ NONNARCOTIC SCHEDULE III 3 ☐ NARCOTIC SCHEDULE III 4 ☐ NONNARCOTIC SCHEDULE IV 5 ☐ SCHEDULE V 6 ☐

3. ☐ (E) CHECK THIS BLOCK IF INDIVIDUAL NAMED HEREON IS A FEDERAL, STATE, OR LOCAL OFFICIAL. IF CHECKED, *also complete Item 6.* →

4. ☐ (Y) CHECK HERE IF YOU REQUIRE ORDER FORMS.

5. ALL APPLICANTS MUST ANSWER THE FOLLOWING:

(a) Are you currently authorized to prescribe, distribute, dispense, conduct research, or otherwise handle the controlled substances in the schedules for which you are applying, under the laws of the state or jurisdiction in which you are operating or propose to operate? ☐YES ☐NO

CURRENT STATE LICENSE or CERTIFICATE NO.

(b) Has the applicant been convicted of a felony in connection with controlled substances under state or federal law? ☐YES ☐NO

(c) If the applicant is a corporation, association, or partnership, has any officer, partner, or stockholder been convicted of a felony in connection with controlled substances under state or federal law? ☐YES ☐NO

(d) Has the applicant ever surrendered a previous CSA registration or had a CSA registration revoked, suspended, or denied? ☐YES ☐NO

(e) If the applicant is a corporation, association, or partnership, has any officer, partner, or stockholder surrendered a previous CSA registration or had a CSA registration revoked, suspended or denied? ☐YES ☐NO

IF ANSWER TO QUESTIONS (b) (c) (d) or (e) *is YES, attach a letter setting forth the circumstances.*

SIGN HERE ▶ *Signature of applicant or authorized individual* *Date*

Title (If the applicant is a corporation, institution, or other entity, enter the TITLE of the person signing on behalf of the applicant ((e.g. President, Dean, Procurement Officer, etc...))

6. CERTIFICATION OF EXEMPT OFFICIAL *(Complete only if Item 3 is checked)*

ONLY OFFICERS, EMPLOYEES AND AGENCIES OF FEDERAL, STATE, OR LOCAL GOVERNMENTS ARE EXEMPT FROM PAYMENT OF REGISTRATION FEES.

(a) Name of governmental unit by whom applicant is employed or of which agency is a part *(e.g., U.S. Public Health Service, Iowa Department of Mental Health, Ohio State University King's County Hospital, Dallas City Health Clinic, etc...)*

(b) Is the official whose signature appears in Item 5 authorized to obtain from official stock, dispense, administer, conduct research, instructional activities or chemical analyses with controlled substances? ☐YES ☐NO

(c) Is he authorized to purchase controlled substances? ☐YES ☐NO

Signature of applicant's certifying superior *Date*

Official Title of Applicant's certifying superior

WARNING: SECTION 843 (a) (4) OF TITLE 21, UNITED STATES CODE, STATES THAT ANY PERSON WHO KNOWINGLY OR INTENTIONALLY FURNISHES FALSE OR FRAUDULENT INFORMATION IN THIS APPLICATION IS SUBJECT TO IMPRISONMENT FOR NOT MORE THAN FOUR YEARS, A FINE OF NOT MORE THAN $30,000.00 OR BOTH.

NOTE: Registration as a teaching institution authorizes purchase and possession of controlled substances for instructional purposes only. Practitioners, teaching institutions or individuals within teaching institutions desiring to conduct research with any Schedule I substance, must obtain a "Researcher" registration by submitting Form DEA-225 with applicable fee.

MAIL the Original and 1 Copy with FEE to the above address. Retain 3rd copy for your records.

Section 3

MULTIPLE REGISTRATION

If practitioners registered to dispense controlled substances also engage in other activities not covered by their registration, it is necessary to obtain additional registrations. The DEA considers the following to be independent activities:

21 C.F.R. 1301.22 (a) Separate registration for independent activities.

(a) The following groups of activities are deemed to be independent of each other:

(1) Manufacturing controlled substances;

(2) Distributing controlled substances;

(3) Dispensing controlled substances listed in schedules II through V;

(4) Conducting research (other than research described in subparagraph (6) of this paragraph) with controlled substances listed in schedules II through V;

(5) Conducting instructional activities with controlled substances listed in schedules II through V;

(6) Conducting research with narcotic drugs listed in schedules II through V for the purpose of continuing the dependence on such drugs of a narcotic drug dependent person in the course of conducting an authorized clinical investigation in the development of a narcotic addict rehabilitation program pursuant to a Notice of Claimed Investigational Exemption for a New Drug approved by the Food and Drug Administration;

(7) Conducting research and instructional activities with controlled substances listed in schedule I;

(8) Conducting chemical analysis with controlled substances listed in any schedule;

(9) Importing controlled substances; and

(10) Exporting controlled substances listed in schedules I through IV.

Any person engaging in more than one class of independent activities, other than in a coincidental manner in compliance with all regulations, must obtain a separate registration for each activity. Subsection (b) of this regulation sets forth further interpretations.

21 C.F.R. 1301.22 (b)

Every person who engages in more than one group of independent activities shall obtain a separate registration for each group of activities, except as provided in this paragraph. Any person, when registered to engage in the group of activities described in each subparagraph in this paragraph shall be authorized to engage in the coincident activities described in that subparagraph without obtaining a registration to engage in such coincident activities, provided that, unless specifically exempted, he complies with all requirements and duties prescribed by law for persons registered to engage in such coincident activities:

(1) A person registered to manufacture or import any controlled substance or basic class of controlled substance shall be authorized to distribute that substance or class, but no other substance or class which he is not registered to manufacture or import;

(2) A person registered to manufacture any controlled substance listed in schedules II through V shall be authorized to conduct chemical analysis and preclinical research (including quality control analysis) with narcotic and nonnarcotic controlled substances listed in those schedules in which he is authorized to manufacture;

(3) A person registered to conduct research with a basic class of controlled substance listed in schedule I shall be authorized to manufacture such class if and to the extent that such manufacture is set forth in the research protocol filed with the application for registration and to distribute such class to other persons registered or authorized to conduct research with such class or registered or authorized to conduct chemical analysis with controlled substances;

(4) A person registered or authorized to conduct chemical analysis with controlled substances shall be authorized to manufacture and import such substances for analytical or instructional purposes, to distribute such substances to other persons registered or authorized to conduct chemical analysis or instructional activities or research with such substances and to persons exempted from registration pursuant to §301.26, to export such substances to persons in other countries performing chemical analysis or enforcing laws relating to controlled substances or drugs in those countries, and to conduct instructional activities with controlled substances; and

(5) A person registered or authorized to conduct research (other than research described in paragraph (a) (6) of this section) with controlled substances listed in schedules II through V shall be authorized to conduct chemical analysis with controlled substances listed in those schedules in which he is authorized to conduct research to manufacture such substances if and to the extent that such manufacture is set forth in a statement filed with the application for registration, and to distribute such substances to other persons registered or authorized to conduct chemical analysis, instructional activities, or research with, such substances and to persons exempted from registration pursuant to §301.26, and to conduct instructional activities with controlled substances;

(6) A person registered to dispense controlled substances listed in schedules II through V shall be authorized to conduct

research (other than research described in paragraph (1) (6) of this section) and to conduct instructional activities with those substances.

(c) A single registration to engage in any group of independent activities may include one or more controlled substances listed in the schedules authorized in that group of independent activities. A person registered to conduct research with controlled substances listed in schedule I may conduct research with any substance listed in schedule I for which he has filed and had approved a research protocol.

It should be noted that by this regulation, subsection (b) (6), a person registered to dispense substances in Schedules II through V may also conduct research with these substances without obtaining separate registration. There is one exception. Research with narcotic drugs listed in Schedules II through V "for the purpose of continuing the dependence on such drugs of a narcotic drug dependent person . . . in the development of a narcotic addict rehabilitation program pursuant to a Notice of Claimed Investigational Exemption for a New Drug approved by the Food and Drug Administration" is prohibited. Although it is permissible with other types of research, research in a methadone maintenance program cannot be conducted under a dispensing registration. The use of methadone, either in research, maintenance, detoxification or treatment is discussed in Chapter 19.

Another area in which separate activities raise a special question concerns hospital service corporations under §501(e) of the Internal Revenue Code. These service corporations are independent entities that purchase drugs on behalf of member hospitals. They then distribute the drugs to each hospital in the group.

Under the CSA, "distribute" means:

§102 (11)

. . . to deliver (other than by administering or dispensing) a controlled substance. The term "distributor" means a person who so delivers a controlled substance.

Since distribution is listed as an independent activity, those persons distributing substances in Schedules I or II must have a separate registration. Such registrants may distribute only Schedule I or II substances listed in the registration. Registration for other controlled substances entitles the applicant to distribute substances in Schedule III, IV, or V without limitation. The same registration requirements for distributors apply to chainstore warehouses.

Without registering as a distributor, pharmacies may distribute controlled substances to another practitioner for dispensing to his patients provided the practitioner is registered to dispense, a record of the distribution is made, an order form is obtained if the substance is in

Schedule II, and the total dosage units so distributed does not exceed 5% of all dosage units distributed or dispensed during the same registration year. If the distributed dosage units will exceed 5%, the pharmacy must register as a distributor.

Manufacturing activities that result in delivery of controlled substances to persons other than the ultimate user would require registration as a manufacturer. This would not, however, include bulk compounding, centralized IV additive services, or other medication preparation if done in the course of the practice of pharmacy for dispensing or administering to the patient.

Conducting independent activities is not the only way a pharmacy might need multiple registration. Separate registration is also needed for each location. Every principal place of business or professional practice where controlled substances are manufactured, distributed or dispensed must be registered. It is not necessary to register warehouses, offices of agents where orders are taken but controlled substances are not kept, or practitioners' offices where substances are prescribed but not administered or dispensed.

The regulations are not very clear on what a principal place of business is. Whether more than one principal place of business exists is a question of fact. Among the factors to be considered are separate addresses, physical distances, separate buildings, and integration of facilities. Separate addresses usually require multiple registration; different buildings in the same area may not. Each store of a chain drug store requires separate registration, but satellite pharmacies generally do not, especially if they are located in the same building, for example, a hospital.

Whether a principal place of business exists so as to require a separate registration depends to a large extent upon physical factors. How close or far are the two locations? Is management and control under the same roof? Are records maintained together? Are personnel interchangeable between locations? Answers to these questions, prior practice, plus a general "feel" help in determining an answer. In case of uncertainty, pharmacists should call the nearest DEA office for assistance.

CHAPTER 16
INVENTORIES AND RECORDS

Section 1
INVENTORIES

UNDER THE CSA, AN INITIAL INVENTORY MUST BE TAKEN AT THE START OF business. Thereafter, each registrant must take a physical inventory every two years. After the first inventory, each subsequent one may be taken on the registrant's regular general physical inventory date nearest to and not more than six months from the biennial inventory date. Inventory records must be kept in written, typewritten, or printed form for two years, but the CSA specifically states that the maintenance of a perpetual inventory is not required. However, a separate inventory is required for each registered location and for each independent activity which is registered.

Each inventory must contain a complete and accurate record of all controlled substances on the premises on the date the inventory is taken. The burden is upon each registrant to know which substances are controlled under law. Although the DEA disclaims any responsibility to provide practitioners with a list of the names of all products containing controlled substances, it has, in cooperation with national pharmacy groups, issued inventory booklets. These listings are not exhaustive and any products on hand that are not on the printed list must be added by the pharmacist.

All registrants must include the same basic inventory information. If the substance is listed in Schedule I or II, an exact count or measure must be made.. However, in the case of dispensers, if a substance in Schedule III, IV, or V is in a broken package of 1000 units or less, an estimated count or measure may be made.

Section 2
RECORDS

In addition to inventory records, each registrant must maintain two other types of records — records of receipt and records of disposition. These three records allow the DEA to account for the drugs on hand with the amount of drugs received and used at any point in time. Hence, the CSA requires complete, accurate records of all controlled substances received and disposed of, including the name of the drug, quantity, strength, dosage form, number of units and date. All such records must be kept for two years for inspection and copying by DEA's employees. (See Exhibit 10, Inspection of Premises.) Records of a financial or shipping nature must be kept at a central location rather than at the registered location, if the registrant obtains approval from the DEA.

Records and inventories for substances in Schedules I or II must be kept separate from all other records. Records that are maintained via computers or other automatic data processing equipment are considered to be separate, but the specific information must be obtainable within a reasonably short period of time.

Records and inventories for substances in Schedules III, IV or V must either be kept "separate" or must be kept in such form that the information is "readily retrievable" from ordinary business records. In addition to the use of electronic and mechanical systems, records can be made readily retrievable if the necessary items are asterisked, red-lined, or in some other manner made visually identifiable apart from other items appearing on the records.

Records must also be kept on a current basis. This does not mean, however, that a perpetual inventory is required. Separate records are required for each registered location as well as for each independent activity for which the practitioner is registered.

Records of receipt which itemize controlled substances received by a pharmacy may consist of official order forms or ordinary business records such as invoices or packing slips. Whatever record is kept, it should be carefully reconciled against the drug actually received, for the pharmacy will be held accountable.

Official order forms are required for substances in Schedules I or II. (See Exhibit 11 and Exhibit 12.) These forms are obtained from the DEA. The DEA has promulgated definitive regulations concerning the execution, filling, endorsing and disposition of order forms which should be carefully followed. When a purchase is made via order form, a copy must be retained by the purchaser and filed separately for a two-year period.

Order forms may be obtained and executed only by the person whose authorized signature appears in the original registration form. This situation presents no particular difficulties if the name of the pharmacist who orders the drugs appears on the registration. However, in large corporate structures such as chain drug stores or hospitals, the pharmacy owner or the hospital administrator may have signed the registration. More appropriately, the practicing pharmacist should be the one to execute the registration form. Then he can obtain and execute order forms for the purchase of Schedule I or II substances.

If someone other than the pharmacist executes the registration, a power of attorney should be made, thus granting the pharmacist power to execute order forms. (See Exhibit 13.)

It is not necessary to use order forms for the purchase of substances in Schedules III, IV, or V. Records of receipt of these substances will probably consist of invoices, purchase orders or packing slips. If separate handwritten or transcribed records are maintained, the original documents need not be kept. If the original documents are kept as the record of receipt and they contain noncontrolled substances, the controlled substances should be made "readily retrievable" by means of some identifying marks as suggested above.

The basic record of disposition, *i.e.,* where the drugs went, is the prescription order. All orders for Schedule II substances must be filed separately. Prescriptions for substances in other schedules may be filed separately or with prescriptions for noncontrolled drugs if they are made readily retrievable. Prescriptions will be deemed readily retrievable if, at the time they are initially filed, the face of the prescription is stamped in red ink in the lower right hand corner with the letter "C" no less than one inch high.

In institutions, basic records of disposition are found in patient medical records. Every drug that is administered is recorded there. However, reconciling the amount of drugs on hand with the amount received and used is difficult when the primary records of disposition are dispersed throughout the medical records. Therefore, it has become accepted practice to distill from the medical record the information required. One type of record in wide use is the "certificate of use" or "proof of use" sheet. This document has drawbacks because of the nursing and pharmacy time required to maintain it and in the relatively low reliability of proof it provides. A more reliable method, and one that does not divert as much professional time from patient care, is the medication administration record (MAR). This document is a subdivision of the patient's medical record on which all medication information is recorded. A direct copy of the MAR can be filed in the pharmacy as the record of disposition. Hospitals that dispense controlled substances to outpatients pursuant to prescriptions, must maintain prescriptions in accordance with the rules applicable to pharmacies.

Another type of record is the computer record. This type of record is considered to be separate or readily retrievable. When the computer record is maintained, separate written records are not necessary.

All records of disposition must bear the name or initials of the individual dispensing or administering the medication.

Exhibit 10

U. S. DEPARTMENT OF JUSTICE
DRUG ENFORCEMENT ADMINISTRATION

NOTICE OF INSPECTION OF CONTROLLED PREMISES	DEA USE ONLY
	FILE NUMBER

NAME OF INDIVIDUAL	TITLE	
NAME OF CONTROLLED PREMISES		DEA REGISTRATION NO.
NUMBER AND STREET		
CITY AND STATE	ZIP CODE DATE	TIME *(initial inspection)*

ACKNOWLEDGEMENT

I, _____ , have been advised
                              (Name)

by DEA _____ , who
                              (Title and Name)

has identified himself to me with his credentials and presented me with this Notice of Inspection containing a copy of sections 302(f) and 510(a), (b) and (c) of the Controlled Substances Act (21 U. S. C. 822(f) and 21 U. S. C. 880 (a), (b) and (c)), printed hereon,* authorizing an inspection of the above-described controlled premises. I hereby acknowledge receipt of this Notice of Inspection. In addition, I hereby certify that I am the _____
                              (President) (Manager) (Owner)

for the premises described in this Notice of Inspection; that I have read the foregoing and understand its contents; that I have authority to act in this matter and have signed this Notice of Inspection pursuant to my authority.

_____
(Signature)

WITNESSES: _____
                              (Date)

_____   _____
(signed)   *(date)*

_____   _____
(signed)   *(date)*

* See reverse

DEA FORM — 82
(FEB 1974)   Previous edition, dated 7/73, may be used until supply is exhausted.

Exhibit 10 *(Continued)*

These sections are quoted below.

SEC. 302. (f) The Attorney General is authorized to inspect the establishment of a registrant or applicant for registration in accordance with the rules and regulations promulgated by him.

SEC. 510. (a) As used in this section, the term "controlled premises" means—
    (1) places where original or other records or documents required under this title are kept or required to be kept, and
    (2) places, including factories, warehouses, or other establishments, and conveyances, where persons registered under section 303 (or exempted from registration under section 302(d)) may lawfully hold, manufacture, or distribute, dispense, administer, or otherwise dispose of controlled substances.

(b)(1) For the purpose of inspecting, copying, and verifying the correctness of records, reports, or other documents required to be kept or made under this title and otherwise facilitating the carrying out of his functions under this title, the Attorney General is authorized, in accordance with this section, to enter controlled premises and to conduct administrative inspections thereof, and of the things specified in this section, relevant to those functions.

(2) Such entries and inspections shall be carried out through officers or employees (hereinafter referred to as "inspectors") designated by the Attorney General. Any such inspector, upon stating his purpose and presenting to the owner, operator, or agent in charge of such premises (A) appropriate credentials and (B) a written notice of his inspection authority (which notice in the case of an inspection requiring, or in fact supported by, an administrative inspection warrant shall consist of such warrant), shall have the right to enter such premises and conduct such inspection at reasonable times.

(3) Except as may otherwise be indicated in an applicable inspection warrant, the inspector shall have the right—
    (A) to inspect and copy records, reports, and other documents required to be kept or made under this title;
    (B) to inspect, within reasonable limits and in a reasonable manner, controlled premises and all pertinent equipment, finished and unfinished drugs and other substances or materials, containers, and labeling found therein, and, except as provided in paragraph (5) of this subsection, all other things therein (including records, files, papers, processes, controls, and facilities) appropriate for verification of the records, reports, and documents referred to in clause (A) or otherwise bearing on the provisions of this title; and
    (C) to inventory any stock of any controlled substance therein and obtain samples of any such substance.

(4) Except when the owner, operator, or agent in charge of the controlled premises so consents in writing, no inspection authorized by this section shall extend to—
    (A) financial data;
    (B) sales data other than shipment data; or
    (C) pricing data.

(c) A warrant under this section shall not be required for the inspection of books and records pursuant to an administrative subpena issued in accordance with section 506, nor for entries and administrative inspections (including seizures of property)—
    (1) with the consent of the owner, operator, or agent in charge of the controlled premises;
    (2) in situations presenting imminent danger to health or safety;
    (3) in situations involving inspection of conveyances where there is reasonable cause to believe that the mobility of the conveyance makes it impracticable to obtain a warrant;
    (4) in any other exceptional or emergency circumstance where time or opportunity to apply for a warrant is lacking; or
    (5) in any other situations where a warrant is not constitutionally required

Exhibit 11

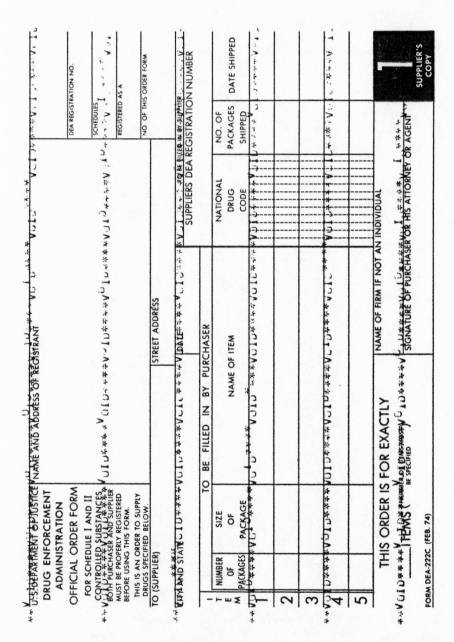

Exhibit 11 *(Continued)*

ENDORSEMENT

(MAY BE MADE ONLY BY THE PERSON OR FIRM TO WHOM THIS ORDER IS ISSUED WHO MUST BE A MANUFACTURER OR DISTRIBUTOR REGISTERED IN SCHEDULE I OR II.)

TO (ALTERNATE SUPPLIER)

ADDRESS (NUMBER AND STREET)

(CITY, STATE AND ZIP CODE)

PLEASE SEND MERCHANDISE REQUESTED ON THE REVERSE SIDE OF THIS SHEET ONLY TO PERSON OR FIRM DESIGNATED AND ONLY AT LOCATION SPECIFIED BY THE ADMINISTRATOR, DRUG ENFORCEMENT ADMINISTRATION.

NAME OF PERSON OR FIRM IF NOT AN INDIVIDUAL	SIGNATURE OF ENDORSER OR HIS ATTORNEY OR AGENT	DEA REGISTRATION NO. OF ENDORSER

NUMBER AND STREET

CITY, STATE AND ZIP CODE

THE PERSON SUPPLYING THE DRUGS OR PREPARATIONS ORDERED ON THIS FORM WILL RETAIN COPY 1 AND SEND COPY 2 OF THE FORM TO THE DEA REGIONAL DIRECTOR OF THE REGION IN WHICH THE SUPPLIER IS LOCATED, PROMPTLY AT THE CLOSE OF THE MONTH DURING WHICH IT IS FILLED.

COMPLETE ALL PARTS

Exhibit 12

U.S. DEPARTMENT OF JUSTICE

DRUG ENFORCEMENT ADMINISTRATION

ORDER FORM REQUISITION

FOR

SCHEDULE I AND II SUBSTANCES

ENTER NAME AND ADDRESS AS SHOWN ON CURRENT REGISTRATION CERTIFICATE. YOU MUST BE REGISTERED IN SCHEDULES I OR II TO OBTAIN ORDER FORMS.

ENTER YOUR DEA REGISTRATION NUMBER

BUSINESS NAME

BUSINESS ADDRESS

CITY   STATE   ZIP CODE

NUMBER OF BOOKS REQUESTED

LIMIT OF 3 BOOKS

UNLESS SPECIFIC AUTHORIZATION OBTAINED FROM DEA REGIONAL OFFICE

(No Charge For Order Forms)

NAME OF FIRM IF NOT AN INDIVIDUAL

SIGNATURE OF PURCHASER OR HIS ATTORNEY OR AGENT   DATE

MAIL TO:

DRUG ENFORCEMENT ADMINISTRATION
P.O. BOX 28083
CENTRAL STATION
WASHINGTON, D.C. 20005

DEA FORM – 222d
(DEC. 1973)

☆ U.S. GOVERNMENT PRINTING OFFICE: 1974–732–168/832 3–1

Exhibit 13

POWER OF ATTORNEY FOR DEA ORDER FORM

. . . .
(Name of registrant)

. . . .
(address of registrant)

. . . .
(DEA registration number)

I,. . . . ., the undersigned,
(name of person granting power)
who is authorized to sign the current application for registration of the above-named registrant under the Controlled Substances Act or Controlled Substances Import and Export Act, have made, constituted, and appointed, and by these presents, do make, constitute, and appoint
. . . ., my true and lawful
(name of attorney-in-fact)
attorney for me in my name, place, and stead, to execute applications for books of official order forms and to sign such order forms in requisition for Schedule I and II controlled substances, in accordance with section 308 of the Controlled Substances Act (21 U.S.C. 828) and Part 305 of Title 21 of the Code of Federal Regulations. I hereby ratify and confirm all that said attorney shall lawfully do or cause to be done by virtue hereof.

. . . .
(Signature of person granting power)

I, ..., hereby affirm

that I am the person named herein as attorney-in-fact and that the signature affixed hereto is my signature.

. . . .
(Signature of attorney in-fact)

Witnesses:

1. . . . .
2. . . . .
Signed and dated on the . . . . day of
. . . . , 19. ., at. . . . .

CHAPTER 17
PRESCRIBING AND DISPENSING

Section 1
DEFINITIONS

THERE ARE A NUMBER OF DEFINITIONS AND CONCEPTS AFFECTING THE OPERATIVE provisions of the law as it relates to prescribing and dispensing. One term that is not in the CSA itself but is introduced in the regulatory scheme is the term "institutional practitioner" which is defined as:

21 C.F.R. 1306.02 (c)
. . . a hospital or other person (other than an individual) licensed, registered, or otherwise permitted, by the United States or the jurisdiction in which it practices, to dispense a controlled substance in the course of professional practice, but does not include a pharmacy.

This term distinguishes hospitals, skilled nursing facilities and intermediate care facilities from other practitioners, such as physicians and dentists, among others, who are defined by regulation as "individual practitioners" in the following manner.

21 C.F.R. 1306.02 (b)
The term "individual practitioner" means a physician, dentist, veterinarian, or other individual licensed, registered, or otherwise permitted, by the United States or the jurisdiction in which he practices, to dispense a controlled substance in the course of professional practice, but does not include a pharmacist, a pharmacy, or an institutional practitioner.

Another term of art of importance to pharmacy practice is that of "dispenser."

21 C.F.R. 1304.02 (c)
The term "dispenser" means an individual practitioner, institutional practitioner, pharmacy or pharmacist who dispenses a controlled substance.

"Pharmacist" has an interesting definition under the DEA regulations.

21 C.F.R. 1306.02 (d)
The term "pharmacist" means any pharmacist licensed by a State to dispense controlled substances and shall include any other person (e.g., a pharmacist intern) authorized by a State to dispense controlled substances under the supervision of a pharmacist licensed by such State.

The term "prescription" is also important. Although the CSA devotes an entire section to "prescriptions" and the legal requirements relating thereto, the term "dispensing" speaks of delivering a controlled substance "pursuant to the lawful order of" of a practitioner. The regulations highlight the difference between these two terms by defining prescription in the following manner:

21 C.F.R. 1306.02 (e)
The term "prescription" means an order for medication which is dispensed to or for an ultimate user but does not include an order for medication which is dispensed for immediate administration to the ultimate user (e.g., an order to dispense a drug to a bed patient for immediate administration in a hospital is not a prescription).

Thus, a prescription is a drug order but a drug order is not necessarily a prescription.

The importance of the foregoing terms and their subtle differences become apparent in practical terms when analyzing the prescription requirements of this law, as discussed below.

Section 2
PRESCRIPTION REQUIREMENTS

A prescription for a controlled substance is lawful only if issued for a legitimate medical purpose by an individual practitioner acting in the usual course of his professional practice. Prescriptions may not be issued for narcotic drugs for the purpose of detoxification or maintenance of narcotic addicts. (These uses are discussed in Chapter 10.) It is also unlawful for practitioners to issue prescriptions to obtain supplies for the purpose of general dispensing to patients.

Although the basic responsibility for proper prescribing is upon individual practitioners, pharmacists have an independent responsibility to check prescriptions that appear improper.

All prescriptions for controlled substances must bear the following information:

1. name of patient
2. address of patient
3. name of practitioner
4. address of practitioner
5. registration number of practitioner
6. name, strength, and quantity of medication
7. directions for use, if any

All prescriptions must be dated with the day when issued and signed manually on that day by the practitioner. If an oral prescription is not permitted, the prescription must be prepared with ink, indelible pencil or a typewriter. If the prescription is an oral one it must be promptly reduced to writing by the pharmacist with all the necessary information except the practitioner's signature. The pharmacist who dispenses a prescription bears responsibility along with the prescriber to see to it that the prescription conforms in all respects with these requirements.

Schedule II substances require written prescriptions prior to dispensing. They may not be refilled. However, the DEA regulations provide for emergency situations. Under such circumstances, a Schedule II drug may be dispensed by a pharmacist upon oral prescription if the quantity dispensed is limited to the emergency period, if the prescription is reduced immediately to writing by the pharmacist and contains all the information required of written prescriptions except the signature of the prescriber, if the pharmacist knows the prescriber or makes a reasonable effort to verify the order's validity, and, if the prescriber issues to the pharmacist a written prescription within 72 hours of the oral order. Such emergency prescriptions must also have written on their face the words "Authorization for Emergency Dispensing" plus the date of the oral order. If the pharmacist does not receive a written prescription from the prescriber within 72 hours, he must notify the DEA regional office.

Substances in Schedules III or IV may be dispensed to outpatients pursuant to written or oral prescriptions. Such prescriptions may be refilled up to five times within six months of issuance.

Schedule V drugs and drugs in Schedules II through IV which are not prescription drugs under the Food, Drug, and Cosmetic Act may be sold to patients without a prescription but only for a medical purpose, provided the dispensing is done personally by a pharmacist (technicians are specifically prohibited under these circumstances), the express quantity limitations are not exceeded, the purchaser is at least 18 years old, suitable identification is obtained from unknown purchasers, and a record is maintained in a bound book setting forth the name and address of the purchaser, the name and quantity of substance dispensed, the date, and the name or initials of the pharmacist. Making a determination of a bona fide medical purpose without a professional diagnosis or physical examination borders on the occult. Yet pharmacists are expected to do so based on visual observation and oral representations. A cautionary note is in order at this point for state law may prohibit such dispensing of certain products.

There are two situations encountered in the institutional setting that require specific mention. The first concerns orders for controlled substances that are written into a patient's medical chart. It is important to keep in mind that chart orders for inpatients are excluded from the definition of prescription as set forth above. Chart orders satisfy the CSA's requirements for a lawful order; separate prescriptions are not required.

The second practice concerns the institutional use of an intern, resident, or foreign-trained physician, or physician on the staff of a Veterans Administration facility. These practitioners may, according to the regulations, dispense and prescribe under the employing hospital's registration provided that:

21 C.F.R. §1301.24 (c)

* * *

(1) Such dispensing or prescribing is done in the usual course of his professional practice;

(2) Such individual practitioner is authorized or permitted to do so by the jurisdiction in which he is practicing;

(3) The hospital or other institution by whom he is employed has verified that the individual practitioner is so permitted to dispense, administer, or prescribe drugs within the jurisdiction;

(4) Such individual practitioner is acting only within the scope of his employment in the hospital or institution;

(5) The hospital or other institution authorizes the intern, resident, or foreign physician to dispense or prescribe under the hospital registration and designates a specific internal code number for each intern, resident, or foreign physician so authorized. The code number shall consist of numbers, letters, or a combination thereof and shall be a suffix to the institution's DEA registration number, preceded by a hyphen (e.g., APO 123456-10 or APO 123456-A12); and

(6) A current list of internal codes and the corresponding individual practitioner is kept by the hospital or other institution and is made available at all times to other registrants and law enforcement agencies upon request for the purpose of verifying the authority of the prescribing individual practitioner.

However, an individual practitioner who is independently registered may not issue prescriptions for outpatients as an agent or employee under the registration of a principal. Such practitioners should issue such prescriptions using their own registrations.

Section 3
DISPENSING REQUIREMENTS

According to DEA regulations, a prescription for controlled substances may only be dispensed by a pharmacist acting in the usual course of his professional practice and who is either registered individually, is employed in a registered pharmacy, or is a registered institutional practitioner.

Some of the dispensing requirements relating to refills, emergency dispensing and reducing oral prescriptions to writing are discussed in the previous section.

Partial filling of prescriptions for controlled substances is permissible if the pharmacist is unable to supply a full quantity. Under such circumstances the pharmacist must make a notation on the face of the prescription of the exact quantity actually dispensed. The balance due may be supplied within 72 hours of the original partial dispensing. If the remaining quantity is not supplied within 72 hours, the pharmacist must notify the prescriber and no further quantity may be dispensed for that prescription.

One basic difficulty in completing drug orders is the verification of the authenticity of a prescription. Bogus prescriptions, as well as stolen and forged orders, have been identified as a particular problem area. In 1973, the DEA announced the results of a survey, "Project Script — A Study of Prescription Fraud Vulnerability" which reported that:

> . . . If a fraud perpetrator attempts a common prescription fraud involving representative drugs from C.S.A. Schedules II through V, the retail pharmacy will honor the prescription 56 percent of the time.

Telephone orders create a similar problem. When a nurse calls in a prescription, has the prescriber actually ordered the drug in the dosage and quantity requested? Did the prescriber actually see the patient or is the nurse, as a faithful servant, doing what she "knows" the practitioner would do? The same applies to physician assistants.

The label on the dispensing container of controlled substances must bear the following information:

1. the date of filling
2. the pharmacy's name
3. the pharmacy's address

4. the serial number of the prescription
5. the name of the patient
6. the name of the prescriber
7. directions for use
8. the statement, "Caution: Federal law prohibits transfer of this drug to any person other than the patient for whom it was prescribed."

The labeling requirements are somewhat different for drugs administered to institutionalized patients. In institutions having their own pharmacy services the usual labeling is generally suitable. Special identification of scheduled drugs may be desirable to assist nurses and others in making proper chart notations.

Where controlled substances are dispensed for administration to an institutionalized patient from an off-site pharmacy which is separately registered, the product, in lieu of the foregoing information, may be labeled to adequately identify the supplier, the product, the patient, and to provide adequate directions for use if:

1. the controlled substance is not in the possession of the patient,
2. appropriate records are maintained,
3. no more than a seven day supply of schedule II drugs is dispensed,
4. no more than a 34-day supply or 100 dosage units of schedule III or IV drugs is dispensed

This latter exception to the full labeling requirements is designed to accomodate the small labeling space of unit-dose packaging with the desirable advantage of safety in use.

CHAPTER 18
SECURITY

Section 1

IN GENERAL

ALL REGISTRANTS MUST PROVIDE EFFECTIVE CONTROLS AND PROCEDURES TO guard against theft and diversion of controlled substances. The DEA has outlined fourteen factors in the regulations which it will take into account in determining whether a control system is suitable.

21 C.F.R. 1301.71 (b)
. . . In evaluating the overall security system of a registrant or applicant, the Administrator may consider any of the following factors as he may deem relevent to the need for strict compliance with security requirements:

(1) The type of activity conducted (e.g., processing of bulk chemicals, preparing dosage forms, packaging, labeling, cooperative buying, etc.);

(2) The type and form of controlled substances handled (e.g., bulk liquids or dosage units, usable powders or nonusable powders);

(3) The quantity of controlled substances handled;

(4) The location of the premises and the relationship such location bears on security needs;

(5) The type of building construction comprising the facility and the general characteristics of the building or buildings;

(6) The type of vault, safe, and secure enclosres or other storage system (e.g., automatic storage and retrieval system) used;

(7) The type of closures on vaults, safes and secure enclosures;

(8) The adequancy of key control systems and/or combination lock control systems;

(9) The adequacy of electric detection and alarm systems, if any including use of supervised transmittal lines and standby power sources;

(10) The extent of unsupervised public access to the facility, including the presence and characteristics of perimeter fencing, if any;

(11) The adequacy of supervision over employees having access to manufacturing and storage areas;

(12) The procedures for handling business guests, visitors, maintenance personnel, and nonemployee service personnel;

(13) The availability of local police protection or of the registrant's or applicant's security personnel, and;

(14) The adequacy of the registrant's or applicant's system for monitoring the receipt, manufacture, distribution, and disposition of controlled substances in its operations.

Section 2

PRACTITIONERS

The foregoing principles apply broadly to all classes of registrants. The following regulations apply more specifically to practitioners.

21 C.F.R. §1301.75 Physical security controls of practitioners

(a) Controlled substances listed in Schedule I shall be stored in a securely locked, substantially constructed cabinet.

(b) Controlled substances listed in Schedules II, III, IV, and V shall be stored in a securely locked, substantially constructed cabinet. However, pharmacies and institutional practitioners (as defined in § 1304.02(e) of this chapter) may disperse such substances throughout the stock of noncontrolled substances in such a manner as to obstruct the theft or diversion of the controlled substances.

(c) This section shall also apply to nonpractitioners authorized to conduct research or chemical analysis under another registration.

§1301.76 Other Security Controls for Practitioners

(a) The registrant shall not employ as an agent or employee who has access to controlled substances any person who has had an application for registration denied, or has had his registration revoked, at any time.

(b) The registrant shall notify the Regional Office of the Bureau in this region of the theft or significant loss of any controlled substances upon discovery of such loss or theft. The registrant shall also complete DEA Form 106 regarding such loss or theft.

The question of security has been of growing concern to pharmacists in recent times. Thefts of controlled substances are on the rise. The community pharmacy has a handy supply of narcotics, depressants and stimulants, and criminals take advantage of this relatively easy resource. Senator Birch Bayh, in addressing the U.S. Senate on October 3, 1973, pointed out that:

> As officials crack down on illegitimate drugs, abusers direct their efforts at the legitimate sources of abusable medicines, in particular pharmacies. During fiscal year 1973 thefts of controlled substances stolen from distribution channels rose by 15 percent — from 2,974 in the first half of the year to 3,403 in the second half. During the same year thefts from pharmacies rose from 57 percent of the total during the first half of the year to 77 percent during the second half. Night break-ins accounted for 70 percent of the total thefts reported with armed robbery being the second most utilized method at 17 percent of the total.

Not only is the security of the drug supplier itself of great importance, but the individual safety of the pharmacist and other employees of the pharmacy has been increasingly threatened.

A number of suggestions have been made to help alleviate the problem. Legislation has been presented to the U.S. Congress that would make theft of controlled substances from pharmacies and other DEA registrants a federal offense. At the present time such robberies and burglaries are violations of local laws. Making such transgressions a matter of federal law would bring federal enforcement capabilities.

The DEA has been working on its own initiative to assist pharmacists in this area. An attempt is being made to apply new techniques of crime prevention and detection to the problems faced by pharmacies. This includes education in the availability and usefulness of burglar alarm systems, safes, etc.

In the area of hospital practice the central storage in the hospital should be under the direct control and supervision of pharmacists. Only authorized personnel should have access to this area.

When controlled substances are stored at nursing units, they, likewise, should be kept securely locked, and only authorized personnel should have access to these drugs. A question arises concerning medication carts and unit dose carts. If these carts are used merely for delivery purposes, it would seem they need not be locked; however, if they are used for storage, they may require locking for security reasons. The answer to this question must be determined in light of various factors, such as the frequency with which the carts are exchanged, the quantity of drugs they hold, the length of time for which the medication will last and other similar factors. Generally, if medications are on carts for brief periods, if they are designated for specific patients and if they are not part of a bulk storage unit, the carts probably do not need locks. On the other hand, safety factors may dictate locking all medications.

If such medications must be locked, it is important to note that they need not be segregated based upon schedule classification. This is significant, for the separation of one patient's medications into various compartments or locations may lead to medication error. For this reason it is desirable that all the medications assigned to one patient be kept together.

All thefts should be reported on forms available from the DEA. (See Exhibit 14.)

Exhibit 14

Office of Management & Budget
Approval   43-RO464

U. S. DEPARTMENT OF JUSTICE
DRUG ENFORCEMENT ADMINISTRATION

REPORT OF THEFT OF CONTROLLED SUBSTANCES

Federal Regulations require registrants to submit a detailed report of any theft of controlled substances to the Drug Enforcement Administration.

Complete this form in triplicate. Forward the original and duplicate copies to the nearest DEA Regional Office. Retain the triplicate copy for your records.

1. Name and address of firm _____
    (Include ZIP Code)
    _____

    _____

2. DEA Registration No. _____

3. Date of theft _____

4. Was theft reported to police?   ☐ Yes   ☐ No

5. Name and address of police dept. _____

    _____

    _____

6. Type of theft *(night break-in, armed robbery, employee theft, customer pilferage, etc.)* _____

7. If Official Controlled Substance Order Forms were stolen, give numbers: _____

    _____

8. What security measures have been taken to prevent future thefts? _____

    _____

9. What identifying marks, symbols or price codes were on the labels of these containers? _____
    (Insert your pricing code)

    _____

Exhibit 14 *(Continued)*

LIST OF CONTROLLED SUBSTANCES LOST

NAME OF SUBSTANCE OR PREPARATION	NAME OF CONTROLLED SUBSTANCE IN PREP.	DOSAGE FORM AND STRENGHT	QUANTITY	TOTAL NET WT. *(Gms.)* OF CONTROLLED INGREDIENT
EX: EMPIRIN ✦ 3	CODEINE	½ GR TAB.	100	3,200
1.				
2.				
3.				
4.				
5.				
6.				
7.				
8.				
9.				
10.				
11.				
12.				
13.				
14.				
15.				
16.				
17.				
18.				
19.				
20.				
21.				
22.				
23.				
24.				
25.				
26.				
27.				
28.				
29.				
30.				
31.				
32.				
33.				
34.				
35.				
36.				
37.				

FOR DEA REGIONAL OFFICE USE ONLY	GRAMS
AMPHETAMINES	
BARBITURATES	
COCAINE	
CODEINE	
DIHYDROCODEINONE	
DILAUDID	
METHADONE	
METHAMPHETAMINE	
MORPHINE	
NUMORPHAN	
OPIUM	
OXYCODONE	
PETHIDINE	
OTHERS *(List)*	

I certify that the foregoing information is correct to the best of my knowledge and belief.

Signature _____

Title _____

Date _____

CHAPTER 19
METHADONE

Section 1

ADDICTION TREATMENT PROGRAMS

IN THE PAST THE NARCOTIC DRUG METHADONE HAS BEEN MARKETED UNDER AN approved new drug application. It has been promoted and distributed for use as an analgesic, antitussive, and for detoxification. In recent years it has been used to wean addicts from heroin and other illegal narcotics. After the transfer to methadone has been achieved the methadone itself is subsequently withdrawn. It has also been used as a mere substitute for heroin in maintenance programs, thus reducing the crime involved in obtaining money for illegal narcotics.

In 1974, methadone came under the control procedures of a new law, the Narcotic Addict Treatment Act of 1974. This law supercedes previous regulatory controls of the DEA and the FDA to the extent that the FDA regulations may be inconsistent with the requirements of the new law.

Under the new scheme, a separate registration is necessary to conduct a narcotic treatment program using any narcotic drug listed in Schedules II through V. A narcotic treatment program is one which engages in maintenance or detoxification with narcotic drugs. Maintenance and detoxification have specific meanings and are defined in regulations.

21 C.F.R. §1301.02
(e) The term "detoxification treatment" means the dispensing for a period not in excess of twenty-one days, of a narcotic drug or narcotic drugs in decreasing doses to an individual in order to alleviate adverse physiological or psychological affects incident to withdrawal from the continuous or sustained use of a narcotic drug and as a method of bringing

191

the individual to a narcotic drug-free state within such period of time.

* * *

(h) The term "maintenance treatment" means the dispensing for a period in excess of twenty-one days, of a narcotic drug or narcotic drugs in the treatment of an individual for dependence upon heroin or other morphine-like drug.

The narcotic treatment program registration includes all activities necessary to conduct a proper treatment program including detoxification, maintenance, purchase of drug supplies, and compounding and dispensing drugs to patients of the program. Narcotics may be dispensed or administered to patients only by a licensed practitioner, registered nurse, licensed practical nurse or a pharmacist. Presumably, state law must allow these activities by such persons.

Each program site located away from the principal location where narcotic drugs are stored or dispensed must be separately registered and must obtain its own supply of narcotic drugs by use of order forms.

Acceptance of narcotic drugs by a treatment program must be made by a licensed practitioner or other individual authorized in writing. Patients must wait for their medication in an area physically separated from the storage and dispensing area.

A log must be maintained by the treatment program containing the following information:

1. name of substance
2. strength of substance
3. dosage form
4. date dispensed
5. adequate identification of patient (consumer)
6. amount consumed
7. amount and dosage form taken home by patient
8. dispenser's initials

Separate batch records of bulk compounding must be maintained. All such records are confidential.

If a narcotic treatment program does not have its own pharmacy service for preparing narcotic drugs for its patients, it may obtain necessary dosage forms from a registered "compounder." This term is defined in the regulations in the following manner.

21 C.F.R. §1301.02

(d) The term "compounder" means any person engaging in maintenance or detoxification treatment who also mixes, prepares, packages or changes the dosage form of a narcotic drug listed in Schedules II, III, IV or V for use in maintenance or detoxification treatment by another narcotic treatment program.

This definition implies that only a treatment program engaging in maintenance and detoxification may distribute narcotic drugs to other treatment programs. This would eliminate the need for community or hospital pharmacies that are not part of a treatment program to dispense methadone for maintenance and detoxification.

The records that must be kept by compounders are set forth with great specificity. The data to be included are the name and quantities received, compounded and dispensed; batch records; name, address and registration number of other registrants with whom the compounder has dealt; and theoretical and actual yields as well as other information.

Section 2

APPROVED MEDICAL USES

In addition to maintenance and detoxification, methadone may also be used for other purposes. Recently, the FDA changed the marketing status of methadone by using a combination of NDA and IND procedures. The antitussive use of methadone is no longer an approved use. It is available for detoxification and temporary maintenance of hospitalized addicts as an adjunct to the primary treatment of some conditions other than addiction. Methadone for the treatment of severe pain on either an inpatient or outpatient basis is also available.

It is not necessary to obtain a separate registration for these latter uses. The purchase, storage, dispensing and administration of methadone for these purposes is covered under the general DEA dispensing registration requirements and should be handled like other narcotics.

PART IV
PROFESSIONAL LIABILITIES

THIS PART OF THE BOOK DISCUSSES VARIOUS LIABILITIES THAT PHARMACISTS might encounter. The discussion centers on those liabilities that derive from the practice of pharmacy. Business and personal liabilities are not included unless they have special interest and applicability to pharmacy.

The liabilities are divided into three major categories. The first concerns the violation of laws. Many of the standards discussed throughout this book are legal requirements. Failure to comply can result in liabilities of various kinds.

The second class of liabilities involves tort liability. Tort liability arises when one's conduct or action transgresses the bounds of acceptable community behavior and that conduct or action harms or injures another, but does not, generally, involve a crime. It is a means whereby a private citizen may obtain redress from a wrongdoer. In addition to legal requirements, many of the standards involved in pharmacy practice are professional or community standards. If a pharmacist violates these standards and thereby injures his patients or other individuals he may be liable.

The third category of liabilities includes product liability arising out of warranty law and strict liability. Whenever a product is sold, the law imposes certain responsibilities, the breach of which may result in accountability.

No discussion about professional liability would be complete without at least the mention of insurance. All practicing pharmacists should have professional liability insurance coverage whether they are owners, supervisors or employees.

Each pharmacist is potentially liable for injuries caused by his own actions. No matter how skilled or how careful a pharmacist is, there is always the possibility of liability arising out of his professional activities. If nothing else has been achieved by this book, hopefully it has demonstrated the plethora of laws, regulations and standards with which today's pharmacists are expected to comply. The risk of liability is directly proportionate to the number of standards that must be met. In pharmacy, the risk is high.

Owners and supervisors may be liable for their agents or employees. Employee pharmacists may not be covered by their employers insurance policy. In this regard unless a written binder is received from an insurance underwriter, employees should assume they are not covered by their employers policy. Employers or their insurance companies may also seek restitution from an employee whose action has resulted in their liability.

Group professional and personal liability insurance is available to pharmacists at reasonable cost from professional pharmacy associations such as the American Pharmaceutical Association and the American Society of Hospital Pharmacists and some state pharmaceutical associations. It is advisable that this or similar insurance coverage be obtained.

CHAPTER 20
VIOLATION OF LAWS

THE MAJOR LAWS DEALING WITH THE PRACTICE OF PHARMACY HAVE BEEN DIS-
cussed in detail throughout this book. This Chapter, therefore, does not
repeat the specific requirements of these laws. The purpose of this
section is to present the variety of legal sanctions that are available
when one does not comply with an applicable law. The sanctions for
violation of laws regulating the distribution of drugs vary from civil
and administrative penalties to costly criminal fines and long term imprisonment.

Legal requirements are almost always enforced by the government;
private citizens ordinarily do not prosecute other persons for violating
the law. Often a law will establish or authorize a governmental agency
to enforce that law. The enforcing agency can merely be an attorney
general's office or a department of justice, or it may be a specialized
regulatory body such as the Food and Drug Administration established
to deal solely with the management of a specific law.

Most state laws discussed in this book, such as pharmacy laws, food
and drug laws, and controlled substances acts provide for criminal
penalties. These penalties may be different from those imposed under
federal law, and they should be examined for applicability to specific
circumstances.

Section 1
PHARMACY ACTS

Penalties for violation of state pharmacy laws vary. In order to
understand the full impact of the pharmacy act of any specific state,
each state's laws, regulations and administration and judicial opinions
must be examined. Nevertheless, a sampling of the kinds of penalties
involved is outlined below.

197

In some states the basic penalty for violation of the pharmacy act by a pharmacist is a civil suit filed by the board of pharmacy for civil fines. For example, in New Jersey, the fine for the first offense is not less than $25 nor more than $100; for the second offense the fine is $100—$300; and for the third offense it is $300—$500. Strangely, the penalty for a nonpharmacist who unlawfully practices pharmacy is less. Nonpayment of the fines can result in confinement in the county jail for up to 100 days. Stiffer penalties apply to violations concerning drugs of abuse.

Some state laws specify that violation of the pharmacy act is punishable as, or constitutes, a misdemeanor. The pharmacy law of Nebraska states:

Neb. Rev. Stat. §71-1147.13
Any person who does or commits any of the acts or things prohibited by this act, or otherwise violates any of the provisions thereof shall be guilty of a misdemeanor and shall, upon conviction thereof, be punished by a fine of not less than one hundred dollars, and not more than five hundred dollars, or by imprisonment in the county jail for not less than thirty days or more than six months, or by both such as fine and imprisonment.

Making violation of the pharmacy act a misdemeanor removes the transgression from the civil area of law and places it in the area of criminal activity.

Possibly worse than the foregoing is the power granted by most pharmacy acts to the board of pharmacy to suspend or revoke one's pharmacy license. For example, the Oklahoma pharmacy law provides:

Okla. Stat. Ann. tit. 59, §353.26
Revocation or suspension of licenses, certificates or permits.

The Board of Pharmacy is specifically granted the power to revoke or suspend any certificate, license or permit issued pursuant to this Act to any holder of such certificate, license or permit who:
(a) violates any provision of this Act,
(b) violates any of the provisions of 63 O.S. §§401 to 470.12 inclusive, 1959,
(c) has been convicted of a felony,
(d) now habitually uses intoxicating liquors or habit-forming drugs,
(e) conducts himself in a manner likely to lower public esteem for the profession of pharmacy,
(f) has been legally adjudged to be not mentally competent, or

(g) exercises conduct and habits inconsistent with the rules of professional conduct established by the Board.

Suspension or revocation of a pharmacist's license is a serious matter, for it denies one the right and opportunity to earn a living in his chosen profession. Because of the gravity of this type of sanction most pharmacy laws also specify an appeal procedure whereby the accused may appeal the decision of the board of pharmacy to a higher authority.

At this point it is appropriate to discuss administrative procedures, which is a broad concept that applies to the manner in which governmental agencies conduct their affairs. This topic is discussed here because most pharmacists, during their career, will be more likely to have contact with state boards of pharmacy than most other governmental agencies affecting their practice. It is important to keep in mind, however, that these same principles apply to most other governmental enforcement agencies, including the federal Food and Drug Administration and the Drug Enforcement Administration. Other state agencies, such as the State Department of Health or the State Department of Education, may also affect pharmacy practice.

When dealing with agencies in different jurisdictions, variations in procedures and the rules that govern agency actions can be expected. The federal government has adopted the Federal Administrative Procedure Act which governs the activities of federal agencies. Many states have similar laws governing state agencies. General principles are discussed below, but local variations should be examined before drawing any firm conclusions.

Agency activity can be divided into two major categories, rulemaking and adjudication. Rulemaking is the process that develops rules or regulations having future effect on the implementation or interpretation of the law or on development of policies and/or procedures of the agency. Many state boards of pharmacy, under their rulemaking powers, have added practice requirements to those contained in the pharmacy laws. Sometimes these requirements are reasonable; other times they are not. The first question to be explored is whether the regulatory requirements are within the scope and power of the board of pharmacy as authorized by the creator of the law, the state legislature. Sometimes regulatory agencies, in their zeal to enforce the law go beyond the power granted to them. Such activity is legally designated as being *ultra vires*. Pharmacy boards are no exception, and any such regulations are unlawful and will be declared so by the courts. Such was the situation in the case of *In re Cloyd Sorensen, Jr.,* a reciprocity case discussed in Chapter 2, Section 1.

A second question to be raised concerning the appropriateness of such requirements in the law or in the regulations is whether they are constitutional. Under our federalist constitution, states may adopt laws reasonably designed to protect the public health, safety and welfare of the citizens of the state. By contrast however, they may not adopt laws or regulations that are, for example, in restraint of trade and which unnecessarily burden interstate commerce.

The second major area of administrative significance is the adjudicatory activity of agencies. This includes the final resolution of questions under a law, generally resulting in an agency "order." The final resolution usually relates to specific persons or specific issues that generally relate to past activities. An adjudication usually results when someone has been accused of violating the law or when someone's license has been denied, suspended or revoked. In the case of the *Pennsylvania Board of Pharmacy v. Cohen,* the Board of Pharmacy ruled that a pharmacist who had sold capsules of lactose and quinine in large quantities, which could have been used for illegal purposes, was guilty of grossly unprofessional conduct. Upon appeal, the court, in reversing the Board's ruling, stated:

> State Board of Pharmacy statutory duty to regulate the practice of pharmacy does not give it the power on a case by case basis to make ongoing evaluation of what constitutes unprofessional conduct; rather, such determinations may only be made by statute or rule, and exercise of the Board's power on a case by case basis not based on statute or rule suffers from constitutional infirmities of vagueness.

In another case, *Gordon v. Dept. of Reg. and Education,* the court upheld the suspension of a pharmacist's license for dispensing drugs without a prescription in violation of federal law, which was considered to be "gross immorality" even though it constituted a misdemeanor rather than a felony.

Important aspects of "due process" come into play in agency adjudications. Under the United States Constitution, neither the federal government nor the state government may deny any person of his life, liberty, or property without due process of law. "Due process" has been defined in varying ways by legal scholars and constitutes an area of jurisprudence that can be very technical and yet at the same time vague. Basically, it is a term that implies fairness and use of an orderly process that has been generally acceptable before one can be denied certain rights.

In our legal system certain procedures have been considered necessary before one can be deprived of his life, liberty or property. These procedures include the use of a competent impartial tribunal, jurisdiction over the person being charged, sufficient notice of the alleged claims, adequate time in which to prepare a defense, the right to be represented by counsel, the opportunity to present evidence and to face and question witnesses before a judge who is fair and impartial.

Most but not all of these factors are applicable to agency proceedings. Certainly, the agency should have proper authority to conduct the proceedings, but it need not use a judge or jury in the traditional sense. There is a question whether the agency member who conducted an investigation may enter the charges as the prosecution might. There is also doubt as to whether the investigator or the person presenting the case might also sit as judge in rendering a decision. Proper notice is required as well as the right to counsel and the opportunity to present evidence and question witnesses.

In a case suspending a pharmacist from participating in the welfare drug program, *State of West Virginia ex. rel. Bowen v. Flowers,* the Supreme Court of Appeals, the state's highest court, ruled that the pharmacist was entitled to a reasonable period of time in which to conduct a proper investigation before a hearing was held. The court directed a hearing to be conducted within 30 days.

The pharmacy law of the state of Washington is quite specific concerning the rights of pharmacists before the Board of Pharmacy may refuse, suspend or revoke their licenses. It says, in part,

Wash. Rev. Code Ann. §18.64.160
. . . In any case of the refusal, suspension or revocation of a license by said board of pharmacy under the provisions of this chapter, said board shall file a brief and concise statement of the grounds and reasons for such refusal, suspension or revocation in the office of the secretary of said board, which said statement, together with the decision of said board in writing, shall remain of record in said office. Before a license can be refused, suspended or revoked by said board of pharmacy under the provisions of this chapter, a complaint of some person under oath must be filed in the office of the secretary of said board of pharmacy, charging the acts of misconduct and facts complained of against the pharmacist or intern accused, in ordinary and concise language, and thereupon said board shall cause to be served upon such accused a written notice and copy of such complaint, which said notice shall contain a statement of the time and place of hearing of the matters and things set forth and charged in such complaint, and said notice shall be so served at least ten days prior to the time of such hearing. Such accused may appear at such hearing, and defend against the accusations of such complaint, personally and by counsel, and may have the sworn testimony of witnesses taken and present other evidence in his behalf at such hearing, and said board may receive the arguments of counsel at such hearing.

The last major ingredient in agency administrative procedures is the right of appeal to a court of law. This process is termed judicial review, and is available in most instances. The pharmacy law in New Hampshire contains the following:

N.H. Rev. Stat. Ann. §318:31 — Appeal.
Within thirty days after the suspension or revocation of a certificate of registration the registrant may appeal to the superior court, and pending such appeal the decision of the commission shall be suspended until the court renders judgment, which shall be final in the case, and if the decision of the commission is not sustained the registrant shall be reinstated. In the case of suspension for addiction to drugs, the certificate shall not be returned on appeal until the court shall find the decision of the commission is not sustained.

Depending upon the law of the jurisdiction and the type of case involved upon appeal, the accused may be entitled to a trial *de novo* (the entire matter will be tried again) or the review may be limited to a review of the agency's interpretation and application of the law. The Federal Administrative Procedure Act states:

5 U.S.C. §706 Scope of Review
To the extent necessary to decision and when presented, the reviewing court shall decide all relevant questions of law, interpret constitutional and statutory provisions, and determine the meaning or applicability of the terms of an agency action. The reviewing court shall—

(1) compel agency action unlawfully withheld or unreasonably delayed; and

(2) hold unlawful and set aside agency action, findings, and conclusions found to be—

(A) arbitrary, capricious, an abuse of discretion, or otherwise not in accordance with law;

(B) contrary to constitutional right, power, privilege, or immunity;

(C) in excess of statutory jurisdiction, authority, or limitations, or short of statutory right;

(D) without observance of procedure required by law;

(E) unsupported by substantial evidence in a case subject to sections 556 and 557 of this title or otherwise reviewed on the record of an agency hearing provided by statute; or

(F) unwarranted by the facts to the extent that the facts are subject to trial de novo by the reviewing court.

In making the foregoing determinations, the court shall review the whole record or those parts of it cited by a party, and due account shall be taken of the rule of prejudicial error. Pub.L. 89-554, Sept. 6, 1966, 80 Stat. 393.

The complexities of administration hearings are apparent, and it is advisable for pharmacists to be represented by legal counsel in such matters.

Section 2

CONTROLLED SUBSTANCES ACT

The Controlled Substances Act is basically directed toward criminal activity. Indeed, the CSA places responsibility for the enforcement and administration of that law in the Drug Enforcement Administration of the United States Department of Justice. This agency is oriented towards law enforcement, rather than being a scientifically oriented agency of government.

The CSA provides for various levels of penalties, the simplest being for first offenders for simple possession of controlled substances. Such individuals are eligible for immediate probation and may, upon certain conditions, have the record of their arrest and conviction expunged from all records except the confidential files of the DEA. The harshest penalties are reserved for those guilty of unlawfully distributing controlled substances to persons under age twenty-one, or those engaging in continuing criminal enterprise, or those found to be special drug offenders.

A separate set of penalties applies to registrants, including pharmacists under the CSA. For violation of the CSA, a registrant is liable in the first instance to a civil fine of not more than $25,000. If the violation was committed knowingly and the trier of fact (*i.e.*, the jury), specifically finds that the violation was so committed, such person may, in addition to the fine, be imprisoned for a term not exceeding one year. A knowing violation of the law after one or more prior convictions subjects the offender to a term of imprisonment of not more than two years, or a fine of $50,000, or both.

The United States Attorney General is empowered, under the CSA, to suspend or revoke a registration if the registrant materially falsified any application filed or required under the CSA, if the registrant has been convicted of a felony under any federal or state law relating to controlled substances, or if the registrant has had his state license or registration revoked or denied and is no longer authorized under state law to deal in controlled substances. The revocation or suspension may be limited by the Attorney General to a specified controlled substance.

The CSA provides for an administrative procedure to be followed in taking action to suspend or revoke a registration. Upon revocation of registration all controlled substances owned by the registrant are forfeited to the United States.

Section 3

FOOD, DRUG, AND COSMETIC ACT

The Food and Drug Administration, the federal agency charged with enforcement of the FDCA, has various remedies, including injunctions, seizures and outright criminal proceedings, to use against transgressors of the law.

Injunctions are available from U.S. District Courts, upon showing of cause, to restrain violations of the FDCA. Temporary restraining orders are also available if irreparable damage is likely to occur between the time of petition and final disposition of the request for an injunction.

The FDA may also seize, and seek a condemnation order against, adulterated or misbranded products. Moreover, where the Secretary of HEW has probable cause to believe an article is dangerous to health or may cause injury or damage to the purchaser or consumer multiple seizures are permissible.

In addition to the foregoing, the FDA may bring criminal proceedings for violations of the act. Unlike penalties of the CSA, those under the Federal Food, Drug, and Cosmetic Act are straightforward. For simple violation of any of the prohibited acts relating to adulteration or misbranding, the penalty is imprisonment for not more than one year or a fine of not more than $1,000, or both. For a violation committed with intent to defraud or mislead, or for violations after final conviction for a prior offense, the penalty is imprisonment for not more than three years, or a fine of not more than $10,000, or both.

There are certain exceptions concerning good faith and guarantees that apply to practitioners. If a pharmacist receives an offending article, he shall not be subject to the stipulated penalties if he received and delivered the product in good faith, and if he furnishes the name and address of the supplier and copies of any pertinent documents to the FDA. Furthermore, a pharmacist will not be liable for use of any product that is misbranded or adulterated or in violation of the new drug provisions if he establishes a guaranty or undertaking signed by and containing the name and address of the person from whom he received, in good faith, the article. The guarantee must state, in effect, that the product is not adulterated, misbranded or in violation of the new drug provisions.

These latter provisions are important to pharmacists. If in doubt concerning the compliance of certain products, pharmacists can request a written guarantee signed by the supplier that the product is not in violation of the FDCA.

Section 4

SOCIAL SECURITY ACT

Pharmacists must also avoid violation of other laws, such as the Social Security Act (SSA), the Internal Revenue Code and antitrust laws. The SSA provides hospital and outpatient prescription medications to beneficiaries under the Medicare and Medicaid programs.

Pharmacists submit claims to program administrators of, for example, insurance companies and state agencies to obtain reimbursement for medicines dispensed under these programs. There have been instances in which excessive fraudulent claims have been submitted by various professionals, including pharmacists. Sometimes the prescription itself has been altered to obtain greater reimbursement, or charges were made for drugs prescribed but never delivered, or prescriptions never issued were fabricated.

Under P.L. 92-603, the 1972 Amendments to the Social Security Act, fraudulent acts and false reporting under Medicare or Medicaid constitutes a misdemeanor punishable by a fine up to $10,000 or imporisonment up to one year, or both. The SSA now reads:

Sec. 1877 (a) Whoever—

"(1) knowingly and willfully makes or causes to be made any false statement or representation of a material fact in any application for any benefit or payment under this title,

"(2) at any time knowingly and willfully makes or causes to be made any false statement or representation of material fact for use in determining rights to any such benefit or payment,

"(3) having knowledge of the occurrence of any event affecting (A) his initial or continued right to any such benefit or payment, or (B) the initial or continued right to any such benefit or payment of any other individual in whose behalf he has applied for or is receiving such benefit or payment, conceals or fails to disclose such event with an intent fraudulently to secure such benefit or payment either in a greater amount or quantity than is due or when no such benefit or payment is authorized, or

"(4) having made application to receive any such benefit or payment for the use and benefit of another and having received it, knowingly and willfully converts such benefit or payment or any part thereof to a use other than for the use and benefit of such other person,

shall be guilty of a misdemeanor and upon conviction thereof shall be fined not more than $10,000 or imprisoned for not more than one year, or both.

When the SSA was amended it added more stringent penalties for unlawful kickbacks and rebates. The law now states:

§1877 (b)

Whoever furnishes items or services to an individual for which payment is or may be made under this title and who solicits, offers, or receives any—

(1) kickback or bribe in connection with the furnishing of such items or services or the making or receipt of such payment, or

(2) rebate of any fee or charge for referring any such individual to another person for the furnishing of such items or services,

shall be guilty of a misdemeanor and upon conviction thereof shall be fined not more than $10,000 or imprisoned for not more than one year, or both.

Section 5

TAX LAWS

Tax laws also have a bearing on the subject of reimbursements for professional services. The Internal Revenue Service (IRS) now requires all third party payors to report to the IRS all payments of $600 or more made to professionals.

IRS Reg. §1.604-1 Return of information as to payments of $600 or more.

* * *

(d) Payments specifically included.

* * *

(2) Fees for professional services paid to attorneys, physicians, and members of other professions are required to be reported in returns of information if paid by persons engaged in a trade or business and paid in the course of such trade or business.

Hence, it becomes apparent that the IRS will likely know of all monies reimbursed to pharmacists for services rendered to Medicare and Medicaid beneficiaries.

It is also important that all income from the sale of drugs be reported. In the case of *Petworth Pharmacy Inc. v. District of Columbia,* the Court stated:

Respondent then proceeded to prove to the Court's satisfaction that Petworth had purchased at wholesale nearly one-quarter million dollars worth of a narcotic-based drug (Robitussin AC) from wholesale distributors, that it had not recorded in the exempt-narcotic records required by law to be maintained by every pharmacy any sales of Robitussin AC, that it declined to sell said product over the counter to police agents posing as customers, that about one-tenth of one percent of its purchases of this product (159 ounces) was listed in Petworth's prescription books, and that only about $4,500 wholesale value of the product remained in stock when a search was conducted in February 1970.

What happened to the remaining $236,500 worth of Robitussin AC?

Based on evidence presented at trial, the Court found that the product was sold secretly in bulk to blackmarket dealers and not included in its cash register receipts. Tax deficiencies plus fraud penalties and interest were assessed against the pharmacy.

Section 6

ANTITRUST LAW

Antitrust laws are also an area of potential concern to pharmacists. These laws include the Sherman Antitrust Act, the Federal Trade Commission Act, and other laws that regulate certain business activities that may be monopolistic, anticompetitive or unfair business practices. Violations of these laws are subject to criminal penalties and civil remedies such as injunctions and suit by injured parties.

One prohibition of particular concern to pharmacists is the prohibition against conspiracies to fix prices. For example, suggested pricing schedules for prescription drugs have been held to be illegal under the antitrust laws in *Northern California Pharmaceutical Association v. United States* and in *United States v. Utah Pharmaceutical Association.*

This issue of price fixing also comes up in the third party prepaid prescription area. Under such prepaid programs a pharmacist is reimbursed for prescriptions filled for persons covered by the program in a manner similar to that used under Medicaid. Payments made to the pharmacist are generally based on the cost of the drug dispensed plus a dispensing fee. All participating pharmacists in a given area generally receive the same reimbursements for their services. Pharmacists participate on a take it or leave it basis; the plan does not negotiate the fee or vary the reimbursement formula on a pharmacy-by-pharmacy basis. If a pharmacist does not participate he loses the prescriptions of persons covered by the plan.

The difficulty under the antitrust law is that the pharmacists in a given area may not join together or work jointly through their professional association to negotiate the fees, because it could constitute price fixing, as the court held in *Blue Cross of Virginia v. Commonwealth of Virginia.*

Alternatively, pharmacists could boycott the plan as a group, although such action could also violate the law. Yet, if pharmacists try to act individually they have no leverage. In order to avoid an illegal boycott, pharmacists in Philadelphia, Pennsylvania, brought suit against the Paid Prescription program in *Ostrow Pharmacies, Inc. v. Frank Beal, Secretary of Welfare, et al.* They felt the fees for welfare prescriptions were arbitrary and unreasonable and were established without complying with the requirements of the Social Security Act and its regulations.

Antitrust problems not only arise in relation to price fixing but may also be encountered if other activities could, in a secondary manner, affect competition. This was the case when the APhA and the Michigan State Pharmaceutical Association attempted to hold hearings on whether certain pharmacists should be expelled from membership in these organizations. These organizations felt that some pharmacists violated their codes of ethics by virtue of being employed by drug stores that advertised prescription services and prescription discount plans. Such advertisements are prohibited by their codes. The chain drug stores, by whom the pharmacists were employed, obtained an injunction against further proceedings by the associations in the cases of *Geoffrey Stebbins, et al. v. Michigan State Pharmaceutical Assoc., et al.* and *Myron D. Winkelman v. Michigan State Pharmaceutical Assoc., et al.* At the same time, the Antitrust Division of the U.S. Department of Justice was notified of and investigating the activity. After the original suit was filed, the parties entered into a settlement agreement in order to avoid long and expensive litigation.

The Robinson-Patman Act is another area of antitrust law that can be troublesome to pharmacy. The law provides

15 U.S.C. 13c (1970)
Nothing in section 13 to 13b and 21a of this title, shall apply to purchases of their supplies for their own use by schools, colleges, universities, public libraries, churches, hospitals, and charitable institutions not operated for profit.

A case was brought under this provision. Pharmaceutical manufacturers allegedly sold their products to hospitals at illegally lower prices than those at which they sold the same products to community pharmacists. In a suit brought by a group of Oregon pharmacists, *Portland Retail Druggists Assoc. v. Abbott Labs., et al.,* the United States Court of Appeals for the Ninth Circuit, reversed the dismissal of the complainant. In doing so the Court of Appeals held that only drugs "dispensed to the hospitals' inpatients in the course of treatment" and those "dispensed in the course of treatment to patients at emergency clinics operated by the hospitals" fall within the price exemptions of Section 13c. Other uses of specially priced drugs were not within the hospital exemption and were unlawful.

The last area of major concern to pharmacists under the antiturst laws concerns restrictive membership requirements imposed by professional associations. Recently four dentists, *Boddicker, et al., v. Arizona State Dental Association, et al.,* brought suit against the American Dental Association and the state and local dental associations, because membership in the state and local organizations would be denied unless they joined the national association. The dentists claim the membership requirements to be violation of the Sherman Antitrust Act as a combination in restraint of trade. The lower court ruled against the petitioning dentists who are appealing the decision.

CHAPTER 21
TORT LIABILITY

Section 1
INTENTIONAL TORTS

AN INTENTIONAL TORT ARISES OUT OF AN ACTION THAT IS UNDERTAKEN FOR THE purpose of achieving a specific result. The action does not have to be done with the intent to do harm, although such intent may be present. The foundation of these torts is the intent to attain a result which invades the interests of another person — interests the law finds desirable to protect.

There are many types of intentional torts. The more prominent include battery, assault, false imprisonment, trespass to land or chattels, conversion, defamation of character, interference with contractual relationships, and invasion of privacy.

Pharmacists, as businessmen, might encounter the tort of false imprisonment, if they find a customer shoplifting and try to stop him; the tort of interference with a contractual relationship, if overly zealous in competing with others. But these are basically derived from business activities and not from the practice of pharmacy.

One intentional tort that might more directly flow from the practice of pharmacy is defamation of character. Under the law of torts, it is defamation, *per se,* to falsely claim that someone has a loathesome disease such as syphilis, gonorrhea, leprosy etc. A pharmacist may receive a prescription for a patient for high doses of penicillin, in the dosage range that would ordinarily be used for venereal disease. If he assumes this is the condition of the patient and makes statements to this effect to other persons, the patient could sue for defamation of character. If, in fact, the patient merely had an upper respiratory infection for which the penicillin had been prescribed, the patient could win the case.

This type of gossip could also result in a tortious invasion of the patient's right to privacy for which the pharmacist could be found liable. This would be in addition to any breach of professional ethics for failure to maintain the confidentiality of the patient's condition.

Section 2

NEGLIGENCE

Although it has been shown that intentional torts may arise out of the practice of pharmacy, liability based upon an unintentional tort, *i.e.*, negligence, is by far the more important area. When negligence arises out of the practice of physicians, lawyers, pharmacists and other professionals, it is commonly referred to as "malpractice." The following discussion concentrates on areas of malpractice which are of major concern in the practice of pharmacy. Additionally, in pharmacy, drugs, devices, cosmetics and other products are generally involved. The term product liability is frequently used. Major principles of product liability, such as breach of warranty and strict liability, are discussed in Chapter 22.

Unlike the torts discussed in the preceding section, negligence is an unintentional tort. In general it is a course of conduct which creates unreasonable risk, by falling below the standard of conduct acceptable by law. It amounts to carelessness or lack of foresight or neglect.

There are a number of elements necessary in order to maintain an action for negligence. There must be an injury to someone, there must be a duty owed to the injured party, this duty must have been breached, and the breach of that duty must have been the proximate cause of the injury. Without these elements, anb action for negligence cannot be maintained. Various aspects of these elements are discussed below. Major emphasis is placed on the duty owed by pharmacists to their patients and the breach thereof. Proximate cause may also arise as an issue as may the question of injury.

Courts vary in the terminology used to describe the duty or standard of care applicable to pharmacists. The court, in *Tremblay v. Kimball,* spoke of "ordinary care."

> . . . the legal measure of the duty of druggists towards their patrons, . . . is properly expressed by the phrase "ordinary care," yet it must not be forgotten that it is "ordinary care" with reference to that special and peculiar business. In determining what degree of prudence, vigilance, and thoughtfulness will fill the requirements of "ordinary care" in compounding medicines and filling prescriptions, it is necessary to consider the poisonous character of so many of the drugs with which may follow the want of due care. In such a case "ordinary care" calls for a degree of vigilance and prudence commensurate with the dangers involved.

However, because the public health and safety are involved, courts will sometimes speak in terms of a higher standard of care than "reasonable" or "due" care. Since pharmacists deal in potent pharmacological agents, such as poisons, narcotics and other potentially dangerous drugs, courts have applied a standard of care variously described as the "highest degree of care" or a "very special degree of responsibility." One author has questioned whether this is substantively different in legal conceptualization from "ordinary care under the circumstances." Whether the relative measurement of the requisite care is a reasonable degree or the highest degree, it gains practical importance only when measured in absolute terms — what acts or omissions constitute negligence.

In discussing the duties and standards applicable to the dispensing of drugs, it is important to establish a reference point, the reasonable man. Obviously, the acts of a pharmacist will not be measured against those of an ordinarily prudent and reasonable layman. A pharmacist's education and training requires more than that. The practice of a pharmacist is measured by the practice of other pharmacists.

Another important factor in determining what is reasonable is the custom or practice in the area in which the pharmacist practices. Recent years have seen the demise of the locality rule to the extent that courts are almost uniformly using a national standard. In such cases, the court and jury will look at what constitutes acceptable practice throughout the country. Their exploration will not be limited to what is occurring in the locality where the allegedly negligent act occurred. Therefore, it is important in practice today to be aware of what is happening on a national basis, for this may be the measurement by which negligence is determined.

In a highly regulated profession like pharmacy, the first place to find specific standards of practice are in federal or state statutes, agency regulations, and municipal or county ordinances. Most of the important ones have been discussed throughout earlier parts of the book.

What is the effect of not meeting the requirements set forth in a law? The violation of a law could be treated in a number of ways depending upon the rule in a particular jurisdiction. It could be negligence, *per se, i.e.,* merely violating the law is all that need be shown by a plaintiff in order to prove his claim of negligence. In other jurisdictions the violation of a statute may constitute a *prima facie* case. This means that once violation of a statute has been shown the burden of proof shifts to the defendant pharmacist, and if he is unable to prove otherwise or establish a sufficient defense, the plaintiff will prevail. Lastly, violation of a law may merely be *evidence* of negligence along with all other testimony, exhibits, etc. In this instance, it does not shift the burden of proof or establish the plaintiff's case.

Generally, if the purpose of the law is to prevent the type of harm sustained by a plaintiff, and if the plaintiff is a member of the class of persons the law intended to protect, violation of the law could constitute negligence *per se*. Otherwise, it may merely be evidence of negligence; under such circumstances evidence is necessary to prove negligence. For example, there are a number of cases involving drugs, chemicals and other products which hold that compliance or lack of compliance with government requirements can be an important factor in determining liability, while others state that custom normally followed by those similarly situated is highly relevant.

One question in this area that arises frequently is whether the use of new drugs in a way other than that contained in the approved labeling or package insert, *i.e.*, noncompliance with government requirements, will result in civil liability. The American Medical Association advises that:

> The information contained in package inserts does not establish the standard of care for physicians in prescribing or administering the drug in question. It does, however, put the physician on notice of the risks involved and may contribute to establishing liability.
>
> Where a physician prescribes or administers a drug in a manner deviating from the recommendations of the manufacturer, he assumes certain legal risks. He may be held liable unless he is able to persuade the court or jury that the deviation is medically justified.

In the case of *Mulder v. Parke, Davis & Co.,* the court states the legal effect of deviation in somewhat stronger terms:

> Where the dosage is prescribed by the manufacturer, testimony of the physician's failure to adhere to its recommendations is sufficient evidence to require him to explain the reason for his deviation. This is particularly true where the manufacturer's warning puts the doctor on notice of potentially lethal effects . . .
>
> Where a drug manufacturer recommends to the medical profession (1) the conditions under which a drug should be prescribed; (2) the disorders it is designed to relieve; (3) the precautionary measures which should be observed; and (4) warns of the dangers which are inherent in its use, a doctor's deviation from such recommendations is prima facie evidence of negligence if there is competent medical testimony that his patient's injury or death resulted from the doctor's failure to adhere to the recommendations.
>
> Under such circumstances, it is incumbent on the doctor to disclose his reasons for departing from the procedures recom-

mended by the manufacturer. Although it will ordinarily be a jury question whether the doctor has justified or excused his deviation, there may be situations where as a matter of law the explanation exonerates him unless rebutted by other evidence.

In applying these principles to pharmacy practice, it appears prudent for a pharmacist to question a physician prescribing a drug in a manner that deviates substantially from the use recommended by the package insert. In really questionable cases, an acknowledgment and assumption of liability form could be obtained from the physician to provide protection to the pharmacist and possibly serve as an element in the defense of any subsequent liability suit. (See Exhibit 15.)

Quasi-legal standards, such as those contained in the Hospital Accreditation Manual of the Joint Commission on Accreditation of Hospitals, may also establish duties, the breach of which may result in liability predicated upon negligence. For example, Standard II of the Manual's Pharmaceutical Services states in part:

> The pharmaceutical service shall be directed by a professionally competent and legally qualified pharmacist.

This apparently places primary responsibility for drugs throughout the institution on the pharmacist, and the hospital may be liable for drug injuries if it fails to employ a licensed pharmacist. This was the situation in the case of *Sullivan v. Sisters of St. Francis.*

Still another source for the standard of care is the profession itself. National and state pharmacy organizations develop and publish standards of professional practice and other policy statements that may be used as a yardstick for measuring the conduct of practitioners. The American Society of Hospital Pharmacists has many such statements, some of which have been reprinted or referenced in the *Lawyers Drug Handbook* published by the Practicing Law Institute.

Codes of ethics may also provide criteria for determining the reasonableness of professional practice. In addition to the Code of Ethics of the American Pharmaceutical Association, most, if not all, state pharmaceutical associations have codes of ethics relating to practice within each state.

The last major area to turn to for guidance in identifying acceptable norms of practice is the common law as expressed in court decisions.

In addition to all the responsibilities that have been discussed in previous sections, there are still a number of other specific duties that should be identified, particularly because of their importance in the area of liability.

A number of states specifically provide by statute that owners of pharmacies and pharmacists are responsible for the quality of drugs sold or dispensed. In states where no duty has been spelled out by the

Exhibit 15

R E L E A S E

I, _____, M.D., authorize _____
        (physician)   (pharmacist)
to dispense _____ in a dosage of
                              (name of medication)
_____ to_____
        (form and strength)   (patient's name)
for the purpose of _____,
                              (intended use)
and hereby release and agree to hold harmless and to indemnify
_____ from all liability whatsoever which may
        (pharmacist)
arise from or be imposed on account of an injury caused by or attributed to the dispensing and/or administration of the drug as prescribed.

_____   _____
Witness   Physician

_____   _____
Date   Date

legislature, the common law duty would apply. Statutory quotations are set forth below from those laws having such provisions.

Alaska: Alaska Stat. §08.80.280 (1962).

§ 08.80.280. Responsibility for Goods, Sold.

An owner, or, if the owner is not a licensed pharmacist, a manager of a pharmacy, is responsible for the quality of drugs, chemicals and other medicines sold or dispensed by him, except those sold in the original packages of the manufacturer, and except those articles and preparations known as patent or proprietary medicines.

Arizona: Ariz. Rev. Stat. Ann. §32-1963 (Supp. 1971).

§ 32-1963. Liability of Manager, Proprietor, or Responsible Pharmacist of a Pharmacy; Variances in Quality of Drugs or Devices Prohibited.

A. The proprietor, manager, and responsible pharmacist of a pharmacy shall be responsible for the quality of drugs and devices sold or dispensed in the pharmacy, except those sold in original packages of the manufacturer.

Florida: Fla. Stat. Ann. §859.08 (Supp. 1972).

§ 859.08. Penalty for Selling Adulterated Drug.

Every registered pharmacist, and the owner or proprietor of any store dealing in drugs or medicines, shall be held responsible for the quality of all drugs, chemicals or medicines he may sell or dispense, with the exception of tnose sold in the original packages of the manufacturer and those known as proprietary; . . .

Hawaii: Hawaii Rev. Stat. §71-11 (1955).

§ 71-11. Duties of Registered Pharmacist.

Every registered pharmacist in charge of a pharmacy shall comply with all laws, and rules and regulations. He shall be responsible for the management of the pharmacy; and every activity thereof which is subject to this chapter shall be under his complete control . . . .

Kansas: Kan. Stat. Ann. §65-1634 (1964).

§ 65-1634. Responsibility for Quality of Drugs Sold; Adulteration or Mislabeling Unlawful.

Every person who shall engage in the sale of drugs, medicines, chemicals, and poisons shall be responsible for the quality of all such drugs, medicines, chemicals and poisons which he may sell, compound or put up except when sold in the original and unbroken pack, package, box or other container of the manufacturer. If any person shall intentionally adulterate or mislabel any drugs, medicines, chemicals or poisons, or cause the same to be adulterated or mislabeled or exposed for sale knowing the same to be adulterated or mislabeled, he shall be guilty of a misdemeanor.

Michigan: Mich. Comp. Laws Ann. §338.1114 (Supp. 1970).

§ 338.1114. Pharmacy, Supervision of Registered Pharmacist, Revocation of License.

. . . The owner of the pharmacy and the pharmacists on duty are responsible for compliance with all state and federal laws regulating the distribution of drugs and the practice of pharmacy.

Minnesota: Minn. Stat. Ann. §151.22 (1970).

§ 151.22. Liability for Quality of Drugs.

Every pharmacist in charge or proprietor of a pharmacy shall be responsible for the quality of all drugs, medicines, chemicals, and poisons procured for use and sold therein, except proprietary medicines or other articles sold in the original package of the manufacturer.

New Jersey: N.J. Rev. Stat. Ann. §45:14-16.1 (1963).

§ 45:14-16.1. Liability for Violations.

For violations of sections 45:14-13, 45:14-14, 45:14-15 and 45: 14-16 of the Revised Statutes, the registered pharmacist or other person who either compounds, fills, dispenses or sells a prescription or who supervises the compounding, filling, dispensing or sale of a prescription by a person other than a pharmacist registered in this State, and the owner of a pharmacy in which a violation occurs, shall be held equally liable, except that no liability shall be attached to the owner of a pharmacy if in the opinion of the board such liability does not exist, and the payment of a penalty for any such violation shall constitute an offense.

New York: N.Y. Educ. Law §6808 (McKinney 1972).

§ 6808. Registering and Operating Establishments.

e. Conduct of a pharmacy. Every owner of a pharmacy is responsible for the strength, quality, purity and the labeling thereof of all drugs, toxic substances, devices and cosmetics, dispensed or sold, subject to the guaranty provisions of this article and the public health law. Every owner of a pharmacy or every pharmacist in charge of a pharmacy shall be responsible for the proper conduct of this pharmacy . . . .

North Carolina: N.C. Gen. Stat. §90-69 (1965).

§ 90-69. Purity of Drugs Protected; Seller Responsible; Adulteration Misdemeanor.

Every person who shall engage in the sale of drugs, chemicals, and medicines shall be held responsible for the quality of all drugs, chemicals and medicines he may sell or dispense, with the exception of those sold in the original packages of the manufacturers, and also those known as "patent or proprietary medicines."

Utah: Utah Code Ann. §58-17-12 (1963).

§ 57-17-12. Proprietor Responsible for Quality of Drugs.

The proprietors of all pharmacies shall be held responsible for the quality of all drugs and chemicals sold or dispensed at their respective places of business, except . . . [dietary foods, packaged drugs, and patent drugs].

Washington: Wash. Rev. Code Ann. §18.64.270 (Supp. 1972).

§ 18.64.270. Responsibility for Drug Purity—Adulteration— Penalty.

Every proprietor of a wholesale or retail drug store shall be held responsible for the quality of all drugs, chemicals or medicines sold or dispensed by him except those sold in original packages of the manufacturer and except those articles or preparations known as patent or proprietary medicines. . . .

West Virginia: W.Va. Code Ann. §30-5-12 (1971).

§ 30-5-12. Responsibility for Quality of Drugs Dispensed: Exception . . .

All persons, whether registered pharmacists or not shall be held responsible for the quality of all drugs, chemicals and medicines they may sell or dispense, with the exception of those sold in the original retail package of the manufacturer.

In addition to quality, the drug dispensed must be the right drug. In the case of *Troppi v. Scarf,* a tranquilizer was dispensed instead of the prescribed oral contraceptive. The patient who became pregnant and delivered a child sued the pharmacist for damages. Damages were awarded which included child support until the child reached the age of majority.

Preparing a physician's order with the correct quantity of ingredients is also a must. As recently as 1961, a prescription was compounded with excessive quantities of bichloride of mercury and salicylic acid which resulted in severe burns to the patient's face. In affirming the lower court finding that the pharmacist was negligent, the appellate court, in *Adams v. American Druggist Insurance Co.,* in an unusual move, increased an award of $650 to $4,000.

Not only must the drug and dosage be accurate, but the route of administration must be correct. A hospital nurse misinterpreted a physician's order. Rather than administering the drug orally as intended, she injected the prescribed amount of the correct medication which resulted in a lethal overdose. This case, *Norton v. Argonaut Insurance Co.,* underscores the desirability of having the pharmacist interpret the physician's order or a direct copy of it, as recommended by the Joint Commission on Accreditation of Hospitals in their Pharmaceutical Services Standard IV, Interpretation.

Once a hospital assumes the provision of a treatment, it must assure the continued availability of the treatment. In one case, *McCord v. State of New York,* involving an investigational drug, the patient was unable, during a long holiday weekend, to obtain the psychotropic agent she was taking because it was maintained by the hospital's research department which was closed. In finding the hospital liable, the court pointed out that, among other factors, had the drug been maintained by the hospital pharmacy it would have been available.

Pharmacists may also be responsible for rational drug therapy, especially in the hospital setting. The case *Darling v. Charleston Com-*

munity Hospital, has suggested a "corporate" responsibility of the hospital for services provided within the hospital. Although this interpretation of the *Darling* case has been questioned, there have been subsequent cases supporting this theory. The implications of the *Darling* case to hospital drug distribution systems have been explored. A system of review for rational drug therapy has been suggested with the pharmacist and nurse being the first level of review. The attending physician, and, ultimately, the pharmacy and therapeutics committee would then review the case, thus assuring patients the benefit of supervision and review should drug therapy be questionable.

In addition to potential liabilities arising out of the use of drugs themselves, pharmacists should be equally as careful concerning the drug information they dispense. For example, increasingly hospital pharmacies publish newsletters discussing drugs for the information of hospital personnel. The issue here is whether the pharmacist would be held liable for any inaccuracies, misinterpretations, or for any misuse of the information contained in the newsletter. One hospital pharmacy uses the following exculpatory language on its publication:

> The material in this newsletter is presented in a condensed form for the information and convenience of . . . physicians. The newsletter is not intended to be all-inclusive, and physicians should continue to consult the professional literature and exercise their own judgment to prescribing or utilizing drugs. The Hospital hereby disclaims any responsibility for the accuracy of the information set forth herein. No statement in this newsletter should be construed as an endorsement by the Hospital of any product, procedure, or practice.

The pharmacist's drug information role, specifically his duty to warn others concerning potential side effects, has gained recognition in a recent Kansas case, *Mahaffey v. Sandoz, Inc.* The patient had taken Sansert for 28 months which resulted in endocardial fibrosis and other damage requiring surgery. The pharmacist was sued, along with the physician and manufacturer, for failure to relate to the prescribing physician his information concerning the fibrotic side-effects caused by the drug. The pharmacist, along with the other defendants, contributed to the $350,000 settlement of the case.

In another case, *Nelson v. Stadner,* a patient who suffered a reaction to prednisone claimed the pharmacist failed to properly set forth the physician's instructions on the dispensing container. The California jury rendered a verdict in favor of the pharmacist who claimed the prescription container was properly labeled and additional instructions had been given on use of the drug after it was dispensed.

It is too early to tell whether the Health Maintenance Organization Act of 1972 will create new liabilities for pharmacists based on additional drug information responsibilities. (See Chapter 2, Section 2.)

After all, it was the intent of Congress, in part, to reduce drug interactions and improve therapy by involving pharmacists in HMO activities.

Drug information is also important in selling OTC drugs, as demonstrated in the case of *Jacobs Pharmacy Company Inc. v. Gipson,* a breach of warranty case, discussed below.

Naturally, before liability can be imposed, an improperly compounded prescription must be the proximate cause of the patient's injury. In a case where a pharmacist dispensed cortisone in a cream base rather than in a lotion, he was not found negligent because the patient's injury was caused by the cortisone itself and not by the form of preparation in which it was dispensed. In other words, the same injury was likely to occur even if the medication had been prepared as ordered. The error by the pharmacist did not, therefore, cause the injury.

In a negligence case the occurence of an injury must be proved. In the *Troppi v. Scarf* birth control pill case, above, the pharmacist argued that having a child, whether wanted or unwanted is a blessing, that having a healthy child was not the kind of "harm" that was compensable under tort law. The court disagreed for the child was unwanted and presented the parents with unexpected financial burdens plus the psychological and emotional stress of rearing a fifth child.

The injury might also be sustained by a third party, someone other than the patient. In the case of *Whitty v. Daw Drug Company, Inc.,* the patient received an anticoagulant instead of the prescribed antispasmotic which resulted in hemorrhaging and ultimately in hospitalization. In the suit against the pharmacist for improperly filling the prescription, the husband was allowed to sue for loss of consortium, loss of his wife's services and companionship.

Consideration of negligence would not be complete without looking at potential liabilities under Professional Standards Review Organizations. (See Chapter 5, Section 2) PSROs will be identifying or developing criteria and standards against which to measure professional services that are provided under government programs. What happens if a pharmacist fails to meet these standards? In addition to not being reimbursed for his services, will his failure to meet the standards be admissible in a law suit, if the deviation results in harm to a patient? This question must await actual litigation for a sure answer.

Some sections of the PSRO law could have an effect upon future liability risks. Section 1167(a) protects from criminal prosecution or civil liability any individual who furnishes information to any PSRO. Such information must be related to the performance of the duties and functions of the PSRO, and cannot be false. Under this provision, if a patient feels the services he received were sub-par or in some other way improper, he will be free to communicate this information to the PSRO. In fact, anyone communicating with the PSRO will be protected. Hopefully, this free flow of information will have a salutory ombudsman-like effect on the provision of health care services and not cause unnecessary disruption of services because of nuisance communications.

Another subsection, §1167(c), contains a limitation on liability. It states that no provider of health care services (this would include pharmacists) shall be civilly liable on account of any action taken by him in compliance with or reliance upon professionally developed norms of care and treatment applied by a PSRO. Such protection only arises if he takes such action in the exercise of his functions as a provider of health care services. Furthermore, he must have exercised due care in all professional conduct taken in compliance with or reliance upon such professionally accepted norms of care and treatment. What this means is a pharmacist would not be liable simply because he complied with PSRO standards even if these standards differed from other recognized standards. He must still use due care in all other respects. In effect, this liability limitation is designed to encourage the use of PSRO standards and not limit any other type of liability.

Section 3

VICARIOUS LIABILITY

It is a basic principle of law that each individual is liable for his own torts. There are circumstances, however, under which pharmacists may incur criminal or civil liability although they, themselves, have done nothing wrong. As an employer of other pharmacists, technicians, and clerks, etc., pharmacists may be liable for the acts of those professionals or employees under their control. This assumed or inherited liability is known as vicarious liability.

Vicarious liability is generally based upon a principal-agent relationship, master-servant relationship or an employer-employee relationship. In such situations, the principal, master, or employer may have to answer for the transgressions of his agent, servant or employee under the doctrine of *respondeat superior.* This doctrine is based upon the rationale that "he who does a thing through another does it himself." The principal's liability, however, is limited to torts committed while the agent is acting within the scope of his authority but not if the agent is acting on his own.

Based on such considerations, an employer or supervisory pharmacist may incur vicarious liability based upon the acts or omissions of employees under his control and supervision. There could be liability for the improper selection, training or supervision of pharmacists or technicians. Written standards and a policy and procedure manual should be developed for selection, training and supervision of personnel. Formal academic training and state certification are also desirable safeguards against liability.

Liability could result from the improper delegation of duties to technicians. In the case of *Duensing v. Huscher* the pharmacist allowed a technician to receive a telephonic prescription order from a physician. The order was filled with Seconal Suppositories rather than aspirin suppositories, resulting in an infant patient's death. Under Missouri law, nonlicensed personnel may fill prescriptions, but only under the supervision of a pharmacist. In this case the pharmacist was not in the store. He had, in effect, delegated an excess of authority to the technician and was found liable.

Finally, a principal would be liable for injuries occurring because he entrusted his servant with a dangerous instrument capable of creating a high degree of risk. Present day drugs are potent pharmacological agents and could fall within this class; therefore, proper controls must be used to safeguard the patients receiving them, especially when technicians are used.

As demonstrated by the case of *Rice v. California Lutheran Hospital*, in the area of institutional practice, the hospital will be liable not only for negligence occurring in the pharmacy but also for negligence in the handling and administration of drugs anywhere in the hospital. The hospital itself could be liable for its failure, in the first instance, to employ a pharmacist as in *Sullivan v. Sisters of St. Francis*. It could also be liable for misuse or underutilization of its pharmacy staff. In the case of *McCord v. State of New York*, the hospital was found liable for the death of a patient taking an investigational psychotropic agent. One of the factors upon which the court based its finding of liability was that the drug was unavailable to the patient during a long holiday weekend, because it was maintained by the research department which was closed. If the drug had been maintained in the pharmacy, which provided service during the weekend, it would have been available and the patient may not have committed suicide.

An important question in hospital practice is whether any of these pharmacy standards apply to other areas of the hospital or whether they are limited solely to the area called the pharmacy. Simple logic and professional advice tells us that if temperature controls are necessary for the preservation of drugs in the pharmacy, they probably have an effect on the same products in other areas of the hospital, such as the emergency room, nursing stations, and operating rooms. For example, nurses should not store nitroglycerine or other unstable products near heat or moisture in order to protect the potency of the products. And, nurses who measure out doses of medication must have equipment sensitive enough to yield the proper quantities before administering them to patients. In fact, such principles have been carried over into certain standards. For example, state and federal laws require that narcotics be locked wherever they are stored in the institution. The interpretation of Standard II of the Joint Commission on Accreditation of Hospitals deals in detail with this subject:

Drugs stored within the pharmacy, and throughout the hospital, must be under the supervision of the pharmacist. They must be stored under proper conditions of sanitation, temperature, light, moisture, ventilation, segregation and security. There should be adequate and properly controlled drug preparation areas, as well as locked storage areas, on the nursing units. These areas, which should be well lighted, should be located in a place where the nursing personnel will not be interrupted when handling drugs. The pharmacist, or his designee, must make periodic inspections of all drug storage and medication centers on nursing care units. A record of these inspections should be maintained in order to verify that:

Disinfectants and drugs for external use are stored separately from internal and injectable medications.

Drugs requiring special conditions for storage to ensure stability are properly stored. For example, biologicals and other thermolabile medications should be stored in a separate compartment within a refrigerator that is capable of maintaining the necessary temperature.

No outdated drugs are stocked.

Distribution and administration of controlled drugs are adequately documented.

Emergency drugs are in adequate and proper supply.

Metric-apothecaries' weight and measure conversion charts are posted wherever they are needed.

Materials and equipment necessary for the administration of the service should be provided. Effective messenger and delivery service should connect the pharmacy with appropriate parts of the hospital.

Up-to-date pharmaceutical reference material should be provided in order to furnish the medical and nursing staffs with adequate information concerning drugs. As a minimum, the following should be available: *United States Pharmacopoeia, National Formulary, American Hospital Formulary Service, and A.M.A. Drug Evaluations.*

In addition, there should be current editions of test and reference books covering theoretical and practical pharmacy; general, organic, pharmaceutical and biological chemistry; toxicology; pharmacology; bacteriology; sterilization and disinfection; as well as other related matters important to good patient care. Authoritative, current antidote information should be readily available in the pharmacy for emergency reference, along with the telephone number of the regional poison control center.

Standards established by the profession itself are also applicable. The American Society of Hospital Pharmacists has a published statement entitled "Minimum Standards for Pharmacies in Hospitals with Guide to Application," which sets forth in detail the minimum requirements, as determined by professional practitioners, necessary to properly provide quality pharmaceutical services to patients of hospitals. Of similar importance is the *Statement on Hospital Drug Control Systems.*

CHAPTER 22
WARRANTY AND
STRICT LIABILITY

Section 1
LAW OF SALES

PHARMACISTS PROVIDE BOTH PRODUCTS AND SERVICES IN THEIR PROFESSIONAL practice. Activities relating to the product, the drug or medication, still overshadow the less readily identifiable services provided by the pharmacist. Indeed, even the services rendered by pharmacists most often relate in some way to drugs whether it be use, misuse or nonuse of medications.

Dispensing medications constitutes a major proportion of all pharmaceutical activities. Such dispensing of prescription drugs or the distribution of OTC medicine involves the sale of a product. The law of sales is, therefore, important to this aspect of practice. The law of sales can be found in the Uniform Commercial Code (UCC) as enacted by the District of Columbia and all states except Louisiana. As with other laws, variations exist from state to state. Nevertheless, the same basic principles are generally applicable.

The UCC contains rules relating to many business transactions, including commercial paper such as checks and notes, bank deposits and collections, letters of credit, bulk transfers and documents of title. Most important to the present topic is the article dealing with sales of goods or personal property, for this would include the sale of pharmaceuticals. The following discussion centers on those aspects of the law of sales that deal specifically with civil liabilities arising out of the sale of products, commonly referred to as product liability.

There are a number of legal principles that deal with liablity for injuries caused by the products a vendor sells. One basis, negligence or malpractice, was discussed in detail in Chapter 21. Negligence involves a wrongdoing, conduct that fell below the community standard for which the defendant is held answerable. Product liability under the law of sales is based upon breach of warranty. Historically, this action was also considered a tort, just as negligence, for it was based on deceit by the seller, a wrongful activity. Now however, breach of warranty is based on contract law. The warranty is a part of the sales contract, the breach of which can result in liability. Such an action, not being a tort, does not require proof of wrongdoing; determination of fault is not necessary.

The basic elements of an action for breach of warranty is proof of the existence of a warranty, that the warranty was breached or broken, and that failure of the warranty was the proximate cause of the injury.

Section 2
WARRANTIES

In basic terms, a warranty is a promise that a proposition of fact is true. In relation to the sale of goods, a representation that the goods are of a certain quality or character, which becomes part of the basis of the sale, is a warranty. Such warranties may be express or implied.

Express warranties arise out of the actions of the parties involved in the sale, namely the buyer and the seller. If the seller makes an affirmation of fact or promise which relates to the goods, a warranty can arise. Likewise a warranty is created if the sale was made pursuant to a description of the goods, *i.e.,* the goods must meet the description. The goods sold must also conform to any sample involved.

In order for an express warranty to arise, it is not necessary to use the words "warranty" or "guarantee." The actions of the parties in attempting to fulfill a description or duplicate a sample creates a warranty. Warranties are not created by virtue of the seller's "puffing." Puffing is a term generally applied to sales talk that constitutes the seller's affirmation that the goods are of "high value" or a seller's commendation of the goods. For example, a pharmacist, in selling an elastic support for the knee, may state that it will give the customer "long service." Without more, this would not generally constitute a warranty.

Unlike express warranties, implied warranties do not arise out of what the seller or buyer said or did; they occur by operation of law. The law will imply, in contracts for the sale of goods, that the goods are "merchantable" and that they are "fit for a particular purpose" for which they were bought. The UCC provisions dealing with implied warranties state:

**Section 2—314. Implied Warranty: Merchantability; Usage of
Trade**

(1) Unless excluded or modified (Section 2—316), a warranty that the goods shall be merchantable is implied in a

contract for their sale if the seller is a merchant with respect to goods of that kind. Under this section the serving for value of food or drink to be consumed either on the premises or elsewhere is a sale.

(2) Goods to be merchantable must be at least such as

(a) pass without objection in the trade under the contract description; and

(b) in the case of fungible goods, are of fair average quality within the description; and

(c) are fit for the ordinary purposes for which such goods are used; and

(d) run, within the variations permitted by the agreement, of even kind, quality and quantity within each unit and among all units involved; and

(e) are adequately contained, packaged, and labeled as the agreement may require; and

(f) conform to the promises or affirmations of fact made on the container or label if any.

(3) Unless excluded or modified (Section 2—316) other implied warranties may arise from course of dealing or usage of trade.

Section 2—315. Implied Warranty: Fitness for Particular Purpose

Where the seller at the time of contracting has reason to know any particular purpose for which the goods are required and that the buyer is relying on the seller's skill or judgment to select or furnish suitable goods, there is unless excluded or modified under the next section an implied warranty that the goods shall be fit for such purpose.

Warranties are not immutable. They may be avoided by exclusion or modification as provided in the U.C.C.

Section 2—316. Exclusion or Modification of Warranties

(1) Words or conduct relevant to the creation of an express warranty and words or conduct tending to negate or limit warranty shall be construed wherever reasonable as consistent with each other; but subject to the provisions of this Article on parol or extrinsic evidence (Section 2—202) negation or limitation is inoperative to the extent that such construction is unreasonable.

(2) Subject to subsection (3), to exclude or modify the implied warranty of merchantability or any part of it the language must mention merchantability and in case of a writing must be conspicuous, and to exclude or modify any implied

warranty of fitness the exclusion must be by a writing and conspicuous. Language to exclude all implied warranties of fitness is sufficient if it states, for example, that "There are no warranties which extend beyond the description on the face hereof."

    (3) Not withstanding subsection (2)

        (a) unless the circumstances indicate otherwise, all implied warranties are excluded by expressions like "as is", "with all faults" or other language which in common understanding calls the buyer's attention to the exclusion of warranties and makes plain that there is no implied warranty; and

        (b) when the buyer before entering into the contract has examined the goods or the sample or model as fully as he desired or has refused to examine the goods there is no implied warranty with regard to defects which an examination ought in the circumstances to have revealed to him; and

        (c) an implied warranty can also be excluded or modified by course of dealing or course of performance or usage of trade.

    (4) Remedies for breach of warranty can be limited in accordance with the provisions of this Article on liquidation or limitation of damages and on contractual modification of remedy (Sections 2—718 and 2—719).

Section 3

APPLICATIONS TO PHARMACY

A basic question that can arise in pharmacy practice under breach of warranty is whether the pharmacist was providing a service or selling a product. If there was no sale of goods there can be no breach of warranty. This type of question has been raised where a hospital patient contracted serum hepatitis from blood transfusions. Many courts have held this to be a service and not the sale of a product. In such cases the hospital could not be sued under the doctrine of breach of warranty, and negligence would have to be proved. In other cases it has been held that such transfusions were, indeed, the sale of a product to which liability for breach of implied warranty of fitness could attach, thus alleviating the injured patient from having to prove negligence.

In applying this principle to pharmacy, what happens if a patient does not, based on the advice of his pharmacist, purchase and use prescription medication and his condition worsens or he dies? Since there was no product sold there is probably no cause of action under warranty against the pharmacist. The pharmacist merely provided a service, his professional advice. Suit may, however, be brought against the pharmacist if he negligently performed this service.

Outside of a few examples of what might be considered purely service, in most cases pharmacists' services will entail the sale of a product and warranty law will apply. In fact, there have been a number of warranty cases involving pharmacists and the sale of both prescription and nonprescription products.

A prescription is usually an order for a specific drug or brand of drug in a specific strength and dosage form. If the pharmacist fills the drug exactly as written, has he fulfilled his obligations under the warranty of fitness for use and merchantability? If the produce is an outdated medication, one that exceeds its expiration dating, is the product fit for any use, let alone the specific use for which it was prescribed? If the medication is an injectable liquid, vitamin B_{12} for example, and the vial, upon visual observation, is found to be discolored or to contain a precipitate, is the product fit for the use for which it is sold, *i.e.*, the use for which such products are intended, presumably the indications in the labeling?

Under these situations involving outdated or decomposed medications, they certainly would not be merchantable. The distinction between fitness and merchantability is not always clear where drugs are concerned.

In one case, *Jacobs Pharmacy Co., Inc. v. Gipson,* the pharmacist sold the patient a bottle of Zephiran Concentrate instead of filling the prescription for Zephiran solution. He told the patient the concentrate was the same as her prescription, although it was many times stronger. The patient applied the solution full strength which resulted in severe burns. In a suit based on breach of warranty the pharmacist was found liable for the patient's injuries, even though the package label indicated dilution of the product was necessary.

Unlike the situation involving prescription drugs where the physician selects the drug for a particular use, the sale of OTC medications constitutes an area in which the pharmacist may be responsible for providing a drug that is fit for a particular use as well as being merchantable. This is clearly the case where a patient describes his symptoms to a pharmacist and asks what he should take. The patient is clearly relying on the pharmacist's knowledge and judgment. Under these circumstances, if the pharmacist recommends a certain medication, there is little doubt that a warranty of fitness for the condition described will attach to such a sale.

What happens if a patient does not request the pharmacist's recommendation but orders an OTC medication by trade name? The general rule is that where a product is purchased by its trade name the purchaser is not relying on the seller's judgment and recommendation, and the warranty of fitness is not, therefore, applicable. There are exceptions, however, where, for example, the patient describes his symptoms and the trade name of a product is used for convenience of description.

The trade name exception does not apply to the warranty of merchantability.

There have also been warranty cases against pharmacists where non-drug products have caused injury. These cases have involved cosmetic bleach creams, *Phillips v. Whelan Drug Co., Inc.;* lipstick, *Reynolds v. Sun Ray Drug Co.;* coffee pot, *McCabe v. Liggett Drug Co.,* and hair waving lotion, *Corneliuson v. Arthur Drug Stores, Inc.* and *Rexall Drug Co. v. Nihill.*

As might be expected, pharmacists do not always lose the law suits in which they have been charged. In *McLeod v. W.S. Merrell Co.,* the community pharmacist was not liable for breach of warranty for harmful side-effects since he dispensed the "MER/29" in the original sealed packets supplied by the manufacturer. In *Foley v. Weaver Drug, Co.,* the purchaser of a shattering bottle of diet pills lost a suit against the drug store for injuries. Even a hospital patient was unsuccessful in suing a hospital, in *Shivers v. Good Shepherd Hospital, Inc.,* for injuries sustained from use of a bacterially contaminated intravenous injection of an anticoagulant.

Section 4
STRICT LIABILITY

Strict liability is a legal hybrid. In some cases it is based upon tort law, in others it is derived from principles of warranty. The strict liability doctrine extends the liability of manufacturers and sellers of goods beyond those to whom the products are sold. Protection extends to members of the household of the purchaser and other consumers. In addition, it eliminates the need to prove negligence. A product may have been made with all the care in the world but is still dangerous to the user or consumer. *The Restatement of Torts, Second,* expresses the principle as follows:

§402A. Special Liability of Seller of Product for Physician Harm to User or Consumer

(1) One who sells any product in a defective condition unreasonably dangerous to the user or consumer or to his property is subject to liability for physical harm thereby caused to the ultimate user or consumer, or to his property, if

   (a) the seller is engaged in the business of selling such a product, and

   (b) it is expected to and does reach the user or consumer without substantial change in the condition in which it is sold.

(2) The rule stated in Subsection (1) applies although

   (a) the seller has exercised all possible care in the preparation and sale of his product, and

(b) the user or consumer has not bought the product from or entered into any contractual relation with the seller.

Caveat:

The Institute expresses no opinion as to whether the rules stated in this Section may not apply
(1) to harm to persons other than users or consumers;
(2) to the seller of a product expected to be processed or otherwise substantially changed before it reaches the user or consumer; or
(3) to the seller of a component part of a product to be assembled.

All that is necessary to make a case in strict tort liability is to show that there was an inherent defect in the product and that use of the product caused harm. Drugs can be inherently dangerous because many are potent pharmacologic agents with serious toxic or side effects and allergic reactions.

As such it is necessary to provide proper directions and warnings. Failure to provide proper warnings can in fact make the use of a drug dangerous. If, for example, a product should be skin-tested for allergic reaction, the product's labeling should contain such instructions. Failure to do so can result in liability.

Sometimes a question arises as to who is liable under the strict liability doctrine. Is the manufacturer liable or is it the retailer? In this case is it the pharmacist or the prescribing physician? Each case may have a different outcome.

SELECTED REFERENCES

PART I

Accreditation Manual for Hospitals, Joint Commission on Accreditation of Hospitals (1971).

"American Society of Hospital Pharmacists Product Selection Survey," *Am. J. Hosp. Pharm.* 29:506 (1972).

Angorn, "The Florida Institutional Pharmacy Law," *Am. J. Hosp. Pharm.* 29:970-72 (1972).

"APhA-ASIM Statement on Prescription Writing and Prescription Labeling," *J. Am. Pharm. Ass'n.,* NS14:654 (Dec. 1974).

"ASHP Workshop on Subprofessional Personnel in Hospital Pharmacy," *Am. J. Hosp. Pharm.* 26:224-32 (1969).

Atkinson, J., "A Model Pharmacy Act," *The Louisiana Pharmacist,* 23:15 (Nov. 1974).

Barker and Valentino, "On a Political and Legal Foundation for Clinical Pharmacy Practice," *J. Am. Pharm. Ass'n.,* NS12:202 (1972).

Berstein, A.H., "Professional Society Membership," *Hospitals, JAHA,* 45:110 (March 1, 1971).

Braverman, "Subprofessionals in Pharmacy," *J. Am. Pharm. Ass'n,* NS9:273 (1969).

Brodie, D.C. and Graber, J.B., *Report of the Task Force on the Pharmacist's Clinical Role,* National Center for Health Services Research & Development, U.S. DHEW (May 1971); also published in *J. Am. Pharm. Ass'n.* NS11:482 (1971).

Covington and Pfeiffer, "The Pharmacist-Acquired Medication History," *Am. J. Hosp. Pharm.* 29:692, 695 (1972).

Davis, "Patient Profile Draws The Whole Picture," *Hospitals, JAHA,* 45:110 (Sept. 1971).

DeMarco, C.T., "Health Maintenance Organization Act of 1973," *Am. J. Hosp. Pharm.* 31:402 (April 1974).

233

DeMarco, C.T., "The Legal Basis for Clinical Pharmacy Practice" *Am. J. Hosp. Pharm.* 30:1067 (Nov. 1973).

DeMarco, C.T., "PSROs and Pharmacy," *Am. J. Hosp. Pharm.* 30:723 (Aug. 1973).

Drug Bioequivalence, Report of the Office of Technical Assessments, U.S. Congress (July 15, 1974).

Fernsler, J.P., "The Use of Professionals in the Practice of Pharmacy 1970," *Proceedings,* National Association of Boards of Pharmacy, 266 (1970).

Final Report of Task Force on Prescription Drugs, Office of the Secretary, U.S. DHEW (Feb. 7, 1969).

Fink, J.L. III, "Some Legal Aspects of the Hospital Formulary System," *Am. J. Hosp. Pharm.,* 31:86 (Jan. 1974).

Francke and Whitney, *Perspectives in Clinical Pharmacy,* Drug Intelligence Publications (1972).

Health Maintenance Organization Act of 1973, P.L. 93-222, S. Rep. No. 93-239 (April 27, 1973); H.R. Rep. No. 93-451 (Aug. 10, 1973); S. Conf. Rep. No. 93-621 (Dec. 13, 1973); H.R. Conf. Rep. No. 03-714 (Dec. 12, 1973).

Knoben, J. E., "PSROs and Pharmacy: An Update," *Hospital Formulary Management* (1975).

Kelly, White and Miller, *An Effective Ongoing Drug Utilization Program in a General Community Hospital,* American Society of Hospital Pharmacists (1975).

Latiolais, "A Pharmacy Coordinated Unit Dose Dispensing and Drug Administration System," *Am. J. Hosp. Pharm.* 27:886 (Nov. 1970).

Livingston, B.P., "Legal Opinion Letter," *Am. J. Hosp. Pharm.* 17:607 (1960).

Martin and Cook, *Remington's Practice of Pharmacy,* 1380-88 (11th ed. 1956).

Medical Malpractice, Report of the Secretary's Commission on Medical Malpractice, DHEW Pub. No. (OS) 73-88 (Jan. 16, 1973).

Nudelman, P., "The New Patient Information Regulation," *Washington Pharmacist,* 9 (Nov.-Dec. 1973).

Peer Review Manual, American Medical Association (1973).

Pharmaceutical Benefits Under State Medical Assistance Programs, National Pharmaceutical Council, Inc. (1970).

The Pharmacist's Role in Product Selection, American Pharmaceutical Association (March 1971).

"Practitioner's and Subprofessional's Roles in Pharmacy" *J. Am. Pharm. Ass'n.* NS9:415-23 (1969).

"Primer on Medicines," *FDA Consumer,* Food and Drug Administration, (Dec.-Jan. 1973-1974).

"Report of Committee on Model for a Modern Pharmacy Law," *J. Am. Pharm. Ass'n.* 11:566 (July 1922).

Report of the Task Force on Specialties in Pharmacy, American Pharmaceutical Association (April 18, 1974).

The Rx Legend, An FDA Manual for Pharmacists, FDA Pub. No. 12 (May 1971).

Ryan, M., "ACA Developing Minimum Practice Standards," *The Voice of the Pharmacist,* 17:1 (Nov. 15, 1974).

Sesti, L.M., "Understanding H.B. 4145," *Michigan Pharmacist,* 7 (Aug. 1974).

Social Security Amendments of 1972, P.L. 92-603, H.R. Rep. No. 92-231 (June 22, 1971); S. Rep. No. 92-1230 (Oct. 5, 6, 17, 1972); H.R. Conf. Rep. No. 92-1605 (Oct. 17, 1972).

"Statement of Guiding Principle on the Operation of the Hospital Formulary System," *Am. J. Hosp. Pharm.* 21:40 (1964).

"Statement of the Pharmacy and Therapeutics Committee," *Am. J. Hosp. Pharm.* 16:122 (1959).

Statement on Hospital Drug Control Systems, American Society of Hospital Pharmacists (1975).

"Statement on Supportive Personnel in Hospital Pharmacy," *Am. J. Hosp. Pharm.* 28:516 (1971).

Steeves, R.F., Vitale, C.L., and Wolff, N.J., *Establishment and Maintenance of Membership Standards in Professional Societies of Pharmacists,* American Pharmaceutical Association (March 1967).

Survey of Pharmacy Laws, National Association of Boards of Pharmacy (July 1, 1973).

Utilization Review, A Handbook for the Medical Staff, American Medical Association (1968).

Willig, S.H., "Ethical and Legal Implications of Drug Substitution," *Food, Drug & Cosmetic Law J.* 284 (June, 1968).

PART II

Anderson, Betty Jane, "May Pharmacist Fill Prescription of Physician Licensed in Another State?" *J.A.M.A.* 227:215 (Jan. 14, 1974).

Anon., "Use of Drugs for Unapproved Indications," *Hospital Formulary Management* 9:16 (Jan. 1974).

Anon., "Use of Drugs for Unapproved Indications: Your Legal Responsibility," *FDA Drug Bulletin* (October 1972).

Archambault, G.F., "Investigational Drugs and the Law," *Cleveland-Marshall L. Rev.* 16:487 (Sept. 1967).

Archambault, G.F., "Investigational Drugs—Legal Implications of Their Use," *Hospital Formulary Management* (Oct. 1974).

Barnett, F.J., "Liability for Adverse Drug Reactions: The Role of the Package Insert," *Journal of Legal Medicine* (March-April 1973).

A Brief Legislative History of the Food, Drug, and Cosmetic Act, Staff of the House of Representatives Commission on Interstate and Foreign Commerce, 93d Cong., 2d Sess. Comm. Print. No. 14 (1974).

Christopher, Thomas W. and Goodrich, William W., *Cases and Materials on Food and Drug Law,* 2nd ed., Commerce Clearing House (1973).

D'Arco and Williams, "The Poison Prevention Packaging Act and Child Resistant Containers," *J. Am. Pharm. Ass'n.* NS12:380 (1972).

"Developments in the Law: The Federal, Food, Drug and Cosmetic Act," *Harvard L. Rev.* 67:632 (1954).

Dowling, Harry F., *Medicines for Man: The Development, Regulation and Use of Prescription Drugs,* Knopf (1970).

"Drug Amendments of 1962-Generic Name Prescribing: Drug Price Panacea?" *Stanford L. Rev.* 16:649 (1964).

"Drug Efficacy and the 1962 Drug Amendments," *Georgetown L.J.* 60:185 (1971).

"The Food and Drug Administration: Law, Science, and Politics in the Evaluation and Control of New Drug Technology," *Northwestern Univ. L. Rev.* 67:858 (1973).

Forte, Wesley E., "The GMP Regulations and the Proper Scope of FDA Rulemaking Authority," *Georgetown L. J.* 56:688 (1968).

"Guidelines for IND's," *FDA Papers* (June 1971).

Guidelines for Organization and Operation of an Institutional Review Committee, *Grants Administration Manual,* Ch. 1-40, U.S. DHEW (1975).

Hotaling, William H., "The Investigational Drug Procedure," *Hospital Formulary Management* (Oct. 1973).

Institutional Guide to DHEW Policy on Protection of Human Subjects, U.S. DHEW.

"Investigational Exemption Procedures for New Drugs," *J.A.M.A.* 213:1902 (1970).

Mintz, Morton, *By Prescription Only,* Beacon Press (1967).

Mintz, Morton, *The Pill: An Alarming Report,* Beacon Press (1969).

"The New Food, Drug, and Cosmetic Legislation," *Law and Contemporary Problems,* 6:1, Duke Univ. School of Law (Winter 1939).

"Nonapproved Uses of F.D.A. Approved Drugs," *J.A.M.A.* 211:1705 (1970).

Patterson, Forrest T., "Dispensing FDA Non-Approved Drugs," *J. Am. Pharm. Ass'n.* NS8:466 (Sept. 1968).

Patterson, Forrest T., "Dispensing for FDA Non-Approved Uses," *J. Am. Pharm. Ass'n.* NS8:422 (Aug. 1968).

Patterson, Forrest T., "Dispensing Investigational Drugs," *J. Am. Pharm. Ass'n.* NS8:526 (Oct. 1968).

"Prescription of Drugs Contrary to Package-Insert Recommendations," *J.A.M.A.* 220:1506 (1972).

Sherman, Max, "A Pharmacist Examines the Package Insert," *J. Am. Pharm. Ass'n.* NS10:458 (Aug. 1970).

The Status of the Poison Prevention Packaging Act as it Applies to Pharmacists, Food and Drug Administration, Bureau of Product Safety (Jan. 14, 1972).

Summer, Fred A., "Federal Regulations Over Clinical Use of Investigational New Drugs Versus Preservation of the Physician-Patient Relationship," *Scalpel & Quill* (Sept. 1973).

Temple, R., "Legal Implications of the Package Insert," *Medical Clinics of North America* 58:1151 (Sept. 1974).

Wetheimer, "Mail Order Rxs are Here to Stay," *American Drug Merchandising* 167:17 (June 15, 1973).

Willig, S.H., "The Influence of the Federal Food, Drug, and Cosmetic Act on the Pharmacists' Current Good Dispensing Practice," *Food, Drug, and Cosmetic Law. J.* 28:636 (Oct. 1973).

Woods, "Pharmacy is Not a Mail-Order Profession," *American Drug Merchandising* 167:17 (June 15, 1973).

PART III

Anderson, R.D. et al., "A.S.H.P. Guidelines for Institutional Use of Controlled Substances," *Am. J. Hosp. Pharm.* 31:582 (June 1974).

Anon., "How Pharmacists Try to Protect Themselves Against Drug Related Crimes, *Pharmacy Times* 40:31 (1974).

Anon., "How to Guard Against Improper, Forged or Altered Rxs," *Pharmacy Times* 39:72 (1973).

Anon., "Twenty Ways to Improve Security in Your Pharmacy," *Pharmacy Times* 39:78 (1973).

The Controlled Substances Act of 1970 . . . A BNDD Manual for the Pharmacist, Drug Enforcement Administration.

DeMarco, C.T., "Comprehensive Drug Abuse Prevention and Control Act of 1970," *Am. J. Hosp. Pharm.* 28:290 (April 1971).

DeMarco, C.T., "State Narcotic and Drug Abuse Laws: A Combination of Ingredients," *Am. J. Hosp. Pharm.* 28:707 (Sept. 1971).

DeMarco and White, "New Methadone Regulations," *Am. J. Hosp. Pharm.* 20:168 (Feb. 1973).

Drug Use in America: Problem in Perspective, Second Report of the National Commission on Marihuana and Drug Abuse, U.S. Government Printing Office (March 1972).

Durrin, "Burglaries and Robberies in Drug Stores, A Federal Overview," *NACDS Security Conference* (Feb. 28, 1975).

Eldridge, W.B., *Narcotics and the Law,* University of Chicago Press (1967).

Fisher, "A Community Approach to Pharmacy Holdups," *Drug Enforcement* 1:6 (1974).

H.R. Rep. No. 91-1444, 91st Cong., 2d Sess. (1970); S. Rep. No. 91-613, 91st Cong., 2d Sess. (1970); Conf. Rep. No. 91-1903, 91st Cong., 2d Sess. (1970).

Lash, R.C., "Our New Federal Narcotic and Drug Laws," *Case and Comment* (Sept.-Oct. 1971).

Marihuana: A Signal of Misunderstandings, First Report of the National Commission on Marihuana and Drug Abuse, U.S. Government Printing Office (March 22, 1972).

Narcotic Don'ts for the Pharmacist, Bureau of Narcotics and Dangerous Drugs.

Patterson, F.T., "Defending Against the Illegal Prescription Order," *J. Am. Pharm. Ass'n.* NS8:147 (March 1968).

Petruconis, S.K., "How to Fit Schedule II into the System," *Hospitals, JAHA,* 48:99 (Aug. 1, 1974).

Practitioners Informational Outline of the Controlled Substances Act of 1970, Bureau of Narcotics and Dangerous Drugs.

Report of the Task Force on Narcotics and Drug Abuse, President's Commission on Law Enforcement and Administration of Justice, U.S. Government Printing Office (1967).

PART IV

Anon., "Expulsion From Medical Society," (Parts 1, 2 and 3), *J.A.M.A.* 229:1502, 1656, 1801 (1974).

Arthur, Wm. R., *The Law of Drugs and Druggists,* West Publishing Company (4th ed. 1955).

Atkinson, J.F., "Fraudulent Claims for Third Party Payments Under Medicaid," *Oregon Pharmacist* (Sept. 1969).

Braucher and Sutherland, *Commercial Transactions,* The Foundation Press, Inc. (1964).

Frumer and Friedman, *Products Liability,* Matthew Bender (1975).

Goodman and Rhingold, *Drug Liability: A Lawyer's Drug Handbook,* (Practicing Law Institute) Litigation Sourcebook Series No. 2 (1970).

Hassan, W.E., *Law for the Pharmacy Student,* Lea and Febiger (1971).

Kerr, "Professional Liability of the Pharmacist," *Michigan Pharmacist* (March 1972).

Kintner, E.W., *Antitrust Primer for Retail Druggist,* National Association of Retail Druggists, Undated.

Oppenheim, S.C., "Antitrust Implications of the Virginia Blue Cross Decision," Unpublished Address, National Pharmacy Insurance Council (Nov. 30, 1970).

Problems of Third Party Prepaid Prescription Programs, Permanent Select Committee on Small Business, 93d Cong., 1st Sess., H. Rep. No. 93-730 (1973).

Prosser, *Law of Torts,* West Publishing Company (4th ed. 1971).

Restatement (Second), Torts, American Law Institute (1965).

Steeves, R.F., *A Pharmacist's Guide to Liability,* Medical Economics (Drug Topics) (1974).

Tucker, Wm., "Dealing with Attorneys in Conduct and Control of Board Hearings in Disciplinary Adjudications," Unpublished Speech, 69th NABP Annual Convention (May 1, 1973).

TABLE OF CASES

U

V

W

This Table of Cases includes cases that are not mentioned in the text but which are incorporated in the listing as an aid to research because of their relevance to pharmacy practice.

ATTORNEY GENERALS' OPINIONS

APPENDIX A

UNIFORM PROFESSIONAL CONTINUING EDUCATION ACT

I. LEGISLATIVE FINDINGS AND DECLARATIONS
The legislature makes the following findings and declarations:

A. The practice of the profession of pharmacy is directly related to the public health and welfare of the citizens of the state of _____and is subject to regulation and control in the public interest.

B. Because of the continuous introduction of new medicinal agents and the changing concepts of the delivery of health-care services in the practice of pharmacy at both the institutional and community levels, it is essential that a pharmacist undertake a continuing-education program in order to maintain his professional competency and improve his professional skills.

C. To assure the continued competency of the pharmacist and to maintain uniform qualifications for registration (licensure) in the profession for the protection of the health and welfare of its citizens, the legislature of the state of_____deems it in the public interest to adopt a continuing-professional-education program.

D. This act shall be liberally construed in order to carry out its stated objects and purposes.

II. TITLE
This act shall be called the "Uniform Pharmacy Continuing Professional Education Act of the State of_____;"

III. DEFINITIONS
As used in this subchapter,

A. The term "board" or "board of pharmacy" means the State Board of Pharmacy (of the Department of_____).

B. The term "continuing professional education" means professional, pharmaceutical postgraduate education in the general areas of the socio-economic and legal aspects of health care; the properties and actions of drugs and dosage forms; and the etiology, characteristics and therapeutics of the disease state.

C. The term "continuing-education unit" means the unit of measurement of credits for continuing-education courses and programs.

D. The term "pharmacist" means those individuals qualified and registered (licensed) to practice the profession of pharmacy.

E. The term "accredited program" means those seminars, classes, meetings, work projects and other educational programs in pharmacy approved by the board for purposes of continuing professional education.

IV. REQUIRED CONTINUING PROFESSIONAL EDUCATION

Commencing_____, 19____, no annual renewal certificate (license) shall issue to a pharmacist pursuant to chapter_____, section_____, and no initial registration (licensure) by reciprocity pursuant to chapter_____, section_____, of the (Enter appropriate name of applicable act), until such pharmacist shall have submitted proof to the board of the receipt of the required number of continuing-education units obtained through the satisfactory completion of an accredited program of continuing professional education during the previous year.

IV. A. CONTINUING PROFESSIONAL EDUCATION
(IN LIEU OF IV.)

Commencing_____, 19____, no annual renewal certificate (license) shall issue to a pharmacist pursuant to chapter_____, section_____, of the (Enter appropriate name of applicable act), until such pharmacist shall have submitted proof to the board of the required number of continuing-education units obtained through the satisfactory completion of an accredited program of continuing professional education during the previous year.

V. RULES AND REGULATIONS

The board shall adopt rules and regulations necessary to carry out the stated objects and purposes and enforce the provisions of this act, which shall include the methods of determining accredited programs, the number of hours of continuing professional education necessary to constitute a continuing-education unit, the number of units required annually of each pharmacist and such other rules and regulations consistent with this act as the board shall determine.

VI. HARDSHIP
ALTERNATIVE CONTINUING
PROFESSIONAL EDUCATION PROGRAMS

The board may grant to a pharmacist who meets all the necessary requirements for registration (licensure), except the continuing professional education requirements, alternate methods of obtaining continuing education units through home-study courses or other such programs, examination or the like, substantially equivalent in scope and content to the continuing-professional-education programs regularly scheduled; provided, however, only those pharmacists shall be eligible for the alternative programs who, upon written application to the board and for good cause shown, demonstrate that they are unable to attend a sufficient number of regularly scheduled continuing-professional-education programs to obtain the requisite number of continuing-education units for registration (licensure). This section and all rules and regulations promulgated hereunder shall be uniformly applied by the board.

VII. SEVERABILITY

If any clause, sentence, paragraph or section of this act shall, for any reason, be adjudged by any court of competent jurisdiction to be unconstitutional and invalid, such judgment shall not affect, repeal or invalidate the remainder thereof but shall be confined in its operation to the clause, sentence, paragraph or section thereof so found unconstitutional and invalid.

APPENDIX B

STATE-BY-STATE COMPILATION OF LAWS

Alabama

Adulteration of food and drugs
ALA. CODE ANN. tit. 2, §§ 303 to 315 (1958, *as amended* Supp. 1971).
Uniform Controlled Substances Act
ALA. CODE ANN. tit. 22, §§ 258(25) to 258(60) (Supp. 1971).
Pharmacy
ALA. CODE ANN. tit. 46, §§ 257 (a1) to 257(a32) (Supp. 1971).

Alaska

Adulteration of food, drugs, and cosmetics
ALASKA STAT. §§ 17.20.010 to 17.20.380 (1962, *as amended* Supp. 1970).
Uniform Narcotic Drug Act
ALASKA STAT. §§ 17.10.010 to 17.10.240 (1962, *as amended* Supp. 1970).
Dangerous drugs
ALASKA STAT. §§ 17.12.010 to 17.12.240 (1962, *as amended* Supp. 1970).
Pharmacy
ALASKA STAT. §§ 08.80.010 to 08.80.490 (1962, *as amended* Supp. 1970).

Arizona

Uniform Narcotic Drug Act
ARIZ. REV. STAT. ANN. §§ 36-1001 to 36-1024 (1956, *as amended* Supp. 1971).
Dangerous Drugs
ARIZ. REV. STAT. ANN. §§ 36-1061 to 36-1062 (1956, *as amended* Supp. 1971).
Poisons
ARIZ. REV. STAT. ANN. §§ 36-1101 to 36-1105 (1956).
Pharmacy
ARIZ. REV. STAT. ANN. §§ 32-1901 to 32-1996 (1956, *as amended* Supp. 1971).

Arkansas

Uniform Narcotic Drug Act
ARK. STAT. ANN. §§ 82-1001 to 82-1068 (1960, *as amended* Supp. 1971).
Uniform Controlled Substances Act
ARK. STAT. ANN. §§ 82-2601 to 82-2638 (Supp. 1971).

Dangerous Drugs
ARK. STAT. ANN. §§ 82-2101 to 82-2117 (Supp. 1971).

Adulteration of food, drugs and cosmetics
ARK. STAT. ANN. §§ 72-1001 to 72-1046 (1960, *as amended* Supp. 1971).

California

Narcotics and dangerous drugs
CAL. HEALTH & SAFETY CODE §§ 11000 to 11925 (West 1964, *as amended* Supp. 1972).
CAL. BUS. & PROF. CODE §§ 4211 to 4242 (West 1962, *as amended* Supp. 1972).

Adulteration of food, drugs, and cosmetics
CAL. HEALTH & SAFETY CODE §§ 26000 to 26851 (West Supp. 1972).

Hazardous substances labeling
CAL. HEALTH & SAFETY CODE §§ 28740 to 28792 (West 1967, *as amended* Supp. 1972).

Pharmacy
CAL. BUS. & PROF. CODE §§ 4000 to 4416 (West 1962, *as amended* Supp. 1972).

Colorado

Adulteration of food and drugs
COLO. REV. STAT. ANN. §§ 66-20-1 to 66-20-24 (1963).

Narcotic drugs
COLO. REV. STAT. ANN. §§ 48-5-1 to 48-5-21 (1963).

Pharmacy
COLO. REV. STAT. ANN. §§ 48-1-1 to 48-4-4, 48-7-1 to 48-7-9 (1963).

Connecticut

Adulteration of food, drugs, and cosmetics
CONN. GEN. STAT. ANN. §§ 19-211 to 19-239 (1969, *as amended* Supp. 1972).

Narcotic drugs
CONN. GEN. STAT. ANN. §§ 19-443 to 19-504 (1969, *as amended* Supp. 1972).

Pharmacy
CONN. GEN. STAT. ANN. §§ 20-163 to 20-185, 19-240 to 19-242 (1969, *as amended* Supp. 1972).

Delaware

Adulteration of food and drugs
DEL. CODE ANN. tit. 16, §§ 3301 to 3322 (1953, *as amended* Supp. 1970).

Narcotics and dangerous drugs
DEL. CODE ANN. tit. 16, §§ 4701 to 4732 (1953, *as amended* Supp. 1970).

Depressants and stimulants
DEL. CODE ANN. tit. 16, §§ 4901 to 4912 (Supp. 1970).

Pharmacy
DEL. CODE ANN. tit. 24, §§ 2501 to 2589 (1953, *as amended* Supp. 1970).

District of Columbia

Adulteration of food and drugs
D.C. CODE ANN. §§ 33-104 to 33-111 (1967, *as amended* Supp. 1972).

Narcotics
D.C. CODE ANN. §§ 33-401 to 33-425 (1967, *as amended* Supp. 1972).

Dangerous drugs
D.C. CODE ANN. §§ 33-701 to 33-712 (1967, *as amended* Supp. 1972).

Pharmacy
D.C. CODE ANN. §§ 2-601 to 2-617 (1967, *as amended* Supp. 1972).

Florida

Adulteration of food, drugs and cosmetics
FLA. STAT. ANN. §§ 500.01 to 500.47 (1972).

Uniform Narcotic Drug Law
FLA. STAT. ANN. §§ 398.01 to 398.24 (1960, *as amended* Supp. 1972).

Poisons; adulterated drugs
FLA. STAT. ANN. §§ 859.01 to 859.08 (1965, *as amended* Supp. 1972).

Pharmacy
FLA. STAT. ANN. §§ 465.011 to 465.24 (1965, *as amended* Supp. 1972).

Georgia

Adulteration of food and drugs
GA. CODE ANN. §§ 101 to 9937 (1957, *as amended* Supp. 1971).

Uniform Narcotic Drug Act
GA. CODE ANN. §§ 801 to 822 (Supp. 1971).

Pharmacy
GA. CODE ANN. §§ 101 to 9917 (Supp. 1971).

Hawaii

Adulteration of food, drugs and cosmetics
HAWAII REV. STAT. §§ 51-1 to 51-30 (1955, *as amended* Supp. 1963).

Poisons
HAWAII REV. STAT. §§ 53-1 to 53-6 (1955, *as amended* Supp. 1963).

Narcotics
HAWAII REV. STAT. §§ 52-1 to 52-39 (1955, *as amended* Supp. 1963).

Pharmacy
HAWAII REV. STAT. §§ 71-1 to 71-20 (1955, *as amended* Supp. 1963).

Idaho

Adulteration of food, drugs and cosmetics
IDAHO CODE §§ 113 to 134 (1961).

Narcotics
IDAHO CODE §§ 3101 to 3105 (Supp. 1971).

Uniform Controlled Substances Act
IDAHO CODE §§ 2701 to 2751 (Supp. 1971).

Pharmacy
IDAHO CODE §§ 2201 to 2215 (1961, *as amended* Supp. 1971).
IDAHO CODE §§ 1701 to 1726 (1957, *as amended* Supp. 1971).

Illinois

Adulteration of food, drugs and cosmetics
ILL. ANN. STAT. ch. 56 1/2, §§ 501 to 526 (Smith-Hurd Supp. 1972).

Controlled Substances Act
ILL. ANN. STAT. ch. 56 1/2, §§ 1100 to 1602 (Smith-Hurd Supp. 1972).

Pharmacy
ILL. ANN. STAT. ch. 91, §§ 55.1 to 55.59 (Smith-Hurd 1966, *as amended* Supp. 1972).

Indiana

Adulteration of food, drugs and cosmetics
IND. ANN. STAT. §§ 35-3101 to 35-3139 (1969, *as amended* Supp. 1972).

Uniform Narcotic Drug Act
IND. ANN. STAT. §§ 10-3519 to 10-3557 (1956, *as amended* Supp. 1972).

Pharmacy
IND. ANN. STAT. §§ 63-1101 to 63-1125 (1961, *as amended* Supp. 1972).

Iowa

Adulteration and labeling of drugs
IOWA CODE ANN. §§ 203.1 to 203.9 (1969, *as amended* Supp. 1973).

Drugs and cosmetics
IOWA CODE ANN. §§ 203A.1 to 203A.19 (1969, *as amended* Supp. 1973).

Uniform Controlled Substances Act
IOWA CODE ANN. §§ 204.101 to 204.602 (Supp. 1973).

Pharmacy
IOWA CODE ANN. §§ 155.1 to 155.35 (1972, *as amended* Supp. 1973).

Kansas

Adulteration of food, drugs and cosmetics
KAN. STAT. ANN. §§ 65-619 to 65-680 (1964, *as amended* Supp. 1970).

Uniform Narcotic Drug Act
KAN. STAT. ANN. §§ 65-2501 to 65-2522 (1964, *as amended* Supp. 1970).

Dangerous drugs
KAN. STAT. ANN. §§ 65-2601 to 65-2607 (1964, *as amended* Supp. 1970).

Pharmacy
KAN. STAT. ANN. §§ 65-1624 to 65-1649 (1964, *as amended* Supp. 1970).

Kentucky

Adulteration of food, drugs and cosmetics
KY. REV. STAT. §§ 217.005 to 217.215 (Supp. 1972).

Labeling hazardous substances
KY. REV. STAT. §§ 217.650 to 217.710 (1972).

Controlled Substances Act
KY. REV. STAT. §§ 218A.010 to 218A.990 (Supp. 1972).

Pharmacy
KY. REV. STAT. §§ 315.010 to 315.991 (1972).

Labeling drugs by generic name
KY. REV. STAT. §§ 217.814 to 217.826 (Supp. 1972).

Louisiana

Adulteration of food and drugs
LA. REV. STAT. §§ 40:601 to 40:642 (1965).

Narcotics
LA. REV. STAT. §§ 40:1001 to 40:1056 (1965, *as amended* Supp. 1972).

Uniform Controlled Dangerous Substances Law
LA. REV. STAT. §§ 40:961 to 40:990 (Supp. 1972).

Pharmacy
LA. REV. STAT. §§ 37:1171 to 37:1229 (1964, *as amended* Supp. 1972).

Maine

Drugs
ME. REV. STAT. ANN. tit. 22, §§ 2201 to 2215 (1965, *as amended* Supp. 1972).

Narcotics
ME. REV. STAT. ANN. tit. 22, §§ 2361 to 2380 (1965, *as amended* Supp. 1972).

Adulterated or misbranded goods
ME. REV. STAT. ANN. tit. 7, §§ 481 to 489 (1964, *as amended* Supp. 1972).

Hazardous Substances Labeling Act
ME. REV. STAT. ANN. tit. 7, §§ 501 to 513 (Supp. 1972).

Pharmacy
ME. REV. STAT. ANN. tit. 32, §§ 2801 to 2903 (1965, *as amended* Supp. 1972).

Maryland

Adulteration of food, drugs and cosmetics
MD. ANN. CODE art. 43, §§ 187 to 191E (Supp. 1972).

Controlled dangerous substances
MD. ANN. CODE art. 27, §§ 276 to 302 (1971, *as amended* Supp. 1972).

Barbitol and hypnotic drugs
MD. ANN. CODE art. 43, §§ 284 to 289 (1971).

Poison
MD. ANN. CODE art. 43, §§ 274 to 283 (1971).

Pharmacy
MD. ANN. CODE art. 43, §§ 249 to 273A (1971, *as amended* Supp. 1972).

Massachusetts

Adulteration of food and drugs
MASS. GEN. LAWS ANN. ch. 94, §§ 186 to 195 (1958, *as amended* Supp. 1972).

Hazardous substances labeling
MASS. GEN. LAWS ANN. ch. 94B, §§ 1 to 21C (Supp. 1972).

Uniform Controlled Substances Act
MASS. GEN. LAWS ANN. ch. 94C, §§ 1 to 47 (Supp. 1972).

Pharmacy
MASS. GEN. LAWS ANN. ch. 112, §§ 12D, 24 to 42A (1971, *as amended*
Supp. 1972); ch. 17, § 13 (Supp. 1972).

Michigan

Adulteration, misbranding of drugs
MICH. COMP. LAWS ANN. §§ 335.1 to 335.10 (1967, *as amended* Supp.
1971).

Narcotics
MICH. COMP. LAWS ANN. §§ 335.51 to 335.78, 335.151 to 335.231 (1967,
as amended Supp. 1971).

Hypnotic drugs
MICH. COMP. LAWS ANN. §§ 335.101 to 335.107 (1967, *as amended*
Supp. 1971).

Pharmacy
MICH. COMP. LAWS ANN. §§ 338.1101 to 338.1130 (1967, *as amended*
Supp. 1970).

Minnesota

Prohibited drugs
MINN. STAT. ANN. §§ 152.01 to 152.20 (1970, *as amended* Supp. 1972).

Pharmacy
MINN. STAT. ANN. §§ 151.01 to 151.40 (1970, *as amended* Supp. 1972).

Mississippi

Adulteration of food and drugs
MISS. CODE ANN. §§ 7107 to 7129 (1953, *as amended* Supp. 1971).

Uniform Controlled Substances Act
MISS. CODE ANN. §§ 6831-51 to 6831-87 (Supp. 1971).

Narcotics
MISS. CODE ANN. §§ 6847, 6848, 6851, 6856, 6857, 6859 (1953).

Pharmacy
MISS. CODE ANN. §§ 8847 to 8877 (1957, *as amended* Supp. 1971).

Missouri

Adulteration of food and drugs
MO. ANN. STAT. §§ 196.010 to 196.180 (1972).

Drugs
  Mo. ANN. STAT. §§ 195.010 to 195.545 (1972).
Pharmacy
  Mo. ANN. STAT. §§ 338.010 to 338.310 (1966, *as amended* Supp. 1972).

Montana

Adulteration of food, drugs and cosmetics
  MONT. REV. CODES ANN. §§ 27-701 to 27-725 (1967, *as amended* Supp. 1971).
Dispensing of drugs by practitioners
  MONT. REV. CODES ANN. §§ 27-901 to 27-906 (Supp. 1971).
Narcotics
  MONT. REV. CODES ANN. §§ 54-101 to 54-138 (1961, *as amended* Supp. 1971).
Pharmacy
  MONT. REV. CODES ANN. §§ 66-1501 to 66-1527 (1970, *as amended* Supp. 1971).

Nebraska

Adulteration of drugs
  NEB. REV. STAT. §§ 71-2401 to 71-2405 (1971).
Narcotics
  NEB. REV. STAT. §§ 28-457 to 28-460 (1965, *as amended* Supp. 1972).
Uniform Controlled Substances Act
  NEB. REV. STAT. §§ 28-4115 to 28-4142 (Supp. 1972).
Poisons
  NEB. REV. STAT. §§ 71-2501 to 71-2512 (1971, *as amended* Supp. 1972).
Pharmacy
  NEB. REV. STAT. §§ 71-1142 to 71-1147.16 (1971, *as amended* Supp. 1972).

Nevada

Adulteration of food, drugs and cosmetics
  NEV. REV. STAT. §§ 585.010 to 585.550 (1971).
Controlled substances
  NEV. REV. STAT. §§ 453.011 to 453.570 (1971).
Pharmacy
  NEV. REV. STAT. §§ 639.001 to 639.310 (1971).

New Hampshire

Adulteration of food and drugs
N.H. REV. STAT. ANN. §§ 146:1 to 146:6 (1964, *as amended* Supp. 1972).

Controlled Drug Act
N.H. REV. STAT. ANN. §§ 318-B:1 to 318-B:30 (Supp. 1972).

Pharmacy
N.H. REV. STAT. ANN. §§ 318:1 to 318:55 (1966, *as amended* Supp. 1972).

New Jersey

Adulteration of food and drugs
N.J. STAT. ANN. §§ 24:1-1 to 24:6D-3 (1940, *as amended* Supp. 1972).

Dangerous Substances Control Law
N.J. STAT. ANN. §§ 24:21-1 to 24:21-45 (Supp. 1972).

Pharmacy
N.J. STAT. ANN. §§ 45:14-1 to 45:14-39 (1963, *as amended* Supp. 1972).

New Mexico

Adulteration of drugs and cosmetics
N.M. STAT. ANN. §§ 54-6-26 to 54-6-51 (Supp. 1971).

Narcotics
N.M. STAT. ANN §§ 54-7-1 to 54-7-50 (1962, *as amended* Supp. 1971).

Pharmacy
N.M. STAT. ANN. §§ 67-9-33 to 67-9-59 (Supp. 1971).

New York

Controlled Substances Act
N.Y. PUB. HEALTH LAW §§ 3300 to 3396 (McKinney Supp. 1972).

Pharmacy
N.Y. EDUC. LAW §§ 6800 to 6825 (McKinney Supp. 1972).

North Carolina

Adulteration of food, drugs and cosmetics
N.C. GEN. STAT. §§ 106-120 to 106-145 (1960).

Controlled Substances Act
N.C. GEN. STAT. §§ 90-86 to 90-113.8 (Supp. 1971).

Pharmacy
N.C. GEN. STAT. §§ 90-53 to 90-85.1 (1965, *as amended* Supp. 1971).

North Dakota

Adulteration of food and drugs
N.D. CENT. CODE §§ 19-02.1-01 to 19-02.1-22 (Supp. 1971).

Uniform Controlled Substances Act
N.D. CENT. CODE §§ 19-03.1-01 to 19-03.1-43 (Supp. 1971).

Labeling hazardous substances
N.D. CENT. CODE §§ 19-21-01 to 19-21-10 (Supp. 1971).

Pharmacy
N.D. CENT. CODE §§ 43-15-01 to 43-15-45 (1960, *as amended* Supp. 1971).

Ohio

Adulteration of food and drugs
OHIO REV. CODE ANN. §§ 3715.01 to 3715.99 (Page 1971, *as amended* Supp. 1971).

Uniform Narcotic Drug Act
OHIO REV. CODE ANN. §§ 3719.01 to 3719.22 (Page 1971, *as amended* Supp. 1971).

Barbiturates
OHIO REV. CODE ANN. §§ 3719.23 to 3719.29 (Page 1971).

Hallucinogens
OHIO REV. CODE ANN. §§ 3719.40 to 3719.99 (Page 1971, *as amended* Supp. 1971).

Poison
OHIO REV. CODE ANN. §§ 3719.30 to 3719.36 (Page 1971).

Labeling hazardous substances
OHIO REV. CODE ANN. §§ 3716.01 to 3716.99 (Page 1971).

Pharmacy
OHIO REV. CODE ANN. §§ 4729.01 to 4729.99 (Page 1954, *as amended* Supp. 1971).

Oklahoma

Adulteration of drugs and cosmetics
OKLA. STAT. ANN. tit. 63, §§ 1-1401 to 1-1414 (1964).

Uniform Controlled Dangerous Substances Act
OKLA. STAT. ANN. tit. 63, §§ 2-101 to 2-610 (Supp. 1972).

Hazardous substances
OKLA. STAT. ANN. tit. 63, §§ 1-1601 to 1-1612 (1964).

Pharmacy
OKLA. STAT. ANN. tit. 59, §§ 353.1 to 353.27 (1971).

Oregon

Uniform Narcotic Drug Act
ORE. REV. STAT. §§ 474.010 to 474.990 (1971).

Narcotics and dangerous drugs
ORE. REV. STAT. §§ 475.010 to 475.990 (1971).

Hazardous substances
ORE. REV. STAT. §§ 689.010 to 689.990 (1971).

Pharmacy
ORE. REV. STAT. §§ 689.010 to 689.990 (1971).

Pennsylvania

Adulteration of drugs and cosmetics
PA. STAT. ANN. tit. 35, §§ 780-1 to 780-30 (1964, *as amended* Supp. 1972).

Dangerous substances
PA. STAT. ANN. tit. 35, §§ 821 to 826, 931 to 933 (1964).

Pharmacy
PA. STAT. ANN. tit. 63, §§ 390-1 to 390-13 (1968).

Rhode Island

Adulteration of food, drugs and cosmetics
R.I. GEN. LAWS ANN. §§ 21-31-1 to 21-31-23 (1968, *as amended* Supp. 1971).

Uniform Narcotic Drug Act
R.I. GEN. LAWS ANN. §§ 21-28-1 to 21-28-68 (1968, *as amended* Supp. 1971).

Barbiturates and hypnotic drugs
R.I. GEN. LAWS ANN. §§ 21-29-1 to 21-29-23 (1968, *as amended* Supp. 1971).

Pharmacy
R.I. GEN. LAWS ANN. §§ 5-19-1 to 5-19-37 (1957, *as amended* Supp. 1971).

South Carolina

Narcotics and controlled substances
S.C. CODE ANN. §§ 32-1510.21 to 32-1510.69 (Supp. 1971).

Pharmacy
S.C. CODE ANN. §§ 56-1301 to 56-1334.7 (1962, *as amended* Supp. 1971).

South Dakota

Adulteration of drugs
S.D. COMP. LAWS ANN. §§ 39-15-1 to 39-15-11 (1969)
Controlled substances
S.D. COMP. LAWS ANN. §§ 39-17-44 to 39-17-155 (Supp. 1971).
Pharmacy
S.D. COMP. LAWS ANN. §§ 36-11-1 to 36-11-66 (1969, *as amended* Supp. 1971).

Tennessee

Adulteration of food, drugs and cosmetics
TENN. CODE ANN. §§ 52-101 to 52-124 (1966, *as amended* Supp. 1972).
Legend drugs
TENN. CODE ANN. §§ 52-1201 to 52-1208 (1966, *as amended* Supp. 1972).
Narcotics
TENN. CODE ANN. §§ 52-1305 to 52-1318 (1966, *as amended* Supp. 1972).
Drug control
TENN. CODE ANN. §§ 52-1404 to 52-1450 (1966, *as amended* Supp. 1972).
Pharmacy
TENN. CODE ANN. §§ 63-1001 to 63-1025 (1955, *as amended* Supp. 1972).

Texas

Adulteration of food and drugs
TEX. REV. CIV. STAT. ANN. art. 4476-5 (1966, *as amended* Supp. 1972).
Drugs, narcotics and poisons
TEX. PENAL CODE ANN. art. 725b to 725e, 726-2 to 726-3, 726d (1961, *as amended* Supp. 1972).
Pharmacy
TEX. REV. CIV. STAT. ANN. art. 454a, 454b (1960, *as amended* Supp. 1972).
TEX. PENAL CODE ANN. art. 755 to 758a (1961).

Utah

Adulteration of food, drugs and cosmetics
UTAH CODE ANN. §§ 4-26-1 to 4-26-22 (Supp. 1967).

Narcotics
UTAH CODE ANN. §§ 58-13a-1 to 58-13a-48 (1963, *as amended* Supp. 1967).

Drug control
UTAH CODE ANN. §§ 58-33-1 to 58-33-8 (Supp. 1967).

Pharmacy
UTAH CODE ANN. §§ 58-12b-1 to 58-12b-3, 58-17-1 to 58-17-27 (1963, *as amended* Supp. 1967).

Vermont

Adulteration of food, drugs and cosmetics
VT. STAT. ANN. tit. 18, §§ 4051 to 4071 (1968, *as amended* Supp. 1972).

Drug control
VT. STAT. ANN. tit. 18, §§ 4201 to 4226 (1968, *as amended* Supp. 1972).

Pharmacy
VT. STAT. ANN. tit. 26, §§ 1891 to 2016 (1967, *as amended* Supp. 1972); tit. 18, §§ 4026 to 4028 (1968).

Virginia

Adulteration of drugs and cosmetics
VA. CODE ANN. §§ 54-524.85 to 54-524.100 (1972).

Drug control
VA. CODE ANN. §§ 54-524.55 to 54-524.84:13, 54-524.101:1 to 54-524.109:8 (1972, *as amended* Supp. 1972).

Pharmacy
VA. CODE ANN. §§ 54-524.1 to 54-524.54 (1972, *as amended* Supp. 1972).

Washington

Adulteration of food, drugs and cosmetics
WASH. REV. CODE ANN. §§ 69.04.001 to 69.04.870 (1962, *as amended* Supp. 1972).

Narcotics
WASH. REV. CODE ANN. §§ 69.33.220, 69.33.300, 69.33.410 to 69.33.440 (1962, *as amended* Supp. 1972).

Poisons and dangerous drugs
WASH. REV. CODE ANN. §§ 69.40.010 to 69.40.065 (1962, *as amended* Supp. 1972).

Uniform Controlled Substances Act
WASH. REV. CODE ANN. §§ 69.50.101 to 69.50.608 (Supp. 1972).
Pharmacy
WASH. REV. CODE ANN. §§ 18.64.001 to 18.64.911 (1961, *as amended*
Supp. 1972).

West Virginia
Adulteration of food and drugs
W. VA. CODE ANN. §§ 16-7-1 to 16-7-11 (1966).
Uniform Controlled Substances Act
W. VA. CODE ANN. §§ 60A-1-101 to 60A-6-605 (Supp. 1972).
Pharmacy
W. VA. CODE ANN. §§ 30-5-1 to 30-5-24 (1971, *as amended* Supp. 1972).

Wisconsin
Narcotics and dangerous substances
WIS. STAT. ANN. §§ 161.001 to 161.45 (1957, *as amended* Supp. 1972).
Pharmacy
WIS. STAT. ANN. §§ 450.01 to 450.18 (1972).

Wyoming
Adulteration of food and drugs
WYO. STAT. ANN. §§ 35-235 to 35-246, 35-254 to 35-262 (1959, *as
amended* Supp. 1971).
Controlled substances
WYO. STAT. ANN. §§ 35-347.1 to 35-347.55 (Supp. 1971).
Pharmacy
WYO. STAT. ANN. §§ 33-304.1 to 33-304.46 (Supp. 1971).

APPENDIX C

SELECTED FEDERAL LAWS, REGULATIONS AND AGENCIES

LAWS

Federal Food, Drug, and Cosmetic Act
21 U.S.C. §§301-392

Controlled Substances Act
Pub. L. No. 91-513, 84 Stat. 1236 (codified in scattered sections of 18, 19, 21, 26, 31, 40, 42, 49 U.S.C.)

Social Security Amendments of 1965 (Medicare and Medicaid)
Pub. L. No. 89-97, 79 Stat. 286 (codified in scattered sections of 18, 26, 42, 45 U.S.C.)

Social Security Amendments of 1972 (Professional Standards Review Organizations)
Pub. L. No. 92-603, 86 Stat. 1329 (codified in scattered sections of 5, 7, 26, 42 U.S.C.)

Health Maintenance Organization Act of 1973
Pub. L. No. 92-222, 87 Stat. 914 (codified in scattered sections of 12, 42, U.S.C.)

Poison Prevention Packaging Act of 1970
Pub. L. No. 91-601, 84 Stat. 1670 (codified in 51 U.S.C. 1471-1476, and scattered sections of 7, 21 U.S.C.)

Alcohol Tax Law
26 U.S.C. §§5214, 5271

Public Health Service Act
42 U.S.C. §§201-300e-14a

Atomic Energy Act of 1954
Pub. L. No. 83-703, 68 Stat. 921, 42 U.S.C. §§2011-2201

Animal Welfare Act of 1970
Pub. L. No. 91-579, 84 Stat. 1560, 7 U.S.C. §§2131-2155

Narcotic Addict Treatment Act of 1974
Pub. L. No. 93-281, 88 Stat. 124, (codified in various sections of 21 U.S.C.)

REGULATIONS

Food and Drug Administration
21 C.F.R. §§1-1230 (1974)

Drug Enforcement Administration
21 C.F.R. §§1301-1316 (1974)

Atomic Energy Commission
10 C.F.R. §§30, 35, 70 and others (1974)

Internal Revenue Service (Alcohol Tax Law)
26 C.F.R. §§213.1-213.176 (1974)

Social Security Administration ((Medicare); Social and Rehabilitation
Service (Medicaid)

Hospitals - 20 C.F.R. §405 (1974)
Skilled Nursing Facilities - 20 C.F.R. §405 (1974)
Intermediate Care Facilities - 45 C.F.R. §§249-250 (1973)
HMOs - 42 C.F.R. §110 (1974)
PSROs - (Fed. Register - Nov. 29, 1974)

Consumer Product Safety Commission (Poison Prevention Packaging Act)
16 C.F.R. §1700 (1974)

AGENCIES

Food and Drug Administration
2600 Fishers Lane
Rockville, Maryland 20852

Drug Enforcement Administration
1405 I Street, N.W.
Washington, D.C. 20537

Social Security Administration
6401 Security Boulevard
Baltimore, Maryland 21235

Internal Revenue Service
111 Constitution Avenue, N.W.
Washington, D.C. 20224

Office of Professional Standards Review
330 Independence Avenue, S.W.
Washington, D.C. 20201

National Institutes of Health
Bethesda, Maryland 20014

Consumer Product Safety Commission
1750 K Street, N.W.
Washington, D.C.

Center for Disease Control
1600 Clifton Road, N.E.
Atlanta, Georgia 30333

Federal Trade Commission
Pennsylvania Avenue at 6th Street, N.W.
Washington, D.C. 20580

Public Health Service
5600 Fishers Lane
Rockville, Maryland 20852

Social and Rehabilitation Service
330 C Street, N.W.
Washington, D.C. 20201

APPENDIX D

SELECTED SECTIONS

FEDERAL FOOD, DRUG, AND COSMETIC ACT, AS AMENDED

CHAPTER I—SHORT TITLE

SECTION 1. This Act may be cited as the Federal Food, Drug, and Cosmetic Act.

CHAPTER II—DEFINITIONS

SEC. 201 [321]. For the purposes of this Act—

(a) (1) The term "State", except as used in the last sentence of section 702(a), means any State or Territory of the United States, the District of Columbia, and the Commonwealth of Puerto Rico.

(2) The term "Territory" means any Territory or possession of the United States, including the District of Columbia, and excluding the Commonwealth of Puerto Rico and the Canal Zone.

(b) The term "interstate commerce" means (1) commerce between any State or Territory and any place outside thereof, and (2) commerce within the District of Columbia or within any other Territory not organized with a legislative body.

(c) The term "Department" means the U.S. Department of Health, Education, and Welfare.

(d) The term "Secretary" means the Secretary of Health, Education, and Welfare.

(e) The term "person" includes individual, partnership, corporation, and association.

(f) The term "food" means (1) articles used for food or drink for man or other animals, (2) chewing gum, and (3) articles used for components of any such article.

NOTE—References in brackets [ ] are to title 21 U.S. Code.

(g) (1) The term "drug" means (A) articles recognized in the official United States Pharmacopeia, official Homeopathic Pharmacopeia of the United States, or official National Formulary, or any supplement to any of them; and (B) articles intended for use in the diagnosis, cure, mitigation, treatment, or prevention of disease in man or other animals; and (C) articles (other than food) intended to affect the structure or any function of the body of man or other animals; and (D) articles intended for use as a component of any articles specified in clause (A), (B), or (C); but does not include devices or their components, parts, or accessories.

(2) The term "counterfeit drug" means a drug which, or the container or labeling of which, without authorization, bears the trademark, trade name, or other identifying mark, imprint, or device, or any likeness thereof, of a drug manufacturer, processor, packer, or distributor other than the person or persons who in fact manufactured, processed, packed, or distributed such drug and which thereby falsely purports or is represented to be the product of, or to have been packed or distributed by, such other drug manufacturer, processor, packer, or distributor.

(h) The term "device" (except when used in paragraph (n) of this section and in sections 301(i), 403(f), 502(c), and 602(c)) means instruments, apparatus, and contrivances, including their components, parts, and accessories, intended (1) for use in the diagnosis, cure, mitigation, treatment, or prevention of disease in man or other animals; or (2) to affect the structure or any function of the body of man or other animals.

(i) The term "cosmetic" means (1) articles intended to be rubbed, poured, sprinkled, or sprayed on, introduced into, or otherwise applied to the human body or any part thereof for cleansing, beautifying, promoting attractiveness, or altering the appearance, and (2) articles intended for use as a component of any such articles; except that such term shall not include soap.

(j) The term "official compendium" means the official United States Pharmacopeia, official Homeopathic Pharmacopeia of the United States, official National Formulary, or any supplement to any of them.

(k) The term "label" means a display of written, printed, or graphic matter upon the immediate container of any article; and a requirement made by or under authority of this Act that any word, statement, or other information appear on the label shall not be considered to be complied with unless such word, statement, or other information also appears on the outside container or wrapper, if any there be, of the retail package of such article, or is easily legible through the outside container or wrapper.

(1) The term "immediate container" does not include package liners.

(m) The term "labeling" means all labels and other written, printed, or graphic matter (1) upon any article or any of its containers or wrappers, or (2) accompanying such article.

(n) If an article is alleged to be misbranded because the labeling is misleading, then in determining whether the labeling is misleading there shall be taken into account (among other things) not only representations made or suggested by statement, word, design, device, or any combination thereof, but also the extent to which the labeling fails to reveal facts material in the light of such representations or material with respect to consequences which may result from the use of the article to which the labeling relates under the conditions of use prescribed in the labeling thereof or under such conditions of use as are customary or usual.

(o) The representation of a drug, in its labeling, as an antiseptic shall be considered to be a representation that it is a germicide, except in the case of a drug purporting to be, or represented as, an antiseptic for inhibitory use as a wet dressing, ointment, dusting powder, or such other use as involves prolonged contact with the body.

(p) ² The term "new drug" means—

---

² Sec. 201(p) amended by secs. 102 (a) and (b) of P.L. 90–399.

"ENACTMENT DATE" AS DEFINED IN DRUG AMENDMENTS ACT OF 1962

Sec. 107 of P.L. 87–781

Sec. 107(c)(1) [As used in this subsection, the term "enactment date" means the date of enactment of this Act; and the term "basic Act" means the Federal Food, Drug, and Cosmetic Act.

(2) An application filed pursuant to section 505(b) of the basic Act which was "effective" within the meaning of that Act on the day immediately preceding the enactment date shall be deemed, as of the enactment date, to be an application "approved" by the Secretary within the meaning of the basic Act as amended by this Act.

(3) In the case of any drug with respect to which an application filed under section 505(b) of the basic Act is deemed to be an approved application on the enactment date by virtue of paragraph (2) of this subsection—

(A) the amendments made by this Act to section 201(p), and to subsections (b) and (d) of section 505, of the basic Act, insofar as such amendments relate to the effectiveness of drugs, shall not, so long as approval of such application is not withdrawn or suspended pursuant to section 505(e) of that Act, apply to such drug when intended solely for use under conditions prescribed, recommended, or suggested in labeling covered by such approved application, but shall apply to any changed use, or conditions of use, prescribed, recommended, or suggested in its labeling, including such conditions of use as are the subject of an amendment or supplement to such application pending on, or filed after, the enactment date; and

(B) clause (3) of the first sentence of section 505(e) of the basic Act, as amended by this Act, shall not apply to such drug when intended solely for use under conditions prescribed, recommended, or suggested in labeling covered by such approved application (except with respect to such use, or conditions of use, as are the subject of an amendment or supplement to such approved application, which amendment or supplement has been approved after the enactment date under section 505 of the basic Act as amended by this Act) until whichever of the following first occurs: (i) the expiration of the two-year period beginning with the enactment date; (ii) the effective date of an order under section 505(e) of the basic Act, other than clause (3) of the first sentence of such section 505(e), withdrawing or suspending the approval of such application.

(4) In the case of any drug which, on the first day immediately pre-

(1) Any drug (except a new animal drug or an animal feed bearing or containing a new animal drug) the composition of which is such that such drug is not generally recognized, among experts qualified by scientific training and experience to evaluate the safety and effectiveness of drugs, as safe and effective for use under the conditions prescribed, recommended, or suggested in the labeling thereof, except that such a drug not so recognized shall not be deemed to be a "new drug" if at any time prior to the enactment of this Act it was subject to the Food and Drugs Act of June 30, 1906, as amended, and if at such time its labeling contained the same representations concerning the conditions of its use; or

(2) Any drug (except a new animal drug or an animal feed bearing or containing a new animal drug) the composition of which is such that such drug, as a result of investigations to determine its safety and effectiveness for use under such conditions, has become so recognized, but which has not, otherwise than in such investigations, been used to a material extent or for a material time under such conditions.

(q) The term "pesticide chemical" means any substance which, alone, in chemical combination or in formulation with one or more other substances, is an "economic poison" within the meaning of the Federal Insecticide, Fungicide, and Rodenticide Act (7 U.S.C., secs. 135–135k) as now in force or as hereafter amended, and which is used in the production, storage, or transportation of raw agricultural commodities.

(r) The term "raw agricultural commodity" means any food in its raw or natural state, including all fruits that are washed, colored, or otherwise treated in their unpeeled natural form prior to marketing.

(s)[3] The term "food additive" means any substance the intended use of which results or may reasonably be expected to result, directly or indirectly, in its becoming a component or otherwise affecting the characteristics of any food (including any substance intended for use in producing, manufacturing, packing, processing, preparing, treating, packaging, transporting, or holding food; and including any source of radiation intended for any such use), if such substance is not generally recognized, among experts qualified by scientific training and experience to evaluate its safety, as having been adequately

ceding the enactment date, (A) was commercially used or sold in the United States, (B) was not a new drug as defined by section 201(p) of the basic Act as then in force, and (C) was not covered by an effective application under section 505 of that Act, the amendments to section 201(p) made by this Act shall not apply to such drug when intended solely for use under conditions prescribed, recommended, or suggested in labeling with respect to such drug on that day.]
[3] Subsec. 201(s)(5) added by sec. 102(c) of P.L. 90–399.

shown through scientific procedures (or, in the case of a substance used in food prior to January 1, 1958, through either scientific procedures or experience based on common use in food) to be safe under the conditions of its intended use; except that such term does not include—

(1) a pesticide chemical in or on a raw agricultural commodity; or

(2) a pesticide chemical to the extent that it is intended for use or is used in the production, storage, or transportation of any raw agricultural commodity; or

(3) a color additive; or

(4) any substance used in accordance with a sanction or approval granted prior to the enactment of this paragraph pursuant to this Act, the Poultry Products Inspection Act (21 U.S.C. 451 and the following) or the Meat Inspection Act of March 4, 1907 (34 Stat. 1260), as amended and extended (21 U.S.C. 71 and the following); or

(5) a new animal drug.

(t) (1) The term "color additive" means a material which—

(A) is a dye, pigment, or other substance made by a process of synthesis or similar artifice, or extracted, isolated, or otherwise derived, with or without intermediate or final change of identity, from a vegetable, animal, mineral, or other source, and

(B) when added or applied to a food, drug, or cosmetic, or to the human body or any part thereof, is capable (alone or through reaction with other substance) of imparting color thereto;

except that such term does not include any material which the Secretary, by regulation, determines is used (or intended to be used) solely for a purpose or purposes other than coloring.

(2) The term "color" includes black, white, and intermediate grays.

(3) Nothing in subparagraph (1) of this paragraph shall be construed to apply to any pesticide chemical, soil or plant nutrient, or other agricultural chemical solely because of its effect in aiding, retarding, or otherwise affecting, directly or indirectly, the growth or other natural physiological processes of produce of the soil and thereby affecting its color, whether before or after harvest.

(u) [4] The term "safe," as used in paragraph (s) of this section and in sections 409, 512, and 706, has reference to the health of man or animal.

(v) [5] * * *

(w) [6] The term "new animal drug" means any drug intended for use for animals other than man, including

---

[4] Sec. 201(u) amended by sec. 102(d) of P.L. 90–399.
[5] Subsec. 201(v) repealed by sec. 701 of P.L. 91–513.
[6] Secs. 201 (w) and (x) added by sec. 102(e) of P.L. 90–399.

any drug intended for use in animal feed but not including such animal feed—

(1) the composition of which is such that such drug is not generally recognized, among experts qualified by scientific training and experience to evaluate the safety and effectiveness of animal drugs, as safe and effective for use under the conditions prescribed, recommended, or suggested in the labeling thereof; except that such a drug not so recognized shall not be deemed to be a "new animal drug" if at any time prior to June 25, 1938, it was subject to the Food and Drug Act of June 30, 1906, as amended, and if at such time its labeling contained the same representations concerning the conditions of its use; or

(2) the composition of which is such that such drug, as a result of investigations to determine its safety and effectiveness for use under such conditions, has become so recognized but which has not, otherwise than in such investigations, been used to a material extent or for a material time under such conditions; or

(3) which drug is composed wholly or partly of any kind of penicillin, streptomycin, chlortetracycline, chloramphenicol, or bacitracin, or any derivative thereof, except when there is in effect a published order of the Secretary declaring such drug not to be a new animal drug on the grounds that (A) the requirement of certification of batches of such drug, as provided for in section 512(n), is not necessary to insure that the objectives specified in paragraph (3) thereof are achieved and (B) that neither subparagraph (1) nor (2) of this paragraph (w) applies to such drug.

(x) [6] The term "animal feed", as used in paragraph (w) of this section, in section 512, and in provisions of this Act referring to such paragraph or section, means an article which is intended for use for food for animals other than man and which is intended for use as a substantial source of nutrients in the diet of the animal, and is not limited to a mixture intended to be the sole ration of the animal.

CHAPTER III—PROHIBITED ACTS AND PENALTIES

PROHIBITED ACTS

SEC. 301. [331]. The following acts and the causing thereof are hereby prohibited:

(a) The introduction or delivery for introduction into interstate commerce of any food, drug, device, or cosmetic that is adulterated or misbranded.

(b) The adulteration or misbranding of any food, drug, device, or cosmetic in interstate commerce.

(c) The receipt in interstate commerce of any food, drug, device, or cosmetic that is adulterated or misbranded, and the delivery or proffered delivery thereof for pay or otherwise.

(d) The introduction or delivery for introduction into interstate commerce of any article in violation of section 404 or 505.

(e) [7] The refusal to permit access to or copying of any record as required by section 703; or the failure to establish or maintain any record, or make any report, required under section 505 (i) or (j), 507 (d) or (g), or 512 (j), (l) or (m) or the refusal to permit access to or verification or copying of any such required record.

(f) The refusal to permit entry or inspection as authorized by section 704.

(g) The manufacture within any Territory of any food, drug, device, or cosmetic that is adulterated or misbranded.

(h) The giving of a guaranty or undertaking referred to in section 303(c)(2), which guaranty or undertaking is false, except by a person who relied upon a guaranty or undertaking to the same effect signed by, and containing the name and address of, the person residing in the United States from whom he received in good faith the food, drug, device, or cosmetic; or the giving of a guaranty or undertaking referred to in section 303(c)(3), which guaranty or undertaking is false.

(i) (1) Forging, counterfeiting, simulating, or falsely representing, or without proper authority using any mark, stamp, tag, label, or other identification device authorized or required by regulations promulgated under the provisions of section 404, 506, 507, or 706.

(2) Making, selling, disposing of, or keeping in possession, control, or custody, or concealing any punch, die, plate, stone, or other thing designed to print, imprint, or reproduce the trademark, trade name, or other identifying mark, imprint, or device of another or any likeness of any of the foregoing upon any drug or container or labeling thereof so as to render such drugs a counterfeit drug.

(3) The doing of any act which causes a drug to be a counterfeit drug, or the sale or dispensing, or the holding for sale or dispensing, of a counterfeit drug.

(j) [8] The using by any person to his own advantage, or revealing, other than to the Secretary or officers or employees of the Department, or to the courts when relevant in any judicial proceeding under this Act, any in-

---

[7] Sec. 301(e) amended by sec. 103(1) of P.L. 90-399.
[8] Sec. 301(j) amended by sec. 103(2) of P.L. 90-399.

formation acquired under authority of section 404, 409, 505, 506, 507, 512, 704, or 706 concerning any method or process which as a trade secret is entitled to protection.

(k) The alteration, mutilation, destruction, obliteration, or removal of the whole or any part of the labeling of, or the doing of any other act with respect to, a food, drug, device, or cosmetic, if such act is done while such article is held for sale (whether or not the first sale) after shipment in interstate commerce and results in such article being adulterated or misbranded.

(l) The using, on the labeling of any drug or in any advertising relating to such drug, of any representation or suggestion that approval of an application with respect to such drug is in effect under section 505, or that such drug complies with the provisions of such section.

(m) The sale or offering for sale of colored oleomargarine or colored margarine, or the possession or serving of colored oleomargarine or colored margarine in violation of section 407(b) or 407(c).

(n) The using, in labeling, advertising or other sales promotion of any reference to any report or analysis furnished in compliance with section 704.

(o) In the case of a prescription drug distributed or offered for sale in interstate commerce, the failure of the manufacturer, packer, or distributor thereof to maintain for transmittal, or to transmit, to any practitioner licensed by applicable State law to administer such drug who makes written request for information as to such drug, true and correct copies of all printed matter which is required to be included in any package in which that drug is distributed or sold, or such other printed matter as is approved by the Secretary. Nothing in this paragraph shall be construed to exempt any person from any labeling requirement imposed by or under other provisions of this Act.

(p) The failure to register in accordance with section 510, the failure to provide any information required by section 510(j), or the failure to provide a notice required by section 510(j)(2).

(q) [9] * * *

INJUNCTION PROCEEDINGS

SEC. 302 [332]. (a) The district courts of the United States and the United States courts of the Territories shall have jurisdiction, for cause shown, and subject to the provisions of section 381 (relating to notice to opposite party) of Title 28, to restrain violations of section 301 of this title, except paragraphs (h), (i), and (j) of said section.

(b) In case of violation of an injunction or restraining order issued under this section, which also constitutes a violation of this Act, trial shall be by the court, or, upon demand of the accused, by a jury. Such trial shall be conducted in accordance with the practice and procedure

[9] Subsec. 301(q) repealed by sec. 701 of P.L. 91-513.

applicable in the case of proceedings subject to the provisions of section 22 of such Act of October 15, 1914, as amended. [This section, which appeared as U.S.C., title 28, sec. 387, has been repealed. It is now covered by Rule 42(b), Federal Rules of Criminal Procedure.]

PENALTIES

SEC. 303 [333]. (a)[10] Any person who violates a provision of section 301 shall be imprisoned for not more than one year or fined not more than $1,000, or both.

(b) [10] Notwithstanding the provisions of subsection (a) of this section, if any person commits such a violation after a conviction of him under this section has become final, or commits such a violation with the intent to defraud or mislead, such person shall be imprisoned for not more than three years or fined not more than $10,000 or both.

(c) No person shall be subject to the penalties of subsection (a) of this section, (1) for having received in interstate commerce any article and delivered it or proffered delivery of it, if such delivery or proffer was made in good faith, unless he refuses to furnish on request of an officer or employee duly designated by the Secretary the name and address of the person from whom he purchased or received such article and copies of all documents, if any there be, pertaining to the delivery of the article to him; or (2) for having violated section 301 (a) or (d), if he establishes a guaranty or undertaking signed by, and containing the name and address of, the person residing in the United States from whom he received in good faith the article, to the effect, in case of an alleged violation of section 301(a), that such article is not adulterated or misbranded, within the meaning of this Act, designating this Act, or to the effect, in case of an alleged violation of section 301(d), that such article is not an article which may not, under the provisions of section 404 or 505, be introduced into interstate commerce; or (3) for having violated section 301(a), where the violation exists because the article is adulterated by reason of containing a color additive not from a batch certified in accordance with regulations promulgated by the Secretary under this Act, if such person establishes a guaranty or undertaking signed by, and containing the name and address of, the manufacturer of the color additive, to the effect that such color additive was from a batch certified in accordance with the applicable regulations promulgated by the Secretary under this Act; or (4) for having violated section 301(b), (c), or (k) by failure to comply with section 502(f) in respect to an

---

[10] Secs. 303 (a) and (b) amended by sec. 701 of P.L. 91-513 effective May 1, 1971.

article received in interstate commerce to which neither
section 503(a) nor section 503(b)(1) is applicable, if the
delivery or proffered delivery was made in good faith
and the labeling at the time thereof contained the same
directions for use and warning statements as were contained in the labeling at the time of such receipt of such
article; or (5) for having violated section 301(i)(2) if
such person acted in good faith and had no reason to believe that use of the punch, die, plate, stone, or other
thing involved would result in a drug being a counterfeit
drug, or for having violated section 301(i)(3) if the person doing the act or causing it to be done acted in good
faith and had no reason to believe that the drug was a
counterfeit drug.

SEIZURE

SEC. 304 [334]. (a)[11] (1) Any article of food, drug,
device, or cosmetic that is adulterated or misbranded
when introduced into or while in interstate commerce or
while held for sale (whether or not the first sale) after
shipment in interstate commerce, or which may not, under
the provisions of section 404 or 505, be introduced into
interstate commerce, shall be liable to be proceeded
against while in interstate commerce, or at any time
thereafter, on libel of information and condemned in
any district court of the United States or United States
court of a Territory within the jurisdiction of which
the article is found: *Provided, however,* That no libel
for condemnation shall be instituted under this Act, for
any alleged misbranding if there is pending in any court
a libel for condemnation proceeding under this Act based
upon the same alleged misbranding, and not more than
one such proceeding shall be instituted if no such proceeding is so pending, except that such limitations shall
not apply (A) when such misbranding has been the basis
of a prior judgment in favor of the United States, in a
criminal, injunction, or libel for condemnation proceeding under this Act, or (B) when the Secretary has probable cause to believe from facts found, without hearing,
by him or any officer or employee of the Department that
the misbranded article is dangerous to health, or that
the labeling of the misbranded article is fraudulent, or
would be in a material respect misleading to the injury
or damage of the purchaser or consumer. In any case
where the number of libel for condemnation proceedings
is limited as above provided the proceeding pending or
instituted shall, on application on the claimant, seasonably made, be removed for trial to any district agreed
upon by stipulation between the parties, or, in case of
failure to so stipulate within a reasonable time, the claim-

---

[11] Sec. 304(a) amended by sec. 4(b) of P.L. 90–639 and sec. 304
(a)(2) and (d)(3) by sec. 701 of P.L. 91–513.

ant may apply to the court of the district in which the seizure has been made, and such court (after giving the United States attorney for such district reasonable notice and opportunity to be heard) shall by order, unless good cause to the contrary is shown, specify a district of reasonable proximity to the claimant's principal place of business to which the case shall be removed for trial.

(2) The following shall be liable to be proceeded against at any time on libel of information and condemned in any district court of the United States or United States court of a Territory within the jurisdiction of which they are found: (A) Any drug that is a counterfeit drug, (B) Any container of a counterfeit drug, and (C) Any punch, die, plate, stone, labeling, container, or other thing used or designed for use in making a counterfeit drug or drugs.

(b) The article, equipment, or other thing proceeded against shall be liable to seizure by process pursuant to the libel, and the procedure in cases under this section shall conform, as nearly as may be, to the procedure in admiralty; except that on demand of either party any issue of fact joined in any such case shall be tried by jury. When libel for condemnation proceedings under this section, involving the same claimant and the same issues of adulteration or misbranding, are pending in two or more jurisdictions, such pending proceedings, upon application of the claimant seasonably made to the court of one such jurisdiction, shall be consolidated for trial by order of such court, and tried in (1) any district selected by the claimant where one of such proceedings is pending; or (2) a district agreed upon by stipulation between the parties. If no order for consolidation is so made within a reasonable time, the claimant may apply to the court of one such jurisdiction, and such court (after giving the United States attorney for such district reasonable notice and opportunity to be heard) shall by order, unless good cause to the contrary is shown, specify a district of reasonable proximity to the claimant's principal place of business, in which all such pending proceedings shall be consolidated for trial and tried. Such order of consolidation shall not apply so as to require the removal of any case the date for trial of which has been fixed. The court granting such order shall give prompt notification thereof to the other courts having jurisdiction of the cases covered thereby.

(c) The court at any time after seizure up to a reasonable time before trial shall by order allow any party to a condemnation proceeding, his attorney or agent, to obtain a representative sample of the article seized and a true copy of the analysis, if any, on which the proceeding is based and the identifying marks or numbers, if any, of the packages from which the samples analyzed were obtained.

(d) (1) Any food, drug, device, or cosmetic condemned under this section shall, after entry of the decree,
be disposed of by destruction or sale as the court may, in
accordance with the provisions of this section, direct and
the proceeds thereof, if sold, less the legal costs and
charges, shall be paid into the Treasury of the United
States; but such article shall not be sold under such decree contrary to the provisions of this Act or the laws
of the jurisdiction in which sold: *Provided*, That after
entry of the decree and upon the payment of the costs
of such proceedings and the execution of a good and
sufficient bond conditioned that such article shall not be
sold or disposed of contrary to the provisions of this Act
or the laws of any State or Territory in which sold, the
court may by order direct that such article be delivered
to the owner thereof to be destroyed or brought into
compliance with the provisions of this Act under the
supervision of an officer or employee duly designated by
the Secretary, and the expenses of such supervision shall
be paid by the person obtaining release of the article
under bond. If the article was imported into the United
States and the person seeking its release establishes (A)
that the adulteration, misbranding, or violation did not
occur after the article was imported, and (B) that he
had no cause for believing that it was adulterated, misbranded, or in violation before it was released from
customs custody, the court may permit the article to be
delivered to the owner for exportation in lieu of destruction upon a showing by the owner that all of the
conditions of section 801(d) can and will be met: *Provided, however*, That the provisions of this sentence shall
not apply where condemnation is based upon violation
of section 402(a) (1), (2), or (6), section 501 (a)(3),
section 502(j), or section 601 (a) or (d); *And provided
further*, That where such exportation is made to the original foreign supplier, then clauses (1) and (2) of section
801(d) and the foregoing proviso shall not be applicable;
and in all cases of exportation the bond shall be conditioned that the article shall not be sold or disposed of
until the applicable conditions of section 801(d) have
been met. Any article condemned by reason of its being
an article which may not, under section 404 or 505, be
introduced into interstate commerce, shall be disposed of
by destruction.

(2) The provisions of paragraph (1) of this subsection shall, to the extent deemed appropriate by the court,
apply to any equipment or other thing which is not
otherwise within the scope of such paragraph and which
is referred to in paragraph (2) of subsection (a).

(3) Whenever in any proceeding under this section,
involving paragraph (2) of subsection (a), the condemnation of any equipment or thing (other than a drug) is

decreed, the court shall allow the claim of any claimant, to the extent of such claimant's interest, for remission or mitigation of such forfeiture if such claimant proves to the satisfaction of the court (i) that he has not committed or caused to be committed any prohibited act referred to in such paragraph (2) and has no interest in any drug referred to therein, (ii) that he has an interest in such equipment or other thing as owner or lienor or otherwise, acquired by him in good faith, and (iii) that he at no time had any knowledge or reason to believe that such equipment or other thing was being or would be used in, or to facilitate, the violation of laws of the United States relating to counterfeit drugs.

(e) When a decree of condemnation is entered against the article, court costs and fees, and storage and other proper expenses, shall be awarded against the person, if any, intervening as claimant of the article.

(f) In the case of removal for trial of any case as provided by subsection (a) or (b)—

(1) The clerk of the court from which removal is made shall promptly transmit to the court in which the case is to be tried all records in the case necessary in order that such court may exercise jurisdiction.

(2) The court to which such case was removed shall have the powers and be subject to the duties for purposes of such case, which the court from which removal was made would have had, or to which such court would have been subject, if such case had not been removed.

HEARING BEFORE REPORT OF CRIMINAL VIOLATION

SEC. 305 [335]. Before any violation of this Act is reported by the Secretary to any United States attorney for institution of a criminal proceeding, the person against whom such proceeding is contemplated shall be given appropriate notice and an opportunity to present his views, either orally or in writing, with regard to such contemplated proceeding.

REPORT OF MINOR VIOLATIONS

SEC. 306 [336]. Nothing in this Act shall be construed as requiring the Secretary to report for prosecution, or for the institution of libel or injunction proceedings, minor violations of this Act whenever he believes that the public interest will be adequately served by a suitable written notice or warning.

PROCEEDINGS IN NAME OF UNITED STATES; PROVISION AS TO SUBPOENAS

SEC. 307 [337]. All such proceedings for the enforcement, or to restrain violations, of this Act shall be by and in the name of the United States. Subpoenas for

witnesses who are required to attend a court of the United
States, in any district, may run into any other district in
any such proceeding.

* * *

CHAPTER V—DRUGS AND DEVICES

ADULTERATED DRUGS AND DEVICES

SEC. 501 [351]. A drug or device shall be deemed to be
adulterated—

(a) [16] (1) If it consists in whole or in part of any filthy,
putrid, or decomposed substance; or (2)(A) if it has
been prepared, packed, or held under insanitary conditions whereby it may have been contaminated with filth,
or whereby it may have been rendered injurious to
health; or (B) if it is a drug and the methods used in, or
the facilities or controls used for, its manufacture, processing, packing, or holding do not conform to or are not
operated or administered in conformity with current good
manufacturing practice to assure that such drug meets
the requirements of this Act as to safety and has the
identity and strength, and meets the quality and purity
characteristics, which it purports or is represented to
possess; or (3) if it is a drug and its container is composed, in whole or in part, of any poisonous or deleterious
substance which may render the contents injurious to
health; or (4) if (A) it is a drug which bears or contains, for purposes of coloring only, a color additive
which is unsafe within the meaning of section 706(a),
or, (B) it is a color additive the intended use of which
in or on drugs is for purposes of coloring only and is unsafe within the meaning of section 706(a); or (5) if it
is a new animal drug which is unsafe within the meaning of section 512; or (6) if it is an animal feed bearing
or containing a new animal drug, and such animal feed
is unsafe within the meaning of section 512.

(b) If it purports to be or is represented as a drug the
name of which is recognized in an official compendium,
and its strength differs from, or its quality or purity falls
below, the standards set forth in such compendium. Such
determination as to strength, quality, or purity shall be
made in accordance with the tests or methods of assay set
forth in such compendium, except that whenever tests or
methods of assay have not been prescribed in such compendium, or such tests or methods of assay as are prescribed are, in the judgment of the Secretary, insufficient
for the making of such determination, the Secretary shall

---

[16] Sec. 501(a) amended by sec. 101(a) of P.L. 90-399.

bring such fact to the attention of the appropriate body charged with the revision of such compendium, and if such body fails within a reasonable time to prescribe tests or methods of assay which, in the judgment of the Secretary, are sufficient for purposes of this paragraph, then the Secretary shall promulgate regulations prescribing appropriate tests or methods of assay in accordance with which such determination as to strength, quality, or purity shall be made. No drug defined in an official compendium shall be deemed to be adulterated under this paragraph because it differs from the standard of strength, quality, or purity therefor set forth in such compendium, if its difference in strength, quality, or purity from such standards is plainly stated on its label. Whenever a drug is recognized in both the United States Pharmacopeia and the Homeopathic Pharmacopeia of the United States it shall be subject to the requirements of the United States Pharmacopeia unless it is labeled and offered for sale as a homeopathic drug, in which case it shall be subject to the provisions of the Homeopathic Pharmacopeia of the United States and not to those of the United States Pharmacopeia.

(c) If it is not subject to the provisions of paragraph (b) of this section and its strength differs from, or its purity or quality falls below, that which it purports or is represented to possess.

(d) If it is a drug and any substance has been (1) mixed or packed therewith so as to reduce its quality or strength or (2) substituted wholly or in part therefor.

MISBRANDED DRUGS AND DEVICES

SEC. 502 [352]. A drug or device shall be deemed to be misbranded—

(a) If its labeling is false or misleading in any particular.

(b) If in a package form unless it bears a label containing (1) the name and place of business of the manufacturer, packer, or distributor; and (2) an accurate statement of the quantity of the contents in terms of weight, measure, or numerical count: *Provided,* That under clause (2) of this paragraph reasonable variations shall be permitted, and exemptions as to small packages shall be established, by regulations prescribed by the Secretary.

(c) If any word, statement, or other information required by or under authority of this Act to appear on the label or labeling is not prominently placed thereon with such conspicuousness (as compared with other words, statements, designs, or devices, in the labeling) and in such terms as to render it likely to be read and understood by the ordinary individual under customary conditions of purchase and use.

(d) If it is for use by man and contains any quantity of the narcotic or hypnotic substance alpha-eucaine, barbituric acid, beta-eucaine, bromal, cannabis, carbromal, chloral, coca, cocaine, codeine, heroin, marihuana, morphine, opium, paraldehyde, peyote, or sulfonmethane; or any chemical derivative of such substance, which derivative has been by the Secretary, after investigation, found to be, and by regulations designated as, habit forming; unless its label bears the name, and quantity or proportion of such substance or derivative and in juxtaposition therewith the statement "Warning—May be habit forming."

(e) (1) If it is a drug, unless (A) its label bears, to the exclusion of any other nonproprietary name (except the applicable systematic chemical name or the chemical formula), (i) the established name (as defined in subparagraph (2)) of the drug, if such there be, and (ii) in case it is fabricated from two or more ingredients, the established name and quantity of each active ingredient, including the quantity, kind, and proportion of any alcohol, and also including whether active or not, the established name and quantity or proportion of any bromides, ether, chloroform, acetanilide, acetophenetidin, amidopyrine, antipyrine, atropine, hyoscine, hyoscyamine, arsenic, digitalis, digitalis glucosides, mercury, ouabain, strophanthin, strychnine, thyroid, or any derivative or preparation of any such substances, contained therein: *Provided*, That the requirement for stating the quantity of the active ingredients, other than the quantity of those specifically named in this paragraph, shall apply only to prescription drugs; and (B) for any prescription drug the established name of such drug or ingredient, as the case may be, on such label (and on any labeling on which a name for such drug or ingredient is used) is printed prominently and in type at least half as large as that used thereon for any proprietary name or designation for such drug or ingredient: and *Provided*, That to the extent that compliance with the requirements of clause (A) (ii) or clause (B) of this subparagraph is impracticable, exemptions shall be established by regulations promulgated by the Secretary.

(2) As used in this paragraph (e), the term "established name", with respect to a drug or ingredient thereof, means (A) the applicable official name designated pursuant to section 508, or (B) if there is no such name and such drug, or such ingredient, is an article recognized in an official compendium, then the official title thereof in such compendium, or (C) if neither clause (A) nor clause (B) of this subparagraph applies, then the common or usual name, if any, of such drug or of such ingredient: *Provided further*, That where clause (B) of this subparagraph applies to an article recognized in the United States Pharmacopeia and in the Homeopathic Pharmacopeia under different official titles, the official title used in the United States Pharmacopeia shall apply

unless it is labeled and offered for sale as a homeopathic drug, in which case the official title used in the Homeopathic Pharmacopeia shall apply.

(f) Unless its labeling bears (1) adequate directions for use; and (2) such adequate warnings against use in those pathological conditions or by children where its use may be dangerous to health, or against unsafe dosage or methods or duration of administration or application, in such manner and form, as are necessary for the protection of users: *Provided*, That where any requirement of clause (1) of this paragraph, as applied to any drug or device, is not necessary for the protection of the public health, the Secretary shall promulgate regulations exempting such drug or device from such requirement.

(g) If it purports to be a drug the name of which is recognized in an official compendium, unless it is packaged and labeled as prescribed therein: *Provided*, That the method of packing may be modified with the consent of the Secretary. Whenever a drug is recognized in both the United States Pharmacopeia and the Homeopathic Pharmacopeia of the United States, it shall be subject to the requirements of the United States Pharmacopeia with respect to packaging, and labeling unless it is labeled and offered for sale as a homeopathic drug, in which case it shall be subject to the provisions of the Homeopathic Pharmacopeia of the United States, and not to those of the United States Pharmacopeia: *Provided further*, That, in the event of inconsistency between the requirements of this paragraph and those of paragraph (e) as to the name by which the drug or its ingredients shall be designated, the requirements of paragraph (e) shall prevail.

(h) If it has been found by the Secretary to be a drug liable to deterioration, unless it is packaged in such form and manner, and its label bears a statement of such precautions, as the Secretary shall by regulations require as necessary for the protection of the public health. No such regulation shall be established for any drug recognized in an official compendium until the Secretary shall have informed the appropriate body charged with the revision of such compendium of the need for such packaging or labeling requirements and such body shall have failed within a reasonable time to prescribe such requirements.

(i) (1) If it is a drug and its container is so made, formed, or filled as to be misleading; or (2) if it is an imitation of another drug; or (3) if it is offered for sale under the name of another drug.

(j) If it is dangerous to health when used in the dosage, or with the frequency or duration prescribed, recommended, or suggested in the labeling thereof.

(k) If it is, or purports to be, or is represented as a drug composed wholly or partly of insulin, unless (1) it is from a batch with respect to which a certificate or release has been issued pursuant to section 506, and (2) such certificate or release is in effect with respect to such drug.

(l) [17] If it is, or purports to be, or is represented as a drug (except a drug for use in animals other than man) composed wholly or partly of any kind of penicillin, streptomycin, chlortetracycline, chloramphenicol, bacitracin, or any other antibiotic drug, or any derivative thereof, unless (1) it is from a batch with respect to which a certificate or release has been issued pursuant to section 507, and (2) such certificate or release is in effect with respect to such drug: *Provided*, That this paragraph shall not apply to any drug or class of drugs exempted by regulations promulgated under section 507 (c) or (d).

(m) If it is a color additive the intended use of which in or on drugs is for the purpose of coloring only, unless its packaging and labeling are in conformity with such packaging and labeling requirements applicable to such color additive, as may be contained in regulations issued under section 706.

(n) In the case of any prescription drug distributed or offered for sale in any State, unless the manufacturer, packer, or distributor thereof includes in all advertisements and other descriptive printed matter issued or caused to be issued by the manufacturer, packer, or distributor with respect to that drug a true statement of (1) the established name as defined in section 502(e), printed prominently and in type at least half as large as that used for any trade or brand name thereof, (2) the formula showing quantitatively each ingredient of such drug to the extent required for labels under section 502(e), and (3) such other information in brief summary relating to side effects, contraindications, and effectiveness as shall be required in regulations which shall be issued by the Secretary in accordance with the procedure specified in section 701(e) of this Act: *Provided*, That (A) except in extraordinary circumstances, no regulation issued under this paragraph shall require prior approval by the Secretary of the content of any advertisement, and (B) no advertisement of a prescription drug, published after the effective date of regulations issued under this paragraph applicable to advertisements of prescription drugs, shall, with respect to the matters specified in this paragraph or covered by such regulations, be subject to the provisions of sections 12 through 17 of the Federal Trade Commission Act, as amended (15 U.S.C. 52–57). This paragraph (n) shall not be applicable to any printed matter which the Secretary determines to be labeling as defined in section 201(m) of this Act.

---

[17] Sec. 502(l) amended by sec. 105(a) of P.L. 90–399.

(o) If it is a drug and was manufactured, prepared, propagated, compounded, or processed in an establishment in any State not duly registered under section 510.

(p) [18] If it is a drug and its packaging or labeling is in violation of an applicable regulation issued pursuant to section 3 or 4 of the Poison Prevention Packaging Act of 1970.

EXEMPTIONS IN CASE OF DRUGS AND DEVICES

SEC. 503 [353]. (a) The Secretary is hereby directed to promulgate regulations exempting from any labeling or packaging requirement of this Act drugs and devices which are, in accordance with the practice of the trade, to be processed, labeled, or repacked in substantial quantities at establishments other than those where originally processed or packed, on condition that such drugs and devices are not adulterated or misbranded, under the provisions of this Act upon removal from such processing, labeling, or repacking establishment.

(b) (1) A drug intended for use by man which—

(A) is a habit-forming drug to which section 502(d) applies; or

(B) because of its toxicity or other potentiality for harmful effect, or the method of its use, or the collateral measures necessary to its use, is not safe for use except under the supervision of a practitioner licensed by law to administer such drug; or

(C) is limited by an approved application under section 505 to use under the professional supervision of a practitioner licensed by law to administer such drug;

shall be dispensed only (i) upon a written prescription of a practitioner licensed by law to administer such drug, or (ii) upon an oral prescription of such practitioner which is reduced promptly to writing and filed by the pharmacist, or (iii) by refilling any such written or oral prescription if such refilling is authorized by the prescriber either in the original prescription or by oral order which is reduced promptly to writing and filed by the pharmacist. The act of dispensing a drug contrary to the provisions of this paragraph shall be deemed to be an act which results in the drug being misbranded while held for sale.

(2) [19] Any drug dispensed by filling or refilling a written or oral prescription of a practitioner licensed by law to administer such drug shall be exempt from the requirements of section 502, except paragraphs (a), (i) (2) and (3), (k), and (l), and the packaging requirements of

---

[18] Sec. 502(p) added by sec. 7 of P.L. 91–601.
[19] Sec. 503(b) (2) amended by sec. 7 of P.L. 91–601.

paragraphs (g), (h), and (p), if the drug bears a label containing the name and address of the dispenser, the serial number and date of the prescription or of its filling, the name of the prescriber, and, if stated in the prescription, the name of the patient, and the directions for use and cautionary statements, if any, contained in such prescription. This exemption shall not apply to any drug dispensed in the course of the conduct of a business of dispensing drugs pursuant to diagnosis by mail, or to a drug dispensed in violation of paragraph (1) of this subsection.

(3) The Secretary may by regulation remove drugs subject to section 502(d) and section 505 from the requirements of paragraph (1) of this subsection when such requirements are not necessary for the protection of the public health.

(4) A drug which is subject to paragraph (1) of this subsection shall be deemed to be misbranded if at any time prior to dispensing its label fails to bear the statement "Caution: Federal law prohibits dispensing without prescription." A drug to which paragraph (1) of this subsection does not apply shall be deemed to be misbranded if at any time prior to dispensing its label bears the caution statement quoted in the preceding sentence.

(5) Nothing in this subsection shall be construed to relieve any person from any requirement prescribed by or under authority of law with respect to drugs now included or which may hereafter be included within the classifications stated in section 3220 of the Internal Revenue Code (26 U.S.C. 3220), or to marihuana as defined in section 3238(b) of the Internal Revenue Code (26 U.S.C. 3238(b)).

NEW DRUGS

SEC. 505 [20] [355]. (a) No person shall introduce or deliver for introduction into interstate commerce any new drug, unless an approval of an application filed pursuant to subsection (b) is effective with respect to such drug.

(b) Any person may file with the Secretary an application with respect to any drug subject to the provisions of subsection (a). Such persons shall submit to the Secretary as a part of the application (1) full reports of investigations which have been made to show whether or not such drug is safe for use and whether such drug is effective in use; (2) a full list of the articles used as components of such drug; (3) a full statement of the

---

[20] See sec. 107 of P.L. 87–781 set out as a note under sec. 201(p) of this Act.

composition of such drug; (4) a full description of the methods used in, and the facilities and controls used for, the manufacture, processing, and packing of such drug; (5) such samples of such drug and of the articles used as components thereof as the Secretary may require; and (6) specimens of the labeling proposed to be used for such drug.

(c) Within one hundred and eighty days after the filing of an application under this subsection, or such additional period as may be agreed upon by the Secretary and the applicant, the Secretary shall either—

(1) approve the application if he then finds that none of the grounds for denying approval specified in subsection (d) applies, or

(2) give the applicant notice of an opportunity for a hearing before the Secretary under subsection (d) on the question whether such application is approvable. If the applicant elects to accept the opportunity for hearing by written request within thirty days after such notice, such hearing shall commence not more than ninety days after the expiration of such thirty days unless the Secretary and the applicant otherwise agree. Any such hearing shall thereafter be conducted on an expedited basis and the Secretary's order thereon shall be issued within ninety days after the date fixed by the Secretary for filing final briefs.

(d) If the Secretary finds, after due notice to the applicant in accordance with subsection (c) and giving him an opportunity for a hearing, in accordance with said subsection, that (1) the investigations, reports of which are required to be submitted to the Secretary pursuant to subsection (b), do not include adequate tests by all methods reasonably applicable to show whether or not such drug is safe for use under the conditions prescribed, recommended, or suggested in the proposed labeling thereof; (2) the results of such tests show that such drug is unsafe for use under such conditions or do not show that such drug is safe for use under such conditions; (3) the methods used in, and the facilities and controls used for, the manufacture, processing, and packing of such drug are inadequate to preserve its identity, strength, quality, and purity; (4) upon the basis of the information submitted to him as part of the application, or upon the basis of any other information before him with respect to such drug, he has insufficient information to determine whether such drug is safe for use under such conditions; or (5) evaluated on the basis of the information submitted to him as part of the application and any other information before him with respect to such drug, there is a lack of substantial evidence that the drug will have the effect it purports or is represented to have under the conditions of use prescribed, recommended, or suggested in the proposed labeling thereof; or (6) based on a fair evaluation of all material facts, such labeling is false or misleading in any particular; he shall issue an order refusing to approve the application. If, after such notice and opportunity for hearing, the Secretary finds that clauses (1) through (6) do not apply, he shall issue an order approving the application. As used in this subsection and subsection (e), the term "substantial evidence" means evidence consisting of adequate and well-controlled investigations, including clinical investigations, by experts qualified by scientific training and experience to evaluate the effectiveness of the drug involved, on the basis of which it could fairly and responsibly be concluded by such experts that the drug will have the effect it purports or is represented to have under the conditions of use prescribed, recommended, or suggested in the labeling or proposed labeling thereof.

(e) The Secretary shall, after due notice and opportunity for hearing to the applicant, withdraw approval of an application with respect to any drug under this section if the Secretary finds (1) that clinical or other experience, tests, or other scientific data show that such drug is unsafe for use under the conditions of use upon the basis of which the application was approved; (2) that new evidence of clinical experience, not contained in such application or not available to the Secretary until after such application was approved, or tests by new methods, or tests by methods not deemed reasonably applicable when such application was approved, evaluated together with the evidence available to the Secretary when the application was approved, shows that such drug is not shown to be safe for use under the conditions of use upon the basis of which the application was approved; or (3) on the basis of new information before him with respect to such drug, evaluated together with the evidence available to him when the application was approved, that there is a lack of substantial evidence that the drug will have the effect it purports or is represented to have under the conditions of use prescribed, recommended, or suggested in the labeling thereof; or (4) that the application contains any untrue statement of a material fact: *Provided*, That if the Secretary (or in his absence the officer acting as Secretary) finds that there is an imminent hazard to the public health, he may suspend the approval of such application immediately, and give the applicant prompt notice of his action and afford the applicant the opportunity for an expedited hearing under this subsection; but the authority conferred by this proviso to suspend the approval of an application shall not be delegated. The Secretary may also, after due notice and opportunity for hearing to the applicant, withdraw the approval of an application with respect to any drug under this section if the Secretary finds (1) that the applicant has failed to establish a system for maintaining required records, or has repeatedly or deliberately failed to maintain such records or to make required reports, in accordance with a regulation or order under subsection (j) or to comply with the notice requirements of section 510(j)(2), or the applicant has refused to permit access to, or copying or verification of, such records as required by paragraph (2) of such sub-section; or (2) that on the basis of new information before him, evaluated together with the evidence before him when the application was approved, the methods used in, or the facilities and controls used for, the manufacture, processing, and packing of such drug are inadequate to assure and preserve its identity, strength, quality, and purity and were not made adequate within a reasonable time after receipt of written notice from the Secretary specifying the matter complained of; or (3) that on the basis of new information before him, evaluated together with the evidence before him when the application was approved, the labeling of such drug, based on a fair evaluation of all material facts, is false or misleading in any particular and was not corrected within a reasonable time after receipt of written notice from the Secretary specifying the matter complained of. Any order under this subsection shall state the findings upon which it is based.

(f) Whenever the Secretary finds that the facts so require, he shall revoke any previous order under subsection (d) or (e) refusing, withdrawing, or suspending approval of an application and shall approve such application or reinstate such approval, as may be appropriate.

(g) Orders of the Secretary issued under this section shall be served (1) in person by any officer or employee of the Department designated by the Secretary or (2) by mailing the order by registered mail or by certified mail addressed to the applicant or respondent at his last-known address in the records of the Secretary.

(h) [21] An appeal may be taken by the applicant from an order of the Secretary refusing or withdrawing approval of an application under this section. Such appeal shall be taken by filing in the United States court of appeals for the circuit wherein such applicant resides or has his principal place of business, or in the United States Court of Appeals for the District of Columbia Circuit, within sixty days after the entry of such order, a written petition praying that the order of the Secretary be set aside. A copy of such petition shall be forthwith transmitted by the clerk of the court to the Secretary, or

---

[21] This amendment shall not apply to any appeal taken prior to the date of enactment of the Drug Amendments of 1962, enacted Oct. 10, 1962.

any officer designated by him for that purpose, and thereupon the Secretary shall certify and file in the court the record upon which the order complained of was entered, as provided in section 2112 of title 28, United States Code. Upon the filing of such petition such court shall have exclusive jurisdiction to affirm or set aside such order, except that until the filing of the record the Secretary may modify or set aside his order. No objection to the order of the Secretary shall be considered by the court unless such objection shall have been urged before the Secretary or unless there were reasonable grounds for failure so to do. The finding of the Secretary as to the facts, if supported by substantial evidence, shall be conclusive. If any person shall apply to the court for leave to adduce additional evidence, and shall show to the satisfaction of the court that such additional evidence is material and that there were reasonable grounds for failure to adduce such evidence in the proceeding before the Secretary, the court may order such additional evidence to be taken before the Secretary and to be adduced upon the hearing in such manner and upon such terms and conditions as to the court may seem proper. The Secretary may modify his findings as to the facts by reason of the additional evidence so taken, and he shall file with the court such modified findings which, if supported by substantial evidence, shall be conclusive, and his recommendation, if any, for the setting aside of the original order. The judgment of the court affirming or setting aside any such order of the Secretary shall be final, subject to review by the Supreme Court of the United States upon certiorari or certification as provided in section 1254 of title 28 of the United States Code. The commencement of proceedings under this subsection shall not, unless specifically ordered by the court to the contrary, operate as a stay of the Secretary's order.

(i) The Secretary shall promulgate regulations for exempting from the operation of the foregoing subsections of this section drugs intended solely for investigational use by experts qualified by scientific training and experience to investigate the safety and effectiveness of drugs. Such regulations may, within the discretion of the Secretary, among other conditions relating to the protection of the public health, provide for conditioning such exemption upon—

(1) the submission to the Secretary, before any clinical testing of a new drug is undertaken, of reports, by the manufacturer or the sponsor of the investigation of such drug, or preclinical tests (including tests on animals) of such drug adequate to justify the proposed clinical testing;

(2) The manufacturer or the sponsor of the investigation of a new drug proposed to be distributed to investigators for clinical testing obtaining a

signed agreement from each of such investigators that patients to whom the drug is administered will be under his personal supervision, or under the supervision of investigators responsible to him, and that he will not supply such drug to any other investigator, or to clinics, for administration to human beings; and

(3) the establishment and maintenance of such records, and the making of such reports to the Secretary, by the manufacturer or the sponsor of the investigation of such drug, of data (including but not limited to analytical reports by investigators) obtained as the result of such investigational use of such drug, as the Secretary finds will enable him to evaluate the safety and effectiveness of such drug in the event of the filing of an application pursuant to subsection (b).

Such regulations shall provide that such exemption shall be conditioned upon the manufacturer, or the sponsor of the investigation, requiring that experts using such drugs for investigational purposes certify to such manufacturer or sponsor that they will inform any human beings to whom such drugs, or any controls used in connection therewith, are being administered, or their representatives, that such drugs are being used for investigational purposes and will obtain the consent of such human beings or their representatives, except where they deem it not feasible or, in their professional judgment, contrary to the best interests of such human beings. Nothing in this subsection shall be construed to require any clinical investigator to submit directly to the Secretary reports on the investigational use of drugs.

(j) (1) In the case of any drug for which an approval of an application filed pursuant to this section is in effect, the applicant shall establish and maintain such records, and make such reports to the Secretary, of data relating to clinical experience and other data or information, received or otherwise obtained by such applicant with respect to such drug, as the Secretary may by general regulation, or by order with respect to such application, prescribe on the basis of a finding that such records and reports are necessary in order to enable the Secretary to determine, or facilitate a determination, whether there is or may be ground for invoking subsection (e) of this section: *Provided, however*, That regulations and orders issued under this subsection and under subsection (i) shall have due regard for the professional ethics of the medical profession and the interests of patients and shall provide, where the Secretary deems it to be appropriate, for the examination, upon request, by the persons to whom such regulations or orders are applicable, of similar information received or otherwise obtained by the Secretary.

(2) Every person required under this section to maintain records, and every person in charge or custody thereof, shall, upon request of an officer or employee designated by the Secretary, permit such officer or employee at all reasonable times to have access to and copy and verify such records.

CERTIFICATION OF DRUGS CONTAINING INSULIN

SEC. 506 [356]. (a) The Secretary of Health, Education, and Welfare, pursuant to regulations promulgated by him, shall provide for the certification of batches of drugs composed wholly or partly of insulin. A batch of any such drug shall be certified if such drug has such characteristics of identity and such batch has such characteristics of strength, quality, and purity, as the Secretary prescribes in such regulations as necessary to adequately insure safety and efficacy of use, but shall not otherwise be certified. Prior to the effective date of such regulations the Secretary, in lieu of certification, shall issue a release for any batch which, in his judgment, may be released without risk as to the safety and efficacy of its use. Such release shall prescribe the date of its expiration and other conditions under which it shall cease to be effective as to such batch and as to portions thereof.

(b) Regulations providing for such certification shall contain such provisions as are necessary to carry out the purposes of this section, including provisions prescribing (1) standards of identity and of strength, quality, and purity; (2) tests and methods of assay to determine compliance with such standards; (3) effective periods for certificates, and other conditions under which they shall cease to be effective as to certified batches and as to portions thereof; (4) administration and procedure; and (5) such fees, specified in such regulations, as are necessary to provide, equip, and maintain an adequate certification service. Such regulations shall prescribe no standard of identity or of strength, quality, or purity for any drug different from the standard of identity, strength, quality, or purity set forth for such drug in an official compendium.

(c) Such regulations, insofar as they prescribe tests or methods of assay to determine strength, quality, or purity of any drug, different from the tests or methods of assay set forth for such drug in an official compendium, shall be prescribed, after notice and opportunity for revision of such compendium, in the manner provided in the second sentence of section 501(b). The provisions of subsections (e), (f), and (g) of section 701 shall be applicable to such portion of any regulation as prescribes any such different test or method, but shall not be applicable to any other portion of any such regulation.

CERTIFICATION OF ANTIBIOTICS

SEC. 507 [357]. (a) [22] The Secretary of Health, Education, and Welfare, pursuant to regulations promulgated by him, shall provide for the certification of batches of drugs (except drugs for use in animals other than man) composed wholly or partly of any kind of penicillin, streptomycin, chlortetracycline, chloramphenicol, bacitracin, or any other antibiotic drug, or any derivative thereof. A batch of any such drug shall be certified if such drug has such characteristics of identity and such batch has such characteristics of strength, quality, and purity, as the Secretary prescribes in such regulations as necessary to adequately insure safety and efficacy of use, but shall not otherwise be certified. Prior to the effective date of such regulations the Secretary, in lieu of certification, shall issue a release for any batch which, in his judgment, may be released without risk as to the safety and efficacy of its use. Such release shall prescribe the date of its expiration and other conditions under which it shall cease to be effective as to such batch and as to portions thereof. For purposes of this section and of section 502(1), the term "antibiotic drug" means any drug intended for use by man containing any quantity of any chemical substance which is produced by a micro-organism and which has the capacity to inhibit or destroy micro-organisms in dilute solution (including the chemically synthesized equivalent of any such substance).

(b) Regulations providing for such certifications shall contain such provisions as are necessary to carry out the purposes of this section, including provisions prescribing (1) standards of identity and of strength, quality, and purity; (2) tests and methods of assay to determine compliance with such standards; (3) effective periods for certificates, and other conditions under which they shall cease to be effective as to certified batches and as to portions thereof; (4) administration and procedure; and (5) such fees, specified in such regulations, as are necessary to provide, equip, and maintain an adequate certification service. Such regulations shall prescribe only such tests and methods of assay as will provide for certification or rejection within the shortest time consistent with the purposes of this section.

(c) Whenever in the judgment of the Secretary, the requirements of this section and of section 502(1) with respect to any drug or class of drugs are not necessary to insure safety and efficacy of use, the Secretary shall promulgate regulations exempting such drug or class of drugs from such requirements. In deciding whether an antibiotic drug, or class of antibiotic drugs, is to be exempted from the requirement of certification the

---

[22] Sec. 507(a) amended by sec. 105(b) of P.L. 90–399.

Secretary shall give consideration, among other relevant factors, to—
(1) whether such drug or class of drugs is manufactured by a person who has, or hereafter shall have, produced fifty consecutive batches of such drug or class of drugs in compliance with the regulations for the certification thereof within a period of not more than eighteen calendar months, upon the application by such person to the Secretary; or
(2) whether such drug or class of drugs is manufactured by any person who has otherwise demonstrated such consistency in the production of such drug or class of drugs, in compliance with the regulations for the certification thereof, as in the judgment of the Secretary is adequate to insure the safety and efficacy of use thereof.
When an antibiotic drug or a drug manufacturer has been exempted from the requirement of certification, the manufacturer may still obtain certification of a batch or batches of that drug if he applies for and meets the requirements for certification. Nothing in this Act shall be deemed to prevent a manufacturer or distributor of an antibiotic drug from making a truthful statement in labeling or advertising of the product as to whether it has been certified or exempted from the requirement of certification.

(d) The Secretary shall promulgate regulations exempting from any requirement of this section and of section 502(1), (1) drugs which are to be stored, processed, labeled, or repacked at establishments other than those where manufactured, on condition that such drugs comply with all such requirements upon removal from such establishments; (2) drugs which conform to applicable standards of identity, strength, quality, and purity prescribed by these regulations and are intended for use in manufacturing other drugs; and (3) drugs which are intended solely for investigational use by experts qualified by scientific training and experience to investigate the safety and efficacy of drugs. Such regulations may, within the discretion of the Secretary, among other conditions relating to the protection of the public health, provide for conditioning the exemption under clause (3) upon—
(1) the submission to the Secretary, before any clinical testing of a new drug is undertaken, of reports, by the manufacturer or the sponsor of the investigation of such drug, of preclinical tests (including tests on animals) of such drug adequate to justify the proposed clinical testing;
(2) the manufacturer or the sponsor of the investigation of a new drug proposed to be distributed to investigators for clinical testing obtaining a signed agreement from each of such investigators that patients to whom the drug is administered will be

under his personal supervision, or under the supervision of investigators responsible to him, and that he will not supply such drug to any other investigator, or to clinics, for administration to human beings; and

(3) the establishment and maintenance of such records, and the making of such reports to the Secretary, by the manufacturer or the sponsor of the investigation of such drug, of data (including but not limited to analytical reports by investigators) obtained as the result of such investigational use of such drug, as the Secretary finds will enable him to evaluate the safety and effectiveness of such drug in the event of the filing of an application for certification or release pursuant to subsection (a).

Such regulations shall provide that such exemption shall be conditioned upon the manufacturer, or the sponsor of the investigation, requiring that experts using such drugs for investigational purposes certify to such manufacturer or sponsor that they will inform any human beings to whom such drugs, or any controls used in connection therewith, are being administered, or their representatives, that such drugs are being used for investigational purposes and will obtain the consent of such human beings or their representatives, except where they deem it not feasible or, in their professional judgment, contrary to the best interests of such human beings. Nothing in this subsection shall be construed to require any clinical investigator to submit directly to the Secretary reports on the investigational use of drugs.

(e) No drug which is subject to section 507 shall be deemed to be subject to any provision of section 505 except.a new drug exempted from the requirements of this section and of section 502(l) pursuant to regulations promulgated by the Secretary: *Provided*, That, for purposes of section 505, the initial request for certification, as thereafter duly amended, pursuant to section 507, of a new drug so exempted shall be considered a part of the application filed pursuant to section 505(b) with respect to the person filing such request and to such drug as of the date of the exemption. Compliance of any drug subject to section 502(l) or 507 with section 501(b) and 502(g) shall be determined by the application of the standards of strength, quality, and purity, the tests and methods of assay, and the requirements of packaging, and labeling, respectively, prescribed by regulations promulgated under section 507.

(f) Any interested person may file with the Secretary a petition proposing the issuance, amendment, or repeal of any regulation contemplated by this section. The petition shall set forth the proposal in general terms and shall state reasonable grounds therefor. The Secretary

shall give public notice of the proposal and an opportunity for all interested persons to present their views
thereon, orally or in writing, and as soon as practicable
thereafter shall make public his action upon such proposal. At any time prior to the thirtieth day after such
action is made public any interested person may file
objections to such action, specifying with particularity
the changes desired, stating reasonable grounds therefor,
and requesting a public hearing upon such objections.
The Secretary shall thereupon, after due notice, hold such
public hearing. As soon as practicable after completion
of the hearing, the Secretary shall by order make public
his action on such objections. The Secretary shall base
his order only on substantial evidence of record at the
hearing and shall set forth as part of the order detailed
findings of fact on which the order is based. The order
shall be subject to the provision of section 701 (f) and
(g).

(g) (1) Every person engaged in manufacturing, compounding, or processing any drug within the purview of
this section with respect to which a certificate or release
has been issued pursuant to this section shall establish
and maintain such records, and make such reports to the
Secretary, of data relating to clinical experience and
other data or information, received or otherwise obtained
by such person with respect to such drug, as the Secretary may by general regulation, or by order with respect
to such certification or release, prescribe on the basis of a
finding that such records and reports are necessary in
order to enable the Secretary to make, or to facilitate, a
determination as to whether such certification or release
should be rescinded or whether any regulation issued
under this section should be amended or repealed: *Provided, however,* That regulations and orders issued under
this subsection and under clause (3) of subsection (d)
shall have due regard for the professional ethics of the
medical profession and the interests of patients and shall
provide, where the Secretary deems it to be appropriate,
for the examination, upon request, by the persons to
whom such regulations or orders are applicable, of similar information received or otherwise obtained by the
Secretary.

(2) Every person required under this section to maintain records, and every person having charge or custody
thereof, shall, upon request of an officer or employee
designated by the Secretary, permit such officer or employee at all reasonable times to have access to and copy
and verify such records.

(h) In the case of a drug for which, on the day immediately preceding the effective date of this subsection,
a prior approval of an application under section 505 had
not been withdrawn under section 505(e), the initial
issuance of regulations providing for certification or

exemption of such drug under this section 507 shall, with respect to the conditions of use prescribed, recommended, or suggested in the labeling covered by such application, not be conditioned upon an affirmative finding of the efficacy of such drug. Any subsequent amendment or repeal of such regulations so as no longer to provide for such certification or exemption on the ground of a lack of efficacy of such drug for use under such conditions of use may be effected only on or after that effective date of clause (3) of the first sentence of section 505(e) which would be applicable to such drug under such conditions of use if such drug were subject to section 505(e), and then only if (1) such amendment or repeal is made in accordance with the procedure specified in subsection (f) of this section (except that such amendment or repeal may be initiated either by a proposal of the Secretary or by a petition of any interested person) and (2) the Secretary finds, on the basis of new information with respect to such drug evaluated together with the information before him when the application under section 505 became effective or was approved, that there is a lack of substantial evidence (as defined in section 505(d)) that the drug has the effect it purports or is represented to have under such conditions of use.

AUTHORITY TO DESIGNATE OFFICIAL NAMES

SEC. 508 [358]. (a) The Secretary may designate an official name for any drug if he determines that such action is necessary or desirable in the interest of usefulness and simplicity. Any official name designated under this section for any drug shall be the only official name of that drug used in any official compendium published after such name has been prescribed or for any other purpose of this Act. In no event, however, shall the Secretary establish an official name so as to infringe a valid trademark.

(b) Within a reasonable time after the effective date of this section, and at such other times as he may deem necessary, the Secretary shall cause a review to be made of the official names by which drugs are identified in the official United States Pharmacopeia, the official Homeopathic Pharmacopeia of the United States, and the official National Formulary, and all supplements thereto, to determine whether revision of any of those names is necessary or desirable in the interest of usefulness and simplicity.

(c) Whenever he determines after any such review that (1) any such official name is unduly complex or is not useful for any other reason, (2) two or more official names have been applied to a single drug, or to two or more drugs which are identical in chemical structure and pharmacological action and which are substantially

identical in strength, quality, and purity, or (3) no official name has been applied to a medically useful drug,
he shall transmit in writing to the compiler of each official compendium in which that drug or drugs are identified and recognized his request for the recommendation of
a single official name for such drug or drugs which will
have usefulness and simplicity. Whenever such a single
official name has not been recommended within one hundred and eighty days after such request, or the Secretary
determines that any name so recommended is not useful
for any reason, he shall designate a single official name
for such drug or drugs. Whenever he determines that the
name so recommended is useful, he shall designate that
name as the official name of such drug or drugs. Such
designation shall be made as a regulation upon public
notice and in accordance with the procedure set forth in
section 4 of the Administrative Procedure Act (5 U.S.C.
1003).

(d) After each such review, and at such other times
as the Secretary may determine to be necessary or desirable, the Secretary shall cause to be compiled, published,
and publicly distributed a list which shall list all revised
official names of drugs designated under this section and
shall contain such descriptive and explanatory matter as
the Secretary may determine to be required for the effective use of those names.

(e) Upon a request in writing by any compiler of an
official compendium that the Secretary exercise the authority granted to him under section 508(a), he shall
upon public notice and in accordance with the procedure
set forth in section 4 of the Administrative Procedure
Act (5 U.S.C. 1003) designate the official name of the
drug for which the request is made.

NONAPPLICABILITY TO COSMETICS

SEC. 509 [359]. This chapter, as amended by the Drug
Amendments of 1962, shall not apply to any cosmetic
unless such cosmetic is also a drug or device or component thereof.

REGISTRATION OF PRODUCERS OF DRUGS [23]

SEC. 510 [360].[24, 25] (a) As used in this section—
    (1) the term "manufacture, preparation, propa-
gation, compounding, or processing" shall include

---

[23] The Congress hereby finds and declares that in order to make regulation of interstate commerce in drugs effective, it is necessary to provide
for registration and inspection of all establishments in which drugs are
manufactured, prepared, propagated, compounded, or processed; that the
products of all such establishments are likely to enter the channels of
interstate commerce and directly affect such commerce; and that the
regulation of interstate commerce in drugs without provision for registration and inspection of establishments that may be engaged only in intrastate commerce in such drugs would discriminate against and depress
interstate commerce in such drugs, and adversely burden, obstruct, and
affect such interstate commerce. Amended by sec. 701 of P.L. 91–513.
[24] Secs. 10 and 11 of P.L. 89–74 apply to certain provisions in sec. 510
and to all of sec. 511. Secs. 10 and 11 of P.L. 89–74 provide that—

repackaging or otherwise changing the container, wrapper, or labeling of any drug package in furtherance of the distribution of the drug from the original place of manufacture to the person who makes final delivery or sale to the ultimate consumer; and

(2) the term "name" shall include in the case of a partnership the name of each partner and, in the case of a corporation, the name of each corporate officer and director, and the State of incorporation.

(b) On or before December 31 of each year every person who owns or operates any establishment in any State engaged in the manufacture, preparation, propagation, compounding, or processing of a drug or drugs shall register with the Secretary his name, places of business, and all such establishments.

(c) Every person upon first engaging in the manufacture, preparation, propagation, compounding, or processing of a drug or drugs in any establishment which he owns or operates in any State shall immediately register with the Secretary his name, place of business, and such establishment.

(d) Every person duly registered in accordance with the foregoing subsections of this section shall immediately register with the Secretary any additional establishment which he owns or operates in any State and in which he begins the manufacture, preparation, propagation, compounding, or processing of a drug or drugs.

(e) The Secretary may assign a registration number to any person or any establishment registered in accordance with this section. The Secretary may also assign a listing number to each drug or class of drugs listed under subsection (j). Any number assigned pursuant to the preceding sentence shall be the same as that assigned pursuant to the National Drug Code.

(f) The Secretary shall make available for inspection, to any person so requesting, any registration filed pursuant to this section, except that any list submitted pursuant to paragraph (3) of subsection (j) and the information accompanying any list or notice filed under paragraph (1) or (2) of that subsection shall be exempt from such inspection unless the Secretary finds that such an exemption would be inconsistent with protection of the public health.

(g) The foregoing subsections of this section shall not apply to—

(1) pharmacies which maintain establishments in conformance with any applicable local laws regulating the practice of pharmacy and medicine and which are regularly engaged in dispensing prescrip-

---

Nothing in this Act shall be construed as authorizing the manufacture, compounding, processing, possession, sale, delivery, or other disposal of any drug in any State in contravention of the laws of such State.

No provision of this Act nor any amendment made by it shall be construed as indicating an intent on the part of the Congress to occupy the field in which such provision or amendment operates to the exclusion of any State law on the same subject matter, unless

tion drugs, upon prescriptions of practitioners licensed to administer such drugs to patients under the care of such practitioners in the course of their professional practice, and which do not manufacture, prepare, propagate, compound, or process drugs for sale other than in the regular course of their business of dispensing or selling drugs at retail;

(2) practitioners licensed by law to prescribe or administer drugs and who manufacture, prepare, propagate, compound, or process drugs solely for use in the course of their professional practice;

(3) persons who manufacture, prepare, propagate, compound, or process drugs solely for use in research, teaching, or chemical analysis and not for sale;

(4) such other classes of persons as the Secretary may by regulation exempt from the application of this section upon a finding that registration by such classes of persons in accordance with this section is not necessary for the protection of the public health.

(h) Every establishment in any State registered with the Secretary pursuant to this section shall be subject to inspection pursuant to section 704 and shall be so inspected by one or more officers or employees duly designated by the Secretary at least once in the 2-year period beginning with the date of registration of such establishment pursuant to this section and at least once in every successive 2-year period thereafter.

(i) Any establishment within any foreign country engaged in the manufacture, preparation, propagation, compounding, or processing of a drug or drugs shall be permitted to register under this section pursuant to regulations promulgated by the Secretary. Such regulations shall require such establishment to provide the information required by subsection (j) and shall include provisions for registration of any such establishment upon condition that adequate and effective means are available, by arrangement with the government of such foreign country or otherwise, to enable the Secretary to determine from time to time whether drugs manufactured, prepared, propagated, compounded, or processed in such establishment, if imported or offered for import into the United States, shall be refused admission on any of the grounds set forth in section 801(a) of this Act.

---

there is a direct and positive conflict between such provision or amendment and such State law so that the two cannot be reconciled or consistently stand together.

No amendment made by this Act shall be construed to prevent the enforcement in the courts of any State of any statute of such State prescribing any criminal penalty for any act made criminal by any such amendment.

²⁵ Subsec. (a)(2) repealed and sec. (a)(3) redesignated as sec. (a)(2) by sec. 701 of P.L. 91–513. Subsec. (b), (c), (d) amended by sec. 701 of P.L. 91–513.

(j)(1) Every person who registers with the Secretary under subsection (b), (c), or (d) shall, at the time of registration under any such subsection, file with the Secretary a list of all drugs (by established name (as defined in section 502(e)) and by any proprietary name) which are being manufactured, prepared, propagated, compounded, or processed by him for commercial distribution and which he has not included in any list of drugs filed by him with the Secretary under this paragraph or paragraph (2) before such time of registration. Such list shall be prepared in such form and manner as the Secretary may prescribe and shall be accompanied by—

(A) in the case of a drug contained in such list and subject to section 505, 506, 507, or 512, a reference to the authority for the marketing of such drug and a copy of all labeling for such drug;

(B) in the case of any other drug contained in such list—

(i) which is subject to section 503(b)(1), a copy of all labeling for such drug, a representative sampling of advertisements for such drug, and, upon request made by the Secretary for good cause, a copy of all advertisements for a particular drug product, or

(ii) which is not subject to section 503(b)(1), the label and package insert for such drug and a representative sampling of any other labeling for such drug:

(C) in the case of any drug contained in such list which is described in subparagraph (B), a quantitative listing of its active ingredient or ingredients, except that with respect to a particular drug product the Secretary may require the submission of a quantitative listing of all ingredients if he finds that such submission is necessary to carry out the purposes of this Act: and

(D) if the registrant filing the list has determined that a particular drug product contained in such list is not subject to section 505, 506, 507 or 512, a brief statement of the basis upon which the registrant made such determination if the Secretary requests such a statement with respect to that particular drug product.

(2) Each person who registers with the Secretary under this subsection shall report to the Secretary once during the month of June of each year and once during the month of December of each year the following information:

(A) A list of each drug introduced by the registrant for commercial distribution which has not been included in any list previously filed by him with the Secretary under this subparagraph or paragraph (1) of this subsection. A list under this subparagraph shall list a drug by its established name (as defined in section 502(e)) and by any proprietary name it may have and shall be accompanied by the other information required by paragraph (1).

(B) If since the date the registrant last made a report under this paragraph (or if he has not made a report under this paragraph, since the effective date of this subsection) he has discontinued the manufacture, preparation, propagation, compounding, or processing for commercial distribution of a drug included in a list filed by him under subparagraph (A) or paragraph (1); notice of such discontinuance, the date of such discontinuance, and the identity (by established name (as defined in section 502(e)) and by any proprietary name) of such drug.

(C) If since the date the registrant reported pursuant to subparagraph (B) a notice of discontinuance he has resumed the manufacture, preparation, propagation, compounding, or processing for commercial distribution of the drug with respect to which such notice of discontinuance was reported; notice of such resumption, the date of such resumption, the identity of such drug (by established name (as defined in section 502(e)) and by any proprietary name), and the other information required by paragraph (1), unless the registrant has previously reported such resumption to the Secretary pursuant to this subparagraph.

(D) Any material change in any information previously submitted pursuant to this paragraph or paragraph (1).

(3) The Secretary may also require each registrant under this section to submit a list of each drug product which (A) the registrant is manufacturing, preparing, propagating, compounding, or processing for commercial distribution, and (B) contains a particular ingredient. The Secretary may not require the submission of such a list unless he has made a finding that the submission of such a list is necessary to carry out the purposes of this Act.

SEC. 511.[26] * * *

NEW ANIMAL DRUGS

SEC. 512.[27] (a)(1) A new animal drug shall, with re-

---

[26] Sec. 511 repealed by Sec. 701 of P.L. 91–513.
[27] Sec. 512 added by sec. 101(b) of P.L. 90–399.
Sec. 108 of P.L. 90–399 states that these amendments shall take effect on the first day of the thirteenth calendar month which begins after July 13, 1968, the date of enactment of this Act (P.L. 90–399).

spect to any particular use or intended use of such drug, be deemed unsafe for the purposes of section 501(a)(5) and section 402(a)(2)(D) unless—

(A) there is in effect an approval of an application filed pursuant to subsection (b) of this section with respect to such use or intended use of such drug,

(B) such drug, its labeling, and such use conform to such approved application, and

(C) in the case of a new animal drug subject to subsection (n) of this section and not exempted therefrom by regulations it is from a batch with respect to which a certificate or release issued pursuant to subsection (n) is in effect with respect to such drug.

A new animal drug shall also be deemed unsafe for such purposes in the event of removal from the establishment of a manufacturer, packer, or distributor of such drug for use in the manufacture of animal feed in any State unless at the time of such removal such manufacturer, packer, or distributor has an unrevoked written statement from the consignee of such drug, or notice from the Secretary, to the effect that, with respect to the use of such drug in animal feed, such consignee—

(i) is the holder of an approved application under subsection (m) of this section; or

(ii) will, if the consignee is not a user of the drug, ship such drug only to a holder of an approved application under subsection (m) of this section.

(2) An animal feed bearing or containing a new animal drug shall, with respect to any particular use or intended use of such animal feed, be deemed unsafe for the purposes of section 501(a)(6) unless—

The term "effective date" means the effective date specified in subsection (a) of this section ; the term "basic Act" means the Federal Food, Drug, and Cosmetic Act ; and other terms used both in this section and the basic Act shall have the same meaning as they have, or had, at the time referred to in the context, under the basic Act.

Any approval, prior to the effective date, of a new animal drug or of an animal feed bearing or containing a new animal drug, whether granted by approval of a new-drug application, master file, antibiotic regulation, or food additive regulation, shall continue in effect, and shall be subject to change in accordance with the provisions of the basic Act as amended by this Act.

In the case of any drug (other than a drug subject to section 512(n) of the basic Act as amended by this Act) intended for use in animals other than man which, on October 9, 1962, (A) was commercially used or sold in the United States, (B) was not a new drug as defined by section 201(p) of the basic Act as then in force, and (C) was not covered by an effective application under section 505 of that Act, the words "effectiveness" and "effective" contained in section 201(w) as added by this Act to the basic Act shall not apply to such drug when intended solely for use under conditions prescribed, recommended, or suggested in labeling with respect to such drug on that day.

Regulations providing for fees (and advance deposits to cover fees) which on the day preceding the effective date applicable under subsection (a) of this section were in effect pursuant to section 507 of the basic Act shall, except as the Secretary may otherwise prescribe, be deemed to apply also under section 512(n) of the basic Act, and appropriations of fees (and of advance deposits to cover fees) available for the purposes specified in such section 507 as in effect prior to the effective date shall also be available for the purposes specified in section 512(n), including preparatory work or proceedings prior to that date.

(A) there is in effect an approval of an application filed pursuant to subsection (b) of this section with respect to such drug, as used in such animal feed,

(B) there is in effect an approval of an application pursuant to subsection (m)(1) of this section with respect to such animal feed, and

(C) such animal feed, its labeling, and such use conform to the conditions and indications of use published pursuant to subsection (i) of this section and to the application with respect thereto approved under subsection (m) of this section.

(3) A new animal drug or an animal feed bearing or containing a new animal drug shall not be deemed unsafe for the purposes of section 501(a) (5) or (6) if such article is for investigational use and conforms to the terms of an exemption in effect with respect thereto under section 512(j).

(b) Any person may file with the Secretary an application with respect to any intended use or uses of a new animal drug. Such person shall submit to the Secretary as a part of the application (1) full reports of investigations which have been made to show whether or not such drug is safe and effective for use; (2) a full list of the articles used as components of such drug; (3) a full statement of the composition of such drug; (4) a full description of the methods used in, and the facilities and controls used for, the manufacture, processing, and packing of such drug; (5) such samples of such drug and of the articles used as components thereof, of any animal feed for use in or on which such drug is intended, and of the edible portions or products (before or after slaughter) of animals to which such drug (directly or in or on animal feed) is intended to be administered, as the Secretary may require; (6) specimens of the labeling proposed to be used for such drug, or in case such drug is intended for use in animal feed, proposed labeling appropriate for such use, and specimens of the labeling for the drug to be manufactured, packed, or distributed by the applicant; (7) a description of practicable methods for determining the quantity, if any, of such drug in or on food, and any substance formed in or on food, because of its use; and (8) the proposed tolerance or withdrawal period or other use restrictions for such drug if any tolerance or withdrawal period or other use restrictions are required in order to assure that the proposed use of such drug will be safe.

(c) Within one hundred and eighty days after the filing of an application pursuant to subsection (b), or such additional period as may be agreed upon by the Secretary and the applicant, the Secretary shall either (1) issue an order approving the application if he then finds that none of the grounds for denying approval specified in subsection (d) applies, or (2) give the applicant notice of an opportunity for a hearing before the Secretary under subsection (d) on the question whether such application is approvable. If the applicant elects to accept the opportunity for a hearing by written request within thirty days after such notice, such hearing shall commence not more than ninety days after the expiration of such thirty days unless the Secretary and the applicant otherwise agree. Any such hearing shall thereafter be conducted on an expedited basis and the Secretary's order thereon shall be issued within ninety days after the date fixed by the Secretary for filing final briefs.

(d)(1) If the Secretary finds, after due notice to the applicant in accordance with subsection (c) and giving him an opportunity for a hearing, in accordance with said subsection, that—

(A) the investigations, reports of which are required to be submitted to the Secretary pursuant to subsection (b), do not include adequate tests by all methods reasonably applicable to show whether or not such drug is safe for use under the conditions prescribed, recommended, or suggested in the proposed labeling thereof;

(B) the results of such tests show that such drug is unsafe for use under such conditions or do not show that such drug is safe for use under such conditions;

(C) the methods used in, and the facilities and controls used for, the manufacture, processing, and packing of such drug are inadequate to preserve its identity, strength, quality, and purity;

(D) upon the basis of the information submitted to him as part of the application, or upon the basis of any other information before him with respect to such drug, he has insufficient information to determine whether such drug is safe for use under such conditions;

(E) evaluated on the basis of the information submitted to him as part of the application and any other information before him with respect to such drug, there is a lack of substantial evidence that the drug will have the effect it purports or is represented to have under the conditions of use prescribed, recommended, or suggested in the proposed labeling thereof;

(F) upon the basis of the information submitted to him as part of the application or any other information before him with respect to such drug, the tolerance limitation proposed, if any, exceeds that reasonably required to accomplish the physical or other technical effect for which the drug is intended;

(G) based on a fair evaluation of all material

facts, such labeling is false or misleading in any particular; or

(H) such drug induces cancer when ingested by man or animal or, after tests which are appropriate for the evaluation of the safety of such drug, induces cancer in man or animal, except that the foregoing provisions of this subparagraph shall not apply with respect to such drug if the Secretary finds that, under the conditions of use specified in proposed labeling and reasonably certain to be followed in practice (i) such drug will not adversely affect the animals for which it is intended, and (ii) no residue of such drug will be found (by methods of examination prescribed or approved by the Secretary by regulations, which regulations shall not be subject to subsections (c), (d), and (h)), in any edible portion of such animals after slaughter or in any food yielded by or derived from the living animals;

he shall issue an order refusing to approve the application. If, after such notice and opportunity for hearing, the Secretary finds that subparagraphs (A) through (H) do not apply, he shall issue an order approving the application.

(2) In determining whether such drug is safe for use under the conditions prescribed, recommended, or suggested in the proposed labeling thereof, the Secretary shall consider, among other relevant factors, (A) the probable consumption of such drug and of any substance formed in or on food because of the use of such drug, (B) the cumulative effect on man or animal of such drug, taking into account any chemically or pharmacologically related substance, (C) safety factors which in the opinion of experts, qualified by scientific training and experience to evaluate the safety of such drugs, are appropriate for the use of animal experimentation data, and (D) whether the conditions of use prescribed, recommended, or suggested in the proposed labeling are reasonably certain to be followed in practice. Any order issued under this subsection refusing to approve an application shall state the findings upon which it is based.

(3) As used in this subsection and subsection (e), the term "substantial evidence" means evidence consisting of adequate and well-controlled investigations, including field investigation, by experts qualified by scientific training and experience to evaluate the effectiveness of the drug involved, on the basis of which it could fairly and reasonably be concluded by such experts that the drug will have the effect it purports or is represented to have under the conditions of use prescribed, recommended, or suggested in the labeling or proposed labeling thereof.

(e)(1) The Secretary shall, after due notice and opportunity for hearing to the applicant, issue an order withdrawing approval of an application filed pursuant to subsection (b) with respect to any new animal drug if the Secretary finds—

(A) that experience or scientific data show that such drug is unsafe for use under the conditions of use upon the basis of which the application was approved;

(B) that new evidence not contained in such application or not available to the Secretary until after such application was approved, or tests by new methods, or tests by methods not deemed reasonably applicable when such application was approved, evaluated together with the evidence available to the Secretary when the application was approved, shows that such drug is not shown to be safe for use under the conditions of use upon the basis of which the application was approved or that subparagraph (H) of paragraph (1) of subsection (d) applies to such drug;

(C) on the basis of new information before him with respect to such drug, evaluated together with the evidence available to him when the application was approved, that there is a lack of substantial evidence that such drug will have the effect it purports or is represented to have under the conditions of use prescribed, recommended, or suggested in the labeling thereof;

(D) that the application contains any untrue statement of a material fact; or

(E) that the applicant has made any changes from the standpoint of safety or effectiveness beyond the variations provided for in the application unless he has supplemented the application by filing with the Secretary adequate information respecting all such changes and unless there is in effect an approval of the supplemental application. The supplemental application shall be treated in the same manner as the original application.

If the Secretary (or in his absence the officer acting as Secretary, finds that there is an imminent hazard to the health of man or of the animals for which such drug is intended, he may suspend the approval of such application immediately, and give the applicant prompt notice of his action and afford the applicant the opportunity for an expedited hearing under this subsection; but the authority conferred by this sentence to suspend the approval of an application shall not be delegated.

(2) The Secretary may also, after due notice and opportunity for hearing to the applicant, issue an order withdrawing the approval of an application with respect to any new animal drug under this section if the Secretary finds—

(A) that the applicant has failed to establish a system for maintaining required records, or has repeatedly or deliberately failed to maintain such records or to make required reports in accordance with a regulation or order under subsection (1), or the applicant has refused to permit access to, or copying or verification of, such records as required by paragraph (2) of such subsection;

(B) that on the basis of new information before him, evaluated together with the evidence before him when the application was approved, the methods used in, or the facilities and controls used for, the manufacture, processing, and packing of such drug are inadequate to assure and preserve its identity, strength, quality, and purity and were not made adequate within a reasonable time after receipt of written notice from the Secretary specifying the matter complained of; or

(C) that on the basis of new information before him, evaluated together with the evidence before him when the application was approved, the labeling of such drug, based on a fair evaluation of all material facts, is false or misleading in any particular and was not corrected within a reasonable time after receipt of written notice from the Secretary specifying the matter complained of.

(3) Any order under this subsection shall state the findings upon which it is based.

(f) Whenever the Secretary finds that the facts so require, he shall revoke any previous order under subsection (d), (e), or (m) refusing, withdrawing, or suspending approval of an application and shall approve such application or reinstate such approval, as may be appropriate.

(g) Orders of the Secretary issued under this section (other than orders issuing, amending, or repealing regulations) shall be served (1) in person by any officer or employee of the department designated by the Secretary or (2) by mailing the order by registered mail or by certified mail addressed to the applicant or respondent at his last known address in the records of the Secretary.

(h) An appeal may be taken by the applicant from an order of the Secretary refusing or withdrawing approval of an application filed under subsection (b) or (m) of this section. The provisions of subsection (h) of section 505 of this Act shall govern any such appeal.

(i) When a new animal drug application filed pursuant to subsection (b) is approved, the Secretary shall by notice, which upon publication shall be effective as a regulation, publish in the Federal Register the name and address of the applicant and the conditions and indications of use of the new animal drug covered by such

application, including any tolerance and withdrawal
period or other use restrictions and, if such new animal
drug is intended for use in animal feed, appropriate
purposes and conditions of use (including special labeling requirements) applicable to any animal feed for use
in which such drug is approved, and such other information, upon the basis of which such application was approved, as the Secretary deems necessary to assure the
safe and effective use of such drug. Upon withdrawal of
approval of such new animal drug application or upon
its suspension, the Secretary shall forthwith revoke or
suspend, as the case may be, the regulation published
pursuant to this subsection (i) insofar as it is based on
the approval of such application.

(j) To the extent consistent with the public health,
the Secretary shall promulgate regulations for exempting from the operation of this section new animal drugs,
and animal feeds bearing or containing new animal
drugs, intended solely for investigational use by experts
qualified by scientific training and experience to investigate the safety and effectiveness of animal drugs. Such
regulations may, in the discretion of the Secretary, among
other conditions relating to the protection of the public
health, provide for conditioning such exemption upon
the establishment and maintenance of such records, and
the making of such reports to the Secretary, by the manufacturer or the sponsor of the investigation of such article, of data (including but not limited to analytical reports by investigators) obtained as a result of such investigational use of such article, as the Secretary finds
will enable him to evaluate the safety and effectiveness
of such article in the event of the filing of an application
pursuant to this section. Such regulations, among other
things, shall set forth the conditions (if any) upon which
animals treated with such articles, and any products of
such animals (before or after slaughter), may be marketed for food use.

(k) While approval of an application for a new animal
drug is effective, a food shall not, by reason of bearing
or containing such drug or any substance formed in or
on the food because of its use in accordance with such
application (including the conditions and indications of
use prescribed pursuant to subsection (i)), be considered
adulterated within the meaning of clause (1) of section
402(a).

(l)(1) In the case of any new animal drug for which
an approval of an application filed pursuant to subsection (b) is in effect, the applicant shall establish and
maintain such records, and make such reports to the
Secretary, of data relating to experience and other data
or information, received or otherwise obtained by such
applicant with respect to such drug, or with respect to

animal feeds bearing or containing such drug, as the
Secretary may by general regulation, or by order with
respect to such application, prescribe on the basis of a
finding that such records and reports are necessary in
order to enable the Secretary to determine, or facilitate
a determination, whether there is or may be ground for
invoking subsection (e) or subsection (m)(4) of this
section. Such regulation or order shall provide, where
the Secretary deems it to be appropriate, for the examination, upon request, by the persons to whom such regulation or order is applicable, of similar information
received or otherwise obtained by the Secretary.

(2) Every person required under this subsection to
maintain records, and every person in charge or custody
thereof, shall, upon request of an officer or employee
designated by the Secretary, permit such officer or employee at all reasonable times to have access to and copy
and verify such records.

(m) (1) Any person may file with the Secretary an
application with respect to any intended use or uses of
an animal feed bearing or containing a new animal drug.
Such person shall submit to the Secretary as part of the
application (A) a full statement of the composition of
such animal feed, (B) an identification of the regulation
or regulations (relating to the new animal drug or drugs
to be used in such feed), published pursuant to subsection (i), on which he relies as a basis for approval of
his application with respect to the use of such drug in
such feed, (C) a full description of the methods used in,
and the facilities and controls used for, the manufacture,
processing, and packing of such animal feed, (D) specimens of the labeling proposed to be used for such animal
feed, and (E) if so requested by the Secretary, samples
of such animal feed or components thereof.

(2) Within ninety days after the filing of an application pursuant to subsection (m)(1), or such additional
period as may be agreed upon by the Secretary and the
applicant, the Secretary shall either (A) issue an order
approving the application if he then finds that none of
the grounds for denying approval specified in paragraph
(3) applies, or (B) give the applicant notice of an opportunity for a hearing before the Secretary under paragraph (3) on the question whether such application is
approvable. The procedure governing such a hearing
shall be the procedure set forth in the last two sentences
of subsection (c).

(3) If the Secretary, after due notice to the applicant
in accordance with paragraph (2) and giving him an opportunity for a hearing in accordance with such paragraph, finds, on the basis of information submitted to
him as part of the application or on the basis of any other
information before him—

(A) that there is not in effect a regulation under subsection (i) (identified in such application) on the basis of which such application may be approved;

(B) that such animal feed (including the proposed use of any new animal drug therein or thereon) does not conform to an applicable regulation published pursuant to subsection (i) referred to in the application, or that the purposes and conditions or indications of use prescribed, recommended, or suggested in the labeling of such feed do not conform to the applicable purposes and conditions or indications of use (including warnings) published pursuant to subsection (i) or such labeling omits or fails to conform to other applicable information published pursuant to subsection (i);

(C) that the methods used in, and the facilities and controls used for, the manufacture, processing, and packing of such animal feed are inadequate to preserve the identity, strength, quality, and purity of the new animal drug therein; or

(D) that, based on a fair evaluation of all material facts, such labeling is false or misleading in any particular;

he shall issue an order refusing to approve the application. If, after such notice and opportunity for hearing, the Secretary finds that subparagraphs (A) through (D) do not apply, he shall issue an order approving the application. An order under this subsection approving an application with respect to an animal feed bearing or containing a new animal drug shall be effective only while there is in effect a regulation pursuant to subsection (i), on the basis of which such application (or a supplement thereto) was approved, relating to the use of such drug in or on such feed.

(4) (A) The Secretary shall, after due notice and opportunity for hearing to the applicant, issue an order withdrawing approval of an application with respect to any animal feed under this subsection if the Secretary finds—

(i) that the application contains any untrue statement of a material fact; or

(ii) that the applicant has made any changes from the standpoint of safety or effectiveness beyond the variations provided for in the application unless he has supplemented the application by filing with the Secretary adequate information respecting all such changes and unless there is in effect an approval of the supplemental application. The supplemental application shall be treated in the same manner as the original application.

If the Secretary (or in his absence the officer acting as Secretary) finds that there is an imminent hazard to the

health of man or of the animals for which such animal
feed is intended, he may suspend the approval of such
application immediately, and give the applicant prompt
notice of his action and afford the applicant the opportunity for an expedited hearing under this subsection;
but the authority conferred by this sentence shall
not be delegated.

(B) The Secretary may also, after due notice and opportunity for hearing to the applicant, issue an order
withdrawing the approval of an application with respect
to any animal feed under this subsection if the Secretary
finds—

> (i) that the applicant has failed to establish a sys-
> tem for maintaining required records, or has repeat-
> edly or deliberately failed to maintain such records
> or to make required reports in accordance with a
> regulation or order under paragraph (5)(A) of this
> subsection, or the applicant has refused to permit ac-
> cess to, or copying or verification of, such records
> as required by subparagraph (B) of such para-
> graph;

> (ii) that on the basis of new information before
> him, evaluated together with the evidence before
> him when such application was approved, the meth-
> ods used in, or the facilities and controls used for,
> the manufacture, processing, and packing of such
> animal feed are inadequate to assure and preserve
> the identity, strength, quality, and purity of the new
> animal drug therein, and were not made adequate
> within a reasonable time after receipt of written no-
> tice from the Secretary, specifying the matter com-
> plained of; or

> (iii) that on the basis of new information before
> him, evaluated together with the evidence before
> him when the application was approved, the labeling
> of such animal feed, based on a fair evaluation of all
> material facts, is false or misleading in any particu-
> lar and was not corrected within a reasonable time
> after receipt of written notice from the Secretary
> specifying the matter complained of.

(C) Any order under paragraph (4) of this subsection
shall state the findings upon which it is based.

(5) In the case of any animal feed for which an approval of an application filed pursuant to this subsection
is in effect—

> (A) the applicant shall establish and maintain
> such records, and make such reports to the Secretary,
> or (at the option of the Secretary) to the appropri-
> ate person or persons holding an approved applica-
> tion filed under subsection (b), as the Secretary may
> by general regulation, or by order with respect to
> such application, prescribe on the basis of a finding

that such records and reports are necessary in order to enable the Secretary to determine, or facilitate a determination, whether there is or may be ground for invoking subsection (e) or paragraph (4) of this subsection.

(B) every person required under this subsection to maintain records, and every person in charge or custody thereof, shall, upon request of an officer or employee designated by the Secretary, permit such officer or employee at all reasonable times to have access to and copy and verify such records.

(n) (1) The Secretary, pursuant to regulations promulgated by him, shall provide for the certification of batches of a new animal drug composed wholly or partly of any kind of penicillin, streptomycin, chlortetracycline, chloramphenicol, or bacitracin, or any derivative thereof. A batch of any such drug shall be certified if an approval of an application filed pursuant to subsection (b) is effective with respect to such drug and such drug has the characteristics of identity and such batch has the characteristics of strength, quality, and purity upon the basis of which the application was approved, but shall not otherwise be certified. Prior to the effective date of such regulations the Secretary, in lieu of certification, shall issue a release for any batch which, in his judgment, may be released without risk as to the safety and efficacy of its use. Such release shall prescribe the date of its expiration and other conditions under which it shall cease to be effective as to such batch and as to portions thereof.

(2) Regulations providing for such certifications shall contain such provisions as are necessary to carry out the purposes of this subsection, including provisions prescribing—

(A) tests and methods of assay to determine compliance with applicable standards of identity and of strength, quality, and purity;

(B) effective periods for certificates, and other conditions under which they shall cease to be effective as to certified batches and as to portions thereof;

(C) administration and procedure; and

(D) such fees, specified in such regulations, as are necessary to provide, equip, and maintain an adequate certification service.

Such regulations shall prescribe only such tests and methods of assay as will provide for certification or rejection within the shortest time consistent with the purposes of this subsection.

(3) Whenever, in the judgment of the Secretary, the requirements of this subsection with respect to any drug or class of drugs are not necessary to insure that such drug conforms to the standards of identity, strength, quality, and purity applicable thereto under paragraph

(1) of this subsection, the Secretary shall promulgate regulations exempting such drug or class of drugs from such requirements. The provisions of subsection (c) of section 507 of this Act (other than the first sentence thereof) shall apply under this paragraph.

(4) The Secretary shall promulgate regulations exempting from any requirement of this subsection—

(A) drugs which are to be stored, processed, labeled, or repacked at establishments other than those where manufactured, on condition that such drugs comply with all such requirements upon removal from such establishments; and

(B) drugs which conform to applicable standards of identity, strength, quality, and purity prescribed pursuant to this subsection and are intended for use in manufacturing other drugs.

(5) On petition of any interested person for the issuance, amendment, or repeal of any regulation contemplated by this subsection, the procedure shall be in accordance with subsection (f) of section 507 of this Act.

(6) Where any drug is subject to this subsection and not exempted therefrom by regulations, the compliance of such drug with sections 501(b) and 502(g) shall be determined by the application of the standards of strength, quality, and purity applicable under paragraph (1) of this subsection, the tests and methods of assay applicable under provisions of regulations referred to in paragraph (2)(A) of this subsection, and the requirements of packaging and labeling on the basis of which the application with respect to such drug filed under subsection (b) of this section was approved.

CHAPTER VI—COSMETICS

ADULTERATED COSMETICS

SEC. 601 [361]. A cosmetic shall be deemed to be adulterated—

(a) If it bears or contains any poisonous or deleterious substance which may render it injurious to users under the conditions of use prescribed in the labeling thereof, or, under such conditions of use as are customary or usual: *Provided*, That this provision shall not apply to coal-tar hair dye, the label of which bears the following legend conspicuously displayed thereon: "Caution—This product contains ingredients which may cause skin irritation on certain individuals and a preliminary test according to accompanying directions should first be made. This product must not be used for dyeing the eyelashes or eyebrows; to do so may cause blindness.", and the labeling of which bears adequate directions for such preliminary testing. For the purposes of this paragraph and paragraph (e) the term "hair dye" shall not include eyelash dyes or eyebrow dyes.

(b) If it consists in whole or in part of any filthy, putrid, or decomposed substance.

(c) If it has been prepared, packed, or held under insanitary conditions whereby it may have become contaminated with filth, or whereby it may have been rendered injurious to health.

(d) If its container is composed, in whole or in part, of any poisonous or deleterious substance which may render the contents injurious to health.

(e) If it is not a hair dye and it is, or it bears or contains, a color additive which is unsafe within the meaning of section 706 (a).

MISBRANDED COSMETICS

SEC. 602 [362]. A cosmetic shall be deemed to be misbranded—

(a) If its labeling is false or misleading in any particular.

(b) If in package form unless it bears a label containing (1) the name and place of business of the manufacturer, packer, or distributor; and (2) an accurate statement of the quantity of the contents in terms of weight, measure, or numerical count: *Provided,* That under clause (2) of this paragraph reasonable variations shall be permitted, and exemptions as to small packages shall be established, by regulations prescribed by the Secretary.

(c) If any word, statement, or other information required by or under authority of this act to appear on the label or labeling is not prominently placed thereon with such conspicuousness (as compared with other words, statements, designs, or devices in the labeling) and in such terms as to render it likely to be read and understood by the ordinary individual under customary conditions of purchase and use.

(d) If its container is so made, formed, or filled as to be misleading.

(e) If it is a color additive, unless its packaging and labeling are in conformity with such packaging and labeling requirements, applicable to such color additive, as may be contained in regulations issued under section 706. This paragraph shall not apply to packages of color additives which, with respect to their use for cosmetics, are marketed and intended for use only in or on hair dyes (as defined in the last sentence of section 601(a)).

(f)[28] If its packaging or labeling is in violation of an applicable regulation issued pursuant to section 3 or 4 of the Poison Prevention Packaging Act of 1970.

---

[28] Sec. 602(f) added by Sec. 7 of P.L. 91–601.

REGULATIONS MAKING EXEMPTIONS

Sec. 603 [363]. The Secretary shall promulgate regulations exempting from any labeling requirement of this act cosmetics which are, in accordance with the practice of the trade, to be processed, labeled, or repacked in substantial quantities at establishments other than those where originally processed or packed, on condition that such cosmetics are not adulterated or misbranded under the provisions of this act upon removal from such processing, labeling, or repacking establishment.

CHAPTER VII—GENERAL ADMINISTRATIVE PROVISIONS

REGULATIONS AND HEARINGS

Sec. 701 [371]. (a) The authority to promulgate regulations for the efficient enforcement of this Act, except as otherwise provided in this section, is hereby vested in the Secretary.

(b) The Secretary of the Treasury and the Secretary of Health, Education, and Welfare shall jointly prescribe regulations for the efficient enforcement of the provisions of section 801, except as otherwise provided therein. Such regulations shall be promulgated in such manner and take effect at such time, after due notice, as the Secretary of Health, Education, and Welfare shall determine.

(c) Hearings authorized or required by this Act shall be conducted by the Secretary or such officer or employee as he may designate for the purpose.

(d) The definitions and standards of identity promulgated in accordance with the provisions of this Act shall be effective for the purposes of the enforcement of this Act, notwithstanding such definitions and standards as may be contained in other laws of the United States and regulations promulgated thereunder.

(e)(1) Any action for the issuance, amendment, or repeal of any regulation under section 401, 403(j), 404(a), 406, 501(b), or 502 (d) or (h) of this Act shall be begun by a proposal made (A) by the Secretary on his own initiative, or (B) by petition of any interested persons, showing reasonable grounds therefor, filed with the Secretary. The Secretary shall publish such proposal and shall afford all interested persons an opportunity to present their views thereon, orally or in writing. As soon as practicable thereafter, the Secretary shall by order act upon such proposal and shall make such order public. Except as provided in paragraph (2), the order shall become effective at such time as may be specified therein, but not prior to the day following the last day on which objections may be filed under such paragraph.

(2) On or before the thirtieth day after the date on which an order entered under paragraph (1) is made public, any person who will be adversely affected by such order if placed in effect may file objections thereto with the Secretary, specifying with particularity the provisions of the order deemed objectionable, stating the grounds therefor, and requesting a public hearing upon such objections. Until final action upon such objections is taken by the Secretary under paragraph (3), the filing of such objections shall operate to stay the effectiveness of those provisions of the order to which the objections are made. As soon as practicable after the time for filing objections has expired the Secretary shall publish a notice in the Federal Register specifying those parts of the order which have been stayed by the filing of objections and, if no objections have been filed, stating that fact.

(3) As soon as practicable after such request for a public hearing, the Secretary, after due notice, shall hold such a public hearing for the purpose of receiving evidence relevant and material to the issues raised by such objections. At the hearing, any interested person may be heard in person or by representative. As soon as practicable after completion of the hearing, the Secretary shall by order act upon such objections and make such order public. Such order shall be based only on substantial evidence of record at such hearing and shall set forth, as part of the order, detailed findings of fact on which the order is based. The Secretary shall specify in the order the date on which it shall take effect, except that it shall not be made to take effect prior to the ninetieth day after its publication unless the Secretary finds that emergency conditions exist necessitating an earlier effective date, in which event the Secretary shall specify in the order his findings as to such conditions.

(f) (1) In a case of actual controversy as to the validity of any order under subsection (e), any person who will be adversely affected by such order if placed in effect may at any time prior to the ninetieth day after such order is issued file a petition with the Circuit Court of Appeals of the United States for the circuit wherein such person resides or has his principal place of business, for a judicial review of such order. A copy of the petition shall be forthwith transmitted by the clerk of the court to the Secretary or other officer designated by him for that purpose. The Secretary thereupon shall file in the court the record of the proceedings on which the Secretary based his order, as provided in section 2112 of title 28, United States Code.

(2) If the petitioner applies to the court for leave to adduce additional evidence, and shows to the satisfaction of the court that such additional evidence is material and that there were reasonable grounds for the failure to adduce such evidence in the proceeding before the Secre-

tary the court may order such additional evidence (and evidence in rebuttal thereof) to be taken before the Secretary, and to be adduced upon the hearing, in such manner and upon such terms and conditions as to the court may seem proper. The Secretary may modify his findings as to the facts, or make new findings, by reason of the additional evidence, so taken, and he shall file such modified or new findings, and his recommendation, if any, for the modification or setting aside of his original order, with the return of such additional evidence.

(3) Upon the filing of the petition referred to in paragraph (1) of this subsection, the court shall have jurisdiction to affirm the order, or to set it aside in whole or in part, temporarily or permanently. If the order of the Secretary refuses to issue, amend, or repeal a regulation and such order is not in accordance with law the court shall by its judgment order the Secretary to take action with respect to such regulation, in accordance with law. The findings of the Secretary as to the facts, if supported by substantial evidence, shall be conclusive [now covered by U.S.C. title 28, sec. 1254].

(4) The judgment of the court affirming or setting aside, in whole or in part, any such order of the Secretary shall be final, subject to review by the Supreme Court of the United States upon certiorari or certification as provided in sections 239 and 240 of the Judicial Code, as amended.

(5) Any action instituted under this subsection shall survive notwithstanding any change in the person occupying the office of Secretary or any vacancy in such office.

(6) The remedies provided for in this subsection shall be in addition to and not in substitution for any other remedies provided by law.

(g) A certified copy of the transcript of the record and proceedings under subsection (e) shall be furnished by the Secretary to any interested party at his request, and payment of the costs thereof, and shall be admissible in any criminal libel for condemnation, exclusion of imports, or other proceeding arising under or in respect of this Act, irrespective of whether proceedings with respect to the order have previously been instituted or become final under subsection (f).

EXAMINATIONS AND INVESTIGATIONS

SEC. 702 [372]. (a) The Secretary is authorized to conduct examinations and investigations for the purposes of this Act through officers and employees of the Department or through any health, food, or drug officer or employee of any State, Territory, or political subdivision thereof, duly commissioned by the Secretary as an officer of the Department. In the case of food packed in the

Commonwealth of Puerto Rico or a Territory the Secretary shall attempt to make inspection of such food at the first point of entry within the United States, when in his opinion and with due regard to the enforcement of all the provisions of this Act, the facilities at his disposal will permit of such inspection. For the purposes of this subsection the term "United States" means the States and the District of Columbia.

(b) Where a sample of a food, drug, or cosmetic is collected for analysis under this Act the Secretary shall, upon request, provide a part of such official sample for examination or analysis by any person named on the label of the article, or the owner thereof, or his attorney or agent; except that the Secretary is authorized, by regulations, to make such reasonable exceptions from, and impose such reasonable terms and conditions relating to, the operation of this subsection as he finds necessary for the proper administration of the provisions of this Act.

(c) For purposes of enforcement of this Act, records of any department or independent establishment in the executive branch of the Government shall be open to inspection by any official of the Department of Health, Education, and Welfare duly authorized by the Secretary to make such inspection.

(d) The Secretary is authorized and directed, upon request from the Commissioner of Patents, to furnish full and complete information with respect to such questions relating to drugs as the Commissioner may submit concerning any patent application. The Secretary is further authorized, upon receipt of any such request, to conduct or cause to be conducted, such research as may be required.

(e) [29, 30] Any officer or employee of the Department designated by the Secretary to conduct examinations, investigations, or inspections under this Act relating to counterfeit drugs may, when so authorized by the Secretary—

(1) carry firearms;

(2) execute and serve search warrants and arrest warrants;

(3) execute seizure by process issued pursuant to libel under section 304;

(4) make arrests without warrant for offenses under this Act with respect to such drugs if the offense is committed in his presence or, in the case of a felony, if he has probable cause to believe that the person so arrested has committed, or is committing, such offense; and

[29] Section 1114 of title 18 of the United States Code is amended by sec. 17(h)(1) of P.L. 91–596. Sec. 1114 of title 18 will read in part "or any officer or employee of the Department of Health, Education, and Welfare or of the Department of Labor assigned to perform investigative, inspection or law enforcement functions".
[30] Subsec. (e) amended by sec. 701 of P.L. 91–513.

(5) make, prior to the institution of libel proceedings under section 304(a)(2), seizures of drugs or containers or of equipment, punches, dies, plates, stones, labeling, or other things, if they are, or he has reasonable grounds to believe that they are, subject to seizure and condemnation under such section 304(a)(2).·In the event of seizure pursuant to this paragraph (5), libel proceedings under section 304 (a)(2) shall be instituted promptly and the property seized be placed under the jurisdiction of the court.

* * *

RECORDS OF INTERSTATE SHIPMENT

SEC. 703 [373].[32] For the purpose of enforcing the provisions of this Act, carriers engaged in interstate commerce, and persons receiving food, drugs, devices, or cosmetics in interstate commerce or holding such articles so received, shall, upon the request of an officer or employee duly designated by the Secretary, permit such officer or employee, at reasonable times, to have access to and to copy all records showing the movement in interstate commerce of any food, drug, device, or cosmetic, or the holding thereof during or after such movement, and the quantity, shipper, and consignee thereof; and it shall be unlawful for any such carrier or person to fail to permit such access to and copying of any such record so requested when such request is accompanied by a statement in writing specifying the nature or kind of food, drug, device, or cosmetic to which such request relates: *Provided*, That evidence obtained under this section, or any evidence which is directly or indirectly derived from such evidence, shall not be used in a criminal prosecution of the person from whom obtained: *Provided further*, That carriers shall not be subject to the other provisions of this Act by reason of their receipt, carriage, holding, or delivery of food, drugs, devices, or cosmetics in the usual course of business as carriers.

FACTORY INSPECTION

SEC. 704 [374]. (a) For purposes of enforcement of this Act, officers or employees duly designated by the Secretary, upon presenting appropriate credentials and a written notice to the owner, operator, or agent in charge, are authorized (1) to enter, at reasonable times, any factory, warehouse, or establishment in which food drugs, devices, or cosmetics are manufactured, processed, packed, or held, for introduction into interstate commerce or after such introduction, or to enter any vehicle, being used to transport or hold such food, drugs, devices, or cosmetics in interstate commerce; and (2) to inspect, at reasonable times and within reasonable limits and in a reasonable manner, such factory, warehouse, establishment, or vehicle and all pertinent equipment, finished and unfinished materials, containers, and labeling therein. In the case of any factory, warehouse, establishment, or consulting laboratory in which prescription drugs are manufactured, processed, packed, or held, inspection shall extend to all things therein (including records, files, papers, processes, controls, and facilities) bearing on whether prescription drugs which are adulterated or misbranded within the meaning of this Act, or which may not be manufactured, introduced into interstate commerce, or sold, or offered for sale by reason of any provision of this Act, have been or are being manufactured, processed, packed, transported, or held in any such place, or otherwise bearing on violation of this Act. No inspection authorized for prescription drugs by the preceding sentence shall extend to (A) financial data, (B) sales data other than shipment data, (C) pricing data, (D) personnel data (other than data as to qualifications of technical and professional personnel performing functions subject to this Act), and (E) research data (other than data, relating to new drugs and antibiotic drugs, subject to reporting and inspection under regulations lawfully issued pursuant to section 505 (i) or (j) or section 507 (d) or (g) of this Act, and data, relating to other drugs, which in the case of a new drug would be subject to reporting or inspection under lawful regulations issued pursuant to section 505(j) of this Act). A separate notice shall be given for each such inspection, but a notice shall not be required for each entry made during the period covered by the inspection. Each such inspection shall be commenced and completed with reasonable promptness. The provisions of the second sentence of this subsection shall not apply to—

(1) pharmacies which maintain establishments in conformance with any applicable local laws regulating the practice of pharmacy and medicine and which are regularly engaged in dispensing prescription drugs, upon prescriptions of practitioners licensed to administer such drugs to patients under the care of such practitioners in the course of their professional practice, and which do not, either through a subsidiary or otherwise, manufacture, prepare, propagate, compound, or process drugs for sale other than in the regular course of their business of dispensing or selling drugs at retail;

(2) practitioners licensed by law to prescribe or administer drugs and who manufacture, prepare, propagate, compound, or process drugs solely for use in the course of their professional practice;

(3) persons who manufacture, prepare, propagate, compound, or process drugs solely for use in research, teaching, or chemical analysis and not for sale;

---

[33] Sec. 703 amended by sec. 230 of P.L. 91–452.

(4) such other classes of persons as the Secretary may by regulation exempt from the application of this section·upon a finding that inspection as applied to such classes of persons in accordance with this section is not necessary for the protection of the public health.

(b) Upon completion of any such inspection of a factory, warehouse, consulting laboratory, or other establishment, and prior to leaving the premises, the officer or employee making the inspection shall give to the owner, operator, or agent in charge a report in writing setting forth any conditions or practices observed by him which, in his judgment, indicate that any food, drug, device, or cosmetic in such establishment (1) consists in whole or in part of any filthy, putrid, or decomposed substance, or (2) has been prepared, packed, or held under insanitary conditions whereby it may have become contaminated with filth, or whereby it may have been rendered injurious to health. A copy of such report shall be sent promptly to the Secretary.

(c) If the officer or employee making any such inspection of a factory, warehouse, or other establishment has obtained any sample in the course of the inspection, upon completion of the inspection and prior to leaving the premises he shall give to the owner, operator, or agent in charge a receipt describing the samples obtained.

(d) Whenever in the ·course of any such inspection of a factory or other establishment where food is manufactured, processed, or packed, the officer or employee making the inspection obtains a sample of any such food, and an analysis is made of such sample for the purpose of ascertaining whether such food consists in whole or in part of any filthy, putrid, or decomposed substance, or is otherwise unfit for food, a copy of the results of such analysis shall be furnished promptly to the owner, operator, or agent in charge.

PUBLICITY

SEC. 705 [375]. (a) The Secretary shall cause to be published from time to time reports summarizing all judgments, decrees, and court orders which have been rendered under this Act, including the nature of the charge and the disposition thereof.

(b) The Secretary may also cause to be disseminated information regarding food, drugs, devices, or cosmetics in situations involving, in the opinion of the Secretary, imminent danger to health, or gross deception of the consumer. Nothing in this section shall be construed to prohibit the Secretary from collecting, reporting, and illustrating the results of the investigations of the Department.

LISTING AND CERTIFICATION OF COLOR ADDITIVES FOR FOODS,
DRUGS, AND COSMETICS

When Color Additives Deemed Unsafe

SEC. 706 [376]. (a) A color additive shall, with respect
to any particular use (for which it is being used or
intended to be used or is represented as suitable) in or on
food or drugs or cosmetics be deemed unsafe for the
purposes of the application of section 402(c), section
501(a)(4), or section 601(e), as the case may be unless—
(1)(A) there is in effect, and such additive and
such use are in conformity with, a regulation issued
under subsection (b) of this section listing such additive for such use, including any provision of such
regulation prescribing the conditions under which
such additive may be safely used, and (B) such additive either (i) is from a batch certified, in accordance with regulations issued pursuant to subsection
(c), for such use, or (ii) has, with respect to such
use, been exempted by the Secretary from the requirement of certification; or
(2) such additive and such use thereof conform
to the terms of an exemption which is in effect pursuant to subsection (f) of this section.
While there are in effect regulations under subsections
(b) and (c) of this section relating to a color additive
or an exemption pursuant to subsection (f) with respect
to such additive, an article shall not, by reason of bearing
or containing such additive in all respects in accordance
with such regulations or such exemption, be considered
adulterated within the meaning of clause (1) of section
402(a) if such article is a food, or within the meaning
of section 601(a) if such article is a cosmetic other than
a hair dye (as defined in the last sentence of section
601(a)).

Listing of Colors

(b) (1) The Secretary shall, by regulation, provide for
separately listing color additives for use in or on food,
color additives for use in or on drugs, and color additives
for use in or on cosmetics, if and to the extent that such
additives are suitable and safe for any such use when
employed in accordance with such regulations.
(2)(A) Such regulations may list any color additive
for use generally in or on food, or in or on drugs, or in
or on cosmetics, if the Secretary finds that such additive
is suitable and may safely be employed for such general
use.
(B) If the data before the Secretary do not establish
that the additive satisfies the requirements for listing
such additive on the applicable list pursuant to subparagraph (A) of this paragraph, or if the proposal is for
listing such additive for a more limited use or uses, such
regulations may list such additive only for any more lim-

ited use or uses for which it is suitable and may safely be employed.

(3) Such regulations shall, to the extent deemed necessary by the Secretary to assure the safety of the use or uses for which a particular color additive is listed, prescribe the conditions under which such additive may be safely employed for such use or uses (including, but not limited to, specifications, hereafter in this section referred to as tolerance limitations, as to the maximum quantity or quantities which may be used or permitted to remain in or on the article or articles in or on which it is used; specifications as to the manner in which such additive may be added to or used in or on such article or articles; and directions or other labeling or packaging requirements for such additive).

(4) The Secretary shall not list a color additive under this section for a proposed use unless the data before him establish that such use, under the conditions of use specified in the regulations, will be safe: *Provided, however,* That a color additive shall be deemed to be suitable and safe for the purpose of listing under this subsection for use generally in or on food, while there is in effect a published finding of the Secretary declaring such substance exempt from the term "food additive" because of its being generally recognized by qualified experts as safe for its intended use, as provided in section 201(s).

(5)(A) In determining, for the purposes of this section, whether a proposed use of a color additive is safe, the Secretary shall consider, among other relevant factors—

(i) the probable consumption of, or other relevant exposure from, the additive and of any substance formed in or on food, drugs, or cosmetics because of the use of the additive;

(ii) the cumulative effect, if any, of such additive in the diet of man or animals, taking into account the same or any chemically or pharmacologically related substance or substances in such diet;

(iii) safety factors which, in the opinion of experts qualified by scientific training and experience to evaluate the safety of color additives for the use or uses for which the additive is proposed to be listed, are generally recognized as appropriate for the use of animal experimentation data; and

(iv) the availability of any needed practicable methods of analysis for determining the identity and quantity of (I) the pure dye and all intermediates and other impurities contained in such color additive, (II) such additive in or on any article of food, drug, or cosmetic, and (III) any substance formed in or on such article because of the use of such additive.

(B) A color additive (i) shall be deemed unsafe, and shall not be listed, for any use which will or may result in ingestion of all or part of such additive, if the additive is found by the Secretary to induce cancer when ingested by man or animal, or if it is found by the Secretary, after tests which are appropriate for the evaluation of the safety of additives for use in food, to induce cancer in man or animal, and (ii) shall be deemed unsafe, and shall not be listed, for any use which will not result in ingestion of any part of such additive, if, after tests which are appropriate for the evaluation of the safety of additives for such use, or after other relevant exposure of man or animal to such additive, it is found by the Secretary to induce cancer in man or animal: *Provided,* That clause (i) of this subparagraph (B) shall not apply with respect to the use of a color additive as an ingredient of feed for animals which are raised for food production, if the Secretary finds that, under the conditions of use and feeding specified in proposed labeling and reasonably certain to be followed in practice, such additive will not adversely affect the animals for which such feed is intended, and that no residue of the additive will be found (by methods of examination prescribed or approved by the Secretary by regulations, which regulations shall not be subject to subsection (d)) in any edible portion of such animals after slaughter or in any food yielded by or derived from the living animal.

(C) (i) In any proceeding for the issuance, amendment, or repeal of a regulation listing a color additive, whether commenced by a proposal of the Secretary on his own initiative or by a proposal contained in a petition, the petitioner, or any other person who will be adversely affected by such proposal or by the Secretary's order issued in accordance with paragraph (1) of section 701(e) if placed in effect, may request, within the time specified in this subparagraph, that the petition or order thereon, or the Secretary's proposal, be referred to an advisory committee for a report and recommendations with respect to any matter arising under subparagraph (B) of this paragraph, which is involved in such proposal or order and which requires the exercise of scientific judgment. Upon such request, or if the Secretary within such time deems such a referral necessary, the Secretary shall forthwith appoint an advisory committee under subparagraph (D) of this paragraph and shall refer to it, together with all the data before him, such matter arising under subparagraph (B) for study thereof and for a report and recommendations on such matter. A person who has filed a petition or who has requested the referral of a matter to an advisory committee pursuant to this subparagraph (C), as well as representatives of the Department of Health, Education, and Welfare, shall have the right to consult with such advisory committee in connection with the matter referred to it. The request for referral under this subparagraph, or the Secretary's referral on his own initiative, may be made at any time before, or within thirty days after, publication of an order of the Secretary acting upon the petition or proposal.

(ii) Within sixty days after the date of such referral, or within an additional thirty days if the committee deems such additional time necessary, the committee shall, after independent study of the data furnished to it by the Secretary and other data before it, certify to the Secretary a report and recommendations, together with all underlying data and a statement of the reasons or basis for the recommendations. A copy of the foregoing shall be promptly supplied by the Secretary to any person who has filed a petition, or who has requested such referral to the advisory committee. Within thirty days after such certification, and after giving due consideration to all data then before him, including such report, recommendation, underlying data, and statement, and to any prior order issued by him in connection with such matter, the Secretary shall by order confirm or modify any order therefore issued or, if no such prior order has been issued, shall by order act upon the petition or other proposal.

(iii) Where—

(I) by reason of subparagraph (B) of this paragraph, the Secretary has initiated a proposal to remove from listing a color additive previously listed pursuant to this section; and

(II) a request has been made for referral of such proposal to an advisory committee; the Secretary may not act by order on such proposal until the advisory committee has made a report and recommendations to him under clause (ii) of this subparagraph and he has considered such recommendations, unless the Secretary finds that emergency conditions exist necessitating the issuance of an order notwithstanding this clause.

(D)[33] The advisory committee referred to in subparagraph (C) of this paragraph shall be composed of experts selected by the National Academy of Sciences, qualified in the subject matter referred to the committee and of adequately diversified professional background, except that in the event of the inability or refusal of the National Academy of Sciences to act, the Secretary shall select the members of the committee. The size of the committee shall be determined by the Secretary. Members of any advisory committee established under this Act, while attending conferences or meetings of their committees or otherwise serving at the request of the Secretary, shall be entitled to receive compensation at rates to be fixed by the Secretary but at rates not exceeding the daily equivalent of the rate specified at the time of such service for grade GS-18 of the General Schedule, including traveltime; and while away from their homes or regular places of business they may be allowed travel expenses,

---

[33] Sec. 706(b)(5)(D) amended by sec. 601(d)(2) of P.L. 91-515.

including per diem in lieu of subsistence, as authorized by section 5703(b) of title 5 of the United States Code for persons in the Government service employed intermittently. The members shall not be subject to any other provisions of law regarding the appointment and compensation of employees of the United States. The Secretary shall furnish the committee with adequate clerical and other assistance, and shall by rules and regulations prescribe the procedure to be followed by the committee.

(6) The Secretary shall not list a color additive under this subsection for a proposed use if the data before him show that such proposed use would promote deception of the consumer in violation of this Act or would otherwise result in misbranding or adulteration within the meaning of this Act.

(7) If, in the judgment of the Secretary, a tolerance limitation is required in order to assure that a proposed use of a color additive will be safe, the Secretary—

(A) shall not list the additive for such use if he finds that the data before him do not establish that such additive, if used within a safe tolerance limitation, would achieve the intended physical or other technical effect; and

(B) shall not fix such tolerance limitation at a level higher than he finds to be reasonably required to accomplish the intended physical or other technical effect.

(8) If, having regard to the aggregate quantity of color additive likely to be consumed in the diet or to be applied to the human body, the Secretary finds that the data before him fail to show that it would be safe and otherwise permissible to list a color additive (or pharmacologically related color additives) of all uses proposed therefor and at the levels of concentration proposed, the Secretary shall, in determining for which use or uses such additive (or such related additives) shall be or remain listed, or how the aggregate allowable safe tolerance for such additive or additives shall be allocated by him among the uses under consideration, take into account, among other relevant factors (and subject to the paramount criterion of safety), (A) the relative marketability of the articles involved as affected by the proposed uses of the color additive (or of such related additives) in or on such articles, and the relative dependence of the industries concerned on such uses; (B) the relative aggregate amounts of such color additive which he estimates would be consumed in the diet or applied to the human body by reason of the various uses and levels of concentration proposed; and (C) the availability, if any, of other color additives suitable and safe for one or more of the uses proposed.

Certification of Colors

(c) The Secretary shall further, by regulation, provide (1) for the certification, with safe diluents or without diluents, of batches of color additives listed pursuant to subsection (b) and conforming to the requirements for such additives established by regulations under such subsection and this subsection, and (2) for exemptior from the requirement of certification in the case of any such additive, or any listing or use thereof, for which he finds such requirement not to be necessary in the interest of the protection of the public health: *Provided*, That, with respect to any use in or on food for which a listed color additive is deemed to be safe by reason of the proviso to paragraph (4) of subsection (b), the requirement of certification shall be deemed not to be necessary in the interest of public health protection.

Procedure for Issuance, Amendment, or Repeal of Regulations

(d) The provisions of section 701 (e), (f), and (g) of this Act shall, subject to the provisions of subparagraph (C) of subsection (b)(5) of this section, apply to and in all respects govern proceedings for the issuance, amendment, or repeal of regulations under subsection (b) or (c) of this section (including judicial review of the Secretary's action in such proceedings) and the admissi bility of transcripts of the record of such proceedings in other proceedings, except that—

(1) if the proceeding is commenced by the filing of a petition, notice of the proposal made by the petition shall be published in general terms by the Secretary within thirty days after such filing, and the Secretary's order (required by paragraph (1) of section 701(e)) acting upon such proposal shall, in the absence of prior referral (or request for referral) to an advisory committee, be issued within ninety days after the date of such filing, except that the Secretary may (prior to such ninetieth day) by written notice to the petitioner, extend such ninety-day period to such time (not more than one hundred and eighty days after the date of filing of the petition) as the Secretary deems necessary to enable him to study and investigate the petition;

(2) any report, recommendations, underlying data, and reasons certified to the Secretary by an advisory committee appointed pursuant to subparagraph (D) of subsection (b)(5) of this section, shall be made a part of the record of any hearing if relevant and material, subject to the provisions of section 7(c) of the Administrative Procedure Act (5 U.S.C sec 1006(c)). The advisory committee shall

designate a member to appear and testify at any such hearing with respect to the report and recommendations of such committee upon request of the Secretary, the petitioner, or the officer conducting the hearing, but this shall not preclude any other member of the advisory committee from appearing and testifying at such hearing;

(3) the Secretary's order after public hearing (acting upon objections filed to an order made prior to hearings) shall be subject to the requirements of section 409(f)(2); and

(4) the scope of judicial review of such order shall be in accordance with the fourth sentence of paragraph (2), and with the provisions of paragraph (3), of section 409(g).

Fees

(e) The admitting to listing and certification of color additives, in accordance with regulations prescribed under this Act, shall be performed only upon payment of such fees, which shall be specified in such regulations, as may be necessary to provide, maintain, and equip an adequate service for such purposes.

Exemptions

(f) The Secretary shall by regulations (issued without regard to subsection (d)) provide for exempting from the requirements of this section any color additive or any specific type of use thereof, and any article of food, drug, or cosmetic bearing or containing such additive, intended solely for investigational use by qualified experts when in his opinion such exemption is consistent with the public health.

[The Color Additive Amendments to the Federal Food, Drug, and Cosmetic Act took effect on the date of enactment, July 12, 1960, subject to the provisions of sec. 203, title II, of P.L. 86–618 which follows:

Provisional Listings of Commercially Established Colors

(a) (1) The purpose of this section is to make possible, on an interim basis for a reasonable period, through provisional listings, the use of commercially established color additives to the extent consistent with the public health, pending the completion of the scientific investigations needed as a basis for making determinations as to listing of such additives under the basic Act [the Federal Food, Drug, and Cosmetic Act] as amended by this Act.[34] A provisional listing (including a deemed provisional listing) of a color additive under this section for

---

[34] Words "this Act" refer to P.L. 86–618.

any use shall, unless sooner terminated or expiring under
the provisions of this section, expire (A) on the closing
date (as defined in paragraph (2) of this subsection) of
(B) on the effective date of a listing of such additive for
such use under section 706 of the basic Act, whichever
date first occurs.

(2) For the purposes of this section, the term "closing
date" means (A) the last day of the two and one-half
year period beginning on the enactment date or (B), with
respect to a particular provisional listing (or deemed provisional listing) of a color additive or use thereof, such
later closing date as the Secretary may from time to time
establish pursuant to the authority of this paragraph.
The Secretary may by regulation, upon application of an
interested person or on his own initiative, from time to
time postpone the original closing date with respect to a
provisional listing (or deemed provisional listing) under
this section of a specified color additive, or of a specified
use or uses of such additive, for such period or periods as
he finds necessary to carry out the purpose of this section,
if in the Secretary's judgment such action is consistent
with the objective of carrying to completion in good
faith, as soon as reasonably practicable, the scientific investigations necessary for making a determination as to
listing such additive, or such specified use or uses thereof,
under section 706 of the basic Act. The Secretary may
terminate a postponement of the closing date at any time
if he finds that such postponement should not have been
granted, or that by reason of a change in circumstances
the basis for such postponement no longer exists, or that
there has been a failure to comply with a requirement for
submission of progress reports or with other conditions
attached to such postponement.

(b) Subject to the other provisions of this section—

(1) any color additive which on the day preceding the enactment date, was listed and certifiable
for any use or uses under section 406(b), 504, or 604,
or under the third proviso of section 402(c), of the
basic Act, and of which a batch or batches had been
certified for such use or uses prior to the enactment
date, and

(2) any color additive which was commercially
used or sold prior to the enactment date for any use
or uses in or on any food, drug, or cosmetic, and
which either (A), on the day preceding the enactment date, was not a material within the purview
of any of the provisions of the basic Act enumerated
in paragraph (1) of this subsection, or (B) is the
color additive known as synthetic beta-carotene,
shall, beginning on the enactment date, be deemed to be
provisionally listed under this section as a color additive
for such use or uses.

(c) Upon request of any person, the Secretary, by regulations issued under subsection (d), shall without delay, if on the basis of the data before him he deems such action consistent with the protection of the public health, provisionally list a material as a color additive for any use for which it was listed, and for which a batch or batches of such material had been certified, under section 406(b), 504, or 604 of the basic Act prior to the enactment date, although such color was no longer listed and certifiable for such use under such sections on the day preceding the enactment date. Such provisional listing shall take effect on the date of publication.

(d) (1) The Secretary shall, by regulations issued or amended from time to time under this section—

(A) insofar as practicable promulgate and keep current a list or lists of the color additives, and of the particular uses thereof, which he finds are deemed provisionally listed under subsection (b), and the presence of a color additive on such a list with respect to a particular use shall, in any proceeding under the basic Act, be conclusive evidence that such provisional listing is in effect;

(B) provide for the provisional listing of the color additives and particular uses thereof specified in subsection (c);

(C) provide with respect to particular uses for which color additives are or are deemed to be provisionally listed, such temporary tolerance limitations (including such limitations at zero level) and other conditions of use and labeling or packaging requirements, if any, as in his judgment are necessary to protect the public health pending listing under section 706 of the basic Act;

(D) provide for the certification of batches of such color additives (with or without diluents) for the uses for which they are so listed or deemed to be listed under this section, except that such an additive which is a color additive deemed provisionally listed under subsection (b)(2) of this section shall be deemed exempt from the requirement of such certification while not subject to a tolerance limitation; and

(E) provide for the termination of a provisional listing (or deemed provisional listing) of a color additive or particular use thereof forthwith whenever in his judgment such action is necessary to protect the public health.

(2) (A) Except as provided in subparagraph (C) of this paragraph, regulations under this section shall, from time to time, be issued, amended, or repealed by the Secretary without regard to the requirements of the basic Act, but for the purposes of the application of section

706(e) of the basic Act (relating to fees) and of determining the availability of appropriations of fees (and of advance deposits to cover fees), proceedings, regulations, and certifications under this section shall be deemed to be proceedings, regulations, and certifications under such section 706. Regulations providing for fees (and advance deposits to cover fees), which on the day preceding the enactment date were in effect pursuant to section 706 of the basic Act, shall be deemed to be regulations under such section 706 as amended by this Act, and appropriations of fees (and advance deposits) available for the purposes specified in such section 706 as in effect prior to the enactment date shall be available for the purposes specified in such section 706 as so amended.

(B) If the Secretary, by regulation—

(i) has terminated a provisional listing (or deemed provisional listing) of a color additive or particular use thereof pursuant to paragraph (1) (E) of this subsection; or

(ii) has, pursuant to paragraph (1) (C) or paragraph (3) of this subsection, initially established or rendered more restrictive a tolerance limitation or other restriction or requirement with respect to a provisional listing (or deemed provisional listing) which listing had become effective prior to such action,

any person adversely affected by such action may, prior to the expiration of the period specified in clause (A) of subsection (a) (2) of this section, file with the Secretary a petition for amendment of such regulation so as to revoke or modify such action of the Secretary, but the filing of such petition shall not operate to stay or suspend the effectiveness of such action. Such petition shall, in accordance with regulations, set forth the proposed amendment and shall contain data (or refer to data which are before the Secretary or of which he will take official notice), which show that the revocation or modification proposed is consistent with the protection of the public health. The Secretary shall, after publishing such proposal and affording all interested persons an opportunity to present their views thereon orally or in writing, act upon such proposal by published order.

(C) Any person adversely affected by an order entered under subparagraph (B) of this paragraph may, within thirty days after its publication, file objections thereto with the Secretary, specifying with particularity the provisions of the order deemed objectionable, stating reasonable grounds for such objections, and requesting a public hearing upon such objections. The Secretary shall hold a public hearing on such objections and shall, on the basis of the evidence adduced at such hearing, act on such objections by published order. Such order may reinstate a terminated provisional listing, or increase or dispense with a previously established temporary tolerance limitation, or make less restrictive any other limitation established by him under paragraph (1) or (3) of this subsection, only if in his judgment the evidence so adduced shows that such actions will be consistent with the protection of the public health. An order entered under this subparagraph shall be subject to judicial review in accordance with section 701(f) of the basic Act except that the findings and order of the Secretary shall be sustained only if based upon a fair evaluation of the entire record at such hearing. No stay or suspension of such order shall be ordered by the court pending conclusion of such judicial review.

(D) On and after the enactment date, regulations, provisional listings, and certifications (or exemptions from certification) in effect under this section shall, for the purpose of determining whether an article is adulterated or misbranded within the meaning of the basic Act by reason of its being, bearing or containing a color additive, have the same effect as would regulations, listings, and certifications (or exemptions from certification) under section 706 of the basic Act. A regulation, provisional listing or termination thereof, tolerance, limitation, or certification or exemption therefrom, under this section shall not be the basis for any presumption or inference in any proceeding under section 706 (b) or (c) of the basic Act.

(3) For the purpose of enabling the Secretary to carry out his functions under paragraphs (1) (A) and (C) of this subsection with respect to color additives deemed provisionally listed, he shall, as soon as practicable after enactment of this Act, afford by public notice a reasonable opportunity to interested persons to submit data relevant thereto. If the data so submitted or otherwise before him do not, in his judgment, establish a reliable basis for including such a color additive or particular use or uses thereof in a list or lists promulgated under paragraph (1)(A), or for determining the prevailing level or levels of use thereof prior to the enactment date with a view to prescribing a temporary tolerance or tolerances for such use or uses under paragraph (1)(C), the Secretary shall establish a temporary tolerance limitation at zero level for such use or uses until such time as he finds that it would not be inconsistent with the protection of the public health to increase or dispense with such temporary tolerance limitation.]

REVISION OF UNITED STATES PHARMACOPEIA; DEVELOPMENT
OF ANALYSIS AND MECHANICAL AND PHYSICAL TESTS

Sec. 707 [377]. The Secretary, in carrying into effect the provisions of this chapter, is authorized hereafter to cooperate with associations and scientific societies in the revision of the United States Pharmacopeia and in the development of methods of analysis and mechanical and physical tests necessary to carry out the work of the Food and Drug Administration. [From the Labor-Federal Security Appropriation Act, 1944.]

CHAPTER VIII—IMPORTS AND EXPORTS

SEC. 801 [381].[35] (a) The Secretary of the Treasury shall deliver to the Secretary of Health, Education, and Welfare, upon his request, samples of food, drugs, devices, and cosmetics which are being imported or offered for import into the United States, giving notice thereof to the owner or consignee, who may appear before the Secretary of Health, Education, and Welfare and have the right to introduce testimony. The Secretary of Health, Education, and Welfare shall furnish to the Secretary of the Treasury a list of establishments registered pursuant to subsection (i) of section 510 and shall request that if any drugs manufactured, prepared, propagated, compounded, or processed in an establishment not so registered are imported or offered for import into the United States, samples of such drugs be delivered to the Secretary of Health, Education, and Welfare, with notice of such delivery to the owner or consignee, who may appear before the Secretary of Health, Education, and Welfare and have the right to introduce testimony. If it appears from the examination of such samples or otherwise that (1) such article has been manufactured, processed, or packed under insanitary conditions, or (2) such article is forbidden or restricted in sale in the country in which it was produced or from which it was exported, or (3) such article is adulterated, misbranded, or in violation of section 505, then such article shall be refused admission, except as provided in subsection (b) of this section. The Secretary of the Treasury shall cause the destruction of any such article refused admission unless such article is exported, under regulations prescribed by the Secretary of the Treasury, within ninety days of the date of notice of such refusal or within such additional time as may be permitted pursuant to such regulations. Clause (2) of the third sentence of this paragraph shall not be construed to prohibit the admission of narcotic drugs the importation of which is permitted under the Controlled Substances Import and Export Act.

(b) Pending decision as to the admission of an article being imported or offered for import, the Secretary of the Treasury may authorize delivery of such article to the owner or consignee upon the execution by him of a good and sufficient bond providing for the payment of such liquidated damages in the event of default as may be re-

---

[35] Sec. 801 amended by sec. 701 of P.L. 91–513.

quired pursuant to regulations of the Secretary of the Treasury. If it appears to the Secretary of Health, Education, and Welfare that an article included within the provisions of clause (3) of subsection (a) of this section can, by relabeling or other action, be brought into compliance with the Act or rendered other than a food, drug, device, or cosmetic, final determination as to admission of such article may be deferred and, upon filing of timely written application by the owner or consignee and the execution by him of a bond as provided in the preceding provisions of this subsection, the Secretary may, in accordance with regulations, authorize the applicant to perform such relabeling or other action specified in such authorization (including destruction or export of rejected articles or portions thereof, as may be specified in the Secretary's authorization). All such relabeling or other action pursuant to such authorization shall in accordance with regulations be under the supervision of an officer or employee of the Department of Health, Education, and Welfare designated by the Secretary, or an officer or employee of the Department of the Treasury designated by the Secretary of the Treasury.

(c) All expenses (including travel, per diem or subsistence, and salaries of officers or employees of the United States) in connection with the destruction provided for in subsection (a) of this section and the supervision of the relabeling or other action authorized under the provisions of subsection (b) of this section, the amount of such expenses to be determined in accordance with regulations, and all expenses in connection with the storage, cartage, or labor with respect to any article refused admission under subsection (a) of this section, shall be paid by the owner or consignee and, in default of such payment, shall constitute a lien against any future importations made by such owner or consignee.

(d) [36] A food, drug, device, or cosmetic intended for export shall not be deemed to be adulterated or misbranded under this Act if it (1) accords to the specifications of the foreign purchaser, (2) is not in conflict with the laws of the country to which it is intended for export, and (3) is labeled on the outside of the shipping package to show that it is intended for export. But if such article is sold or offered for sale in domestic commerce, this subsection shall not exempt it from any of the provisions of this Act. Nothing in this subsection shall authorize the exportation of any new animal drug, or an animal feed bearing or containing a new animal drug, which is unsafe within the meaning of section 512 of this Act.

---

[36] Sec. 801 (d) amended by sec 106 of P.L. 90–399.

CHAPTER IX—MISCELLANEOUS

SEPARABILITY CLAUSE

SEC. 901 [391]. If any provision of this Act is declared unconstitutional, or the applicability thereof to any person or circumstances is held invalid, the constitutionality of the remainder of the Act and the applicability thereof to other persons and circumstances shall not be affected thereby.

EFFECTIVE DATE AND REPEALS

SEC. 902 [392]. (a) This Act shall take effect twelve months after the date of its enactment. The Federal Food and Drug Act of June 30, 1906, as amended (U.S.C., 1934 ed., title 21, secs. 1–15), shall remain in force until such effective date, and except as otherwise provided in this subsection, is hereby repealed effective upon such date: *Provided*, That the provisions of section 701 shall become effective on the enactment of this Act, and thereafter the Secretary [of Agriculture] is authorized hereby to (1) conduct hearings and to promulgate regulations which shall become effective on or after the effective date of this Act as the Secretary [of Agriculture] shall direct, and (2) designate prior to the effective date of this Act food having common or usual names and exempt such food from the requirements of clause (2) of section 403(i) for a reasonable time to permit the formulation, promulgation, and effective application of definitions and standards of identity therefor as provided by section 401: *Provided further*, That sections 502(j), 505, and 601(a), and all other provisions of this Act to the extent that they may relate to the enforcement of such sections, shall take effect on the date of the enactment of this Act, except that in the case of a cosmetic to which the proviso of section 601(a) relates, such cosmetic shall not, prior to the ninetieth day after such date of enactment, be deemed adulterated by reason of the failure of its label to bear the legend prescribed in such proviso: *Provided further*, That the Act of March 4, 1923 (U.S.C., 1945 ed. (title 21, sec. 321a; 32 Stat. 1500, ch. 268), defining butter and providing a standard therefor; the Act of July 24, 1919 (U.S.C., 1946 ed., title 21, sec. 321b; 41 Stat. 271, ch. 26), defining wrapped meats [37] as in package form; and the amendment to the Food and Drug Act, section 10A, approved August 27, 1935 (U.S.C., 1946 ed., title 21, sec. 372a [38] [49 Stat. 871, ch. 739]), shall remain in force and effect and be applicable to the provisions of this Act.

---

[37] See secs. 201a and 201b.
[38] See footnote 31.

(b) Meats and meat food products shall be exempt from the provisions of this Act to the extent of the application or the extension thereto of the Meat Inspection Act, approved March 4, 1907, as amended (U.S.C., 1946 ed., title 21, secs. 71–96; 34 Stat. 1260 *et seq.*).
[SEC. 7. Public Law 85–929 (21 U.S.C. 451 note): Nothing in this Act shall be construed to exempt any meat or meat food product or any person from any requirement imposed by or pursuant to the Poultry Products Inspection Act (21 U.S.C. 451 and the following) or the Meat Inspection Act of March 4, 1907, 34 Stat. 1260, as amended and extended (21 U.S.C. 71 and the following).]

(c)[39] Nothing contained in this Act shall be construed as in any way affecting, modifying, repealing, or superseding the provisions of section 351 of Public Health Service Act (relating to viruses, serums, toxins, and analogous products applicable to man); the virus, serum, toxin, and analogous products provisions, applicable to domestic animals, of the Act of Congress approved March 4, 1913 (37 Stat. 832–833); the Filled Cheese Act of June 6, 1896 (U.S.C., 1946 ed., title 26, ch. 17, secs. 2350–2362); the Filled Milk Act of March 4, 1923 (U.S.C. 1946 ed., title 21, ch. 3, secs. 61–64); or the Import Milk Act of February 15, 1927 (U.S.C., 1946 ed., title 21, ch. 4, secs. 141–149).

(Approved June 25, 1938.)

---

[39] Sec. 902(c) amended by sec. 107 of P.L. 90–399. Nothing in the amendments made by the Drug Amendments of 1962 to the Federal Food, Drug, and Cosmetic Act shall be construed as invalidating any provision of State law which would be valid in the absence of such amendments unless there is a direct and positive conflict between such amendments and such provision of State law.

[Excerpt from P.L. 88-136, October 11, 1963]

REVOLVING FUND FOR CERTIFICATION AND OTHER SERVICES

For the establishment of a revolving fund for certification and other services, there is hereby appropriated the aggregate of fees (including advance deposits to cover such fees) paid during the fiscal year 1964, and each succeeding fiscal year, for services in connection with the listing, certification, or inspection of certain products and the establishment of tolerances for pesticides, in accordance with sections 406, 408, 506, 507, 702A, and 706 of the Federal Food, Drug, and Cosmetic Act, as amended 21 U.S.C. 346a, 356, 357, 372a, and 376), and the unexpended balance of such fees (or advance deposits) heretofore appropriated shall be credited to such revolving fund. This fund shall be available without fiscal year limitation for salaries and expenses necessary to carry out the Secretary's responsibilities in connection with such listings, certifications, inspections, or establishment of tolerances, including the conduct of scientific research, development of methods of analysis, purchase of chemicals, fixtures, furniture, and scientific equipment and apparatus; expenses of advisory committees; refund of advance deposits for which no services have been rendered: *Provided*, That any supplies, furniture, fixtures, and equipment on hand or on order on June 30, 1963, and purchased or ordered under appropriations for "Salaries and Expenses, Certification, Inspection, and Other Services," shall be used to capitalize the revolving fund.

APPENDIX E
CONTROLLED SUBSTANCES ACT
SELECTED SECTIONS

Public Law 91-513
91st Congress, H. R. 18583
October 27, 1970

An Act

84 STAT. 1236

To amend the Public Health Service Act and other laws to provide increased research into, and prevention of, drug abuse and drug dependence; to provide for treatment and rehabilitation of drug abusers and drug dependent persons; and to strengthen existing law enforcement authority in the field of drug abuse.

Be it enacted by the Senate and House of Representatives of the United States of America in Congress assembled, That this Act may be cited as the "Comprehensive Drug Abuse Prevention and Control Act of 1970".

Comprehensive Drug Abuse Prevention and Control Act of 1970.

TABLE OF CONTENTS

* * *

TITLE II—CONTROL AND ENFORCEMENT

PART A—SHORT TITLE; FINDINGS AND DECLARATION; DEFINITIONS

PART B—AUTHORITY TO CONTROL; STANDARDS AND SCHEDULES

337

84 STAT. 1237

Pub. Law 91-513   October 27, 1970

TABLE OF CONTENTS—Continued

TITLE II—CONTROL AND ENFORCEMENT—Continued

October 27, 1970   Pub. Law 91-513
                                                    84 STAT. 1242

TITLE II—CONTROL AND ENFORCEMENT

PART A—SHORT TITLE; FINDINGS AND DECLARATION; DEFINITIONS

SHORT TITLE

SEC. 100. This title may be cited as the "Controlled Substances Act". Citation of title.

FINDINGS AND DECLARATIONS

SEC. 101. The Congress makes the following findings and declarations:

(1) Many of the drugs included within this title have a useful and legitimate medical purpose and are necessary to maintain the health and general welfare of the American people.

(2) The illegal importation, manufacture, distribution, and possession and improper use of controlled substances have a substantial and detrimental effect on the health and general welfare of the American people.

(3) A major portion of the traffic in controlled substances flows through interstate and foreign commerce. Incidents of the traffic which are not an integral part of the interstate or foreign flow, such as manufacture, local distribution, and possession, nonetheless have a substantial and direct effect upon interstate commerce because—

(A) after manufacture, many controlled substances are transported in interstate commerce,

(B) controlled substances distributed locally usually have been transported in interstate commerce immediately before their distribution, and

(C) controlled substances possessed commonly flow through interstate commerce immediately prior to such possession.

(4) Local distribution and possession of controlled substances contribute to swelling the interstate traffic in such substances.

(5) Controlled substances manufactured and distributed intrastate cannot be differentiated from controlled substances manufactured and distributed interstate. Thus, it is not feasible to distinguish, in terms of controls, between controlled substances manufactured and distributed interstate and controlled substances manufactured and distributed intrastate.

(6) Federal control of the intrastate incidents of the traffic in controlled substances is essential to the effective control of the interstate incidents of such traffic.

(7) The United States is a party to the Single Convention on Narcotic Drugs, 1961, and other international conventions designed to 18 UST 1407. establish effective control over international and domestic traffic in controlled substances.

DEFINITIONS

SEC. 102. As used in this title:

(1) The term "addict" means any individual who habitually uses any narcotic drug so as to endanger the public morals, health, safety, or welfare, or who is so far addicted to the use of narcotic drugs as to have lost the power of self-control with reference to his addiction.

(2) The term "administer" refers to the direct application of a controlled substance to the body of a patient or research subject by—

(A) a practitioner (or, in his presence, by his authorized agent), or

(B) the patient or research subject at the direction and in the presence of the practitioner, whether such application be by injection, inhalation, ingestion, or any other means.

(3) The term "agent" means an authorized person who acts on behalf of or at the direction of a manufacturer, distributor, or dispenser; except that such term does not include a common or contract carrier, public warehouseman, or employee of the carrier or warehouseman, when acting in the usual and lawful course of the carrier's or warehouseman's business.

(4) The term "Bureau of Narcotics and Dangerous Drugs" means the Bureau of Narcotics and Dangerous Drugs in the Department of Justice.

Post, p. 1247.
(5) The term "control" means to add a drug or other substance, or immediate precursor, to a schedule under part B of this title, whether by transfer from another schedule or otherwise.

(6) The term "controlled substance" means a drug or other substance, or immediate precursor, included in schedule I, II, III, IV, or V of part B of this title. The term does not include distilled spirits, wine, malt beverages, or tobacco, as those terms are defined or used in
68A Stat. 595.
26 USC 5001.
subtitle E of the Internal Revenue Code of 1954.

(7) The term "counterfeit substance" means a controlled substance which, or the container or labeling of which, without authorization, bears the trademark, trade name, or other identifying mark, imprint, number, or device, or any likeness thereof, of a manufacturer, distributor, or dispenser other than the person or persons who in fact manufactured, distributed, or dispensed such substance and which thereby falsely purports or is represented to be the product of, or to have been distributed by, such other manufacturer, distributor, or dispenser.

(8) The terms "deliver" or "delivery" mean the actual, constructive, or attempted transfer of a controlled substance, whether or not there exists an agency relationship.

(9) The term "depressant or stimulant substance" means—

(A) a drug which contains any quantity of (i) barbituric acid or any of the salts of barbituric acid; or (ii) any derivative of barbituric acid which has been designated by the Secretary as habit forming under section 502(d) of the Federal Food, Drug,
52 Stat. 1050.
and Cosmetic Act (21 U.S.C. 352(d)); or

(B) a drug which contains any quantity of (i) amphetamine or any of its optical isomers; (ii) any salt of amphetamine or any salt of an optical isomer of amphetamine; or (iii) any substance which the Attorney General, after investigation, has found to be, and by regulation designated as, habit forming because of its stimulant effect on the central nervous system; or

(C) lysergic acid diethylamide; or

(D) any drug which contains any quantity of a substance which the Attorney General, after investigation, has found to have, and by regulation designated as having, a potential for abuse because of its depressant or stimulant effect on the central nervous system or its hallucinogenic effect.

(10) The term "dispense" means to deliver a controlled substance to an ultimate user or research subject by, or pursuant to the lawful order of, a practitioner, including the prescribing and administering of a controlled substance and the packaging, labeling, or compounding necessary to prepare the substance for such delivery. The term "dispenser" means a practitioner who so delivers a controlled substance to an ultimate user or research subject.

(11) The term "distribute" means to deliver (other than by administering or dispensing) a controlled substance. The term "distributor" means a person who so delivers a controlled substance.

October 27, 1970   Pub. Law 91-513

84 STAT. 1244

(12) The term "drug" has the meaning given that term by section 201(g)(1) of the Federal Food, Drug, and Cosmetic Act.   52 Stat. 1041;

(13) The term "felony" means any Federal or State offense clas- 79 Stat. 234.
sified by applicable Federal or State law as a felony.   21 USC 321.

(14) The term "manufacture" means the production, preparation, propagation, compounding, or processing of a drug or other substance, either directly or indirectly or by extraction from substances of natural origin, or independently by means of chemical synthesis or by a combination of extraction and chemical synthesis, and includes any packaging or repackaging of such substance or labeling or relabeling of its container; except that such term does not include the preparation, compounding, packaging, or labeling of a drug or other substance in conformity with applicable State or local law by a practitioner as an incident to his administration or dispensing of such drug or substance in the course of his professional practice. The term "manufacturer" means a person who manufactures a drug or other substance.

(15) The term "marihuana" means all parts of the plant Cannabis sativa L., whether growing or not; the seeds thereof; the resin extracted from any part of such plant; and every compound, manufacture, salt, derivative, mixture, or preparation of such plant, its seeds or resin. Such term does not include the mature stalks of such plant, fiber produced from such stalks, oil or cake made from the seeds of such plant, any other compound, manufacture, salt, derivative, mixture, or preparation of such mature stalks (except the resin extracted therefrom), fiber, oil, or cake, or the sterilized seed of such plant which is incapable of germination.

(16) The term "narcotic drug" means any of the following, whether produced directly or indirectly by extraction from substances of vegetable origin, or independently by means of chemical synthesis, or by a combination of extraction and chemical synthesis:

(A) Opium, coca leaves, and opiates.

(B) A compound, manufacture, salt, derivative, or preparation of opium, coca leaves, or opiates.

(C) A substance (and any compound, manufacture, salt, derivative, or preparation thereof) which is chemically identical with any of the substances referred to in clause (A) or (B).

Such term does not include decocainized coca leaves or extracts of coca leaves, which extracts do not contain cocaine or ecgonine.

(17) The term "opiate" means any drug or other substance having an addiction-forming or addiction-sustaining liability similar to morphine or being capable of conversion into a drug having such addiction-forming or addiction-sustaining liability.

(18) The term "opium poppy" means the plant of the species Papaver somniferum L., except the seed thereof.

(19) The term "poppy straw" means all parts, except the seeds, of the opium poppy, after mowing.

(20) The term "practitioner" means a physician, dentist, veterinarian, scientific investigator, pharmacy, hospital, or other person licensed, registered, or otherwise permitted, by the United States or the jurisdiction in which he practices or does research, to distribute, dispense, conduct research with respect to, administer, or use in teaching or chemical analysis, a controlled substance in the course of professional practice or research.

(21) The term "production" includes the manufacture, planting, cultivation, growing, or harvesting of a controlled substance.

(22) The term "immediate precursor" means a substance—

(A) which the Attorney General has found to be and by regulation designated as being the principal compound used, or produced primarily for use, in the manufacture of a controlled substance;

(B) which is an immediate chemical intermediary used or likely to be used in the manufacture of such controlled substance; and

(C) the control of which is necessary to prevent, curtail, or limit the manufacture of such controlled substance.

(23) The term "Secretary", unless the context otherwise indicates, means the Secretary of Health, Education, and Welfare.

(24) The term "State" means any State, territory, or possession of the United States, the District of Columbia, the Commonwealth of Puerto Rico, the Trust Territory of the Pacific Islands, and the Canal Zone.

(25) The term "ultimate user" means a person who has lawfully obtained, and who possesses, a controlled substance for his own use or for the use of a member of his household or for an animal owned by him or by a member of his household.

(26) The term "United States", when used in a geographic sense, means all places and waters, continental or insular, subject to the jurisdiction of the United States.

INCREASED NUMBERS OF ENFORCEMENT PERSONNEL

SEC. 103. (a) During the fiscal year 1971, the Bureau of Narcotics and Dangerous Drugs is authorized to add at least 300 agents, together with necessary supporting personnel, to the number of enforcement personnel currently available to it.

Appropriation. (b) There are authorized to be appropriated not to exceed $6,000,000 for the fiscal year 1971 and for each fiscal year thereafter to carry out the provisions of subsection (a).

PART B—AUTHORITY TO CONTROL;

STANDARDS AND SCHEDULES

AUTHORITY AND CRITERIA FOR CLASSIFICATION OF SUBSTANCES

SEC. 201. (a) The Attorney General shall apply the provisions of this title to the controlled substances listed in the schedules established by section 202 of this title and to any other drug or other substance added to such schedules under this title. Except as provided in subsections (d) and (e), the Attorney General may by rule—

(1) add to such a schedule or transfer between such schedules any drug or other substance if he—

(A) finds that such drug or other substance has a potential for abuse, and

(B) makes with respect to such drug or other substance the findings prescribed by subsection (b) of section 202 for the schedule in which such drug is to be placed; or

(2) remove any drug or other substance from the schedules if he finds that the drug or other substance does not meet the requirements for inclusion in any schedule.

Hearing opportunity. Rules. 80 Stat. 381. 5 USC 551. Rules of the Attorney General under this subsection shall be made on the record after opportunity for a hearing pursuant to the rulemaking procedures prescribed by subchapter II of chapter 5 of title 5 of the United States Code. Proceedings for the issuance, amendment, or

October 27, 1970   Pub. Law 91-513

repeal of such rules may be initiated by the Attorney General (1) on his own motion, (2) at the request of the Secretary, or (3) on the petition of any interested party.

(b) The Attorney General shall, before initiating proceedings under Evaluation. subsection (a) to control a drug or other substance or to remove a drug or other substance entirely from the schedules, and after gathering the necessary data, request from the Secretary a scientific and medical evaluation, and his recommendations, as to whether such drug or other substance should be so controlled or removed as a controlled substance. In making such evaluation and recommendations, the Secretary shall consider the factors listed in paragraphs (2), (3), (6), (7), and (8) of subsection (c) and any scientific or medical considerations involved in paragraphs (1), (4), and (5) of such subsection. The recommendations of the Secretary shall include recommendations with respect to the appropriate schedule, if any, under which such drug or other substance should be listed. The evaluation and the recommendations of the Secretary shall be made in writing and submitted to the Attorney General within a reasonable time. The recommendations of the Secretary to the Attorney General shall be binding on the Attorney General as to such scientific and medical matters, and if the Secretary recommends that a drug or other substance not be controlled, the Attorney General shall not control the drug or other substance. If the Attorney General determines that these facts and all other relevant data constitute substantial evidence of potential for abuse such as to warrant control or substantial evidence that the drug or other substance should be removed entirely from the schedules, he shall initiate proceedings for control or removal, as the case may be, under subsection (a).

(c) In making any finding under subsection (a) of this section or under subsection (b) of section 202, the Attorney General shall consider the following factors with respect to each drug or other substance proposed to be controlled or removed from the schedules:

(1) Its actual or relative potential for abuse.
(2) Scientific evidence of its pharmacological effect, if known.
(3) The state of current scientific knowledge regarding the drug or other substance.
(4) Its history and current pattern of abuse.
(5) The scope, duration, and significance of abuse.
(6) What, if any, risk there is to the public health.
(7) Its psychic or physiological dependence liability.
(8) Whether the substance is an immediate precursor of a substance already controlled under this title.

(d) If control is required by United States obligations under international treaties, conventions, or protocols in effect on the effective date of this part, the Attorney General shall issue an order controlling Order. such drug under the schedule he deems most appropriate to carry out such obligations, without regard to the findings required by subsection (a) of this section or section 202(b) and without regard to the procedures prescribed by subsections (a) and (b) of this section.

(e) The Attorney General may, without regard to the findings required by subsection (a) of this section or section 202(b) and without regard to the procedures prescribed by subsections (a) and (b) of this section, place an immediate precursor in the same schedule in which the controlled substance of which it is an immediate precursor is placed or in any other schedule with a higher numerical designation. If the Attorney General designates a substance as an immediate precursor and places it in a schedule, other substances shall not be placed in a schedule solely because they are its precursors.

5

84 STAT. 1247

Pub. Law 91-513   October 27, 1970

(f) If, at the time a new-drug application is submitted to the Secretary for any drug having a stimulant, depressant, or hallucinogenic effect on the central nervous system, it appears that such drug has an abuse potential, such information shall be forwarded by the Secretary to the Attorney General.

(g)(1) The Attorney General shall by regulation exclude any non-narcotic substance from a schedule if such substance may, under the Federal Food, Drug, and Cosmetic Act, be lawfully sold over the counter without a prescription.

52 Stat. 1040.
21 USC 321.
Dextromethor-
phan, excep-
tion.

(2) Dextromethorphan shall not be deemed to be included in any schedule by reason of enactment of this title unless controlled after the date of such enactment pursuant to the foregoing provisions of this section.

SCHEDULES OF CONTROLLED SUBSTANCES

Establishment.

SEC. 202. (a) There are established five schedules of controlled substances, to be known as schedules I, II, III, IV, and V. Such schedules shall initially consist of the substances listed in this section. The schedules established by this section shall be updated and republished on a semiannual basis during the two-year period beginning one year after the date of enactment of this title and shall be updated and republished on an annual basis thereafter.

Placement on
schedules,
findings re-
quired.

(b) Except where control is required by United States obligations under an international treaty, convention, or protocol, in effect on the effective date of this part, and except in the case of an immediate precursor, a drug or other substance may not be placed in any schedule unless the findings required for such schedule are made with respect to such drug or other substance. The findings required for each of the schedules are as follows:

(1) SCHEDULE I.—

(A) The drug or other substance has a high potential for abuse.

(B) The drug or other substance has no currently accepted medical use in treatment in the United States.

(C) There is a lack of accepted safety for use of the drug or other substance under medical supervision.

(2) SCHEDULE II.—

(A) The drug or other substance has a high potential for abuse.

(B) The drug or other substance has a currently accepted medical use in treatment in the United States or a currently accepted medical use with severe restrictions.

(C) Abuse of the drug or other substances may lead to severe psychological or physical dependence.

(3) SCHEDULE III.—

(A) The drug or other substance has a potential for abuse less than the drugs or other substances in schedules I and II.

(B) The drug or other substance has a currently accepted medical use in treatment in the United States.

(C) Abuse of the drug or other substance may lead to moderate or low physical dependence or high psychological dependence.

(4) SCHEDULE IV.—

(A) The drug or other substance has a low potential for abuse relative to the drugs or other substances in schedule III.

(B) The drug or other substance has a currently accepted medical use in treatment in the United States.

(C) Abuse of the drug or other substance may lead to limited physical dependence or psychological dependence relative to the drugs or other substances in schedule III.

(5) SCHEDULE V.—

(A) The drug or other substance has a low potential for abuse relative to the drugs or other substances in schedule IV.

(B) The drug or other substance has a currently accepted medical use in treatment in the United States.

(C) Abuse of the drug or other substance may lead to limited physical dependence or psychological dependence relative to the drugs or other substances in schedule IV.

(c) Schedules I, II, III, IV, and V shall, unless and until amended pursuant to section 201, consist of the following drugs or other substances, by whatever official name, common or usual name, chemical name, or brand name designated:

SCHEDULE I

(a) Unless specifically excepted or unless listed in another   Opiates.
schedule, any of the following opiates, including their isomers, esters, ethers, salts, and salts of isomers, esters, and ethers, whenever the existence of such isomers, esters, ethers, and salts is possible within the specific chemical designation:

   (1) Acetylmethadol.
   (2) Allylprodine.
   (3) Alphacetylmathadol.
   (4) Alphameprodine.
   (5) Alphamethadol.
   (6) Benzethidine.
   (7) Betacetylmethadol.
   (8) Betameprodine.
   (9) Betamethadol.
   (10) Betaprodine.
   (11) Clonitazene.
   (12) Dextromoramide.
   (13) Dextrorphan.
   (14) Diampromide.
   (15) Diethylthiambutene.
   (16) Dimenoxadol.
   (17) Dimepheptanol.
   (18) Dimethylthiambutene.
   (19) Dioxaphetyl butyrate.
   (20) Dipipanone.
   (21) Ethylmethylthiambutene.
   (22) Etonitazene.
   (23) Etoxeridine.
   (24) Furethidine.
   (25) Hydroxypethidine.
   (26) Ketobemidone.
   (27) Levomoramide.
   (28) Levophenacylmorphan.
   (29) Morpheridine.
   (30) Noracymethadol.
   (31) Norlevorphanol.
   (32) Normethadone.
   (33) Norpipanone.
   (34) Phenadoxone.
   (35) Phenampromide.

Pub. Law 91-513   October 27,

84 STAT. 1249

(36) Phenomorphan.
(37) Phenoperidine.
(38) Piritramide.
(39) Proheptazine.
(40) Properidine.
(41) Racemoramide.
(42) Trimeperidine.

Opium derivatives.
(b) Unless specifically excepted or unless listed in another schedule, any of the following opium derivatives, their salts, isomers, and salts of isomers whenever the existence of such salts, isomers, and salts of isomers is possible within the specific chemical designation:

(1) Acetorphine.
(2) Acetyldihydrocodeine.
(3) Benzylmorphine.
(4) Codeine methylbromide.
(5) Codeine-N-Oxide.
(6) Cyprenorphine.
(7) Desomorphine.
(8) Dihydromorphine.
(9) Etorphine.
(10) Heroin.
(11) Hydromorphinol.
(12) Methyldesorphine.
(13) Methylhydromorphine.
(14) Morphine methylbromide.
(15) Morphine methylsulfonate.
(16) Morphine-N-Oxide.
(17) Myrophine.
(18) Nicocodeine.
(19) Nicomorphine.
(20) Normorphine.
(21) Pholcodine.
(22) Thebacon.

Hallucinogenic substances.
(c) Unless specifically excepted or unless listed in another schedule, any material, compound, mixture, or preparation, which contains any quantity of the following hallucinogenic substances, or which contains any of their salts, isomers, and salts of isomers whenever the existence of such salts, isomers, and salts of isomers is possible within the specific chemical designation:

(1) 3,4-methylenedioxy amphetamine.
(2) 5-methoxy-3,4-methylenedioxy amphetamine.
(3) 3,4,5-trimethoxy amphetamine.
(4) Bufotenine.
(5) Diethyltryptamine.
(6) Dimethyltryptamine.
(7) 4-methyl-2,5-dimethoxyamphetamine.
(8) Ibogaine.
(9) Lysergic acid diethylamide.
(10) Marihuana.
(11) Mescaline.
(12) Peyote.
(13) N-ethyl-3-piperidyl benzilate.
(14) N-methyl-3-piperidyl benzilate.
(15) Psilocybin.
(16) Psilocyn.
(17) Tetrahydrocannabinols.

ctober 27, 1970   Pub. Law 91-513
                                                    84 STAT. 1250

SCHEDULE II

(a) Unless specifically excepted or unless listed in another   Substances,
schedule, any of the following substances whether produced   vegetable origin
directly or indirectly by extraction from substances of vege-   or chemical
table origin, or independently by means of chemical syn-   synthesis.
thesis, or by a combination of extraction and chemical
synthesis:

  (1) Opium and opiate, and any salt, compound,
derivative, or preparation of opium or opiate.
  (2) Any salt, compound, derivative, or preparation thereof which is chemically equivalent or identical with any of the substances referred to in clause
(1), except that these substances shall not include
the isoquinoline alkaloids of opium.
  (3) Opium poppy and poppy straw.
  (4) Coca leaves and any salt, compound, derivative, or preparation of coca leaves, and any salt, compound, derivative, or preparation thereof which is
chemically equivalent or identical with any of
these substances, except that the substances shall not
include decocainized coca leaves or extraction of coca
leaves, which extractions do not contain cocaine or
ecgonine.

(b) Unless specifically excepted or unless listed in another   Opiates.
schedule, any of the following opiates, including their isomers, esters, ethers, salts, and salts of isomers, esters and
ethers, whenever the existence of such isomers, esters, ethers,
and salts is possible within the specific chemical designation:

  (1) Alphaprodine.
  (2) Anileridine.
  (3) Bezitramide.
  (4) Dihydrocodeine.
  (5) Diphenoxylate.
  (6) Fentanyl.
  (7) Isomethadone.
  (8) Levomethorphan.
  (9) Levorphanol.
  (10) Metazocine.
  (11) Methadone.
  (12) Methadone-Intermediate, 4-cyano - 2 - dimethyl-
amino-4,4-diphenyl butane.
  (13) Moramide-Intermediate, 2 - methyl - 3 - morpho-
lino-1, 1-diphenylpropane-carboxylic acid.
  (14) Pethidine.
  (15) Pethidine-Intermediate-A, 4 - cyano-1-methyl-4-
phenylpiperidine.
  (16) Pethidine-Intermediate-B, ethyl - 4-phenylpiper-
idine-4-carboxylate.
  (17) Pethidine-Intermediate-C, 1-methyl - 4 - phenyl-
piperidine-4-carboxylic acid.
  (18) Phenazocine.
  (19) Piminodine.
  (20) Racemethorphan.
  (21) Racemorphan.

(c) Unless specifically excepted or unless listed in another   Methampheta-
schedule, any injectable liquid which contains any quantity   mine.
of methamphetamine, including its salts, isomers, and salts
of isomers.

Pub. Law 91-513   October 27, 1970

84 STAT.1251

SCHEDULE III

Stimulants.   (a) Unless specifically excepted or unless listed in another schedule, any material, compound, mixture, or preparation which contains any quantity of the following substances having a stimulant effect on the central nervous system:

(1) Amphetamine, its salts, optical isomers, and salts of its optical isomers.

(2) Phenmetrazine and its salts.

(3) Any substance (except an injectable liquid) which contains any quantity of methamphetamine, including its salts, isomers, and salts of isomers.

(4) Methylphenidate.

Depressants.   (b) Unless specifically excepted or unless listed in another schedule, any material, compound, mixture, or preparation which contains any quantity of the following substances having a depressant effect on the central nervous system:

(1) Any substance which contains any quantity of a derivative of barbituric acid, or any salt of a derivative of barbituric acid.

(2) Chorhexadol.

(3) Glutethimide.

(4) Lysergic acid.

(5) Lysergic acid amide.

(6) Methyprylon.

(7) Phencyclidine.

(8) Sulfondiethylmethane.

(9) Sulfonethylmethane.

(10) Sulfonmethane.

Nalorphine.   (c) Nalorphine.

Narcotic drugs.   (d) Unless specifically excepted or unless listed in another schedule, any material, compound, mixture, or preparation containing limited quantities of any of the following narcotic drugs, or any salts thereof:

(1) Not more than 1.8 grams of codeine per 100 milliliters or not more than 90 milligrams per dosage unit, with an equal or greater quantity of an isoquinoline alkaloid of opium.

(2) Not more than 1.8 grams of codeine per 100 milliliters or not more than 90 milligrams per dosage unit, with one or more active, nonnarcotic ingredients in recognized therapeutic amounts.

(3) Not more than 300 milligrams of dihydrocodeinone per 100 milliliters or not more than 15 milligrams per dosage unit, with a fourfold or greater quantity of an isoquinoline alkaloid of opium.

(4) Not more than 300 milligrams of dihydrocodeinone per 100 milliliters or not more than 15 milligrams per dosage unit, with one or more active, nonnarcotic ingredients in recognized therapeutic amounts.

(5) Not more than 1.8 grams of dihydrocodeine per 100 milliliters or not more than 90 milligrams per dosage unit, with one or more active, nonnarcotic ingredients in recognized therapeutic amounts.

(6) Not more than 300 milligrams of ethylmorphine per 100 milliliters or not more than 15 milligrams per dosage unit, with one or more active, nonnarcotic ingredients in recognized therapeutic amounts.

(7) Not more than 500 milligrams of opium per 100 milliliters or per 100 grams, or not more than 25 milligrams per dosage unit, with one or more active, nonnarcotic ingredients in recognized therapeutic amounts.

(8) Not more than 50 milligrams of morphine per 100 milliliters or per 100 grams with one or more active, nonnarcotic ingredients in recognized therapeutic amounts.

SCHEDULE IV

(1) Barbital.
(2) Chloral betaine.
(3) Chloral hydrate.
(4) Ethchlorvynol.
(5) Ethinamate.
(6) Methohexital.
(7) Meprobamate.
(8) Methylphenobarbital.
(9) Paraldehyde.
(10) Petrichloral.
(11) Phenobarbital.

SCHEDULE V

Any compound, mixture, or preparation containing any of the following limited quantities of narcotic drugs, which shall include one or more nonnarcotic active medicinal ingredients in sufficient proportion to confer upon the compound, mixture, or preparation valuable medicinal qualities other than those possessed by the narcotic drug alone: Narcotic drugs containing nonnarcotic active medicinal ingredients.

(1) Not more than 200 milligrams of codeine per 100 milliliters or per 100 grams.

(2) Not more than 100 milligrams of dihydrocodeine per 100 milliliters or per 100 grams.

(3) Not more than 100 milligrams of ethylmorphine per 100 milliliters or per 100 grams.

(4) Not more than 2.5 milligrams of diphenoxylate and not less than 25 micrograms of atropine sulfate per dosage unit.

(5) Not more than 100 milligrams of opium per 100 milliliters or per 100 grams.

(d) The Attorney General may by regulation except any compound, mixture, or preparation containing any depressant or stimulant substance in paragraph (a) or (b) of schedule III or in schedule IV or V from the application of all or any part of this title if (1) the compound, mixture, or preparation contains one or more active medicinal ingredients not having a depressant or stimulant effect on the central nervous system, and (2) such ingredients are included therein in such combinations, quantity, proportion, or concentration as to vitiate the potential for abuse of the substances which do have a depressant or stimulant effect on the central nervous system. Stimulants or depressants containing active medicinal ingredients, exception.

Pub. Law 91-513   October 27, 1970
84 STAT. 1253

PART C—REGISTRATION OF MANUFACTURERS, DISTRIBUTORS, AND
DISPENSERS OF CONTROLLED SUBSTANCES

RULES AND REGULATIONS

Rules and
regulations.

SEC. 301. The Attorney General is authorized to promulgate rules
and regulations and to charge reasonable fees relating to the registration and control of the manufacture, distribution, and dispensing of
controlled substances.

PERSONS REQUIRED TO REGISTER

Annual
registration.

SEC. 302. (a) Every person who manufactures, distributes, or dispenses any controlled substance or who proposes to engage in the
manufacture, distribution, or dispensing of any controlled substance,
shall obtain annually a registration issued by the Attorney General in
accordance with the rules and regulations promulgated by him.

(b) Persons registered by the Attorney General under this title to
manufacture, distribute, or dispense controlled substances are authorized to possess, manufacture, distribute, or dispense such substances
(including any such activity in the conduct of research) to the extent
authorized by their registration and in conformity with the other
provisions of this title.

Registration,
exceptions.

(c) The following persons shall not be required to register and may
lawfully possess any controlled substance under this title:

(1) An agent or employee of any registered manufacturer, distributor, or dispenser of any controlled substance if such agent or
employee is acting in the usual course of his business or
employment.

(2) A common or contract carrier or warehouseman, or an
employee thereof, whose possession of the controlled substance is
in the usual course of his business or employment.

Ante, p. 1245.

(3) An ultimate user who possesses such substance for a purpose
specified in section 102(25).

Waiver.

(d) The Attorney General may, by regulation, waive the requirement for registration of certain manufacturers, distributors, or dispensers if he finds it consistent with the public health and safety.

Separate
registration.

(e) A separate registration shall be required at each principal place
of business or professional practice where the applicant manufactures,
distributes, or dispenses controlled substances.

Inspection.

(f) The Attorney General is authorized to inspect the establishment
of a registrant or applicant for registration in accordance with the
rules and regulations promulgated by him.

REGISTRATION REQUIREMENTS

Factors con-
sistent with
public inter-
est.

SEC. 303. (a) The Attorney General shall register an applicant to
manufacture controlled substances in schedule I or II if he determines
that such registration is consistent with the public interest and with
United States obligations under international treaties, conventions, or
protocols in effect on the effective date of this part. In determining the
public interest, the following factors shall be considered:

Controls.
Importation
and bulk manu-
facture, limi-
tation.

(1) maintenance of effective controls against diversion of particular controlled substances and any controlled substance in
schedule I or II compounded therefrom into other than legitimate
medical, scientific, research, or industrial channels, by limiting the
importation and bulk manufacture of such controlled substances
to a number of establishments which can produce an adequate and
uninterrupted supply of these substances under adequately com-

October 27, 1970   Pub. Law 91-513

petitive conditions for legitimate medical, scientific, research, and
industrial purposes;

(2) compliance with applicable State and local law;   Compliance.

(3) promotion of technical advances in the art of manufactur-   Technology.
ing these substances and the development of new substances;

(4) prior conviction record of applicant under Federal and   Applicants,
State laws relating to the manufacture, distribution, or dispensing   prior convic-
of such substances;   tion record.

(5) past experience in the manufacture of controlled substances,   Experience.
and the existence in the establishment of effective control against
diversion; and

(6) such other factors as may be relevant to and consistent with
the public health and safety.

(b) The Attorney General shall register an applicant to distribute   Factors
a controlled substance in schedule I or II unless he determines that   consistent
the issuance of such registration is inconsistent with the public inter-   to public
est. In determining the public interest, the following factors shall   interest.
be considered:

(1) maintenance of effective control against diversion of particular controlled substances into other than legitimate medical,
scientific, and industrial channels;

(2) compliance with applicable State and local law;

(3) prior conviction record of applicant under Federal or
State laws relating to the manufacture, distribution, or dispensing
of such substances;

(4) past experience in the distribution of controlled substances;
and

(5) such other factors as may be relevant to and consistent with
the public health and safety.

(c) Registration granted under subsections (a) and (b) of this   Prohibition.
section shall not entitle a registrant to (1) manufacture or distribute
controlled substances in schedule I or II other than those specified in
the registration, or (2) manufacture any quantity of those controlled
substances in excess of the quota assigned pursuant to section 306.   Post, p. 1257.

(d) The Attorney General shall register an applicant to manufacture controlled substances in schedule III, IV, or V, unless he determines that the issuance of such registration is inconsistent with the
public interest. In determining the public interest, the following factors shall be considered:

(1) maintenance of effective controls against diversion of particular controlled substances and any controlled substance in
schedule III, IV, or V compounded therefrom into other than
legitimate medical, scientific, or industrial channels;

(2) compliance with applicable State and local law;

(3) promotion of technical advances in the art of manufacturing these substances and the development of new substances;

(4) prior conviction record of applicant under Federal or State
laws relating to the manufacture, distribution, or dispensing of
such substances;

(5) past experience in the manufacture, distribution, and dispensing of controlled substances, and the existence in the establishment of effective controls against diversion; and

(6) such other factors as may be relevant to and consistent with
the public health and safety.

(e) The Attorney General shall register an applicant to distribute
controlled substances in schedule III, IV, or V, unless he determines
that the issuance of such registration is inconsistent with the public
interest. In determining the public interest, the following factors shall
be considered:

Pub. Law 91-513   October 27, 1970

84 STAT. 1255

(1) maintenance of effective controls against diversion of particular controlled substances into other than legitimate medical, scientific, and industrial channels;

(2) compliance with applicable State and local law;

(3) prior conviction record of applicant under Federal or State laws relating to the manufacture, distribution, or dispensing of such substances;

(4) past experience in the distribution of controlled substances; and

(5) such other factors as may be relevant to and consistent with the public health and safety.

Research. (f) Practitioners shall be registered to dispense or conduct research with controlled substances in schedule II, III, IV, or V if they are authorized to dispense or conduct research under the law of the State in which they practice. Separate registration under this part for practitioners engaging in research with nonnarcotic controlled substances in schedule II, III, IV, or V, who are already registered under this **Pharmacies.** part in another capacity, shall not be required. Pharmacies (as distinguished from pharmacists) when engaged in commercial activities, shall be registered to dispense controlled substances in schedule II, III, IV, or V if they are authorized to dispense under the law of the **Research** State in which they regularly conduct business. Registration applica- **applications.** tions by practitioners wishing to conduct research with controlled substances in schedule I shall be referred to the Secretary, who shall determine qualifications and competency of each practitioner requesting registration, as well as the merits of the research protocol. The Secretary, in determining the merits of each research protocol, shall consult with the Attorney General as to effective procedures to adequately safeguard against diversion of such controlled substances from legitimate medical or scientific use. Registration for the purpose of bona fide research with controlled substances in schedule I by a practitioner deemed qualified by the Secretary may be denied by the Attorney General only on a ground specified in section 304(a).

DENIAL, REVOCATION, OR SUSPENSION OF REGISTRATION

SEC. 304. (a) A registration pursuant to section 303 to manufacture, distribute, or dispense a controlled substance may be suspended or revoked by the Attorney General upon a finding that the registrant—

(1) has materially falsified any application filed pursuant to **Post, p. 1285.** or required by this title or title III;

(2) has been convicted of a felony under this title or title III or any other law of the United States, or of any State, relating to any substance defined in this title as a controlled substance; or

(3) has had his State license or registration suspended, revoked, or denied by competent State authority and is no longer authorized by State law to engage in the manufacturing, distribution, or dispensing of controlled substances.

(b) The Attorney General may limit revocation or suspension of a registration to the particular controlled substance with respect to which grounds for revocation or suspension exist.

Service of (c) Before taking action pursuant to this section, or pursuant to a **order.** denial of registration under section 303, the Attorney General shall serve upon the applicant or registrant an order to show cause why registration should not be denied, revoked, or suspended. The order to show cause shall contain a statement of the basis thereof and shall call upon the applicant or registrant to appear before the Attorney

October 27, 1970　　　　　　　　　Pub. Law 91-513

84 STAT. 1256

General at a time and place stated in the order, but in no event less than thirty days after the date of receipt of the order. Proceedings to deny, revoke, or suspend shall be conducted pursuant to this section in accordance with subchapter II of chapter 5 of title 5 of the United States Code. Such proceedings shall be independent of, and not in lieu of, criminal prosecutions or other proceedings under this title or any other law of the United States.

80 Stat. 381.
5 USC 551.

(d) The Attorney General may, in his discretion, suspend any registration simultaneously with the institution of proceedings under this section, in cases where he finds that there is an imminent danger to the public health or safety. Such suspension shall continue in effect until the conclusion of such proceedings, including judicial review thereof, unless sooner withdrawn by the Attorney General or dissolved by a court of competent jurisdiction.

Registration, suspension.

(e) The suspension or revocation of a registration under this section shall operate to suspend or revoke any quota applicable under section 306.

(f) In the event the Attorney General suspends or revokes a registration granted under section 303, all controlled substances owned or possessed by the registrant pursuant to such registration at the time of suspension or the effective date of the revocation order, as the case may be, may, in the discretion of the Attorney General, be placed under seal. No disposition may be made of any controlled substances under seal until the time for taking an appeal has elapsed or until all appeals have been concluded except that a court, upon application therefor, may at any time order the sale of perishable controlled substances. Any such order shall require the deposit of the proceeds of the sale with the court. Upon a revocation order becoming final, all such controlled substances (or proceeds of sale deposited in court) shall be forfeited to the United States; and the Attorney General shall dispose of such controlled substances in accordance with section 511(e).

Post, p. 1277.

LABELING AND PACKAGING REQUIREMENTS

SEC. 305. (a) It shall be unlawful to distribute a controlled substance in a commercial container unless such container, when and as required by regulations of the Attorney General, bears a label (as defined in section 201(k) of the Federal Food, Drug, and Cosmetic Act) containing an identifying symbol for such substance in accordance with such regulations. A different symbol shall be required for each schedule of controlled substances.

Symbol.

52 Stat. 1041.
21 USC 321.

(b) It shall be unlawful for the manufacturer of any controlled substance to distribute such substance unless the labeling (as defined in section 201(m) of the Federal Food, Drug, and Cosmetic Act) of such substance contains, when and as required by regulations of the Attorney General, the identifying symbol required under subsection (a).

(c) The Secretary shall prescribe regulations under section 503(b) of the Federal Food, Drug, and Cosmetic Act which shall provide that the label of a drug listed in schedule II, III, or IV shall, when dispensed to or for a patient, contain a clear, concise warning that it is a crime to transfer the drug to any person other than the patient.

65 Stat. 648.
21 USC 353.

(d) It shall be unlawful to distribute controlled substances in schedule I or II, and narcotic drugs in schedule III or IV, unless the bottle or other container, stopper, covering, or wrapper thereof is securely sealed as required by regulations of the Attorney General.

Unlawful distribution.

Pub. Law 91-513   October 27, 1970

84 STAT. 1257

QUOTAS APPLICABLE TO CERTAIN SUBSTANCES

Production
quota.

SEC. 306. (a) The Attorney General shall determine the total quantity and establish production quotas for each basic class of controlled substance in schedules I and II to be manufactured each calendar year to provide for the estimated medical, scientific, research, and industrial needs of the United States, for lawful export requirements, and for the establishment and maintenance of reserve stocks. Production quotas shall be established in terms of quantities of each basic class of controlled substance and not in terms of individual pharmaceutical dosage forms prepared from or containing such a controlled substance.

(b) The Attorney General shall limit or reduce individual production quotas to the extent necessary to prevent the aggregate of individual quotas from exceeding the amount determined necessary each year by the Attorney General under subsection (a). The quota of each registered manufacturer for each basic class of controlled substance in schedule I or II shall be revised in the same proportion as the limitation or reduction of the aggregate of the quotas. However, if any registrant, before the issuance of a limitation or reduction in quota, has manufactured in excess of his revised quota, the amount of the excess shall be subtracted from his quota for the following year.

Manufacturing
quota.

(c) On or before July 1 of each year, upon application therefor by a registered manufacturer, the Attorney General shall fix a manufacturing quota for the basic classes of controlled substances in schedules I and II that the manufacturer seeks to produce. The quota shall be subject to the provisions of subsections (a) and (b) of this section. In fixing such quotas, the Attorney General shall determine the manufacturer's estimated disposal, inventory, and other requirements for the calendar year; and, in making his determination, the Attorney General shall consider the manufacturer's current rate of disposal, the trend of the national disposal rate during the preceding calendar year, the manufacturer's production cycle and inventory position, the economic availability of raw materials, yield and stability problems, emergencies such as strikes and fires, and other factors.

(d) The Attorney General shall, upon application and subject to the provisions of subsections (a) and (b) of this section, fix a quota for a basic class of controlled substance in schedule I or II for any registrant who has not manufactured that basic class of controlled substance during one or more preceding calendar years. In fixing such quota, the Attorney General shall take into account the registrant's reasonably anticipated requirements for the current year; and, in making his determination of such requirements, he shall consider such factors specified in subsection (c) of this section as may be relevant.

Quota,
increase.

(e) At any time during the year any registrant who has applied for or received a manufacturing quota for a basic class of controlled substance in schedule I or II may apply for an increase in that quota to meet his estimated disposal, inventory, and other requirements during the remainder of that year. In passing upon the application the Attorney General shall take into consideration any occurrences since the filing of the registrant's initial quota application that may require an increased manufacturing rate by the registrant during the balance of the year. In passing upon the application the Attorney General may also take into account the amount, if any, by which the determination of the Attorney General under subsection (a) of this section exceeds the aggregate of the quotas of all registrants under this section.

Controlled
substances,
incidental
production,
exception.

(f) Notwithstanding any other provisions of this title, no registration or quota may be required for the manufacture of such quantities of controlled substances in schedules I and II as incidentally and necessarily result from the manufacturing process used for the manufacture of a controlled substance with respect to which its manufacturer is duly registered under this title. The Attorney General may, by regulation, prescribe restrictions on the retention and disposal of such incidentally produced substances.   Restrictions.

RECORDS AND REPORTS OF REGISTRANTS

SEC. 307. (a) Except as provided in subsection (c)—   Inventory.
(1) every registrant under this title shall, on the effective date of this section, or as soon thereafter as such registrant first engages in the manufacture, distribution, or dispensing of controlled substances, and every second year thereafter, make a complete and accurate record of all stocks thereof on hand, except that the regulations prescribed under this section shall permit each such biennial inventory (following the initial inventory required by this paragraph) to be prepared on such registrant's regular general physical inventory date (if any) which is nearest to and does not vary by more than six months from the biennial date that would otherwise apply;
(2) on the effective date of each regulation of the Attorney General controlling a substance that immediately prior to such date was not a controlled substance, each registrant under this title manufacturing, distributing, or dispensing such substance shall make a complete and accurate record of all stocks thereof on hand; and
(3) on and after the effective date of this section, every registrant under this title manufacturing, distributing, or dispensing a controlled substance or substances shall maintain, on a current basis, a complete and accurate record of each such substance manufactured, received, sold, delivered, or otherwise disposed of by him, except that this paragraph shall not require the maintenance of a perpetual inventory.
(b) Every inventory or other record required under this section (1) shall be in accordance with, and contain such relevant information as may be required by, regulations of the Attorney General, (2) shall (A) be maintained separately from all other records of the registrant, or (B) alternatively, in the case of nonnarcotic controlled substances, be in such form that information required by the Attorney General is readily retrievable from the ordinary business records of the registrant, and (3) shall be kept and be available, for at least two years, for inspection and copying by officers or employees of the United States authorized by the Attorney General.   Availability.
(c) The foregoing provisions of this section shall not apply—   Nonapplicability.
(1) (A) with respect to narcotic controlled substances in schedule II, III, IV, or V, to the prescribing or administering of such substances by a practitioner in the lawful course of his professional practice; or
(B) with respect to nonnarcotic controlled substances in schedule II, III, IV, or V, to any practitioner who dispenses such substances to his patients, unless the practitioner is regularly engaged in charging his patients, either separately or together with charges for other professional services, for substances so dispensed;
(2) (A) to the use of controlled substances, at establishments registered under this title which keep records with respect to such substances, in research conducted in conformity with an exemption granted under section 505(i) or 512(j) of the Federal Food, Drug, and Cosmetic Act;

52 Stat. 1052;
76 Stat. 783.
82 Stat. 343.
21 USC 355,
360b.

(B) to the use of controlled substances, at establishments registered under this title which keep records with respect to such substances, in preclinical research or in teaching; or

(3) to the extent of any exemption granted to any person, with respect to all or part of such provisions, by the Attorney General by or pursuant to regulation on the basis of a finding that the application of such provisions (or part thereof) to such person is not necessary for carrying out the purposes of this title.

(d) Every manufacturer registered under section 303 shall, at such time or times and in such form as the Attorney General may require, make periodic reports to the Attorney General of every sale, delivery, or other disposal by him of any controlled substance, and each distributor shall make such reports with respect to narcotic controlled substances, identifying by the registration number assigned under this title the person or establishment (unless exempt from registration under section 302(d)) to whom such sale, delivery, or other disposal was made.

(e) Regulations under sections 505(i) and 512(j) of the Federal Food, Drug, and Cosmetic Act, relating to investigational use of drugs, shall include such procedures as the Secretary, after consultation with the Attorney General, determines are necessary to insure the security and accountability of controlled substances used in research to which such regulations apply.

52 Stat. 1052;
76 Stat. 783.
82 Stat. 343.
21 USC 355,
360b.

ORDER FORMS

Unlawful
distribution.

SEC. 308. (a) It shall be unlawful for any person to distribute a controlled substance in schedule I or II to another except in pursuance of a written order of the person to whom such substance is distributed, made on a form to be issued by the Attorney General in blank in accordance with subsection (d) and regulations prescribed by him pursuant to this section.

Nonapplicability.

(b) Nothing in subsection (a) shall apply to—

Post, p.1285.

(1) the exportation of such substances from the United States in conformity with title III;

(2) the delivery of such a substance to or by a common or contract carrier for carriage in the lawful and usual course of its business, or to or by a warehouseman for storage in the lawful and usual course of its business; but where such carriage or storage is in connection with the distribution by the owner of the substance to a third person, this paragraph shall not relieve the distributor from compliance with subsection (a).

Preservation
and availability.

(c) (1) Every person who in pursuance of an order required under subsection (a) distributes a controlled substance shall preserve such order for a period of two years, and shall make such order available for inspection and copying by officers and employees of the United States duly authorized for that purpose by the Attorney General, and by officers or employees of States or their political subdivisions who are charged with the enforcement of State or local laws regulating the production, or regulating the distribution or dispensing, of controlled substances and who are authorized under such laws to inspect such orders.

Duplicate,
preservation
and availability.

(2) Every person who gives an order required under subsection (a) shall, at or before the time of giving such order, make or cause to be made a duplicate thereof on a form to be issued by the Attorney General in blank in accordance with subsection (d) and regulations prescribed by him pursuant to this section, and shall, if such order is accepted, preserve such duplicate for a period of two years and make it available for inspection and copying by the officers and employees mentioned in paragraph (1) of this subsection.

October 27, 1970   **Pub. Law 91-513**
                                    84 STAT. 1260

(d)(1) The Attorney General shall issue forms pursuant to sub- Forms,
sections (a) and (c)(2) only to persons validly registered under issuance.
section 303 (or exempted from registration under section 302(d)).
Whenever any such form is issued to a person, the Attorney General
shall, before delivery thereof, insert therein the name of such person, and it shall be unlawful for any other person (A) to use such
form for the purpose of obtaining controlled substances or (B) to
furnish such form to any person with intent thereby to procure the
distribution of such substances.

(2) The Attorney General may charge reasonable fees for the Fees.
issuance of such forms in such amounts as he may prescribe for the
purpose of covering the cost to the United States of issuing such forms,
and other necessary activities in connection therewith.

(e) It shall be unlawful for any person to obtain by means of order Unlawful act.
forms issued under this section controlled substances for any purpose
other than their use, distribution, dispensing, or administration in the
conduct of a lawful business in such substances or in the course of his
professional practice or research.

PRESCRIPTIONS

SEC. 309. (a) Except when dispensed directly by a practitioner,
other than a pharmacist, to an ultimate user, no controlled substance
in schedule II, which is a prescription drug as determined under the
Federal Food, Drug, and Cosmetic Act, may be dispensed without the 52 Stat. 1040.
written prescription of a practitioner, except that in emergency situa- 21 USC 301.
tions, as prescribed by the Secretary by regulation after consultation
with the Attorney General, such drug may be dispensed upon oral
prescription in accordance with section 503(b) of that Act. Prescrip- 65 Stat. 648.
tions shall be retained in conformity with the requirements of section 21 USC 353.
307 of this title. No prescription for a controlled substance in schedule
II may be refilled.

(b) Except when dispensed directly by a practitioner, other than
a pharmacist, to an ultimate user, no controlled substance in schedule
III or IV, which is a prescription drug as determined under the Federal Food, Drug, and Cosmetic Act, may be dispensed without a written or oral prescription in conformity with section 503(b) of that
Act. Such prescriptions may not be filled or refilled more than six
months after the date thereof or be refilled more than five times after
the date of the prescription unless renewed by the practitioner.

(c) No controlled substance in schedule V which is a drug may be
distributed or dispensed other than for a medical purpose.

(d) Whenever it appears to the Attorney General that a drug not
considered to be a prescription drug under the Federal Food, Drug,
and Cosmetic Act should be so considered because of its abuse potential, he shall so advise the Secretary and furnish to him all available
data relevant thereto.

PART D—OFFENSES AND PENALTIES

PROHIBITED ACTS A—PENALTIES

SEC. 401. (a) Except as authorized by this title, it shall be unlawful
for any person knowingly or intentionally—
    (1) to manufacture, distribute, or dispense, or possess with
    intent to manufacture, distribute, or dispense, a controlled sub
    stance; or
    (2) to create, distribute, or dispense, or possess with intent to
    distribute or dispense, a counterfeit substance.

Pub. Law 91-513   October 27, 1970

84 STAT. 1261

Post, p. 1265.

Penalties.

Post, p. 1285.

Special parole
term.

(b) Except as otherwise provided in section 405, any person who violates subsection (a) of this section shall be sentenced as follows:

(1)(A) In the case of a controlled substance in schedule I or II which is a narcotic drug, such person shall be sentenced to a term of imprisonment of not more than 15 years, a fine of not more than $25,000, or both. If any person commits such a violation after one or more prior convictions of him for an offense punishable under this paragraph, or for a felony under any other provision of this title or title III or other law of the United States relating to narcotic drugs, marihuana, or depressant or stimulant substances, have become final, such person shall be sentenced to a term of imprisonment of not more than 30 years, a fine of not more than $50,000, or both. Any sentence imposing a term of imprisonment under this paragraph shall, in the absence of such a prior conviction, impose a special parole term of at least 3 years in addition to such term of imprisonment and shall, if there was such a prior conviction, impose a special parole term of at least 6 years in addition to such term of imprisonment.

(B) In the case of a controlled substance in schedule I or II which is not a narcotic drug or in the case of any controlled substance in schedule III, such person shall be sentenced to a term of imprisonment of not more than 5 years, a fine of not more than $15,000, or both. If any person commits such a violation after one or more prior convictions of him for an offense punishable under this paragraph, or for a felony under any other provision of this title or title III or other law of the United States relating to narcotic drugs, marihuana, or depressant or stimulant substances, have become final, such person shall be sentenced to a term of imprisonment of not more than 10 years, a fine of not more than $30,000, or both. Any sentence imposing a term of imprisonment under this paragraph shall, in the absence of such a prior conviction, impose a special parole term of at least 2 years in addition to such term of imprisonment and shall, if there was such a prior conviction, impose a special parole term of at least 4 years in addition to such term of imprisonment.

(2) In the case of a controlled substance in schedule IV, such person shall be sentenced to a term of imprisonment of not more than 3 years, a fine of not more than $10,000, or both. If any person commits such a violation after one or more prior convictions of him for an offense punishable under this paragraph, or for a felony under any other provision of this title or title III or other law of the United States relating to narcotic drugs, marihuana, or depressant or stimulant substances, have become final, such person shall be sentenced to a term of imprisonment of not more than 6 years, a fine of not more than $20,000, or both. Any sentence imposing a term of imprisonment under this paragraph shall, in the absence of such a prior conviction, impose a special parole term of at least one year in addition to such term of imprisonment and shall, if there was such a prior conviction, impose a special parole term of at least 2 years in addition to such term of imprisonment.

(3) In the case of a controlled substance in schedule V, such person shall be sentenced to a term of imprisonment of not more than one year, a fine of not more than $5,000, or both. If any person commits such a violation after one or more convictions of him for an offense punishable under this paragraph, or for a crime under any other provision of this title or title III or other law of the United States relating to narcotic drugs, marihuana, or depressant or stimulant substances, have become final, such person shall be sentenced to a term of imprisonment of not more than 2 years, a fine of not more than $10,000, or both.

October 27, 1970   Pub. Law 91-513
84 STAT. 1262

(4) Notwithstanding paragraph (1)(B) of this subsection, any   Marihuana,
person who violates subsection (a) of this section by distributing   simple pos-
a small amount of marihuana for no remuneration shall be treated   session.
as provided in subsections (a) and (b) of section 404.

(c) A special parole term imposed under this section or section 405   Special parole
may be revoked if its terms and conditions are violated. In such cir-   term.
cumstances the original term of imprisonment shall be increased by
the period of the special parole term and the resulting new term of
imprisonment shall not be diminished by the time which was spent on
special parole. A person whose special parole term has been revoked
may be required to serve all or part of the remainder of the new
term of imprisonment. A special parole term provided for in this section or section 405 shall be in addition to, and not in lieu of, any
other parole provided for by law.

PROHIBITED ACTS B—PENALTIES

SEC 402. (a) It shall be unlawful for any person—
(1) who is subject to the requirements of part C to distribute
or dispense a controlled substance in violation of section 309;
(2) who is a registrant to distribute or dispense a controlled
substance not authorized by his registration to another registrant
or other authorized person or to manufacture a controlled substance not authorized by his registration;
(3) who is a registrant to distribute a controlled substance in
violation of section 305 of this title;
(4) to remove, alter, or obliterate a symbol or label required by
section 305 of this title;
(5) to refuse or fail to make, keep, or furnish any record,
report, notification, declaration, order or order form, statement,
invoice, or information required under this title or title III;   *Post,* p. 1285.
(6) to refuse any entry into any premises or inspection authorized by this title or title III;
(7) to remove, break, injure, or deface a seal placed upon controlled substances pursuant to section 304(f) or 511 or to remove   *Ante,* p. 1256.
or dispose of substances so placed under seal; or   *Post,* p. 1276.
(8) to use, to his own advantage, or to reveal, other than to
duly authorized officers or employees of the United States, or to
the courts when relevant in any judicial proceeding under this
title or title III, any information acquired in the course of an
inspection authorized by this title concerning any method or
process which as a trade secret is entitled to protection.

(b) It shall be unlawful for any person who is a registrant to manufacture a controlled substance in schedule I or II which is—
(1) not expressly authorized by his registration and by a quota
assigned to him pursuant to section 306; or
(2) in excess of a quota assigned to him pursuant to section 306.

(c)(1) Except as provided in paragraph (2), any person who vio-   Penalty.
lates this section shall, with respect to any such violation, be subject
to a civil penalty of not more than $25,000. The district courts of the   Jurisdiction
United States (or, where there is no such court in the case of any ter-   of courts.
ritory or possession of the United States, then the court in such territory or possession having the jurisdiction of a district court of the
United States in cases arising under the Constitution and laws of the
United States) shall have jurisdiction in accordance with section 1355
of title 28 of the United States Code to enforce this paragraph.   62 Stat. 934.

Pub. Law 91-513   October 27, 1970
84 STAT. 1263

Penalty.

Post, p.1285.

Penalty.

Exception.

(2)(A) If a violation of this section is prosecuted by an information or indictment which alleges that the violation was committed knowingly and the trier of fact specifically finds that the violation was so committed, such person shall, except as otherwise provided in subparagraph (B) of this paragraph, be sentenced to imprisonment of not more than one year or a fine of not more than $25,000, or both.

(B) If a violation referred to in subparagraph (A) was committed after one or more prior convictions of the offender for an offense punishable under this paragraph (2), or for a crime under any other provision of this title or title III or other law of the United States relating to narcotic drugs, marihuana, or depressant or stimulant substances, have become final, such person shall be sentenced to a term of imprisonment of not more than 2 years, a fine of $50,000, or both.

(3) Except under the conditions specified in paragraph (2) of this subsection, a violation of this section does not constitute a crime, and a judgment for the United States and imposition of a civil penalty pursuant to paragraph (1) shall not give rise to any disability or legal disadvantage based on conviction for a criminal offense.

PROHIBITED ACTS C—PENALTIES

Sec. 403. (a) It shall be unlawful for any person knowingly or intentionally—

Ante, p. 1259.

(1) who is a registrant to distribute a controlled substance classified in schedule I or II, in the course of his legitimate business, except pursuant to an order or an order form as required by section 308 of this title;

(2) to use in the course of the manufacture or distribution of a controlled substance a registration number which is fictitious, revoked, suspended, or issued to another person;

(3) to acquire or obtain possession of a controlled substance by misrepresentation, fraud, forgery, deception, or subterfuge;

(4) to furnish false or fraudulent material information in, or omit any material information from, any application, report, record, or other document required to be made, kept, or filed under this title or title III; or

(5) to make, distribute, or possess any punch, die, plate, stone, or other thing designed to print, imprint, or reproduce the trademark, trade name, or other identifying mark, imprint, or device of another or any likeness of any of the foregoing upon any drug or container or labeling thereof so as to render such drug a counterfeit substance.

(b) It shall be unlawful for any person knowingly or intentionally to use any communication facility in committing or in causing or facilitating the commission of any act or acts constituting a felony under any provision of this title or title III. Each separate use of a communication facility shall be a separate offense under this subsection. For purposes of this subsection, the term "communication facility" means any and all public and private instrumentalities used or useful in the transmission of writing, signs, signals, pictures, or sounds of all kinds and includes mail, telephone, wire, radio, and all other means of communication.

"Communication facility."

Penalty.

(c) Any person who violates this section shall be sentenced to a term of imprisonment of not more than 4 years, a fine of not more than $30,000, or both; except that if any person commits such a violation after one or more prior convictions of him for violation of this section, or for a felony under any other provision of this title or title III or other law of the United States relating to narcotic drugs,

October 27, 1970   Pub. Law 91-513
84 STAT. 1264

marihuana, or depressant or stimulant substances, have become final,
such person shall be sentenced to a term of imprisonment of not more   Penalty.
than 8 years, a fine of not more than $60,000, or both.

PENALTY FOR SIMPLE POSSESSION; CONDITIONAL DISCHARGE AND EXPUNG-
      ING OF RECORDS FOR FIRST OFFENSE

Sec. 404. (a) It shall be unlawful for any person knowingly or
intentionally to possess a controlled substance unless such substance
was obtained directly, or pursuant to a valid prescription or order,
from a practitioner, while acting in the course of his professional
practice, or except as otherwise authorized by this title or title III.   Post, p. 1285.
Any person who violates this subsection shall be sentenced to a term
of imprisonment of not more than one year, a fine of not more than
$5,000, or both, except that if he commits such offense after a prior
conviction or convictions under this subsection have become final, he
shall be sentenced to a term of imprisonment of not more than 2 years,
a fine of not more than $10,000, or both.

(b)(1) If any person who has not previously been convicted of
violating subsection (a) of this section, any other provision of this
title or title III, or any other law of the United States relating to
narcotic drugs, marihuana, or depressant or stimulant substances, is
found guilty of a violation of subsection (a) of this section after trial
or upon a plea of guilty, the court may, without entering a judgment
of guilty and with the consent of such person, defer further proceedings and place him on probation upon such reasonable conditions as
it may require and for such period, not to exceed one year, as the
court may prescribe. Upon violation of a condition of the probation,
the court may enter an adjudication of guilt and proceed as otherwise
provided. The court may, in its discretion, dismiss the proceedings
against such person and discharge him from probation before the
expiration of the maximum period prescribed for such person's probation. If during the period of his probation such person does not violate
any of the conditions of the probation, then upon expiration of such
period the court shall discharge such person and dismiss the proceedings against him. Discharge and dismissal under this subsection shall
be without court adjudication of guilt, but a nonpublic record thereof   Nonpublic
shall be retained by the Department of Justice solely for the purpose   record,
of use by the courts in determining whether or not, in subsequent   retention.
proceedings, such person qualifies under this subsection. Such discharge or dismissal shall not be deemed a conviction for purposes of
disqualifications or disabilities imposed by law upon conviction of a
crime (including the penalties prescribed under this part for second
or subsequent convictions) or for any other purpose. Discharge and
dismissal under this section may occur only once with respect to any
person.

(2) Upon the dismissal of such person and discharge of the pro-   First offense,
ceedings against him under paragraph (1) of this subsection, such   expunging of
person, if he was not over twenty-one years of age at the time of the   records, order.
offense, may apply to the court for an order to expunge from all
official records (other than the nonpublic records to be retained by
the Department of Justice under paragraph (1)) all recordation relating to his arrest, indictment or information, trial, finding of guilty,
and dismissal and discharge pursuant to this section. If the court
determines, after hearing, that such person was dismissed and the
proceedings against him discharged and that he was not over twenty-
one years of age at the time of the offense, it shall enter such order.

The effect of such order shall be to restore such person, in the contemplation of the law, to the status he occupied before such arrest or indictment or information. No person as to whom such order has been entered shall be held thereafter under any provision of any law to be guilty of perjury or otherwise giving a false statement by reason of his failures to recite or acknowledge such arrest, or indictment or information, or trial in response to any inquiry made of him for any purpose.

DISTRIBUTION TO PERSONS UNDER AGE TWENTY-ONE

SEC. 405. (a) Any person at least eighteen years of age who violates section 401(a)(1) by distributing a controlled substance to a person under twenty-one years of age is (except as provided in subsection (b)) punishable by (1) a term of imprisonment, or a fine, or both, up to twice that authorized by section 401(b), and (2) at least twice any special parole term authorized by section 401(b), for a first offense involving the same controlled substance and schedule.

(b) Any person at least eighteen years of age who violates section 401(a)(1) by distributing a controlled substance to a person under twenty-one years of age after a prior conviction or convictions under subsection (a) of this section (or under section 303(b)(2) of the Federal Food, Drug, and Cosmetic Act as in effect prior to the effective date of section 701(b) of this Act) have become final, is punishable by (1) a term of imprisonment, or a fine, or both, up to three times that authorized by section 401(b), and (2) at least three times any special parole term authorized by section 401(b), for a second or subsequent offense involving the same controlled substance and schedule.

82 Stat. 1361.
21 USC 333.

ATTEMPT AND CONSPIRACY

SEC. 406. Any person who attempts or conspires to commit any offense defined in this title is punishable by imprisonment or fine or both which may not exceed the maximum punishment prescribed for the offense, the commission of which was the object of the attempt or conspiracy.

ADDITIONAL PENALTIES

SEC. 407. Any penalty imposed for violation of this title shall be in addition to, and not in lieu of, any civil or administrative penalty or sanction authorized by law.

CONTINUING CRIMINAL ENTERPRISE

SEC. 408. (a)(1) Any person who engages in a continuing criminal enterprise shall be sentenced to a term of imprisonment which may not be less than 10 years and which may be up to life imprisonment, to a fine of not more than $100,000, and to the forfeiture prescribed in paragraph (2); except that if any person engages in such activity after one or more prior convictions of him under this section have become final, he shall be sentenced to a term of imprisonment which may not be less than 20 years and which may be up to life imprisonment, to a fine of not more than $200,000, and to the forfeiture prescribed in paragraph (2).

Penalty.

Forfeiture.

(2) Any person who is convicted under paragraph (1) of engaging in a continuing criminal enterprise shall forfeit to the United States—

(A) the profits obtained by him in such enterprise, and

October 27, 1970   **Pub. Law 91-513**
                                                    84 STAT. 1266

(B) any of his interest in, claim against, or property or contractual rights of any kind affording a source of influence over, such enterprise.

(b) For purposes of subsection (a), a person is engaged in a continuing criminal enterprise if—

    (1) he violates any provision of this title or title III the punishment for which is a felony, and   Post, p.1285.

    (2) such violation is a part of a continuing series of violations of this title or title III—

        (A) which are undertaken by such person in concert with five or more other persons with respect to whom such person occupies a position of organizer, a supervisory position, or any other position of management, and

        (B) from which such person obtains substantial income or resources.

(c) In the case of any sentence imposed under this section, imposition or execution of such sentence shall not be suspended, probation shall not be granted, and section 4202 of title 18 of the United States Code and the Act of July 15, 1932 (D.C. Code, secs. 24–203—24–207), shall not apply.   65 Stat. 150,
                                                       47 Stat. 697;
(d) The district courts of the United States (including courts in   61 Stat. 378;
the territories or possessions of the United States having jurisdiction   67 Stat. 91;
under subsection (a)) shall have jurisdiction to enter such restrain-   79 Stat. 113.
ing orders or prohibitions, or to take such other actions, including   Jurisdiction
the acceptance of satisfactory performance bonds, in connection with   of courts.
any property or other interest subject to forfeiture under this section, as they shall deem proper.

DANGEROUS SPECIAL DRUG OFFENDER SENTENCING

Sec. 409. (a) Whenever a United States attorney charged with the prosecution of a defendant in a court of the United States for an alleged felonious violation of any provision of this title or title III committed when the defendant was over the age of twenty-one years has reasons to believe that the defendant is a dangerous special drug offender such United States attorney, a reasonable time before trial or acceptance by the court of a plea of guilty or nolo contendere, may sign and file with the court, and may amend, a notice (1) specifying   Notice.
that the defendant is a dangerous special drug offender who upon conviction for such felonious violation is subject to the imposition of a sentence under subsection (b) of this section, and (2) setting out with particularity the reasons why such attorney believes the defendant to be a dangerous special drug offender. In no case shall the fact   Prohibition.
that the defendant is alleged to be a dangerous special drug offender be an issue upon the trial of such felonious violation, be disclosed to the jury, or be disclosed before any plea of guilty or nolo contendere or verdict or finding of guilty to the presiding judge without the consent of the parties. If the court finds that the filing of the notice as a public record may prejudice fair consideration of a pending criminal matter, it may order the notice sealed and the notice shall not be subject to subpena or public inspection during the pendency of such criminal matter, except on order of the court, but shall be subject to inspection by the defendant alleged to be a dangerous special drug offender and his counsel.

(b) Upon any plea of guilty or nolo contendere or verdict or finding   Hearing
of guilty of the defendant of such felonious violation, a hearing shall   without jury.
be held, before sentence is imposed, by the court sitting without a jury.

Pub. Law 91-513   October 27, 1970
84 STAT. 1267

Notice.

Presentence
report,
inspection.

Penalty.

Sentence.

Conditions.

The court shall fix a time for the hearing, and notice thereof shall be given to the defendant and the United States at least ten days prior thereto. The court shall permit the United States and counsel for the defendant, or the defendant if he is not represented by counsel, to inspect the presentence report sufficiently prior to the hearing as to afford a reasonable opportunity for verification. In extraordinary cases, the court may withhold material not relevant to a proper sentence, diagnostic opinion which might seriously disrupt a program of rehabilitation, any source of information obtained on a promise of confidentiality, and material previously disclosed in open court. A court withholding all or part of a presentence report shall inform the parties of its action and place in the record the reasons therefor. The court may require parties inspecting all or part of a presentence report to give notice of any part thereof intended to be controverted. In connection with the hearing, the defendant and the United States shall be entitled to assistance of counsel, compulsory process, and cross-examination of such witnesses as appear at the hearing. A duly authenticated copy of a former judgment or commitment shall be prima facie evidence of such former judgment or commitment. If it appears by a preponderance of the information, including information submitted during the trial of such felonious violation and the sentencing hearing and so much of the presentence report as the court relies upon, that the defendant is a dangerous special drug offender, the court shall sentence the defendant to imprisonment for an appropriate term not to exceed twenty-five years and not disproportionate in severity to the maximum term otherwise authorized by law for such felonious violation. Otherwise it shall sentence the defendant in accordance with the law prescribing penalties for such felonious violation. The court shall place in the record its findings, including an identification of the information relied upon in making such findings, and its reasons for the sentence imposed.

(c) This section shall not prevent the imposition and execution of a sentence of imprisonment for life or for a term exceeding twenty-five years upon any person convicted of an offense so punishable.

(d) Notwithstanding any other provision of this section, the court shall not sentence a dangerous special drug offender to less than any mandatory minimum penalty prescribed by law for such felonious violation. This section shall not be construed as creating any mandatory minimum penalty.

(e) A defendant is a special drug offender for purposes of this section if—

(1) the defendant has previously been convicted in courts of the United States or a State or any political subdivision thereof for two or more offenses involving dealing in controlled substances, committed on occasions different from one another and different from such felonious violation, and punishable in such courts by death or imprisonment in excess of one year, for one or more of such convictions the defendant has been imprisoned prior to the commission of such felonious violation, and less than five years have elapsed between the commission of such felonious violation and either the defendant's release, or parole or otherwise, from imprisonment for one such conviction or his commission of the last such previous offense or another offense involving dealing in controlled substances and punishable by death or imprisonment in excess of one year under applicable laws of the United States or a State or any political subdivision thereof; or

(2) the defendant committed such felonious violation as part of a pattern of dealing in controlled substances which was crimi-

October 27, 1970   Pub. Law 91-513
                                              84 STAT. 1268

nal under applicable laws of any jurisdiction, which constituted
a substantial source of his income, and in which he manifested
special skill or expertise; or
    (3) such felonious violation was, or the defendant committed
such felonious violation in furtherance of, a conspiracy with three
or more other persons to engage in a pattern of dealing in controlled substances which was criminal under applicable laws of
any jurisdiction, and the defendant did, or agreed that he would,
initiate, organize, plan, finance, direct, manage, or supervise all
or part of such conspiracy or dealing, or give or receive a bribe
or use force in connection with such dealing.
A conviction shown on direct or collateral review or at the hearing to
be invalid or for which the defendant has been pardoned on the ground
of innocence shall be disregarded for purposes of paragraph (1) of
this subsection. In support of findings under paragraph (2) of this
subsection, it may be shown that the defendant has had in his own
name or under his control income or property not explained as derived
from a source other than such dealing. For purposes of paragraph (2)
of this subsection, a substantial source of income means a source of   Substantial
income which for any period of one year or more exceeds the mini-   source of
mum wage, determined on the basis of a forty-hour week and fifty-   income.
week year, without reference to exceptions, under section 6(a)(1) of
the Fair Labor Standards Act of 1938 for an employee engaged in   80 Stat. 838.
commerce or in the production of goods for commerce, and which for   29 USC 206.
the same period exceeds fifty percent of the defendant's declared
adjusted gross income under section 62 of the Internal Revenue Code
of 1954. For purposes of paragraph (2) of this subsection, special skill   68A Stat. 17;
or expertise in such dealing includes unusual knowledge, judgment or   83 Stat. 655.
ability, including manual dexterity, facilitating the initiation, orga-   26 USC 62.
nizing, planning, financing, direction, management, supervision, exe-   Dealing.
cution or concealment of such dealing, the enlistment of accomplices in
such dealing, the escape from detection or apprehension for such dealing, or the disposition of the fruits or proceeds of such dealing. For
purposes of paragraphs (2) and (3) of this subsection, such dealing
forms a pattern if it embraces criminal acts that have the same or
similar purposes, results, participants, victims, or methods of commission, or otherwise are interrelated by distinguishing characteristics
and are not isolated events.
    (f) A defendant is dangerous for purposes of this section if a period   Defendant,
of confinement longer than that provided for such felonious violation   dangerous.
is required for the protection of the public from further criminal conduct by the defendant.
    (g) The time for taking an appeal from a conviction for which   Appeal.
sentence is imposed after proceedings under this section shall be measured from imposition of the original sentence.
    (h) With respect to the imposition, correction, or reduction of a   Sentence,
sentence after proceedings under this section, a review of the sentence   review.
on the record of the sentencing court may be taken by the defendant
or the United States to a court of appeals. Any review of the sentence
taken by the United States shall be taken at least five days before
expiration of the time for taking a review of the sentence or appeal
of the conviction by the defendant and shall be diligently prosecuted
The sentencing court may, with or without motion and notice extend
the time for taking a review of the sentence for a period not to exceed
thirty days from the expiration of the time otherwise prescribed by
law. The court shall not extend the time for taking a review of the
sentence by the United States after the time has expired. A court

Pub. Law 91-513   October 27, 1970
84 STAT. 1269

extending the time for taking a review of the sentence by the United States shall extend the time for taking a review of the sentence or appeal of the conviction by the defendant for the same period. The taking of a review of the sentence by the United States shall be deemed the taking of a review of the sentence and an appeal of the conviction by the defendant. Review of the sentence shall include review of whether the procedure employed was lawful, the findings made were clearly erroneous, or the sentencing court's discretion was abused. The court of appeals on review of the sentence may, after considering the record, including the entire presentence report, information submitted during the trial of such felonious violation and the sentencing hearing, and the findings and reasons of the sentencing court, affirm the sentence, impose or direct the imposition of any sentence which the sentencing court could originally have imposed, or remand for further sentencing proceedings and imposition of sentence, except that a sentence may be made more severe only on review of the sentence taken by the United States and after hearing. Failure of the United States to take a review of the imposition of the sentence shall, upon review taken by the United States of the correction or reduction of the sentence, foreclose imposition of a sentence more severe than that previously imposed. Any withdrawal or dismissal of review of the sentence taken by the United States shall foreclose imposition of a sentence more severe than that reviewed but shall not otherwise foreclose the review of the sentence or the appeal of the conviction. The court of appeals shall state in writing the reasons for its disposition of the review of the sentence. Any review of the sentence taken by the United States may be dismissed on a showing of the abuse of the right of the United States to take such review.

INFORMATION FOR SENTENCING

70 Stat. 929,
42 USC 242a.

Post, p. 1285.

SEC. 410. Except as otherwise provided in this title or section 303(a) of the Public Health Service Act, no limitation shall be placed on the information concerning the background, character, and conduct of a person convicted of an offense which a court of the United States may receive and consider for the purpose of imposing an appropriate sentence under this title or title III.

PROCEEDINGS TO ESTABLISH PRIOR CONVICTIONS

SEC. 411. (a)(1) No person who stands convicted of an offense under this part shall be sentenced to increased punishment by reason of one or more prior convictions, unless before trial, or before entry of a plea of guilty, the United States attorney files an information with the court (and serves a copy of such information on the person or counsel for the person) stating in writing the previous convictions to be relied upon. Upon a showing by the United States attorney that facts regarding prior convictions could not with due diligence be obtained prior to trial or before entry of a plea of guilty, the court may postpone the trial or the taking of the plea of guilty for a reasonable period for the purpose of obtaining such facts. Clerical mistakes in the information may be amended at any time prior to the pronouncement of sentence.

Prohibition

(2) An information may not be filed under this section if the increased punishment which may be imposed is imprisonment for a term in excess of three years unless the person either waived or was afforded prosecution by indictment for the offense for which such increased punishment may be imposed.

October 27, 1970   Pub. Law 91-513
                                    ─────────────────
                                        84 STAT. 1270

(b) If the United States attorney files an information under this   Previous
section, the court shall after conviction but before pronouncement of   conviction,
sentence inquire of the person with respect to whom the information   affirmation
was filed whether he affirms or denies that he has been previously   or denial.
convicted as alleged in the information, and shall inform him that any
challenge to a prior conviction which is not made before sentence is
imposed may not thereafter be raised to attack the sentence.

(c)(1) If the person denies any allegation of the information of   Denial,
prior conviction, or claims that any conviction alleged is invalid, he   written
shall file a written response to the information. A copy of the response   response.
shall be served upon the United States attorney. The court shall hold a   Hearing.
hearing to determine any issues raised by the response which would
except the person from increased punishment. The failure of the
United States attorney to include in the information the complete
criminal record of the person or any facts in addition to the convictions to be relied upon shall not constitute grounds for invalidating
the notice given in the information required by subsection (a)(1). The   Court without
hearing shall be before the court without a jury and either party may   jury.
introduce evidence. Except as otherwise provided in paragraph (2) of   Evidence,
this subsection, the United States attorney shall have the burden of   introduction.
proof beyond a reasonable doubt on any issue of fact. At the request
of either party, the court shall enter findings of fact and conclusions
of law.

(2) A person claiming that a conviction alleged in the information   Constitution of
was obtained in violation of the Constitution of the United States   U.S., violation.
shall set forth his claim, and the factual basis therefor, with particularity in his response to the information. The person shall have the
burden of proof by a preponderance of the evidence on any issue of
fact raised by the response. Any challenge to a prior conviction, not
raised by response to the information before an increased sentence
is imposed in reliance thereon, shall be waived unless good cause be
shown for failure to make a timely challenge.

(d)(1) If the person files no response to the information, or if   Sentence,
the court determines, after hearing, that the person is subject to in-   imposition.
creased punishment by reason of prior convictions, the court shall
proceed to impose sentence upon him as provided by this part.

(2) If the court determines that the person has not been convicted
as alleged in the information, that a conviction alleged in the information is invalid, or that the person is otherwise not subject to an
increased sentence as a matter of law, the court shall, at the request
of the United States attorney, postpone sentence to allow an appeal
from that determination. If no such request is made, the court shall
impose sentence as provided by this part. The person may appeal from
an order postponing sentence as if sentence had been pronounced and
a final judgment of conviction entered.

(e) No person who stands convicted of an offense under this part   Statute of
may challenge the validity of any prior conviction alleged under this   limitations.
section which occurred more than five years before the date of the
information alleging such prior conviction.

PART E—ADMINISTRATIVE AND ENFORCEMENT PROVISIONS

PROCEDURES

SEC. 501. (a) The Attorney General may delegate any of his func-   Attorney
tions under this title to any officer or employee of the Department of   General,
Justice.   functions,
                                                                        delegation.

Pub. Law 91-513   October 27, 1970
84 STAT. 1271

Regulations.

(b) The Attorney General may promulgate and enforce any rules, regulations, and procedures which he may deem necessary and appropriate for the efficient execution of his functions under this title.

Gifts, etc., acceptance.

(c) The Attorney General may accept in the name of the Department of Justice any form of devise, bequest, gift, or donation where the donor intends to donate property for the purpose of preventing or controlling the abuse of controlled substances. He may take all appropriate steps to secure possession of such property and may sell, assign, transfer, or convey any such property other than moneys.

EDUCATION AND RESEARCH PROGRAMS OF THE ATTORNEY GENERAL

SEC. 502. (a) The Attorney General is authorized to carry out educational and research programs directly related to enforcement of the laws under his jurisdiction concerning drugs or other substances which are or may be subject to control under this title. Such programs may include—

(1) educational and training programs on drug abuse and controlled substances law enforcement for local, State, and Federal personnel;

(2) studies or special projects designed to compare the deterrent effects of various enforcement strategies on drug use and abuse;

(3) studies or special projects designed to assess and detect accurately the presence in the human body of drugs or other substances which are or may be subject to control under this title, including the development of rapid field identification methods which would enable agents to detect microquantities of such drugs or other substances;

(4) studies or special projects designed to evaluate the nature and sources of the supply of illegal drugs throughout the country;

(5) studies or special projects to develop more effective methods to prevent diversion of controlled substances into illegal channels; and

(6) studies or special projects to develop information necessary to carry out his functions under section 201 of this title.

Ante, p. 1245.

(b) The Attorney General may enter into contracts for such educational and research activities without performance bonds and without regard to section 3709 of the Revised Statutes (41 U.S.C. 5).

Research populations, identification, prohibition.

(c) The Attorney General may authorize persons engaged in research to withhold the names and other identifying characteristics of persons who are the subjects of such research. Persons who obtain this authorization may not be compelled in any Federal, State, or local civil, criminal, administrative, legislative, or other proceeding to identify the subjects of research for which such authorization was obtained.

Controlled substances, exception.

(d) The Attorney General, on his own motion or at the request of the Secretary, may authorize the possession, distribution, and dispensing of controlled substances by persons engaged in research. Persons who obtain this authorization shall be exempt from State or Federal prosecution for possession, distribution, and dispensing of controlled substances to the extent authorized by the Attorney General.

COOPERATIVE ARRANGEMENTS

SEC. 503. (a) The Attorney General shall cooperate with local, State, and Federal agencies concerning traffic in controlled substances and in suppressing the abuse of controlled substances. To this end, he is authorized to

October 27, 1970   Pub. Law 91-513

84 STAT. 1272

(1) arrange for the exchange of information between governmental officials concerning the use and abuse of controlled substances;

(2) cooperate in the institution and prosecution of cases in the courts of the United States and before the licensing boards and courts of the several States;

(3) conduct training programs on controlled substance law enforcement for local, State, and Federal personnel;

(4) maintain in the Department of Justice a unit which will accept, catalog, file, and otherwise utilize all information and statistics, including records of controlled substance abusers and other controlled substance law offenders, which may be received from Federal, State, and local agencies, and make such information available for Federal, State, and local law enforcement purposes; and

(5) conduct programs of eradication aimed at destroying wild or illicit growth of plant species from which controlled substances may be extracted.

(b) When requested by the Attorney General, it shall be the duty of any agency or instrumentality of the Federal Government to furnish assistance, including technical advice, to him for carrying out his functions under this title; except that no such agency or instrumentality shall be required to furnish the name of, or other identifying information about, a patient or research subject whose identity it has undertaken to keep confidential.

     Assistance.

     Prohibition.

ADVISORY COMMITTEES

SEC. 504. The Attorney General may from time to time appoint committees to advise him with respect to preventing and controlling the abuse of controlled substances. Members of the committees may be entitled to receive compensation at the rate of $100 for each day (including traveltime) during which they are engaged in the actual performance of duties. While traveling on official business in the performance of duties for the committees, members of the committees shall be allowed expenses of travel, including per diem instead of subsistence, in accordance with subchapter I of chapter 57 of title 5, United States Code.

     Appointment.

     Compensation.

     Travel expenses, etc.

     80 Stat. 498;
     83 Stat. 190.
     5 USC 5701.

ADMINISTRATIVE HEARINGS

SEC. 505. (a) In carrying out his functions under this title, the Attorney General may hold hearings, sign and issue subpenas, administer oaths, examine witnesses, and receive evidence at any place in the United States.

(b) Except as otherwise provided in this title, notice shall be given and hearings shall be conducted under appropriate procedures of subchapter II of chapter 5, title 5, United States Code.

     80 Stat. 381.
     5 USC 551.

SUBPENAS

SEC. 506. (a) In any investigation relating to his functions under this title with respect to controlled substances, the Attorney General may subpena witnesses, compel the attendance and testimony of witnesses, and require the production of any records (including books, papers, documents, and other tangible things which constitute or contain evidence) which the Attorney General finds relevant or material to the investigation. The attendance of witnesses and the production of records may be required from any place in any State or in any territory

Pub. Law 91-513   October 27, 1970

84 STAT. 1273

Exception.

Fees.

or other place subject to the jurisdiction of the United States at any designated place of hearing; except that a witness shall not be required to appear at any hearing more than 500 miles distant from the place where he was served with a subpena. Witnesses summoned under this section shall be paid the same fees and mileage that are paid witnesses in the courts of the United States.

Service.

(b) A subpena issued under this section may be served by any person designated in the subpena to serve it. Service upon a natural person may be made by personal delivery of the subpena to him. Service may be made upon a domestic or foreign corporation or upon a partnership or other unincorporated association which is subject to suit under a common name, by delivering the subpena to an officer, to a managing or general agent, or to any other agent authorized by appointment or by law to receive service of process. The affidavit of the person serving the subpena entered on a true copy thereof by the person serving it shall be proof of service.

Refusal to obey subpena.

Order.

Failure to obey order, penalty. Jurisdiction.

(c) In the case of contumacy by or refusal to obey a subpena issued to any person, the Attorney General may invoke the aid of any court of the United States within the jurisdiction of which the investigation is carried on or of which the subpenaed person is an inhabitant, or in which he carries on business or may be found, to compel compliance with the subpena. The court may issue an order requiring the subpenaed person to appear before the Attorney General to produce records, if so ordered, or to give testimony touching the matter under investigation. Any failure to obey the order of the court may be punished by the court as a contempt thereof. All process in any such case may be served in any judicial district in which such person may be found.

JUDICIAL REVIEW

SEC. 507. All final determinations, findings, and conclusions of the Attorney General under this title shall be final and conclusive decisions of the matters involved, except that any person aggrieved by a final decision of the Attorney General may obtain review of the decision in the United States Court of Appeals for the District of Columbia or for the circuit in which his principal place of business is located upon petition filed with the court and delivered to the Attorney General within thirty days after notice of the decision. Findings of fact by the Attorney General, if supported by substantial evidence, shall be conclusive.

POWERS OF ENFORCEMENT PERSONNEL

SEC. 508. Any officer or employee of the Bureau of Narcotics and Dangerous Drug designated by the Attorney General may—
(1) carry firearms;
(2) execute and serve search warrants, arrest warrants, administrative inspection warrants, subpenas, and summonses issued under the authority of the United States;
(3) make arrests without warrant (A) for any offense against the United States committed in his presence, or (B) for any felony, cognizable under the laws of the United States, if he has probable cause to believe that the person to be arrested has committed or is committing a felony;
(4) make seizures of property pursuant to the provisions of this title; and
(5) perform such other law enforcement duties as the Attorney General may designate.

October 27, 1970   Pub. Law 91-513
                                         84 STAT. 1274

SEARCH WARRANTS

SEC. 509. (a) A search warrant relating to offenses involving controlled substances may be served at any time of the day or night if the judge or United States magistrate issuing the warrant is satisfied that there is probable cause to believe that grounds exist for the warrant and for its service at such time.

(b) Any officer authorized to execute a search warrant relating to   Authority to
offenses involving controlled substances the penalty for which is   break and
imprisonment for more than one year may, without notice of his author-   enter under
ity and purpose, break open an outer or inner door or window of a   certain
building, or any part of the building, or anything therein, if the judge   conditions.
or United States magistrate issuing the warrant (1) is satisfied that
there is probable cause to believe that (A) the property sought may
and, if such notice is given, will be easily and quickly destroyed or
disposed of, or (B) the giving of such notice will immediately endanger the life or safety of the executing officer or another person, and
(2) has included in the warrant a direction that the officer executing
it shall not be required to give such notice. Any officer acting under
such warrant, shall, as soon as practicable after entering the premises,
identify himself and give the reasons and authority for his entrance
upon the premises.

ADMINISTRATIVE INSPECTIONS AND WARRANTS

SEC. 510. (a) As used in this section, the term "controlled premises"   "Controlled
means—   premises."
    (1) places where original or other records or documents
required under this title are kept or required to be kept, and
    (2) places, including factories, warehouses, or other establishments, and conveyances, where persons registered under section
303 (or exempted from registration under section 302(d))
may lawfully hold, manufacture, or distribute, dispense, administer, or otherwise dispose of controlled substances.
(b)(1) For the purpose of inspecting, copying, and verifying the
correctness of records, reports, or other documents required to be kept
or made under this title and otherwise facilitating the carrying out of
his functions under this title, the Attorney General is authorized, in
accordance with this section, to enter controlled premises and to conduct administrative inspections thereof, and of the things specified in
this section, relevant to those functions.
(2) Such entries and inspections shall be carried out through officers
or employees (hereinafter referred to as "inspectors") designated by
the Attorney General. Any such inspector, upon stating his purpose
and presenting to the owner, operator, or agent in charge of such
premises (A) appropriate credentials and (B) a written notice of his
inspection authority (which notice in the case of an inspection requiring, or in fact supported by, an administrative inspection warrant shall
consist of such warrant), shall have the right to enter such premises
and conduct such inspection at reasonable times.
(3) Except as may otherwise be indicated in an applicable inspection warrant, the inspector shall have the right—
    (A) to inspect and copy records, reports, and other documents
required to be kept or made under this title;
    (B) to inspect, within reasonable limits and in a reasonable
manner, controlled premises and all pertinent equipment, finished
and unfinished drugs and other substances or materials, containers, and labeling found therein, and, except as provided in para-

84 STAT. 1275

graph (5) of this subsection, all other things therein (including records, files, papers, processes, controls, and facilities) appropriate for verification of the records, reports, and documents referred to in clause (A) or otherwise bearing on the provisions of this title; and

(C) to inventory any stock of any controlled substance therein and obtain samples of any such substance.

(4) Except when the owner, operator, or agent in charge of the controlled premises so consents in writing, no inspection authorized by this section shall extend to—

(A) financial data;

(B) sales data other than shipment data; or

(C) pricing data.

(c) A warrant under this section shall not be required for the inspection of books and records pursuant to an administrative subpena issued in accordance with section 506, nor for entries and administrative inspections (including seizures of property)—

(1) with the consent of the owner, operator, or agent in charge of the controlled premises;

(2) in situations presenting imminent danger to health or safety;

(3) in situations involving inspection of conveyances where there is reasonable cause to believe that the mobility of the conveyance makes it impracticable to obtain a warrant;

(4) in any other exceptional or emergency circumstance where time or opportunity to apply for a warrant is lacking; or

(5) in any other situations where a warrant is not constitutionally required.

Administrative inspection warrants, issuance and execution.

(d) Issuance and execution of administrative inspection warrants shall be as follows:

(1) Any judge of the United States or of a State court of record, or any United States magistrate, may, within his territorial jurisdiction, and upon proper oath or affirmation showing probable cause, issue warrants for the purpose of conducting administrative inspections authorized by this title or regulations thereunder, and seizures of property appropriate to such inspections. For the purposes of this section, the term "probable cause" means a valid public interest in the effective enforcement of this title or regulations thereunder sufficient to justify administrative inspections of the area, premises, building, or conveyance, or contents thereof, in the circumstances specified in the application for the warrant.

"Probable cause."

(2) A warrant shall issue only upon an affidavit of an officer or employee having knowledge of the facts alleged, sworn to before the judge or magistrate and establishing the grounds for issuing the warrant. If the judge or magistrate is satisfied that grounds for the application exist or that there is probable cause to believe they exist, he shall issue a warrant identifying the area, premises, building, or conveyance to be inspected, the purpose of such inspection, and, where appropriate, the type of property to be inspected, if any. The warrant shall identify the items or types of property to be seized, if any. The warrant shall be directed to a person authorized under subsection (b)(2) to execute it. The warrant shall state the grounds for its issuance and the name of the person or persons whose affidavit has been taken in support thereof. It shall command the person to whom it is directed to inspect the area, premises, building, or conveyance identified for the purpose specified, and, where appropriate, shall direct the seizure of the property specified. The warrant shall direct that it be served during normal business hours. It shall designate the judge or magistrate to whom it shall be returned.

October 27, 1970   Pub. Law 91-513
                                                        84 STAT. 1276

(3) A warrant issued pursuant to this section must be executed and returned within ten days of its date unless, upon a showing by the United States of a need therefor, the judge or magistrate allows additional time in the warrant. If property is seized pursuant to a warrant, the person executing the warrant shall give to the person from whom or from whose premises the property was taken a copy of the warrant and a receipt for the property taken or shall leave the copy and receipt at the place from which the property was taken. The return of the warrant shall be made promptly and shall be accompanied by a written inventory of any property taken. The inventory shall be made in the presence of the person executing the warrant and of the person from whose possession or premises the property was taken, if they are present, or in the presence of at least one credible person other than the person making such inventory, and shall be verified by the person executing the warrant. The judge or magistrate, upon request, shall deliver a copy of the inventory to the person from whom or from whose premises the property was taken and to the applicant for the warrant.

(4) The judge or magistrate who has issued a warrant under this   Warrants,
section shall attach to the warrant a copy of the return and all papers   filing.
filed in connection therewith and shall file them with the clerk of the
district court of the United States for the judicial district in which
the inspection was made.

FORFEITURES

SEC. 511. (a) The following shall be subject to forfeiture to the United States and no property right shall exist in them:

(1) All controlled substances which have been manufactured, distributed, dispensed, or acquired in violation of this title.

(2) All raw materials, products, and equipment of any kind which are used, or intended for use, in manufacturing, compounding, processing, delivering, importing, or exporting any controlled substance in violation of this title.

(3) All property which is used, or intended for use, as a container for property described in paragraph (1) or (2).

(4) All conveyances, including aircraft, vehicles, or vessels, which are used, or are intended for use, to transport, or in any manner to facilitate the transportation, sale, receipt, possession, or concealment of property described in paragraph (1) or (2), except that—

(A) no conveyance used by any person as a common carrier in the transaction of business as a common carrier shall be forfeited under the provisions of this section unless it shall appear that the owner or other person in charge of such conveyance was a consenting party or privy to a violation of this title or title III; and   Post, p. 1285.

(B) no conveyance shall be forfeited under the provisions of this section by reason of any act or omission established by the owner thereof to have been committed or omitted by any person other than such owner while such conveyance was unlawfully in the possession of a person other than the owner in violation of the criminal laws of the United States, or of any State.

(5) All books, records, and research, including formulas, micro film, tapes, and data which are used, or intended for use, in violation of this title

(b) Any property subject to forfeiture to the United States under this title may be seized by the Attorney General upon process issued pursuant to the Supplemental Rules for Certain Admiralty and Maritime Claims by any district court of the United States having jurisdiction over the property, except that seizure without such process may be made when—

(1) the seizure is incident to an arrest or a search under a search warrant or an inspection under an administrative inspection warrant;

(2) the property subject to seizure has been the subject of a prior judgment in favor of the United States in a criminal injunction or forfeiture proceeding under this title;

(3) the Attorney General has probable cause to believe that the property is directly or indirectly dangerous to health or safety; or

(4) the Attorney General has probable cause to believe that the property has been used or is intended to be used in violation of this title.

In the event of seizure pursuant to paragraph (3) or (4) of this subsection, proceedings under subsection (d) of this section shall be instituted promptly.

Property, custody of Attorney General.

(c) Property taken or detained under this section shall not be repleviable, but shall be deemed to be in the custody of the Attorney General, subject only to the orders and decrees of the court or the official having jurisdiction thereof. Whenever property is seized under the provisions of this title, the Attorney General may—

(1) place the property under seal;

(2) remove the property to a place designated by him; or

(3) require that the General Services Administration take custody of the property and remove it to an appropriate location for disposition in accordance with law.

(d) All provisions of law relating to the seizure, summary and judicial forfeiture, and condemnation of property for violation of the customs laws; the disposition of such property or the proceeds from the sale thereof; the remission or mitigation of such forfeitures; and the compromise of claims and the award of compensation to informers in respect of such forfeitures shall apply to seizures and forfeitures incurred, or alleged to have been incurred, under the provisions of this title, insofar as applicable and not inconsistent with the provisions hereof; except that such duties as are imposed upon the customs officer or any other person with respect to the seizure and forfeiture of property under the customs laws shall be performed with respect to seizures and forfeitures of property under this title by such officers, agents, or other persons as may be authorized or designated for that purpose by the Attorney General, except to the extent that such duties arise from seizures and forfeitures effected by any customs officer.

(e) Whenever property is forfeited under this title the Attorney General may—

(1) retain the property for official use;

(2) sell any forfeited property which is not required to be destroyed by law and which is not harmful to the public, but the proceeds from any such sale shall be used to pay all proper expenses of the proceedings for forfeiture and sale including expenses of seizure, maintenance of custody, advertising and court costs;

(3) require that the General Services Administration take custody of the property and remove it for disposition in accordance with law; or

October 27, 1970   Pub. Law 91-513

84 STAT. 1278

(4) forward it to the Bureau of Narcotics and Dangerous Drugs for disposition (including delivery for medical or scientific use to any Federal or State agency under regulations of the Attorney General).

(f) All controlled substances in schedule I that are possessed, transferred, sold, or offered for sale in violation of the provisions of this title shall be deemed contraband and seized and summarily forfeited to the United States. Similarly, all substances in schedule I, which are seized or come into the possession of the United States, the owners of which are unknown, shall be deemed contraband and summarily forfeited to the United States.   Controlled substances, forfeiture.

(g)(1) All species of plants from which controlled substances in schedules I and II may be derived which have been planted or cultivated in violation of this title, or of which the owners or cultivators are unknown, or which are wild growths, may be seized and summarily forfeited to the United States.

(2) The failure, upon demand by the Attorney General or his duly authorized agent, of the person in occupancy or in control of land or premises upon which such species of plants are growing or being stored, to produce an appropriate registration, or proof that he is the holder thereof, shall constitute authority for the seizure and forfeiture.

(3) The Attorney General, or his duly authorized agent, shall have authority to enter upon any lands, or into any dwelling pursuant to a search warrant, to cut, harvest, carry off, or destroy such plants.

INJUNCTIONS

SEC. 512. (a) The district courts of the United States and all courts exercising general jurisdiction in the territories and possessions of the United States shall have jurisdiction in proceedings in accordance with the Federal Rules of Civil Procedure to enjoin violations of this title.   Jurisdiction of courts.

(b) In case of an alleged violation of an injunction or restraining order issued under this section, trial shall, upon demand of the accused, be by a jury in accordance with the Federal Rules of Civil Procedure.   28 USC app.

ENFORCEMENT PROCEEDINGS

SEC. 513. Before any violation of this title is reported by the Director of the Bureau of Narcotics and Dangerous Drugs to any United States attorney for institution of a criminal proceeding, the Director may require that the person against whom such proceeding is contemplated be given appropriate notice and an opportunity to present his views, either orally or in writing, with regard to such contemplated proceeding.   Notice.

IMMUNITY AND PRIVILEGE

SEC. 514. (a) Whenever a witness refuses, on the basis of his privilege against self-incrimination, to testify or provide other information in a proceeding before a court or grand jury of the United States, involving a violation of this title, and the person presiding over the proceeding communicates to the witness an order issued under this section, the witness may not refuse to comply with the order on the basis of his privilege against self-incrimination. But no testimony or other information compelled under the order issued under subsection (b) of this section or any information obtained by the exploitation of such testimony or other information, may be used against the witness in any criminal case, including any criminal case brought in a court of a State, except a prosecution for perjury, giving a false statement, or otherwise failing to comply with the order.   Refusal to testify, prohibition.

Pub. Law 91-513   October 27, 1970

84 STAT. 1279

Order.

(b) In the case of any individual who has been or may be called to testify or provide other information at any proceeding before a court or grand jury of the United States, the United States district court for the judicial district in which the proceeding is or may be held shall issue, upon the request of the United States attorney for such district, an order requiring such individual to give any testimony or provide any other information which he refuses to give or provide on the basis of his privilege against self-incrimination.

(c) A United States attorney may, with the approval of the Attorney General or the Deputy Attorney General, or any Assistant Attorney General designated by the Attorney General, request an order under subsection (b) when in his judgment—

(1) the testimony or other information from such individual may be necessary to the public interest; and

(2) such individual has refused or is likely to refuse to testify or provide other information on the basis of his privilege against self-incrimination.

BURDEN OF PROOF; LIABILITIES

SEC. 515. (a)(1) It shall not be necessary for the United States to negative any exemption or exception set forth in this title in any complaint, information, indictment, or other pleading or in any trial, hearing, or other proceeding under this title, and the burden of going forward with the evidence with respect to any such exemption or exception shall be upon the person claiming its benefit.

Ante, p. 1264.

(2) In the case of a person charged under section 404(a) with the possession of a controlled substance, any label identifying such substance for purposes of section 503(b)(2) of the Federal Food, Drug,

65 Stat. 648.
21 USC 353.

and Cosmetic Act shall be admissible in evidence and shall be prima facie evidence that such substance was obtained pursuant to a valid prescription from a practitioner while acting in the course of his professional practice.

(b) In the absence of proof that a person is the duly authorized holder of an appropriate registration or order form issued under this title, he shall be presumed not to be the holder of such registration or form, and the burden of going forward with the evidence with respect to such registration or form shall be upon him.

(c) The burden of going forward with the evidence to establish that a vehicle, vessel, or aircraft used in connection with controlled substances in schedule I was used in accordance with the provisions of this title shall be on the persons engaged in such use.

Criminal
liability,
prohibition,
exception.
62 Stat. 803.

(d) Except as provided in sections 2234 and 2235 of title 18, United States Code, no civil or criminal liability shall be imposed by virtue of this title upon any duly authorized Federal officer lawfully engaged in the enforcement of this title, or upon any duly authorized officer of any State, territory, political subdivision thereof, the District of Columbia, or any possession of the United States, who shall be lawfully engaged in the enforcement of any law or municipal ordinance relating to controlled substances.

PAYMENTS AND ADVANCES

Informers,
payment.

SEC. 516. (a) The Attorney General is authorized to pay any person, from funds appropriated for the Bureau of Narcotics and Dangerous Drugs, for information concerning a violation of this title, such sum or sums of money as he may deem appropriate, without reference to any moieties or rewards to which such person may otherwise be entitled by law

(b) Moneys expended from appropriations of the Bureau of Narcotics and Dangerous Drugs for purchase of controlled substances and subsequently recovered shall be reimbursed to the current appropriation for the Bureau.

(c) The Attorney General is authorized to direct the advance of funds by the Treasury Department in connection with the enforcement of this title.

Funds, advancement, authority of Attorney General.

PART F—ADVISORY COMMISSION

ESTABLISHMENT OF COMMISSION ON MARIHUANA AND DRUG ABUSE

SEC. 601. (a) There is established a commission to be known as the Commission on Marihuana and Drug Abuse (hereafter in this section referred to as the "Commission"). The Commission shall be composed of—

Membership.

> (1) two Members of the Senate appointed by the President of the Senate;
> (2) two Members of the House of Representatives appointed by the Speaker of the House of Representatives; and
> (3) nine members appointed by the President of the United States.

At no time shall more than one of the members appointed under paragraph (1), or more than one of the members appointed under paragraph (2), or more than five of the members appointed under paragraph (3) be members of the same political party.

(b)(1) The President shall designate one of the members of the Commission as Chairman, and one as Vice Chairman. Seven members of the Commission shall constitute a quorum, but a lesser number may conduct hearings.

Quorum.

(2) Members of the Commission who are Members of Congress or full-time officers or employees of the United States shall serve without additional compensation but shall be reimbursed for travel, subsistence, and other necessary expenses incurred in the performance of the duties vested in the Commission. Members of the Commission from private life shall receive $100 per diem while engaged in the actual performance of the duties vested in the Commission, plus reimbursement for travel, subsistence, and other necessary expenses incurred in the performance of such duties.

Travel expenses, etc.

Compensation.

(3) The Commission shall meet at the call of the Chairman or at the call of a majority of the members thereof.

Meetings.

(c)(1) The Commission shall have the power to appoint and fix the compensation of such personnel as it deems advisable, without regard to the provisions of title 5, United States Code, governing appointments in the competitive service, and the provisions of chapter 51 and subchapter III of chapter 53 of such title, relating to classification and General Schedule pay rates.

Personnel.

80 Stat. 443, 467.
5 USC 5101, 5331.

(2) The Commission may procure, in accordance with the provisions of section 3109 of title 5, United States Code, the temporary or intermittent services of experts or consultants. Persons so employed shall receive compensation at a rate to be fixed by the Commission, but not in excess of $75 per diem, including traveltime. While away from his home or regular place of business in the performance of services for the Commission, any such person may be allowed travel expenses, including per diem in lieu of subsistence, as authorized by section 5703(b) of title 5, United States Code, for persons in the Government service employed intermittently.

35 F. R. 6247.
Experts and consultants.
80 Stat. 416.
Travel expenses, etc.
80 Stat. 499;
83 Stat. 190.

(3) The Commission may secure directly from any department or agency of the United States information necessary to enable it to

Information, availability.

84 STAT. 1281

carry out its duties under this section. Upon request of the Chairman of the Commission, such department or agency shall furnish such information to the Commission.

Marihuana, study.

(d) (1) The Commission shall conduct a study of marihuana including, but not limited to, the following areas:

(A) the extent of use of marihuana in the United States to include its various sources, the number of users, number of arrests, number of convictions, amount of marihuana seized, type of user, nature of use;

(B) an evaluation of the efficacy of existing marihuana laws;

(C) a study of the pharmacology of marihuana and its immediate and long-term effects, both physiological and psychological;

(D) the relationship of marihuana use to aggressive behavior and crime;

(E) the relationship between marihuana and the use of other drugs; and

(F) the international control of marihuana.

Report to President and Congress.

(2) Within one year after the date on which funds first become available to carry out this section, the Commission shall submit to the President and the Congress a comprehensive report on its study and investigation under this subsection which shall include its recommendations and such proposals for legislation and administrative action as may be necessary to carry out its recommendations.

Drug abuse, study and investigation. Interim reports. Final report to President and Congress. Termination. Expenditures, limitation.

(e) The Commission shall conduct a comprehensive study and investigation of the causes of drug abuse and their relative significance. The Commission shall submit to the President and the Congress such interim reports as it deems advisable and shall within two years after the date on which funds first become available to carry out this section submit to the President and the Congress a final report which shall contain a detailed statement of its findings and conclusions and also such recommendations for legislation and administrative actions as it deems appropriate. The Commission shall cease to exist sixty days after the final report is submitted under this subsection.

(f) Total expenditures of the Commission shall not exceed $1,000,000.

PART G—CONFORMING, TRANSITIONAL AND EFFECTIVE DATE, AND GENERAL PROVISIONS

REPEALS AND CONFORMING AMENDMENTS

Repeals.
79 Stat. 227,
232, 228;
82 Stat. 1361.
Penalties.
82 Stat. 1361.

SEC. 701. (a) Sections 201(v), 301(q), and 511 of the Federal Food, Drug, and Cosmetic Act (21 U.S.C. 321(v), 331(q), 360(a) are repealed.

(b) Subsections (a) and (b) of section 303 of the Federal Food, Drug, and Cosmetic Act (21 U.S.C. 333) are amended to read as follows:

"SEC. 303. (a) Any person who violates a provision of section 301 shall be imprisoned for not more than one year or fined not more than $1,000, or both.

"(b) Notwithstanding the provisions of subsection (a) of this section, if any person commits such a violation after a conviction of him under this section has become final, or commits such a violation with the intent to defraud or mislead, such person shall be imprisoned for not more than three years or fined not more than $10,000 or both."

79 Stat. 233.

(c) Section 304(a)(2) of the Federal Food, Drug, and Cosmetic Act (21 U.S.C. 334(a)(2)) is amended (1) by striking out clauses (A) and (D), (2) by striking out "of such depressant or stimulant

October 27, 1970   Pub. Law 91-513
                                    ‾‾‾‾‾‾‾‾‾‾‾‾‾‾‾‾‾‾‾‾‾‾‾‾
                                         84 STAT. 1282

drug or" in clause (C), (3) by adding "and" after the comma at the
end of clause (C), and (4) by redesignating clauses (B), (C), and
(E) as clauses (A), (B), and (C), respectively.

(d) Section 304(d)(3)(iii) of the Federal Food, Drug, and Cos-   79 Stat. 233.
metic Act (21 U.S.C. 334(d)(3)(iii)) is amended by striking out
"depressant or stimulant drugs or".

(e) Section 510 of the Federal Food, Drug, and Cosmetic Act (21
U.S.C. 360) is amended (1) in subsection (a) by striking out para-   76 Stat. 794;
graph (2), by inserting "and" at the end of paragraph (1), and by   79 Stat. 231.
redesignating paragraph (3) as paragraph (2); (2) by striking out
"or in the wholesaling, jobbing, or distributing of any depressant or
stimulant drug" in the first sentence of subsection (b); (3) by striking
out the last sentence of subsection (b); (4) by striking out "or in the
wholesaling, jobbing, or distributing of any depressant or stimulant
drug" in the first sentence of subsection (c); (5) by striking out the
last sentence of subsection (c); (6) by striking out "(1)" in subsection
(d) and by inserting a period after "drug or drugs" in that subsection
and deleting the remainder of that subsection; and (7) by striking out
"AND CERTAIN WHOLESALERS" in the section heading.

(f) Section 702 of the Federal Food, Drug, and Cosmetic Act (21
U.S.C. 372) is amended by striking out "to depressant or stimulant   79 Stat. 234.
drugs or" in subsection (e).

(g) Section 201(a)(2) of the Federal Food, Drug, and Cosmetic
Act (21 U.S.C. 321(a)(2)) is amended by inserting a period after   76 Stat. 796;
"Canal Zone" the first time these words appear and deleting all there- 82 Stat. 1362.
after in such section 201(a)(2).

(h) The last sentence of section 801(a) of the Federal Food, Drug,
and Cosmetic Act (21 U.S.C. 381(a)) is amended (1) by striking out   52 Stat. 1058.
"This paragraph" and inserting in lieu thereof "Clause (2) of the
third sentence of this paragraph,", and (2) by striking out "section 2
of the Act of May 26, 1922, as amended (U.S.C. 1934, edition, title 21,
sec. 173)" and inserting in lieu thereof "the Controlled Substances
Import and Export Act".

(i)(1) Section 1114 of title 18, United States Code, is amended by   65 Stat. 721.
striking out "the Bureau of Narcotics" and inserting in lieu thereof
"the Bureau of Narcotics and Dangerous Drugs".

(2) Section 1952 of such title is amended—   75 Stat. 498.
    (A) by inserting in subsection (b)(1) "or controlled substances   18 USC 1952.
(as defined in section 102(6) of the Controlled Substances Act)"
immediately following "narcotics"; and
    (B) by striking out "or narcotics" in subsection (c).

(j) Subsection (a) of section 302 of the Public Health Service Act   Drugs, study.
(42 U.S.C. 242(a)) is amended to read as follows: 58 Stat. 692.
"SEC. 302. (a) In carrying out the purposes of section 301 with
respect to drugs the use or misuse of which might result in drug abuse
or dependency, the studies and investigations authorized therein shall
include the use and misuse of narcotic drugs and other drugs. Such
studies and investigations shall further include the quantities of crude
opium, coca leaves, and their salts, derivatives, and preparations, and
other drugs subject to control under the Controlled Substances Act   Ante, p. 1242.
and Controlled Substances Import and Export Act, together with re-   Post, p. 1285.
serves thereof, necessary to supply the normal and emergency medicinal and scientific requirements of the United States. The results Report to
of studies and investigations of the quantities of narcotic drugs or Attorney General.
other drugs subject to control under such Acts, together with reserves
of such drugs, that are necessary to supply the normal and emergency
medicinal and scientific requirements of the United States, shall be

Pub. Law 91-513   October 27, 1970

reported not later than the first day of April of each year to the Attorney General, to be used at his discretion in determining manufacturing quotas or importation requirements under such Acts."

PENDING PROCEEDINGS

SEC. 702. (a) Prosecutions for any violation of law occurring prior to the effective date of section 701 shall not be affected by the repeals or amendments made by such section, or abated by reason thereof.

(b) Civil seizures or forfeitures and injunctive proceedings commenced prior to the effective date of section 701 shall not be affected by the repeals or amendments made by such section, or abated by reason thereof.

(c) All administrative proceedings pending before the Bureau of Narcotics and Dangerous Drugs on the date of enactment of this Act shall be continued and brought to final determination in accord with laws and regulations in effect prior to such date of enactment. Where a drug is finally determined under such proceedings to be a depressant or stimulant drug, as defined in section 201(v) of the Federal Food, Drug, and Cosmetic Act, such drug shall automatically be controlled under this title by the Attorney General without further proceedings and listed in the appropriate schedule after he has obtained the recommendation of the Secretary. Any drug with respect to which such a final determination has been made prior to the date of enactment of this Act which is not listed in section 202 within schedules I through V shall automatically be controlled under this title by the Attorney General without further proceedings, and be listed in the appropriate schedule, after he has obtained the recommendations of the Secretary.

Ante, p. 1281.

Ante, p. 1247.

PROVISIONAL REGISTRATION

SEC. 703. (a) (1) Any person who—

(A) is engaged in manufacturing, distributing, or dispensing any controlled substance on the day before the effective date of section 302, and

(B) is registered on such day under section 510 of the Federal Food, Drug, and Cosmetic Act or under section 4722 of the Internal Revenue Code of 1954,

shall, with respect to each establishment for which such registration is in effect under any such section, be deemed to have a provisional registration under section 303 for the manufacture, distribution, or dispensing (as the case may be) of controlled substances.

Ante, p. 1282.

68A Stat. 555.

(2) During the period his provisional registration is in effect under this section, the registration number assigned such person under such section 510 or under such section 4722 (as the case may be) shall be his registration number for purposes of section 303 of this title.

(b) The provisions of section 304, relating to suspension and revocation of registration, shall apply to a provisional registration under this section.

(c) Unless sooner suspended or revoked under subsection (b), a provisional registration of a person under subsection (a)(1) of this section shall be in effect until—

(1) the date on which such person has registered with the Attorney General under section 303 or has had his registration denied under such section, or

October 27, 1970   **Pub. Law 91-513**

84 STAT. 1284

(2) such date as may be prescribed by the Attorney General for registration of manufacturers, distributors, or dispensers, as the case may be, whichever occurs first.

EFFECTIVE DATES AND OTHER TRANSITIONAL PROVISIONS

SEC. 704. (a) Except as otherwise provided in this section, this title shall become effective on the first day of the seventh calendar month that begins after the day immediately preceding the date of enactment.

(b) Parts A, B, E, and F of this title, section 702, this section, and sections 705 through 709, shall become effective upon enactment.

(c) Sections 305 (relating to labels and labeling), and 306 (relating to manufacturing quotas) shall become effective on the date specified in subsection (a) of this section, except that the Attorney General may by order published in the Federal Register postpone the effective date of either or both of these sections for such period as he may determine to be necessary for the efficient administration of this title.

Ante, p. 1256.

Publication in
Federal Register.

CONTINUATION OF REGULATIONS

SEC. 705. Any orders, rules, and regulations which have been promulgated under any law affected by this title and which are in effect on the day preceding enactment of this title shall continue in effect until modified, superseded, or repealed.

SEVERABILITY

SEC. 706. If a provision of this Act is held invalid, all valid provisions that are severable shall remain in effect. If a provision of this Act is held invalid in one or more of its applications, the provision shall remain in effect in all its valid applications that are severable.

SAVING PROVISION

SEC. 707. Nothing in this Act, except this part and, to the extent of any inconsistency, sections 307(e) and 309 of this title, shall be construed as in any way affecting, modifying, repealing, or superseding the provisions of the Federal Food, Drug, and Cosmetic Act.

52 Stat. 1040
21 USC 301.

APPLICATION OF STATE LAW

SEC. 708. No provision of this title shall be construed as indicating an intent on the part of the Congress to occupy the field in which that provision operates, including criminal penalties, to the exclusion of any State law on the same subject matter which would otherwise be within the authority of the State, unless there is a positive conflict between that provision of this title and that State law so that the two cannot consistently stand together.

APPROPRIATIONS AUTHORIZATION

SEC. 709. There are authorized to be appropriated for expenses of the Department of Justice in carrying out its functions under this title (except section 103) not to exceed $60,000,000 for the fiscal year ending June 30, 1972, $70,000,000 for the fiscal year ending June 30, 1973, and $90,000,000 for the fiscal year ending June 30 1974.

Ante, p. 1245.